P9-CDL-206

WHAT WE KNEW

Also by Eric A. Johnson

Nazi Terror: The Gestapo, Jews,
and Ordinary Germans

Urbanization and Crime: Germany, 1871–1914

The Civilization of Crime: Violence in Town and
Country since the Middle Ages
(coeditor)

Social Control in Europe, 1800–2000 (coeditor)

Also by Karl-Heinz Reuband

Drogenkonsum und Drogenpolitik:
Deutschland und die Niederlande im Vergleich

Soziale Realität im Interview:
Empirische Analysen methodischer Probleme
(coeditor)

Die deutsche Gesellschaft in
vergleichender Perspective (coeditor)

WHAT WE KNEW

Terror, Mass Murder, and Everyday Life in Nazi Germany

AN ORAL HISTORY

Eric A. Johnson and Karl-Heinz Reuband

BASIC

BOOKS

A Member of the
Perseus Books Group

Published by Basic Books,
A Member of the Perseus Books Group

Books published by Basic Books are available at special discounts for bulk purchases in
the United States by corporations, institutions, and other organizations. For more information, please contact the Special Markets Department at the Perseus Books Group,
11 Cambridge Center, Cambridge, MA 02142, or special.markets@perseusbooks.com.

Cataloging-in-Publication data for this book is available from the Library of Congress.

ISBN 0-465-08571-7

05 06 07 08 / 10 9 8 7 6 5 4 3 2 1

In memory of Walter and Thea Reuband
and John Clark Johnson

+ + + Contents

Part Two: "Ordinary Germans'" Testimonies

Part Three: Jewish Survivors' Survey Evidence

Part Four: "Ordinary Germans'" Survey Evidence

Conclusion: What Did They Know?

✛ ✛ ✛ Acknowledgments

This book has been a truly international and cooperative undertaking that has taken many years for us to complete. We have incurred many debts along the way. Although we alone are responsible for any errors of fact or interpretation in its final version, it is a much better book than it would have been without the gracious help and support of many people and institutions on both sides of the Atlantic to whom we are deeply thankful.

First we would like to thank all of the people we interviewed for this book. We hope we have represented them fairly. Also at the top of our list we need to recognize all of those who acted as our research assistants at various stages of the project, many of whom helped us conduct our interviews. Without them, this book would never have been written. Among these people are Nina Almasy, Ana Perez Belmonte, Katje Bögner, Andrea Dykstra, Abby Feguer, Linda Garrett, Iris Hildebrand, Volker Hüfken, Christian Knopp, Stefan Kroll, Burghard Margies, Michael Riesenkönig, Falk Schützenmeister, Dave Stockton, Ute Strewe, and Christiane Wever.

Also deserving of special recognition is Ray Brandon. Ray not only provided the original translation of most of the German-language interviews we have published, and of the book's last three chapters, he also offered numerous valuable additions to the manuscript.

Of the many institutions that have housed and supported our project, we first need to thank the Zentralarchiv für empirische Sozialforschung at the

University of Cologne where we began the project and whose managing director, Ekkehard Mochmann, and research staff gave us generous assistance on numerous levels. Among our coworkers at the Zentralarchiv in Cologne we would particularly like to thank Franz Bauske, Jörg Blasius, Stefan Lampe, Rainer Metz, Ralph Ponemereo, Maria Rohlinger, and Willi Schröder.

Other institutions that supported us in our research and writing are the School of Social Science at the Institute for Advanced Study, the Netherlands Institute for Advanced Study, the United States Holocaust Museum, the Technical University of Dresden, the Heinrich-Heine University of Düsseldorf, Harvard University's Center for European Studies, and Central Michigan University. While several of these institutions helped house our project and also gave us needed financial support, our major funding for the project came from the National Endowment for the Humanities, the National Science Foundation, and the Alexander von Humboldt Foundation as part of the "Transcoop Program" designed to promote collaboration between scholars from Germany and the United States.

We are also extremely thankful to many people who gave us important suggestions and advice, several of whom read all or significant parts of the manuscript. Among these are friends and colleagues such as Joseph Blasi, Cyrelene Amoah-Boampong, Steve Aschheim, Andrea Böltken, Arif Dirlik, Richard Evans, Steve Hochstadt, Reinhart Koselleck, Gerd Krumeich, Konrad Jarausch, Pieter Spierenburg, Mel Richter, Steve Scherer, Mark Soderstrom, Helmut Thome, and our literary agent Georges Borchardt.

Our particularly heartfelt gratitude goes to Chip Rossetti, our editor at Basic Books. His effort has gone way beyond that of a typical editor. His guidance, patience, insight, and encouragement have been truly remarkable. No words could thank him adequately.

Finally, we want to thank our families. Our wives and partners—Mary and Nora—and our children—Benjamin and Jonathan—sustained us with love and cheer over the more than a decade we have devoted to this book. Our parents—Thea and Walter Reuband and Frances Barrett and John Clark Johnson—raised us, inspired us, and suffered through the times we write about.

✛ ✛ ✛ Introduction

On June 14, 1994, we interviewed a man named Adam Grolsch for about four hours in his home in Krefeld, Germany. He candidly told us many things about his experiences as a radio operator in the German army during World War II, including how he had frequently listened to BBC broadcasts during the war and how he had personally observed the shooting of thousands of Jews from the Pinsk ghetto in October 1942. Six days after his interview, he sat down and wrote us a brief letter, which we received two days later at our office at the Center for Historical Social Research at the University of Cologne. His ostensible reason for writing was to make a minor correction to what he had said about the BBC broadcasts he had listened to while he was stationed on the eastern front. In addition to this, however, he wanted to communicate that the interview had brought back painful memories that continued to trouble him deeply. At the end of his letter, he wrote, "After our intensive discussion about the Holocaust in Pinsk that I experienced directly, I was haunted the entire night by nightmares. What must it be like for the surviving victims?"

A year later, on July 24, 1995, we interviewed a man named Herbert Klein in a hotel room in Saddle Brook, New Jersey. This interview also lasted for about four hours and was also very candid. Furthermore, it also brought back painful memories to the interviewee, especially because Herbert Klein was just such a surviving victim of the Holocaust that Adam Grolsch had in mind when he had written to us a year earlier. Born two years later than Adam Grolsch, in 1922,

Herbert Klein had been raised in the German city of Nuremberg. His father led the local Jewish community during the entire Nazi period before he and his family were deported to the Theresienstadt ghetto in June 1943. In our wide-ranging interview with him, Herbert Klein talked at length about his experiences as a Jewish man in Nazi Germany and explained that he was one of a very small number of Jews from Nuremberg to survive the Holocaust.

After our interview, he too could not rest easily. Over the next three days, he phoned us several times about minor corrections and additions he wanted to make to his interview, and then he invited us to visit him at his home before we left the New York/New Jersey area. When we finally went there, much of our discussion revolved around a magazine article he gave us to read about a man of good conscience who had written objectively about the Holocaust but had caused considerable pain to some by not understanding some things correctly about what and whom he had written.

Adam Grolsch and Herbert Klein are only two of the nearly two hundred people we interviewed face-to-face and only two of the more than three thousand people we surveyed in writing about their experiences during the Hitler years in Nazi Germany. They are two of the many people, both Jewish and non-Jewish, we have had contact with in the course of the research on this book who have made crystal clear the importance of getting things right, both factually and interpretively.

Although we have tried our level best to "get it right," some of the evidence that we have uncovered leaves room for differing interpretations, and we ourselves continue to disagree on a few issues. The most significant of these relates to the questions of just how much the German population knew about the mass murder of the European Jews while the Holocaust was being perpetrated during World War II and exactly how and when they came to know about it.[1] Nevertheless, despite modest interpretive differences, we are in broad agreement about the answers to the other questions this book confronts, several of which are central to the understanding of dictatorial terror, Nazi society, and the Holocaust. Among these are the following: Did most Germans support or oppose Hitler and the Nazi regime? What aspects of Nazi society did German people find most to their liking? How much and what forms of terror did they experience? Did Jews and non-Jews have experiences with Nazi terror that were similar? Did both Jews and non-Jews live in constant fear of denunciation and arrest? How widespread and popular was anti-Semitism, how was it manifested, and to what extent did it abate or grow worse over time?[2]

The questions we address and the evidence we present are of vital importance, for our study is the first to ask systematically a large cross section of the German population, both Jewish and non-Jewish, about their everyday lives in Nazi Germany and about their brushes with Nazi terror, as well as their knowledge about the mass murder of the Jews. Furthermore, we believe that our study is unique in another way: it has been conducted in an international and cross-disciplinary fashion, combining the expertise of an American specialist in the history of modern German and Nazi society with that of a German specialist in public opinion and sociological research. Ever since we wrote the first grant proposal in 1991 seeking the funds necessary to begin our research,[3] we have worked closely together on every stage of the project, sometimes in Germany, sometimes in the United States, and sometimes in other countries as well.

During the time we have worked on this project, a new conception of the Nazi dictatorship has been developing in the international scholarly community to which our evidence lends powerful support. If this new understanding of how Nazi society functioned gains wider acceptance, which we believe it should, it will have policy import as well as scholarly significance.

Until recently, scholarship on Nazi society in particular and twentieth-century dictatorial societies in general was heavily influenced by the theorists of the "totalitarian school" that emerged during the early years of the Cold War in the 1950s. Basing their argumentation more on logic and anecdote than on systematic empirical evidence, leading exponents of this school like the political philosopher Hannah Arendt and the political scientist Zbigniew Brzezinski viewed the dictatorial regimes and not the people who lived under them to be the problem and construed terror and coercion to be the essential features of Nazi, Soviet, and other dictatorial societies.[4] Many scholars followed their lead and wrote historical accounts emphasizing the supposed omnipotence of secret police agencies like the Nazi Gestapo and the Soviet KGB and the fear that allegedly blanketed the entire populations of these "totalitarian" societies.[5] Eventually a paradigm developed based on logic that seemed inescapable.

Although this paradigm remains influential among policymakers and the lay public, it no longer reigns supreme in the scholarly community. Because of the pioneering efforts of a number of historians from several countries who have systematically worked through previously neglected or unavailable archival materials (e.g., Gestapo and police case files, court and party records, mood and morale reports, and other documentary evidence), a fundamentally new view of the Nazi dictatorship is emerging that stresses complicity and consent more than coercion and compulsion.[6] We are now beginning to understand, for example, that the Gestapo was far more limited in its resources and powers than was once thought, and that to be effective it had to concentrate on policing targeted enemies like Jews and communists while leaving most of the German population considerable latitude to go about their private lives. They were able to do this because Hitler and his ideology had widespread support from the German population.

This is not to argue that the Nazi regime was not oppressive. Neither is it to argue that the German citizenry always agreed with the Nazi regime's most abhorrent policies and acts, above all with the wholesale slaughter of European Jewry. Still, the interview and survey evidence that our study has been built on adds to and buttresses the new view of Nazi society that archival investigation in the past decade or so has begun to create. As Ian Kershaw concludes on the final page of his recent biography of Adolf Hitler, "The previously unprobed depths of inhumanity probed by the Nazi regime could draw upon wide-ranging complicity at all levels of society."[7] Shocking as it may seem, dictatorships can be quite popular.[8]

Thus, by simply asking the German people themselves in an organized and social-scientific way about their experiences and their level of understanding and knowledge about the mundane as well as historic events that they lived through personally, we are able to demonstrate that the Third Reich was not a living hell for all·who lived in it, as many scholars have argued in the past. Even though it brought enormous pain, suffering, and death to many—especially if they were Jewish—it had the strong support of millions of common German citizens for most of its existence, and most Germans did not have to be compelled to remain loyal to Hitler and his regime. Far from living in a state of constant fear and discontent, most Germans led happy and even normal lives in Nazi Germany. As one man we interviewed for this book told us in the comfort of his home in Michigan in May 2001, "To us, it was the most exciting time of our lives. . . . You see, when the Nazis came to power, I was five years old. I grew up in this. So it was a normal way of life for me."[9]

In some ways, therefore, there were two Nazi societies, one for most Germans and another for Jews and a relatively limited number of others who either opposed the Nazi regime on ideological or moral grounds or belonged to minority groups that the Nazis acted against ruthlessly.[10] One of the great tragedies in the history of modern German society is that great numbers of those who lived in that other Nazi society had been proud, patriotic Germans who were consequently dumbfounded when Hitler and the Nazi regime turned them into outcasts. In the words of another man who had also emigrated to America after the war but happened to be Jewish, "It came to us German Jews as a tremendous shock that this anti-Semitic policy was introduced. It took us a long time to grasp this new direction. It was unthinkable, because we were so utterly German—more German than some of the Germans themselves."[11]

The greatest tragedy of all was the Holocaust, which ultimately destroyed the lives of millions of Jews across the continent of Europe. This unspeakable crime against humanity could not have been possible without the indifference and complicity of a large part of the German population. That few Germans protested meaningfully against the Holocaust has been well documented.[12] Still, the extent to which the German population shared Hitler's hatred of the Jews and avidly supported his anti-Semitic measures remains a hotly contested issue.[13] Our evidence, based especially on the testimony of the Jewish participants in our surveys and interviews, will qualify, though not completely contradict, the views of scholars like Daniel Jonah Goldhagen who allege that anti-Semitic views were widely shared among the mainstream German population.

Of equal and perhaps even greater significance for our study, however, is the question of whether the German population was aware of the mass murder of the Jews of Europe while it was being carried out. Certainly the Nazis took pains to keep this a secret both from the German population and the world in general. Otherwise, powerful opposition might have mounted from many quarters to bring their murderous policy to a halt: more Jews might have gone into hiding or might have refused to go to the deportation trains; non-Jews in Germany and outside of Germany might have gathered in open protest or might have swelled the ranks of the limited resistance movements; more pressure might have been placed on Allied governments to bomb the concentration camps; and so on.

But how successful were the Nazis in keeping the Holocaust a secret? Certainly they were successful at least in keeping up the pretense among the German population that the Holocaust was a secret both during the war and for decades after it was over. At Nuremberg and in subsequent war crimes trials and investigations, large numbers of Nazis leaders and functionaries, from Albert Speer to garden-variety Gestapo officers, avoided death sentences and often any punishment at all because it could not be proven that they had known about the mass murder that they had helped carry out.[14] For many years after the war, the words "we didn't know about it" became a national German refrain.

Now the immediate danger of being punished for Nazi crimes has diminished and Germany and its population have long since been welcomed back into the family of civilized nations. Most Germans who lived through the Third Reich have either died or are nearing the end of their lives. Consequently far more people are willing to say what they really knew back then about the Holocaust. Maybe they would have done this sooner had they been asked under the right circumstances. Now at last we have asked them, and hence the title of this book of oral history about the World War II generation in Germany is *What We Knew: Terror, Mass Murder, and Everyday Life in Nazi Germany*.

Finding out what the non-Jewish and Jewish populations of Nazi Germany knew and experienced has not been an easy task, either intellectually or emotionally. Just talking with our interviewees has been traumatic, since many of them have related very painful stories. But, precisely because the issues involved are so sensitive, it was of crucial importance for us to conduct the research for this book in a rigorous fashion. Completing this project has taken us more than a decade.

If the main purpose of our book had been readability, it would have been published several years ago. Rather, it is the product of a truly massive research effort combining oral history and systematic survey techniques to provide convincing evidence that can help answer some of the most central questions about Nazi society.

When we began our research in 1993, we knew what kinds of questions we wanted to ask, but we did not know if people would be willing to answer them. In the end, however, the response we received from both Jews and non-Jews was truly gratifying. We received a positive response rate of nearly 50 percent in the written surveys, and a large proportion of the people we surveyed indicated that they would be willing to speak with us at length in subsequent face-to-face interviews about their views and experiences. By the time we had more or less completed our surveys and interviews in 2001, more than three thousand people had answered our written surveys and we had conducted in-depth interviews with nearly two hundred. We have spent the past three years analyzing the survey results, editing the interviews, and writing the book.

To ensure that the views and experiences of the people we surveyed and interviewed reflect those of the majority of Jews and non-Jews who had lived in Nazi Germany, we decided to conduct our surveys with large and representative samples of the populations of several different German cities and to conduct two additional surveys with separate groups of German Jewish Holocaust survivors. The first survey we conducted was in the city of Cologne in the spring and summer of 1993.

Following standard survey research design, we began our surveying effort with a pilot study. We drew up a sample questionnaire and sent it to about three hundred Cologne residents born in or before 1928 who were randomly selected from a list of people provided to us by the Cologne Statistical Bureau. Although people born in 1928, who are the youngest people we contacted, were teenagers when the Third Reich ended in 1945, which some might consider too young to know or experience very much, they represent a small fraction of the people we surveyed. Most of the people we surveyed in the pretest and in the subsequent larger surveys had already reached adulthood during the years of the Third Reich. In the larger surveys we conducted, the median birth year of the people we surveyed was between 1920 and 1922, depending on the city.

After we concluded our pretest survey, we analyzed the results carefully and made changes in the questionnaire to promote clarity. A year later, in the fall of 1994, we mounted the first of our major survey efforts with over three thousand randomly selected residents of the cities of Cologne and Krefeld. We chose these cities because they were near our base of operations at the time, at the University of Cologne, and because one of us (Johnson) was also working on a related project dealing with the police and court records of those and other

Rhineland communities in the Third Reich.[15] The response rate we received in these surveys mirrored that of the pilot study survey, although it was slightly lower (closer to 50 percent than 60 percent) because we decided to send only two reminders to those who had not answered the survey, instead of three (which would have been prohibitively expensive), even though this lowered the response rate minimally.

We were satisfied with the response to our Cologne and Krefeld surveys, but we still had two important concerns. First, few of the respondents were Jewish, since there are few Jews living in any German city. Second, even though about half of the people who answered the Cologne and Krefeld surveys had lived in other communities during the Third Reich and thus had only moved to Cologne or Krefeld after 1945, we feared that the results we received might not be representative enough of other German communities. Consequently, in the years following our Cologne and Krefeld surveys, we took steps to remedy these potential problems by conducting two subsequent surveys with large random samples of the populations of Dresden (1995) and Berlin (1999), and with two additional surveys specifically targeted to German Jewish survivors.

The survey results from Dresden and Berlin turned out to be very similar to those of Cologne and Krefeld, which added measurably to the statistical reliability of our survey effort in general. They also boost our confidence in our findings for three reasons. One is that the residents of Dresden and Berlin are predominantly Protestant, whereas those of Cologne and Krefeld are largely Catholic. Another is that Dresden and Berlin lie in the east of Germany geographically, Cologne and Krefeld in the west. The final reason is that Hitler and his Nazi Party received far lower voter support in Weimar elections from the western and Catholic-dominated cities of Cologne and Krefeld than from the eastern, Protestant-leaning cities of Dresden and Berlin.

The two surveys that we administered to Jewish survivors took place in 1995 and 1996. Although we employed a questionnaire that was almost identical to that used in the German cities, it was written in English instead of German because most survivors have lived for the past fifty years in the United States, Great Britain, Israel, or some other non–German speaking country. The first of the two surveys, the longer one, was mailed with the gracious help of the United States Holocaust Memorial Museum research staff, which wrote a letter endorsing our study for inclusion with the survey and safeguards our list of Jewish survivors. The second and smaller survivor study was conducted with the surviving Jewish population of the city of Krefeld. The addresses of the Krefeld survivors were provided to us by one of the survivors.

After we had completed our written survey, we could feel that we had truly questioned a representative sample of Jews and non-Jews who had lived in the Third Reich. The only significant caveat is that they represent a somewhat younger population than had been the average in Germany between 1933 and 1945. Still, most of the people we surveyed had reached adulthood before the Third Reich ended, and, because our sample is so large, it is possible to control for the possible distortions caused by this age factor.

The Jewish survivors and the non-Jewish Germans we canvassed included men and women from all corners of Germany and from all walks of life, people who had lived in nearly every large German city during the Third Reich as well as others from numerous small towns and medium-size cities. Their educational, socioeconomic, and religious backgrounds reflect both the Jewish and non-Jewish populations who experienced Nazism firsthand. Finally, they are varied in their political backgrounds and present affiliations, not dissimilar to the way they and their families had been in the Third Reich.

The nearly two hundred people we interviewed at length also originated from all over Germany and came from all types of educational, socioeconomic, religious, and political backgrounds. Except for a handful, all of them had taken our written surveys. The interviews we conducted with them were carried out over the entire span of our survey effort. After we completed our original pretest of the written survey in Cologne in 1993, we selected twenty of the respondents for subsequent face-to-face interviews. We conducted the balance of the non-Jewish interviews between 1995 and 2001, after we completed our main surveys in the relevant cities. Most of the Jewish survivor interviews were conducted in the United States, especially in the New York/New Jersey area in the summer of 1995. We also conducted several interviews in other localities in the United States, Germany, and other countries; a research assistant even conducted an interview in Chile in 2002.

As with our written surveys, we took pains in our interviews to ensure that the answers we received were reliable and valid. We were especially mindful of the so-called interviewer effect, in which the responses of the interviewees are influenced by the personality and values of the interviewer. To control for this, we conducted only a third of the interviews ourselves and trained a few others from different personal and disciplinary backgrounds to conduct the rest. The largest number of interviews were conducted by four people, two women and two men. The two women, Ana Perez Belmonte and Christiane Wever, were advanced history students at the University of Cologne who had worked for several years as our research assistants and were knowledgeable about the historical issues involved. The two men, Christian Knopf and Michael Riesenkönig, were graduate students in psychology at Cologne but had not worked on our project previously and knew somewhat less than the two women about the history of the Third Reich and the Holocaust.* In our view, whatever

*Four other people should also be recognized here as they carried out many of the interviews in Dresden and Berlin. They also had extensive training in either history or the social sciences. The are Falk Schützenmeister, Iris Hildebrandt, Katja Bögner and Ute Stewe.

disadvantages their lack of advanced historical training might have caused were offset by their relative independence from us and by the fresh insights they had as trained psychologists. Furthermore, in the course of their graduate training, both of them had already gained considerable experience in conducting interviews related to other issues.

At the beginning of each interview we told the interviewee that our questions would focus on three main issues. First we asked them to describe their everyday lives in the Third Reich; second, we asked them to discuss any specific experiences they or people known to them had with Nazi terror; third, we asked them to tell us about any experiences they might have had during the Holocaust and what they had come to know, if anything, before the end of the war about the mass murder of Jews.

The interviews were all recorded on audiotape. The shortest interviews lasted for about an hour. The longer ones lasted for many hours; some stretched over a few days. We always tried to give the interviewees a choice of possible interview venues. Locations included university office buildings, restaurants, and even hotel rooms and suites. Most invited us to their homes. Although the interviews always centered on the questions enumerated above, they proceeded in a conversational manner and sometimes moved in quite unexpected directions. In the end, therefore, the interviewees were given the chance to tell us the stories that they wanted to tell us about their lives, although our questions encouraged them to concentrate on the issues of everyday life, terror, and mass murder.

Unfortunately we can publish only a fraction of the interviews we conducted, and each interview has been edited for clarity and brevity. We elected to change the names of all of the interviewees to safeguard their anonymity, even though some of them might have preferred to have their real names published. Nevertheless, the forty interviews we have selected for this volume (twenty with Jews and twenty with non-Jews) are, we believe, reasonably representative of the entire body of interviews that we conducted originally. They reflect the range of opinions and experiences that we encountered in our written surveys with thousands of people.

The book is divided into four parts, each subdivided into several chapters, followed by a brief conclusion chapter summarizing our major findings and arguments. Parts 1-2 contain the forty interview narratives, with one part each for Jews and non-Jews. Parts 3-4 analyze the Jewish and non-Jewish questionnaires and draw on the interview material for supportive illustrations. Most of these references pertain to the forty interviews included here, but we also quote some statements made by people whose interviews we did not publish. Relatively more of these are found in the chapters in Part 4 dealing with the non-Jewish population, because we interviewed more non-Jews than Jews, and we didn't want to lose their voices entirely. Additionally, in the latter group, many of these interviews also contain important commentary and evidence that pertains to our analysis.

Although the focus throughout the book is on average people, their experiences and observations tell us much about an extraordinary period in human history. Many of them, especially Germans who were not Jewish, lived mundane, even quite normal lives under the Nazi dictatorship. But many became involved or participated in truly horrifying events.

Among the Jews we interviewed are several who managed to escape the Holocaust by emigrating during the 1930s to such countries as the United States, Great Britain, and China, and several who emigrated to countries in western and eastern Europe that eventually fell under Nazi occupation and ended up deporting their Jews to ghettos and concentration camps. Of the Jews we interviewed who did not leave Germany before the war began, nearly all eventually wound up in concentration camps, even though a few tried to avoid this by going into hiding once it became clear that deportation to the east was usually tantamount to a death sentence. One woman survived by jumping off a train taking her and other Jews to Auschwitz and another woman survived by working in a massage parlor run by an SS man in Berlin. More typically, however, the deported Jews who survived somehow eluded selection to the gas chambers and endured years of backbreaking forced labor, chronic malnutrition, widespread disease, and barbaric mistreatment.

Compared with these experiences, those of the non-Jewish Germans we interviewed and surveyed were usually rather mild. Although most of them violated the ubiquitous laws of the Third Reich at one point or another by listening to foreign radio broadcasts, telling jokes critical of Hitler and other Nazi leaders, spreading news about the mass murder of Jews, or involving themselves in other kinds of outlawed activities, few of them were caught or punished and most tell us that they did not fear being arrested. Instead of living their lives in fear and dread, most tell us that they in fact supported Hitler and many aspects of Nazi ideology. Still, a significant minority abhorred the Nazi regime and a handful took part in underground resistance activity.

Among the people we interviewed, most had not been members of or functionaries in the Nazi Party. But some were, and others were the children of such people. Many, however, had belonged to the Hitler Youth or other party organizations, and several had been soldiers during the war or the wives and daughters of soldiers. A few were policemen, concentration camp guards, and members of army units that slaughtered Jews; others had special experiences during the Holocaust.

As will become evident in the pages of this book, large numbers of Jews and non-Jews in Nazi Germany eventually came to know quite a lot about the Holocaust during the course of World War II. Since they were the primary victims of it, Jews generally tried harder to find out about it and usually did, but not always before they were deported to the places where it was being carried out. Since people of their background were the prime perpetrators of it, non-Jews did not necessarily seek out news about the mass murder. Nevertheless, after Auschwitz began to gas its first Jewish victims in mid-1942, it became ever harder for them to remain uninformed as news of it came from so many quarters. Some witnessed it happening or even participated directly in it, and, not infrequently, described it to others. Some heard about it second or third hand—from soldiers on leave from the eastern front, foreign news broadcasts, well-informed friends, relatives, and clergymen, and occasionally Gestapo officers and Nazi Party officials. Sometimes the news reached them soon after the murders commenced in 1941 and 1942. Other times it came to them late in the war after most of the Jews had been killed. Sometimes it was passed along in the form of rumors that were whispered under people's breath. Other times it was discussed openly with specific information provided about the concentration camps and the mass shootings and gassings. Not everyone came to know, but a great many did. If people wanted to know, very often they could find out.

Part ONE

JEWISH SURVIVORS' TESTIMONIES

✦ 1 ✦

JEWS WHO LEFT GERMANY BEFORE
KRISTALLNACHT

WILLIAM BENSON

Never to forget, never to forgive.

Born in 1924 and raised in Leipzig as the son of a successful businessman, William Benson fled with his family to Italy in 1937. During the war he fought with the partisans in Italy. After the war he emigrated to the United States and became an engineer.

You can't trust these Germans. Whatever they tell you, they're lying. They tell you what you want to hear, that's all they're doing: they're all innocent; nobody knew anything; they were always against Hitler. All that you hear is nonsense.

In 1934 or 1935, I remember Hitler came to Leipzig. I was a little kid there and there was a big square, I think it was called the Augustus Platz. There was Hitler and he was preaching there. I could not understand a word he was saying because he spoke a very bad German. You know, he'd scream. So I saw peo-

3

ple with tears coming down their faces, tears, and I came home and told my parents that Hitler was speaking and I saw people crying and I couldn't understand why. I wanted to know why they were so hypnotized by that man.

I used to collect photographs. I had an album with all the Nazi pictures of them marching with the banners. To me it was like a big thing, an adventure. I didn't know what it was about; who he was. As a matter of fact, the German Jews during the early years of Hitler were petitioning Hitler to form a Jewish brigade. You must have heard about that one. Some of those German Jews were more German than Jews. They had medals and they were really gung-ho—real, real Germans, especially the rich ones—because Hitler was against communism. Anybody with money would say, "Oh, good, Hitler. He's a good guy to have around."

How were you treated by your German neighbors and classmates?

I used to have a friend; he was a very good friend, a real German. I used to invite him home; he was my best buddy. I remember one time I came home after my mother had sent me out to get some milk—at that time we had to get the milk in a pot, you know, they'd pour the milk and then you had to carry it. So I had got the milk and then kids surrounded me and they called me *Schweinjude* [Jewish pig] and took the milk and poured it over my head. When I came home I was crying and said, "What is a *Schweinjude*?"—I didn't know what that meant—"Who's a *Jude*? What's a *Schweinjude*? Who am I?" I didn't know who I was. I was only a kid. I didn't know what I was, Jew or not Jew.

There were many times when I was beaten up coming from school. I remember one teacher who had something against me because I was a Jew in his class—there were a couple of Jews in his class. Every time when I must have been unruly, he used to pull me up front and bend me over and whip me with a bamboo stick. One time he whipped me so much that when I came home I had welts on my back.

My father took me out of the school. At that time the Jews had opened up their own school because Hitler stated a decree that Jews couldn't go to the German schools, and this school became one of the best schools in the town. It even accepted German kids into that school, and, as a matter of fact, we even had German teachers. At the German school, I remember they always picked on me. But I didn't know if it was because I was a Jew. I was a skinny kid, and when you're a skinny kid, you know. I don't know if they picked on me because I was a Jew or because I was a skinny kid. But they always picked on me.

I also remember they had these stores, where they had always written *Juden verboten*. During Christmastime I remember there was a big department store with a lot of toys in the window and I wanted to see the toy department, and it was written there, *Juden verboten*. And I used to go in, and I used to believe I could because I was sneaking, I was cheating. I walked in, and I looked at all these toys, and I played with the toys, and then I walked out like I had stolen something.

Where did your family live? Did you live in isolation from the Germans or were you integrated with the Germans?

We had a house in a suburb of Leipzig called Nauenhof—my father was pretty well off. But, in 1929, during the Depression, he lost that house and we moved to Leipzig. But we still had a good business so we lived in a very nice neighborhood in a very big apartment. I remember it, seven rooms, a tremendous big place. It was very nice.

We were very integrated. Especially in the business where my father was, they were always very integrated. My father had German friends and they even came to our house—businesspeople, customers. My father always entertained. And that is why my father perished—because he believed in his Germans! Even in 1942 when he gave himself up, he still believed in them.

He was born in Poland. Germany is not my country. It's an abortion, Germany. I'm sorry, but when I talk about Germany, I get very bitter.

I know I have a temper, but I will tell you one thing. I was born in Germany; I was brought up there for thirteen years and it's in me. When I hear German music it does something to me; I like it: I like these marching songs. I say to my wife, "I hear these songs on the radio. I like it." She says, "What's the matter with you?" She gets mad at me. And I say, "I can't help it. It's in me." I am so embarrassed. When people ask me where I was born, I'm embarrassed to say I'm born in Germany. I actually am embarrassed.

You also lived in Italy.

What happened is that in 1937 my father sent the three children, the three sons, to Italy to summer camp, all three of us. And then he figured he was going to follow. So he just followed, he escaped. He left his business with all his furs and everything just left behind and he came to Italy and started anew. That was 1937 to 1939. He started a business again. He was good at making money—not like me, I mean, he was the opposite. Whatever I touch turns bad and whatever he touched turned to gold. All my life I had that problem. So we started again. I went back to school in Italy for a couple of years. First I went to a school in Milan. This was an Italian school, a private school, and I learned Italian. The second year I went to the public school. But then when Mussolini got together with Hitler, he said that all the Jews that came after 1914 to Italy had to leave. So where do you go? Nobody wanted to take a Jew. So we smuggled ourselves over the border, over the Alps to France. But, of course, going over the border we got caught, the whole family—my two brothers, my parents, we were all together.

I will tell you one thing. If I couldn't have come over here, I would have lived in Italy. That's the only country in Europe where a Jew can live, where there's no Jewish discrimination, no anti-Semitism. There is less anti-Semitism in Italy because the Italians look like Jews themselves, especially the ones in the south. Oh the big noses!

Anyway we got caught right at the border, on top. It took us two days and two nights, and the last night our guides abandoned us. We were up on a mountain—no roads or nothing—so we waited until they came. And then the French soldiers came, and they caught us and they arrested everybody—it was something like twenty people. But if people had a few things, they let them go and they gave them a piece of paper that allowed them to live there for six months (every six months this had to be renewed). And those that didn't, went to jail for a few weeks, and they let them go also.

So there we were in France, still all together in a place that became the free zone when the war started. But then one night in August 1942 they came to our apartment and they broke the doors down (I had just graduated high school at that time, from France). So anyway, my dad asked me, "What do you want to do?" I said, "I'd like to go skiing." So we found a place up by Chamonix, just near the border.

While I was up there, it happened, the story happened. My father wired me: "Don't come back." You know, I was a spoiled kid; I never did a day of work; I was always taken care of; I didn't know anything. Here I am up there, with no money. "Don't come back." You know, that was a black, black day in my life in August 1942. As a matter of fact, I even have papers of the transport where my father and my brothers went to Auschwitz. From there they vanished.

That was a difficult time. After that I went to the owner of the place where I was staying and she took a liking to me. I was a young guy, eighteen years old, and she was in her thirties. She saved me really. She had some family in Grenoble and so I stayed there for a while. But then I was caught in September 1943 by the Italians and put into a camp. Luckily I escaped with a friend of mine just two weeks before they emptied out the camp and sent the inmates to Auschwitz. I ended up with the partisans, the underground in Italy, in the mountains for eighteen months from September 1943 until the end of the war.

Thank God, the group I was with didn't want to fight. They just wanted to survive the war. So we lost maybe 25–30 percent of our people, not because of fighting but because the Germans came up these mountains periodically and anything that had pants—was a male and had pants—they shot.

How did you get to the United States?

I came in on the German quota. Even though I was stateless according to the Germans, I was not stateless according to the Americans. They go by the country where you are born. I had papers that I was born in Germany.

Everybody wanted to come at that time. To us, Roosevelt was a god. To a Jew in Europe, Roosevelt was a god. But nobody really knew what he really was. I don't want to use the word, but he was a son of a bitch. I mean, he turned back the Jews when they came on the *St. Louis.* There were some nine hundred Jews on that ship. They came to the land of the free, and he didn't let them in and most of them perished.

I was lucky enough to live two lives. One life was up to 1945. I should have been dead, but I survived and I started all over again. So my new life started in 1946. My second life, this is the life I'm not supposed to have had. And I tell you, the early years, I was very depressed. I was very depressed, very depressed and it was bad. I was all alone. I asked myself, "Why have I survived?" It was rough. They were very bad times. I was very bitter. Today, years later, people tell me, "Oh, Bill, it's time to forgive. Forget and forgive." I get so irritated, so mad. I teach my children, you never forgive, you never forget. And they should teach their children about Germany never to forget, never to forgive, never as long as our children can teach their children and keep on teaching their children. I don't want them to forgive, ever. This is something you don't forgive.

The mere word, German, it's killing, it's murdering. That's all it is. And don't think the children today are any better than their parents were. The hate for the Jews is still in them—it's just covered. Their anti-Semitism is still there. If, God forbid, there were another Hitler, it would come right out again.

I'm very bitter. I'm so very bitter. All those years, I can't get over it. My whole life was ruined. I had a good life, a good family. I was well-off. I never had to worry about anything. But the first ten, twelve years in this country, we were starving. I was ready to throw myself under the front of the railroad. But I didn't. The instinct of survival is very strong. At the last minute, you don't do it.

I cringe when I hear German spoken. I can't stand it if on television they interview a German with subtitles. I look at the guy and I say, "You son of a bitch. You killer." Especially when I see a guy who's sixty, sixty-five, seventy. I know they were all in it, most of them—99 percent. When things got bad, all of a sudden they said, "Oh, we didn't hear, we didn't know about that. We never liked what he was doing." But they were all with Hitler. When things were going good, even the ones that hated Hitler said maybe he's not so bad after all. When everything turned around in '44, then all of a sudden they hitched up to fight him. They should make a big park out of all of Germany, a beautiful park—the location is perfect—and use all the Germans as fertilizer. That is what I felt and what I still feel.

MARGARETE LEIB

They strangled my father with a packaging cord.

Margarete Leib was born in 1910 and raised in Karlsruhe. Her father, an attorney and former Social Democratic Party Reichstag deputy, was murdered in a concentration camp in 1934. Before emigrating from France to the United States in September 1941, she was involved in communist resistance activities in Berlin.

We didn't exactly fit the average family. In 1933, my father was still in the Reichstag, and I met all kinds of Reichstag deputies. For the short time I saw him before he was arrested, my father thought, "Okay, we have another government now, but no government lasts forever. There'll be other elections." He did not foresee what was going to happen, not even when he was in the concentration camp. He always changed between realizing that it might last and thinking that it will not last.

The government in Baden was taken over completely on March 9–10, 1933, and they then arrested a number of SPD [Social Democratic Party] and KPD [Communist Party] politicians and some Jews. My impression is that at that time it was not so much the Jews [who were being arrested]. There were some denunciations, and some people went right away to the party and said so-and-so did such-and-such, and then they were arrested. [Usually, however,] they were let out again after a few days. But the politicians were kept.

Were you present when the Gestapo or the police came to arrest your father?

No, I was still in Berlin taking examinations. On March 10, my mother called and told me, and then I left right away and went home. My father was first imprisoned in Karlsruhe, from March 10 until May 16. My mother was allowed to visit him twice a week, and I went every day. In the jail where he was in *Untersuchungshaft* [investigative detention], there were still some employees that my father knew from being an attorney. They were allowed to receive their meals from their families. So I went three times a day on my bike to the jail and brought breakfast, lunch, and dinner. This lasted until May 16. But on May 16—they had announced it already a day earlier—they were moved. They took those seven SPD people, including my father, on an open truck through Karlsruhe. They took them through the city and through all the little villages between Karlsruhe and Bruchsal and Heidelberg. In most villages, there were people who yelled and screamed at these people. It was really terrible. In Karlsruhe, there was an enormous upheaval both for and against it.

I saw it all. I was in my father's office, because it faced the street, and I was looking out the window. A colleague of my father's was there too. His name was Marx. He was at one window with some of the employees. There was a lot of commotion in the office, and I went over there, because I thought my father would probably look up when he went past his office. I stood at another window and then I made a kind of small movement, and my father looked up, very shyly. That was like a shock to me. Then several of them ran upstairs, and Marx went out to meet them on the stairs, and they immediately seized him and threw him on the truck as well.

Your father was then driven through Karlsruhe and the other places and then taken to a concentration camp. What was it like for him in the concentration camp?

That had been a former palace [in Kislau], a bishop's palace or an archbishop's. Among the prisoners, things were very good, and he was also older, not yet fifty-one. But of course the Nazis, the SA and so on, were horrible. Very soon thereafter, they got a commandant. His name was Mohr. He was a very decent man. Somehow he was in the police, the higher police. I am still in contact with his wife and daughter and their family. Whenever I'm there, it's either for dinner or afternoon coffee.

How could the commandant of a concentration camp be decent? That's not something you would expect.

There were in fact individuals who were decent. You can't lump everybody together. Of course, a lot of unbelievably horrible things were done, and, in my opinion, Germans in general have no civil courage. In France, there was an underground resistance movement; in Germany, there was hardly anything. They followed along as if they had been ordered to by the grand duke or the kaiser. Everybody is obedient in Germany. I have to put it that way. That's why people [only] said anything [about the regime] at home. But then it got so bad that they often couldn't say anything in front of their children anymore. They had been trained in the Hitler Youth to tell on their parents. Dreadful!

How many people were there in the concentration camp? Did you have contact with your father at the time?

That was variable. It was rather on the small side. At one point one hundred [prisoners], at another point two hundred. My mother always went there when she was allowed to. I was also there a few times. I was allowed to go there especially when there was something that had to be discussed about business, something about the office or about money.

Did the Gestapo ever come to your house?

No. I once wrote a letter. After the death of my father at the end of March 1934, I received a notification from the insurance company about the seizure of my father's life insurance, and so I wrote to them. Then it went further. I went to the Gestapo. There were five or six or more of those characters there, and I made a scene. I both cried and cursed. "I'm staying here until this is settled," I said. They all knew that my father had been killed. It was very embarrassing for them in my presence. They wanted nothing more than to be rid of me. Finally, one of them suggested that he would call the insurance agency. They then released the money and kept only about a thousand marks. They had to pay the insurance money to the Gestapo. Not only was one held there as a prisoner and then killed, one then had to pay for having stayed there as well, so and so much money for each day. That's why I was so furious. They then had the nerve to have themselves paid for this.

Where was he shot? In the concentration camp?

He wasn't shot. They strangled him with a packaging cord. But so that they could conceal what had happened, they hung him up from a window frame and then called a doctor.

And what did the commandant of the concentration camp do?

They knew that he wouldn't go along with that. So they said to him, "You're freshly married, aren't you? Wouldn't you like to have a few weeks of vacation?" "Gladly," he said. They had a small house in the northern part of the Black Forest and that is where he and his wife went during the time that this happened. During this period, they had Sauer as the commandant, and that's how it was able to happen. When Mohr found out about it, he immediately said to his wife and those around him, "If I had been there, that wouldn't have happened." We even have that from him in writing. He heard about this in that house there. They didn't even have a telephone there. A policeman came from a neighboring town and told him. He then got terribly upset about it, and he and his wife came straight back.

But it was presented as suicide?

Absolutely. It was played up in all the newspapers. I have it all [the clippings] here.

Did you and your mother believe that it was a suicide?

No. That same night, these three or four characters went to a pub and got drunk and talked about it, and other people overheard them. The next day, somebody from the place called a colleague of my father's and told him about it. So we knew about it from the start. It was made known immediately, but what could we do? The doctor they called was from the prison in Bruchsal. He, of course, merely noted the death and didn't say anything about it. One can certainly tell the difference between hanging and strangling.

My father's colleague had received the corpse and taken it to the morgue at the cemetery in Karlsruhe. And the next day a doctor in Karlsruhe, who was no Jewish doctor, went there under the pretext that he was going to change my father's clothes or something because he had been in his pajamas. So he examined him, and he [saw] the indications and he wrote up a report. Unfortunately, this was lost in the bombings. But there was a doctor in Berlin, and I wrote to him, and he confirmed it for me once again.

Were there any consequences when he determined that your father was killed?

There were none. Sauer then had me summoned, in writing, and I went there. There had been a correspondence with the camp. Later this would not have happened, but the paltry things that my father had there were then given to us: books, articles of clothing, and so on. Then I wrote to them that such-and-such was missing. What especially was missing was his hat. My father had worn a broad-brimmed, brown hat. I have heard that they fought over it in the camp.

Sauer's only question related to his having heard that I wanted to take him to court. That, of course, could have had a lot of repercussions. I believe that he was thinking about those things [that were missing]. But then I said [to myself], "No. How can I take this guy to court under these circumstances?" That would have been crazy. Nevertheless, I must have given it some thought. Then he said, "So we're of the same opinion." He wanted to shake hands, but I ignored him and left.

Did you have any more contact with him after that? What was it like then? Were you afraid yourself about being arrested by the Gestapo?

No. I wasn't quite twenty-four at the time. I wasn't afraid of them. I had the feeling that nothing could happen to me. They wouldn't have dared either. . . . A Swiss newspaper wrote that there were three thousand people at the funeral, three thousand people, a great procession with people everywhere. Of course, the Gestapo was there as well. Actually it was no burial, for he was cremated at the Karlsruhe crematorium. My mother, my sister, and I were there. My brother was already gone. He had gone to Strasbourg in 1933 and then later to Paris.

Didn't one actually have to be rather cautious about saying anything?

We did talk with my father's friends, social democrats and the like, and those from his office. Of course, one kept quiet around strangers.

We then also had to move because we couldn't pay for the apartment anymore. Although my father had a good income, he had not really saved much and all the money he still had in the bank went to taxes. The taxes were high. And that was also really bad for me. I then searched for weeks for an apartment, and when I would see something, I would then tell them that we were Jews, however. Some of them would then reply, "That doesn't bother us any." But others would say, "No." Someone then told me about a rental association and I went to see them. To my great astonishment, he said to me, "That doesn't matter at all to us."

We then went to live in a small house in a modern housing development just outside of Karlsruhe, and, since we were somewhat out of town, I would then ride a bike to my father's office, where I continued to work for a while. The office continued to exist. Dr. Nachman, who was a partner and a Jew, continued to run the practice until it became impossible for him as well.

Were you politically active at the time?

No. It was only when I then went to Berlin that I wanted to do something, and then I looked around for a contact. This was in the fall of 1934. [I then became involved in] a communist group. I would always see only one person, and everyone would also use an alias. My job was the following: They would give me illegal newspapers that had been reproduced with purple letters. I was then supposed to send them to Paris. The contact in Paris would then send them money to support them. What I would do was buy some elegant magazines such as *Die Dame* and then stick the papers into a number of different pages of the magazines and then mail them off as common printed matter. They wanted the French communists to see that something was being done in Germany.

I once had these papers under my arm when I was in the subway. [In the subway] in Germany, you go through a kind of barrier—I was an attractive, young thing—and the man who punched the tickets said to me, "Oh, what kind of interesting papers are those?" My heart stood still. If he had seen what they were!

Anyway, I mailed those magazines in a completely open manner. I bought them, laid the information in them, closed them up with a tape around them, and put the address on them. I assumed that nobody would think about opening up *Die Dame*.

That was all rather dangerous. Weren't you afraid at that time?

No. During this scene in the subway, it suddenly became clear to me, "For God's sake, if he sees that!" But, in general, no. I was engaged at the time but not yet married. My fiancé was in Berlin for a while as a civil service trainee or in Magdeburg, where he was from. He would come to visit me every now and then. I also heard once that the porter or the porter's wife had made some remarks about this. But nothing happened to us.

I was still there during the Olympic Games. Since it was clear to me that I couldn't do anything in Paris as a lawyer, I then also learned to do massage and studied gymnastics. I did a lot myself. I went to a kind of school and took my exams in Berlin. You then had to do some practical work. [I did that at] a Jewish hospital near Alexanderplatz. There were only a lot of young people there, but nothing would be talked about very openly anymore. You had to take care, because somebody could have been an informant who might denounce you to someone in the Nazi Party. And the people in Berlin didn't know me. It wasn't like in Karlsruhe.

I finished with all of that in 1936. Then I got a French visa, liquidated the apartment, and went first to Düsseldorf where my aunt was still living. After that I went to Paris. I spent the summer vacation in St. Tropez with my husband, as we had gotten married. One of my cousins had a house there.

Then the war came in 1939, and all kinds of difficulties took place. My husband was sent to a camp as a native German. [He wasn't Jewish] and they locked up everyone who was a native German. I then stayed all winter in St. Tropez. And then, in May 1940, we no longer had anything to do with Germany. Then the Germans broke into Belgium, Holland, and northern France and the French locked everybody up, including the women. Eventually I was imprisoned in two camps. But I was only in the camps for two months because my husband had already been recognized as being loyal. So I was then released, but not my husband. He had to join a kind of military unit, but one without weapons.

What did you know about the murder of the Jews?

Before 1941, you hadn't heard anything. Between 1942 and 1945, I was already here [in America]. I arrived here with great difficulty with my mother on September 12, 1941. My mother had gone to France right after my father's death. My sister was nine years younger than me. She was killed. [While] they were still in Marseilles, she had a baby. Eventually she couldn't feed her child any longer and she didn't want to go on anymore. So she took the child to a children's home. Then she was picked up during a raid and sent to a temporary camp in Nancy, and from there to Poland and the gas chamber. That she was deported is something I only know about from books.

HENRY SINGER

The anti-Semitism in Germany was there before Hitler came to power. He just openly sanctioned it.

Born in 1919 and raised in Berlin as the son of a master tailor, Henry Singer fled to Italy in June 1938 and spent several years during the war in an Italian concentration camp before emigrating to the United States and becoming a clothing designer.

My father, who lived for thirty years in Germany, was a Polish citizen. In 1938 they told him to leave the country or they would arrest him and put him in a concentration camp. The only country where he could go as a Polish citizen was Italy. So my father and my brother, who was two years older than I, got a visa to go to Italy. The Germans did not allow us to take out any money. I followed about three months later.

I had two sisters still in Germany, but they put me on a train. I was trembling from fear. I was sitting in a corner by the window and there was a man sitting across from me in the train that I was sure was a secret Gestapo agent. I didn't even move; I didn't even say one word. I went through Switzerland to Italy. They had wanted to send me through Austria, but I didn't want to go through Austria because it was already a mess. This was in June 1938.

We went to Genoa, Italy. We didn't know the language, not even one word. We couldn't get a job, because they wouldn't give you a job. The government would not allow you to take a job because there was a lot of unemployment. The only thing that you could do was go into business for yourself.

My father in Germany was a master tailor, what they call a *Schneidermeister*. At one time he had seventeen people working for him. The only thing we could do in Italy was open up a tailor shop for women and men. He had to borrow the money from the Jewish community in that town. They needed tailors in Italy like a hole in the head, so it was not easy for us to make a living. We lived above the store—it was like an attic.

In the meantime, Germany became allied with Italy and consequently the Italian government was forced to emulate the laws that Hitler had, the racial laws against the Jews. The agents came along and said, "You have to get out of here. You have to get out of the store. If not, they're going to arrest you and they're going to put you in jail and then from jail they'll put you in a camp." In the meantime, the Polish government, which was very anti-Semitic, would not renew our passports anymore, and this made it difficult to go anywhere. We became stateless. We were only able to obtain a passport for travel from the Italian government that stated we were stateless. Since nobody wanted anybody with a passport that said "stateless," we couldn't go anywhere.

Then, in 1940, or just before Italy entered the war on the side of Germany, the secret agents came to us and said, "We want you and your brother (not my father) to be in front of the police headquarters on that day and at that time. If you don't come, we know who you are, and we know where you live, and emu we're going to arrest you and put you in jail first for an undetermined period, and then we will send you to a concentration camp." So that's what we had to do. But we were not alone. There were another fifty in the same situation. They took us to the main railroad station and put us on a train. We had no idea where we were going.

Finally the train came to a stop in Naples. I found out that they were uncoupling my train car from the car where my brother was and I went to my end of the train and he went to his end of the train and we reached out and blessed each other because we didn't know if we were going to see each other again. Later I found out that they sent my brother to Campania. I was sent down to Calabria to a concentration camp that they just had built.

This concentration camp was in a huge valley that was malaria infested. The director of the camp tried to be very harsh and very mean verbally—he tried to emulate the Germans. There was nothing there, two barracks, no water, no nothing. The water had to be trucked in every day. But they were building more barracks every day, and the camp grew to about ninety barracks eventually. I spent thirty-eight months there. The name of the camp was Bellamonte. I must say in all fairness, however, that the Italians treated us very humanely.

Unfortunately, my father was in northern Italy, and, as the war went on, northern Italy was occupied by the Germans and southern Italy was occupied by the Allies. The dividing line was Rome. Rome was declared an open city because the Vatican was there. We were liberated way before the north. During that time the German military arrested my father and sent him to Poland to a concentration camp. To this day I am still trying to find out what happened to him. They told me he died. The German government wrote me a letter saying he died on May 8, 1945, which I don't believe because May 8, 1945 was the day of the official end of the war.

Like I said before and wish to emphasize, the Italian people were very generous and very humane and very hospitable. If it wasn't for them, we would not be here. So I must pay tribute to them. They're the ones who saved our lives. Even the secret agents were very humane. I cannot emphasize this enough. I wish to make this comment: In Germany the government was very bad, but the people were bad too; in Italy the government was forced to be bad to emulate Hitler's laws and so on, but the people were very good. In Germany you didn't have to force the people to execute orders, because there are stories in Germany and Poland, which are documented, where the people took babies and ripped them apart. Now nobody gave an order to any soldier or to any person to take a baby and rip it apart. You have to be able to do that. The Italian people would never ever be able to do that.

My wife has a story to tell that would take four tape recorders to hear. She's from Poland, but she came to Italy as a baby and lived eighteen years in Italy before she left. She was hidden in a convent by the nuns. She worked for the partisans. One day a German soldier caught her and wanted to rape her. When she said no, he took out a gun and said, "You let your pants down or I'll shoot you." So she said, "Go ahead and shoot." And he did, he did shoot her. They had to rush her to the hospital. She was afraid to be discovered that she was Jewish. After the operation she ran away from there, from the hospital. She went to the convent and the nuns hid her until the end of the war.

In Berlin, before I left, I went to a design school. I was very young, but I had talent for it. In the two years I went to the school it was very good, but then everything had to be shut down because of Hitler. All the businesses, everything had to be closed. It took me twenty years to get back into my field, because when I came to the United States, I had to go back to school because everything is different here. I had to learn the technical side of design, drafting. Otherwise, I was a designer, earned a living, supported my family, sent my children to college, had vacations, and everything. But for three years I had to go to school. I had a job during the day, and, after the job, I went to school and never came home before ten o'clock in the evening. But it paid off.

Could you discuss your experiences in Nazi Germany a bit more?

I can tell you about an incident when I was about eight years old—that's way before Hitler came to power. We were playing barefoot in the street. It was summertime, and we were playing all kinds of games. There was a neighbor kid, and we were playing games together. When he lost a game he became abusive; he couldn't take it (the Germans were bad losers). After the game he became abusive. He walked this way and then that way and then he turned around and said, "Einbahnstrasse nach Palestina" [take a one-way street to Palestine]. He was the same age as us. Where did he learn this? He learned this from his parents, from his father. But you know, it proves again that he knew that is where we belonged. I also want to say it's ingrained in them. You know what they say in Poland? The children, when they are suckling the mother's breast, are drinking in anti-Semitism. And that holds true to this day.

America is different than Germany. I'll tell you why. It is because America is composed of a lot of small ethnic minorities; a lot of ethnic minorities form the majority. What does it mean? Everybody is an American and at the same time everybody is something else. National patriotism in this country is so far apart from the German nationalism. Why? Everybody in Germany is a German. If you're not German, you're somebody else. Not here. Not in this country.

One thing I must say to you is this: There are some German Jews born in Germany. Their parents were born in Germany, their grandparents were born in Germany, and they participated in World War I and had many citations. They were fanatical patriots for Germany—it's something not to believe. They were so patriotic that they would give their life for Germany, and a lot of them were professors, doctors, scientists, judges; they were very high up. It hurt the German economy tremendously. The biggest department stores in Berlin were founded by Jews. I was just in Berlin in October 1993 because my mother is buried there. She died of natural causes before Hitler. I couldn't go there for about fifty years. But in 1993, I went with my wife and I saw all these stores, fantastic department stores, that were founded by Jews. The Jews aided the economy of Germany.

But in all honesty I want to say that not all Germans were as bad as you see being depicted in the movies and the films. The majority was, but there were some that were not. So it's not fair to accuse all of them.

One of my sisters survived the war in Berlin because she was hidden by a German family through to the end of the war. She was working for Siemens, a big electrical company. This factory was in a suburb of Berlin. She worked there like everybody else and then the word got around at the train station. They said, "You better be careful. They're looking to arrest Jews." Finally they arrested them. They put them on a truck, and of course she knew what was going to happen. Everything was dark. Because they were driving through the woods and the road was bumpy, they had to go a little slow. So she took her chances and jumped off the truck and ran into the woods. Of course they saw that she had jumped and they couldn't put on the lights, so they shot at her. They shot at random. Of course she was hit. They shot her on the side and she fell down in the woods. It had to be in 1940 or 1941, I cannot pinpoint it. She probably passed out. And then, in the morning, a woman found her and took her home. This woman kept her hidden throughout the war. My sister came here after the war and kept sending the woman packages, but then that woman died too.

Like I say, they were not all bad. The majority, yes, but you cannot condemn all of them because the majority was bad. The anti-Semitism in Germany was there before Hitler came to power. He just openly sanctioned it, and he also asked them to kill. It was all retribution. He gave orders to the police.

They were against the Jews, always have been. And the indifference. If you are indifferent to a wrong, then you are part of it. If you know about it and you are indifferent, then you become part of it, part of the anti-Semitism. I'll tell you something else. It goes much further than this. It's not only the Germans that hated Jews. Almost the whole world hated Jews. The concentration camps—Auschwitz, Dachau, Buchenwald—Britain knew about it, France knew about it, the Americans knew about it. They could have done something about it. They could have bombed the camps because they were burning the bodies anyway. But they didn't do it. You know why? Because they said, "Leave Hitler alone because he's doing a good job for us killing all the Jews. He gets the blame and we get what we want." That's it in a nutshell, and nobody's going to tell me any different.

How do you feel about Germany today?

I have mixed feeling about that. I was there in 1993 because I wanted to visit my mother's grave, and my old neighborhood where I was born doesn't exist anymore. The school that I went to was also destroyed, was bombed. Berlin is a beautiful city, don't misunderstand me. It's one of the nicest cities in the world. It's nice and clean and organized. It has a lot of lakes like no other city in the world. The public transportation system is fantastic. I went back to where I used to live. The building looked like brand-new; they had just painted it. The people are very efficient, but ice cold. I was afraid to crack a joke. What am I going to do in a city like that?

KARL MEYER

In Cologne they never had this anti-Semitism.

Born in 1915 and raised in Cologne, Karl Meyer was arrested in August 1938 for underground resistance activity. After spending two months in a Cologne jail, he emigrated to Shanghai.

I was arrested for *Vorbereitung für Hochverrat* [treason], but there was never a trial. As a matter of fact, when the Gestapo officer arrested me he said he didn't even know why the hell they were taking me. He then asked me about some people that I knew and whether I was a communist or had anything to do with them. Of course I had, but I didn't tell him that. I only told him about some woman I knew whose house had been razed and made into a hole in the ground and who had gone to Ulan Bator.

I wasn't a party member. I knew some people who were in the underground and some people who were communists in '32 and '33, but I wasn't a party member or anything. I mean I collected money for some people in the Red Help, Rote Hilfe [resistance organization], which collected money to try to help some people who were in prisons and early concentration camps and so on. But I couldn't tell them that, so I told them about the lady I knew who lived in Ulan Bator.

So you were involved in resistance activity?

Yeah, sure. Among other things, I wrote letters to my friends about the conditions in Germany. I had friends in Luxembourg mostly, and some guys who had emigrated to Holland. And I probably repeated some rumors and some jokes and some things, and I kept copies. So when they arrested me, they searched my house and they found some of this correspondence. I also had a whole folder on Dimitrov and the Reichstag fire trial that they found, and a book by H.G. Wells called *The Dictators* that they took.

They were trying to make a case that I had maligned the führer or something like that in the early years, in '33 and '34. But I was arrested in '38, five years later. What happened was my father died in an accident in '32, and then my mother rented out a room in our house to get some money. One guy who lived in our house in early 1933 was an old-time socialist whose wife had been arrested. But he hadn't been arrested at that time, and what I found out was that this guy, five years later, denounced me as a fellow traveler or communist or that I had done some illegal things. That was the accusation, but even the Gestapo guy said he couldn't understand why. So when they came to my house in August 1938 and arrested me, I had no idea why he had denounced me. Maybe he became a Nazi or maybe they had arrested him, I don't know. He didn't live in our house for a long time. What had happened was that he and I had listened to Radio Moscow and stuff like that. That's what he told them.

How difficult was it to receive Radio Moscow?

Sometimes it wasn't very clear. They played *The International*, and then they came on. At that time I didn't speak any other language, so it must have been in German. It was dangerous. This guy living in our house had a radio—apparently a short-wave radio or whatever—and so we both listened to it. On my regular radio, I couldn't get it.

We had some contacts. I went abroad a couple of times during the Nazi period to Belgium, Holland, Luxembourg, and there I read, of course, the antifascist press. I knew it was illegal. I once came back from Belgium and I had all kinds of newspapers stuck in my hatband or someplace, and they caught me at the border. But there was an old guy there, and he took it away and said, "You have some cigarettes that can be donated to the veterans, so get on the next train and go home." I was lucky. Through these contacts and through reading papers from abroad, we knew about the concentration camps and other things. I also had friends who had been in concentration camps and had come out.

But you were never put in a concentration camp?

No, I was lucky. As a matter of fact, I left Germany on November 6, 1938, three days before *Kristallnacht* and I then went to Shanghai. When I was in jail, some guys from the Jewish community who had good relations with the Gestapo promised the Gestapo that if they would release whoever was in jail, they would get them out of the country. When I was released in October, they told me to get a passage and get out. The only place in the world I could go to was Shanghai at the time.

I was only there from December '38 to September–October '40, a year and a half, and then I came to the United States. I wasn't there during the war years. Anyway, when we arrived in December '38, there were maybe a couple hundred refugees in Shanghai, like some Jewish professional men, doctors, and lawyers who got there in '34 or '35. But in the next nine months about twenty thousand came. You see, that was after the *Kristallnacht*. When these people could get out of concentration camps, they left Germany and Austria right away and often the only place for them to go was Shanghai because you didn't need a visa.

In my case my mother went to the Nord-Deutsche Lloyd and bought a ticket for me for about eight hundred marks, and that was it. I then went by train to Genoa and caught the ship. I got a passport, which was only good for six months. When we later got to America, the German consul, instead of renewing the passport, put it in his drawer and said, "You're not a citizen anymore."

Shanghai, except for the part around the Chinese town and around the outlying areas, was occupied by the Japanese. But the international settlement was ruled by the consuls of Britain, Germany, Italy, and the United States. They were the government there. The French concession was part of France, it was different, but you could move freely between those areas. You didn't need any visa or any papers.

Why didn't more Jews go to Shanghai?

Well, in the first place, until the war broke out in 1940–1941, nobody was thinking about the Holocaust or anything like that. People like my mother had lived there all their lives; they were Germans. They didn't want to leave if they didn't have to. Some people saw it coming and left in '34, '35. But then, in '38 after the *Kristallnacht,* a lot of people left. The people who left before got to, I think, Luxembourg or France or Holland or Belgium. They got caught up later in 1940 when the Germans invaded, and then they wound up getting to Spain and Cuba or they wound up in concentration camps in the east.

What people don't understand is why would people who are born in a country, grew up there, are citizens of this country, have their culture, their language, and everything, want to leave or should leave? You know? It's a hard decision. For me, I was still a young man. It was an adventure.

Could you describe the Gestapo officer who arrested you?

He was probably in his thirties and he was relatively nice when he interrogated me in his office. I was lucky. I was never abused physically. Some people I knew were beaten up and tortured and God knows what. The Gestapo used tactics like saying, "You don't speak loud enough, speak louder." Or, "You stink from the mouth, don't breathe on me"—this kind of intimidation. You never knew what they did or didn't know. He asked me about all my friends and so I gave him some names of people I knew. They were abroad, so they couldn't touch them.

This took place in the Gestapo headquarters in Cologne, but I was never put against a door and then hit or anything like that. As a matter of fact, what happened was that after I was released, I had to get a Reich *Steurerklärung* [tax statement] that I didn't owe any taxes or anything like that. I had to go to the finance office to get this because I never paid taxes. My mother maybe did, but I didn't. So the guy there told me, "Well, I can't do that, it takes time." And I told him that the Gestapo told me to get out. He then said, "Oh, the Gestapo. Well, get a notice from them." When I went back to this Gestapo guy and told him the tax man wanted a written statement, he said, "We don't give any written statements, but I'll call him." I then went back on my bicycle to the tax office there and the guy was as white as a sheet and said, "Yeah the Gestapo called and said it's all right." I mean there was such a fear of the Gestapo and this business in Germany. It was amazing.

But, in Cologne, they never had this anti-Semitism. I mean, I could go on the street, riding my bike and the Hitler Youths came marching by and some guy comes over to me and says, "Why don't you salute the flag?" I told them, "I'm Jewish." "Oh, excuse me," they said. In other places, they would have beat you to a pulp.

Did Cologne really have no anti-Semitism?

No, because it was a Catholic city and the archbishop was not a friend of the Nazis. They were more liberal in Cologne, and also in Hamburg. But in Berlin and in Munich with the Bavarians, of course, they were rabid anti-Semites.

I lived five years under the Nazis. As a matter of fact, I worked for a lawyer across from the Justice Department and I had to go there every morning and pick up briefs and deliver briefs and stuff like that. Those guys were glad when I came in. I said, "Good morning." I didn't say "Heil Hitler." They didn't always know that you're a Jew. I mean, sometimes they were glad that they could say "good day" instead of "Heil Hitler." But when the war started, things became different, I'm sure.

I want to tell you another thing. Where we lived in Cologne-Bayenthal, our neighbor happened to be the postmaster in Cologne-Zollstock, where I used to work. I went to the post office every day to deliver and pick up mail. One day he calls me in his office and he says, "Look, I'm very embarrassed to say this. I value you as neighbors. But please tell your mother not to take it amiss if I don't say hello to her. After all, I'm an official here and I could lose my job. So please don't take it as if we have anything against you." This was the feeling in Germany that some people who had a position couldn't do that; they couldn't be friendly with Jews or be seen talking to Jews or what have you.

Did you not come into contact with at least some anti-Semites?

Oh, yeah. Once in '32, when I was an antifascist, I once got slugged by a Nazi. But, otherwise, during the five years of the Nazi time I lived through, I was never attacked or anything. I was kicked out of school at the end of '33, but that was something else, you know.

Let's go back to the Gestapo man. What did he look like? Did he wear a uniform?

No. Those guys were all wearing civilian clothes—no SS uniforms or anything—just like our detectives. The room I was interrogated in was like an office. We went in and sat at a desk in a large room and there were some other desks and other people at Gestapo headquarters. I think he took notes or just talked. He knew he didn't have much of a case or anything except for the stuff they took from my house—you know, the books and that photo of Dimitrov and some of the correspondence.

He had arrested me with another officer. These two guys had taken me out of the house. They looked in my house and took these couple of books and things and then put me in a wagon that was a kind of early version of a jeep, and took me down to the jail there at the Appelhofplatz. They used no handcuffs. They just put me in a cell with a lot of homosexuals they had rounded up at that time. Then they took me over to the Gestapo headquarters and interrogated me and put me in a cell and then they put me in Klingelpütz [jail]. I was about six or eight weeks in solitary and I was considered a political prisoner with an

X over my door. That means no visitors, no writing privileges, no nothing. Then after some weeks I got out and was put with two other guys in a cell that was meant for one. I had a mattress on the floor.

Let me tell you another thing, the wardens were elderly men and they were relatively nice. One time, one of them forgot to take me out of the cell, so he had me walk around with a couple of shackled murderers in the yard. Another time, when we three were in the cell, they came around and we had bedbugs. So they had to do something and so they used blowtorches on the bedsteads and said, "Hey, you Jews, keep it clean." But they were nice.

The Gestapo man who arrested and interrogated me was civil in a way and he didn't use any force on me, any physical abuse. One time he came to the jail and asked me again, "Why did this guy denounce you?" I said, "I don't know." He didn't get anything else out of me. I didn't tell him exactly what I had done or what I was involved in. I put it down on some other people that in the meantime had left the country. But I don't know why he didn't use physical force against me. Maybe he happened to be a more decent guy. Or maybe I was too insignificant. I only saw him once or twice again after that when I needed to deal with this tax business. I went up to Gestapo headquarters and reported to him and that was all.

What do you recall about the boycott of Jewish stores in April 1933? Did that make a strong impression on you?

No, not really, because I wasn't involved in any trade. At that time, after I was out of school, I was an apprentice at a company that made things for the shoemaker trade and the bosses were Jewish, but nobody was boycotting. You see, the early boycott really was more of professional people. Then later I worked for a couple of Jewish lawyers in '37 and '38 and I was in an office. Their clientele was mostly Jewish, of course.

As I said, the climate in Cologne was different than in other parts of Germany. You see, the Nazis were anti-Catholic and the Catholic cardinal was not a Nazi. They had a joke that when Göring came to town, he wanted the cardinal's uniform. Göring was a nut about uniforms. But, as I said, they were more Catholic and more liberal going back to the Napoleonic times and the occupation by the French. So in the Rhineland, and in Cologne in particular, they were more liberal and not anti-Semitic to that extent. That I know and remember.

Could you say a little more about resistance and the climate of fear and terror? Did you know, for example, other Jews who were involved in the Rote Hilfe organization?

There was that one young lady who went to Ulan Bator. She was very much involved in it. She was a communist, and she had a communist lover. Otherwise, I don't know anybody. The other ones were Gentiles. The Rote Hilfe collected money just to help political prisoners or their families. . . . In '33 everything was illegal after the Nazis came to power. Then anybody who was a social democrat or a communist was an enemy, and anything they did was illegal.

How about you? You said that the fear was amazing? Did you feel that fear?

No! As I said, I had no fear until I was arrested. I walked around freely and did whatever I did. As I said, I went a couple of times to Luxembourg, Holland, and Belgium. Nobody knew about the impending doom. I knew some of my friends had been arrested and some were in camps. And some people were able to emigrate and go to Israel, or, if they were lucky, to America. Like anything else, when you're young, you think nothing ever happens to you. Yes, I was involved in resistance, but only for the first couple of years. After that it died out and the people who were involved were not there anymore or you couldn't do it anymore.

If they hadn't arrested you, do you think you would have left anyway?

No. I think I would have stayed there. The people who emigrated in those days were people who had 100,000 marks in assets and they gave 80,000 to the Reich and took only 20,000 abroad. I didn't expect to leave. You see, when the Germans started this *Drang nach Osten*, they considered Poles and Russians *Untermenschen*, not the same racially, culturally, and intellectually as they were. In the war when they started killing, they didn't give a damn who they killed. If there were a lot of Jews that they killed, I can't explain why most of these Germans did this and the others in Germany didn't know about it or pretended not to know. After the war I had a correspondence with a guy who lived near Dachau in Munich. He claimed he didn't know about Dachau!

Did you believe him?

No, of course not. They closed their eyes. When I was in Germany, we knew about the concentration camps. For example, they told a friend of mine who came out of concentration camp: "Don't talk about it. Don't say anything. If you do, we will put you back in." There was this fear of the Gestapo and the Nazis that people just shut their eyes. Also the Nazis and the Germans are great at putting a fence around things. Not an open, mesh fence like here, but a wall, so you can't see in and you don't know what's going on behind this wall. So people didn't believe it or didn't know about it, or pretended not to know. As long as their lives were not touched by it, fine. In a way it's like here with the people who don't know about discrimination against blacks or Hispanics. They disregard it. To them it doesn't exist. They close their eyes to it.

+2+

Jews Who Left Germany After *Kristallnacht*

ARMIN HERTZ

My toes were frozen . . . all of them fell off.

Born in 1924 and raised by his divorced mother in Berlin, Armin Hertz escaped to Belgium in December 1938 but was deported to Auschwitz in late October 1942. He also survived Buchenwald concentration camp and one of the death marches near the end of the war.

When Hitler came to power in Germany in 1933, I was a young boy, barely nine years old. My mother and father got divorced earlier in 1930. I had a brother three years younger than myself. We lived with my mother and we had a furniture store in our family. All of my mother's brothers and sisters also had furniture stores in Berlin.

After Hitler came to power, there was the boycott in April of that year. I remember that very vividly because I saw the Nazi Party members in their brown uniforms and armbands standing in front of our store with signs: "Kauft nicht bei Juden" [Don't buy from Jews]. That, of course, was very frightening to us. They marched back and forth all day long. They also put graffiti on the windows of the stores and wrote down "Jude" [Jew] and things like that. Nobody entered the shop. As a matter of fact, there was a competitor across the street—she must have been a member of the Nazi Party already by then—who used to come over and chase people away and say, "Don't buy here, these are Jews." After that we continued to run the store, and we went to school—my brother and I went to public school. The anti-Semitism was very vivid in school. In fact, it was so strong that we couldn't continue to go to that public school. It got very uncomfortable.

Was the anti-Semitism mostly from the teachers or the other schoolchildren?

Both. They were trying to teach us Nazi songs. I vividly remember this song they were marching in the street with. The Hitler Youth, young boys actually of our age, were singing, "Das Judenblut vom Messer spritzt, geht's uns nochmal so gut" [The Jews' blood spurting from the knife makes us feel especially good]. They were also singing it in the school. There were not many other Jews in my school, and then my mother took us out of that school and we went to a Jewish school in Berlin. A decree had come out that Jewish teachers were not allowed to teach anymore in public schools. Therefore, there was no shortage of teachers in the Jewish schools. We went to that Jewish school and for us, of course, that was better. This went on until 1938.

During the *Kristallnacht*, our store was destroyed, glass was broken, the synagogues were set on fire. There was a synagogue in the same street where we lived. It was on the first floor of a commercial building; downstairs were stores, and upstairs was a synagogue. In the back of that building, there was a factory so they could not set that synagogue on fire because people were living and working there. But they threw everything out of the window—the Torah scrolls, the prayer books, the benches, everything was lying in the street.

My mother was very worried about her sister, because she had two little children and in the back of the building where she lived there was also a synagogue. So we tried to get in touch with her by phone the next day, but nobody answered. My mother got desperate and said to me, "Get your bicycle and go to Aunt Bertha to see what's going on." As I was riding along the business district, I saw all the stores destroyed, windows broken, everything lying in the street. They were even going into the stores and running away with the merchandise. Finally, I got to my aunt's house and I saw a large crowd assembled in front of the store. The fire department was there; the police were there. The fire department was pouring water on the adjacent building. The synagogue in the back was on fire, but they were not putting the water on the synagogue. The police were there watching it. I mingled with the crowd. I didn't want to be too obvious. I didn't want to get into trouble. But I heard from people talking that the people who lived there were all evacuated, all safe in the neighborhood with friends. So I went right back and reported to my mother.

After *Kristallnacht* our store was destroyed and it was impossible to stay in Berlin because there was no way of earning a living. We had to get out! My mother had a brother in Berlin who had obtained a visa to come to the U.S. just before November 9. He needed passage to go to the U.S., so he went to Antwerp, Belgium, and he waited over there to go on one of the Holland America lines to New York. So she got in touch with him and told him what had happened. She said, "You have got to help us. We have got to get out of Berlin. We can't stay here. We have to do something." So they devised a plan. I was fourteen and my brother was twelve.

My mother went to the Anhalter Bahnhof in Berlin and bought us a return railroad ticket to Paris. The plan was that my brother and I would go to the Anhalter Bahnhof and take the midnight train to Paris, which made a stop in Brussels, Belgium. My uncle would be in Brussels and take us off the train. When we got to the border between Belgium and Germany and the passport control came to ask for our papers, we told them that we were visiting a relative in Paris for a short time and then coming back. Our only papers were our ID cards marked with a red *J* to indicate that we were Jewish. We showed that to the two fellows there and they looked at each other and said, "They're going to Paris. Let the French worry about them." So we got through the border that way and went to Brussels.

When the train pulled in to the station, my aunt and uncle were right on the platform and they took us off the train and took us to Antwerp where they lived temporarily in a room they had rented in a rooming house until their ship came to take them to New York. The lady who owned the rooming house also had another room upstairs under the roof, and she let us stay there and my uncle paid her something.

My mother couldn't have gone with us as it would never have worked. [Instead] she went to Aachen, which is on the border between Belgium and Germany, and there she met a group of four or five people and a guide they had paid to take them during the night over the border into Belgium. But they got caught by the German border police and were sent back to Berlin. So she was in Berlin, my uncle left for New York, and we were in a really touchy situation. [We hoped that] maybe there would be another occasion for her to escape, but it didn't happen because, after that, they tied up the border so tight as there were so many people [trying to escape].

In Antwerp there were many Jewish refugees who had run away and stayed there. The Belgian police were pretty lenient. They gave us a temporary permit to stay there for three months. You could get this as long as the Jewish committee would give you a paper saying that they would support you, that you would not be a burden to the state, and that you were not working. After three months, they would renew the permit.

What happened to your mother?

She went to England in 1939. First she got a document from the Berlin police president allowing her to leave the country. You had to show that you had paid all your taxes, that you did not owe any money, that you were of good character, and that you were in good health. And then, through friends and relatives, she found an English family that helped her apply to work in their household in London, and this is what she did.

We were able to correspond with her from Belgium, but the English government would not give us permission to go there to join her. Although there was a Jewish committee that was helping us, we were stuck and it was a desperate situation. We were still young and we now had nobody there in Belgium. Our uncle was in America, our mother was in London, and we were in Antwerp. And then, on May 10, 1940, the war broke out in Belgium. The Germans overran the Netherlands, Belgium, and France within ten days. So this committee in Antwerp had placed us with another family, a Jewish family. Some of the children were fortunate because they were placed with a nice family with children that wanted to help. But we were not that fortunate. We were placed with a family that was poor and did this for money. Then the war broke out and they didn't get paid anymore because the committee that handled this had got money from America, from a fund. So we had to leave and we were actually living in the street. It was very, very bad.

So the family threw you out in a way.

Yes. They said they had no money and couldn't afford to support us. Since the war was on, everything was now rationed and we couldn't even get ration cards. When we went to the authorities to apply for the ration cards, they wouldn't give them to us because they thought that we were trying to have some kind of a scheme to get extra ration cards. They could not believe that two young children would be living by themselves. We told them we lived in the street. I did some hard jobs that I wasn't supposed to do but did anyway to get a little extra money to live on.

[Eventually] we found a place that was inexpensive and we were able to afford with the money I earned. They called it a mansard; it was underneath the roof. It was a terrible place. We were eaten up by bedbugs every night. We had to go begging for food. Then my brother got taken in by a Jewish family that had no children and he was taken care of at least. I was now alone, but I found a job in a bakery and I slept in the bakery, right on the benches where they baked the bread. It was warm in the winter and at least there was always a little bread left over. That went on until June 1942.

In the meantime, the German occupation forces imposed the same laws against the Jews that they had done in Germany: they made you wear the Jewish star, Jews were not allowed to go out in the street after seven or eight, and they started to round up people to send away. At that time we didn't know anything about concentration camps. We had no idea what was happening in Poland, in the east. They said they were sending people away to work; they would be in labor camps and get their rations there and wouldn't have to worry. In the beginning people actually volunteered because they had no money and the official rations were very small. To buy extra food on the black market was very expensive and they had no money. They thought that if they would go to work, they would get better food. After a while, we found out that those people who went voluntarily to these work camps never returned. So people stopped volunteering.

Then they started to round people up. They would take a block area, surround it with troops of the Wehrmacht, and they also had help from Belgian collaborators in the Rex Party. In one of those roundups, I was caught. They only wanted men at that time. They sent us by train to France to help build the Atlantic wall, a wall as thick as a house that went from Holland all the way through Belgium and France. They thought that the Allied invasion would come from that side.

It was very heavy work. The supervision of this camp was done by Organisation Todt. We had to build a fence around it ourselves. It was close to the beaches where they had to build defense positions. Our job was to carry water and cement. Sand they got from the beaches, but the cement we had to carry in cement bags. The sanitary conditions in that camp were very poor—for toilets we had to dig a huge ditch. I contracted typhoid fever there. The guards got afraid because of that. There were five of us who had typhoid fever. They then took us to a French hospital and put us up in the basement. That was the first time in weeks that we slept in a clean bed. In the beginning we couldn't eat because we had such high temperatures.

When we got better after a few weeks the guards showed up again and said, "We're sending you back to Belgium. You have to go back to the camp now." We did go back to Belgium, but not back to the camp. They put us on regular passenger trains, with fifteen to twenty people in each compartment for eight, and brought us to Mechelen, which was an old army camp from World War I that the Germans used as an assembly point for all the Jews—men, women, and children—they had rounded up while we were in France. From there they added to our train another train with box cars, freight cars. This was the six-teenth transport from Mechelen. They gave us a card with a string to put around our neck, and we got a number—my number was 569. That was on October 31, 1942. There were 848 men, 94 women, and 41 children. Of the men, 54 returned. None of the women returned; none of the children returned. From 983, a total of 54 men returned.

When we got to Auschwitz, the train stopped and they opened up the cars. Everybody had to get out. Right away they separated the women and the chil-dren to one side and the men had to go to the other side. Then we saw some men trying to whisper to us who were working around the train with striped uniforms on and their hair shaved off. They were saying, "Walk!" We couldn't figure out what that meant, but we soon found out. The camp was a short dis-tance away. Anyone who was tired or felt that he couldn't walk was to go to the other side and supposedly there would be trucks that would pick them up and bring them to the camp. The people that were able to walk were to march. We got the message and we lined up to march to the camp. The other people that could not walk, or didn't want to, we never saw again. They went straight to the gas chamber.

When you took the train to Auschwitz, did you know what would happen there?

No, no idea. We had never heard of Auschwitz. We didn't know that a place like Auschwitz existed in 1942 at that time. They had said that there were shootings in Russia, in Ukraine where the Germans had advanced way back into Russia. There were rumors around in Belgium. We thought it was horrible, but we couldn't really believe it.

They did not just march us there to the camp and the gate with the large sign over it: Arbeit macht frei. They forced us. They had these truncheons and they hit you over the head if you didn't walk fast enough. They brought us into a quarantine block. We went into the main camp, Auschwitz 1. In Auschwitz 1 they had brick barracks. Two floors, a ground floor that held about four hun-dred people and six hundred people upstairs. Then came the barbers and they shaved our hair off. Then they put numbers on our arm—I had number 72552. All that put us in shock because nobody would expect that. They took every-thing away from us. We got these pajama-like uniforms and wooden shoes like those Dutch shoes, very uncomfortable to work with. And then we got a big speech from a man who was in charge of the block. He said, "You are going to work here. This is a work camp. There is no escape from here. The only way you can get out of here is through the chimney." We didn't even understand what he meant by that.

Then they put us into work details. First I worked digging ditches for waterlines. There was a lot of construction going on at that time around Auschwitz. They were building factories, they were enlarging the camp, and they were building another camp. It was very hard work and the rations they gave us were not enough to survive on. Every day they gave you a piece of bread that was divided into four pieces. Each one of us got one quarter—that was the ration for the day. Then you had a bowl—everybody had a bowl. Every day they gave you one liter of so-called soup. With the bread, they gave you what they called tea. Sometimes it was so bitter, you couldn't even drink it. It was made of leaves of trees, whatever they had. It was practically impossible to survive on this.

Auschwitz is in Poland; it was very cold there. This was now going into November and December. In Auschwitz they made a *Maurerschule* teaching young people how to lay bricks. I applied for it and they took me in because I was young. We got the same rations as the other people who were working outside, but we were protected from the elements because we were working inside. The teachers were all prisoners. In Auschwitz the administration inside the camp was done by prisoners. These prisoners were criminals, German criminals. In Auschwitz there were also non-Jews; these guys were the capos, the block elders. They would let their frustration out on us. That was very bad. Sometimes they were worse than the guards.

After a few weeks, they sent us out on a work commando. They were building a factory. We found out that this factory was actually built for Krupp. When we got there, the bricklayers were Polish citizens working for the Germans who were paid daily by the hour. We had to hand them the bricks and the mortar. These Polish civilians went home every night to Kattowitz or to the city of Auschwitz. They saw what was going on there.

I stayed in Auschwitz for over two years, which was very rare. I knew all the ins and outs. I was like a rat—I was able to run around that camp blind. Then, on January 18, 1945, they evacuated Auschwitz because at that time the Russian army had advanced in the east. We could already hear the bombardments and the artillery fire from the heavy cannons. They marched us toward Germany. That was the death march. Anybody who could not follow was just shot and left on the roadside. There was snow and ice; it was very cold. They gave us double rations when we left. Of course, that was not much because we marched for days and days. We slept nights in open fields and hundreds of people just died, left lying on the road, shot.

Who were the guards on the death march?

Mostly SS guards. If you ran away, you were very obvious. You could be recognized immediately as a prisoner. It wasn't that simple to just run away. But some people did and managed to hide and get civilian clothes somehow because there were thousands [of us on the death march].

We went to the town of Breslau. There they put us on open cars and we got a lift to another camp, a very big camp. It was way overcrowded, terrible. They put us in a barrack with nothing for us to sleep on. We had to sit down on the floor and we couldn't even lie down. After a day or two they were looking for workers and we right away volunteered. They wanted about two hundred people to work in a factory nearby. We thought there couldn't be a place worse than this one was, so get out of it. When we arrived at the factory, it had been closed already for weeks. Soon we found out what they wanted us to do. The next morning they took us out to a clearance in the woods. They gave us shovels and they had us dig there. It was February 17, 1945. We left on February 26. Then they took us to a town named Reichenau. There they put us again on open cars, about one hundred people in one car, with no food and a bucket in the middle for sanitary needs. We rode on that train for about six days and five nights. People were dying like flies. We had no water, no food, nothing. Once in a while it snowed, so we had a little water from the snow.

The train stopped many times en route. Sometimes it stopped near a station on a siding and they left the train standing there for a whole day because they needed that locomotive to push another train, a through train or a supply train for the army. While we were there and when we saw a civilian nearby, we used to scream and yell, but they wouldn't give us anything. Finally, the train arrived in Buchenwald, Germany, near Weimar. In our car, there were 107 people. Anytime somebody died, we took their clothing off, put it around us to keep warm, and put the dead bodies over to one side. When we arrived in Buchenwald, they opened up the train and the few people that were still alive could hardly walk. I, myself—my toes were frozen—have no toes left; all of them fell off.

In Buchenwald, the administration of the camp was political prisoners, not all necessarily communists, but democrats, socialists, lawyers, and intellectuals who were against the Nazi regime. These were nice people. They really wanted to help us, not like in Auschwitz. They had very little that they could give us, but whatever they had they shared. They tried to do the best they could. I myself couldn't walk. They had taken off my shoes; they had to cut them off actually because my feet were frozen and my toes almost fell off by themselves. They put us in a barrack, 1600 in Buchenwald in the *kleine Lager*, a big camp they called "little camp." We had bunks where four to five people slept in a line with a little straw for a bed; there were four levels. The commandant decided that the sick people didn't need the full ration anymore because they didn't work. They didn't give us any bread anymore. They only gave us that soup, so-called soup. We were very, very sick. If that would have lasted another day or two, I would not have made it.

On April 11, the American army came into Buchenwald. I was so delirious at that time, I didn't even realize that these Americans were liberating us. I thought these were other guards that were sent in because we heard a lot of shooting going on. We thought the SS would send them out on the front and send others to guard us. But it turned out that these were Americans and they were liberating us. They were very good to us. Right away they took the very sick people like myself out and brought us into Weimar, into civilian hospitals. There were regular beds and German doctors and nurses who took care of us. These nurses and doctors claimed they didn't know there was such a camp. Nobody knew what went on. But we knew that throughout the years the prisoners from Buchenwald went into the city of Weimar and cleaned the streets, dug ditches there, did excavations, and whatever. If they dropped a bomb, they took them out there to defuse the bombs. So they must have seen them because they also were wearing these striped uniforms. But they claimed they did not know.

We were very fortunate they sent us to this hospital, because the other prisoners that were a bit healthier, who could walk by themselves, they put up in the SS barracks. The SS, they put into the camp. The Americans would not let us hit the SS men. I remember the guy next to me wanted to and the American officer held back his hands and told him, "Don't do that. If you do that, you come to the same level that they are." The American soldiers wanted to be good to us. They gave us all the food they had. That was a big problem because many people died because they ate all this food. They could not digest it because their intestines were all tied up. In the hospital they knew how to handle this. They gave us special food—just cereal with water and maybe skim milk. Every day they slightly increased the fat content of the rations that they gave us until we got better. I was there for not too long. On May 5 I was already back in Brussels.

The Belgian government and the Dutch and the French had sent delegations to Buchenwald to find out if there were any citizens there. I told them a little lie; I told them I was a Belgian citizen. There was no way for them to check this because nobody had any papers. The Americans took us on transport trains back to Brussels. In Brussels they put us up in hospitals. I stayed in a hospital for a while. Then they put us in a villa outside of Brussels. I stayed there for almost a year. I had to learn how to walk again.

In the meantime, I got in contact with my uncle and I found my brother. He had survived in Belgium hiding in the Ardennes, the Belgian mountains, and he managed to stay there throughout the war. I also found my mother in England. My uncle who was in the U.S. sent us papers to come here. That's how we got here. Then I got married and started a new life. I have two lovely daughters and four grandchildren.

We try not to remember. It's not easy. For thirty-six years, I couldn't talk about it. I'm able to speak freely about it now. My wife can tell you that for years I used to wake up at night soaked in sweat. When I came to this country, if I saw a policeman on the street, I used to walk over to the other side of the street. It was not easy.

JOSEF STONE

All the people on the sidewalks started yelling at us—normal Germans, children and adults, and women also.

Born the son of a salesman in Frankfurt in 1921, Josef Stone emigrated to the United States in 1939 soon after his father returned from Dachau concentration camp.

I had been in a Jewish school from the very first day in school in 1928. We were liberal Jews; we were not Orthodox. I had neither sisters nor brothers; I was the only son. Germans looked at Jews in a sort of bad way. A Jew was always a Jew in Germany. I remember that even before 1933 when I went to my grandparents who lived in the country, that the general population when I came there knew I was Jewish and always made remarks. Especially children made the remarks to me. It was in such a way that I never walked alone on the streets, even in the little town where my grandparents lived. Children always gave me a hard time. They wouldn't hit me; they just annoyed me with words and yelled obscene things at me. But, at that time, I was too young to even fathom the whole idea. I didn't really get involved until I would say thirteen or fourteen. By that time I started realizing what really was going on, and my parents started to say that eventually we would all have to leave, except it was a couple of years more until we finally found our relatives here who gave us the necessary affidavit.

We never felt comfortable. At least I didn't. And then after November 10, 1938, nobody felt comfortable and we all had to leave. My entire family, except for my parents, perished. My parents were the only people of my family who managed to get out.

Do you remember the Gestapo or the SA walking down the street?

Oh yes, very clearly. I remember when they were having their big parades in the evening, their flags, their music, and torchlight parades at night. We all stayed in and we knew they were having parades. Nobody went outside. No one felt secure, no one. You didn't trust your next-door neighbor because you didn't know what they were going to do to you. Neighbors who formerly came to your house, and were neighborly and friendly, all of a sudden refrained from even saying hello to you. They acted as if they didn't know you. I can't say that they were really trying to do something to you, but they were afraid that if they would show you any kind of friendliness that they would have a problem. And yet, I would have to say that after the war, after everything was over, a friend of my father's and a friend of my wife's tried everything possible to get in touch with us, and they succeeded. They had to reestablish connections after the war. But during the Nazi regime, no one would have dared to do anything.

As a matter of fact, that one gentleman, my father's friend, he helped my father in getting his restitution from Germany [after the war]. And my wife's friend is still in touch with us to this day. Even though my wife has passed away, she still writes me or occasionally calls me. When I was in Germany, I visited her. So we sort of reestablished connections because we knew these people were not really against us openly, except that they were afraid for their own lives if they would have shown any sign of friendliness.

What was the *Hausmeister* [superintendent] of your apartment building like?

He owned the building, and, as a matter of fact, they had a café. Before 1933 we very often went downstairs into the café and had coffee and cake. But later on, even though they didn't throw us out, there was no feeling of friendship. Again, whether it was forced on them, we don't know. But we didn't go back, we didn't go into their café anymore.

Did you feel proud or ashamed to be a Jew?

I didn't feel ashamed to be a Jew, of course not. But it was very dangerous. I have always been conscious of it. I would never make a secret out of it. I have sometimes wondered how they could tell who I was. Especially in the city of Frankfurt with over half a million inhabitants, how could they tell who was Jewish? But people still found out.

I remember on November 10, 1938, at the *Kristallnacht*, that I didn't know anything about it that morning. Early in the morning I was walking down the street and two SA men came to me and stopped me. "Come with us," they said. I didn't know them; they didn't know me, but they must have known I was a Jew. I don't know how they knew, but they knew.

So you were arrested by the Gestapo during *Kristallnacht*?

They kept me for the rest of the day, but by evening they let me go. Then, on my way home, I saw all the destruction on the streets. I wasn't aware of that in the morning. They had taken us to what, at that time, they called a *Festhalle*. Now they call it the exhibition [hall]. There must have been thousands of peo-

ple there, all Jewish people. They lined them up and just said, "Stand there."
Nobody said anything. Nobody did anything. They didn't give us food or anything. We just stood there for the whole day. And I'm sure the others stood
there longer. But by late evening or early evening, I don't remember the time,
they called me and asked, "How old are you?" At that time in 1938, I was sixteen and I was able to get out and go home. And that was that.

Did they hit you?

No, I never got hit. At first when they combed the street, they took us to some
sort of assembly point where they already had another twenty, thirty, or forty
people. I don't remember exactly how many they marched there. It really wasn't
that far away. While we walked there, and, of course, after the walk, all the people on the sidewalks started yelling at us—normal Germans, children and
adults, and women also. There were no exceptions: man, woman, and child.
They knew who we were because they walked us down as a group of forty or
fifty people [and because those who marched us] wore uniforms, SA uniforms.
The people just walking down the streets who saw us coming just let loose with
insults. Maybe they were told that we were marching through the streets and
that they should just yell at us. But I don't know, it could have been spontaneous. But who can tell?

What happened to your father?

My father was arrested a couple of days later and taken to Dachau. While he
was away, I went to the American consulate in Stuttgart and checked out our
papers and I was assured at that time that our number, our registration number,
would be called in early 1939. With that information, and with the fact that my
father was a *Frontkämpfer* [frontline soldier] from World War I, I went to the
police and gave them all the information, and they said that on that basis he
would be released shortly. It still took a couple of weeks. I imagine that he was
away for about four or five weeks and then he came home. While we were in
Germany, my father never spoke about it. He never said a word. He said, "I'm
not talking about it. It's forgotten now." But look, we were all glad. Once he
came home, we made our entire efforts to get out, to get rid of our things, and
to make sure that our relatives who lived in a small town in Württemberg could
take over our apartment. We left the furniture; we left everything for them to
take over. We left it for them because they had nothing. They had smashed
their furniture and what not. But that was a small town—everybody knew
everyone. They moved in there as we moved out.

My father was a salesman. He had a business on his own too. But later on I
think he became associated with another company. The exact details I don't

remember anymore. But he was associated with another company and that's where he met the gentleman I spoke to you before about. Whether he was a partner or what, I don't remember exactly. But that's where the friendship started exactly. He didn't help us get out, but he helped us after the war to get back what we could. Before that he was afraid of his own shadow. I mean, he never did anything openly to my father. As a matter of fact, he just kept quiet in his own way. He didn't try to hurt us. But, after the war, he did try to find us and he helped my father recover whatever could be recovered. It wasn't very much. But there were certain amounts of money he could collect as restitution. And so he did the paperwork, so my father didn't have to go to Germany.

Do you remember how your father looked when he came back from Dachau?

I can never forget that. My father always had a mustache and he never had too much hair. Yet whatever he had was shaved off. His mustache was shaved off, that much I remember. He looked very pale. I do know he never regrew the mustache, but, of course, his hair, whatever he had, grew again. And I remember that when he came home, it was late in the evening. I remember when he rang the doorbell he looked strange to us. Although he never had much hair, he never was completely bald. He was just bald and without a mustache. I had never seen my father without a mustache before that time.

What did your father say about Dachau when you were in the United States?

He never said a word to me that I remember. I figured he just wanted to get this whole thing behind him and that once we were out of Germany all he could think about was how to rebuild his life here. Let me put it to you this way: When I came here in 1939, the first couple of years were very bad, especially for my father, who had trouble finding employment. I was always lucky. I had employment within the first few weeks. And then, of course, I was drafted in the army and I fought in North Africa and Italy in the U.S. Army. Naturally, during the war, it was easy for my father to find employment. But in the first two years or so, it was very hard for him. Luckily, we kept our heads above water.

All I know is that we considered ourselves lucky to come here, and, from the first moment we came here, we struggled to get our relatives out too—that's my mother's sister and her children. By that time my mother's parents had passed away, and my father had a sister who did not live near us. Our entire free time was spent in trying to get them over here. But then the war intervened and none of them survived.

Were you of German nationality?

I had a German passport that I came to the United States with, with a big red *J* on it. My father was born in Frankfurt, and his parents were born in Frankfurt. I became a U.S. citizen as soon as I joined the army back in 1943. In 1943 I was in the United States Army. I was fighting as an American, for America in North Africa and in Italy.

So you see yourself as an American?

Oh, yes, certainly. As a matter of fact, when I am in Germany, I don't speak German, not in hotels and not even in stores. I make it my business to speak English only for the simple reason that it is none of their business that I was born there. If I have to write something in German—they sent me a questionnaire for that visit to Frankfurt that had to be filled out in German—I first write it down in English and then translate it. But I can still speak, sometimes with difficulty, and I understand. As a matter of fact, I feel funny when I hear people speak German who don't think I understand. I understand every word they are saying, but they don't know that.

What do you think of the Germans today?

I have mixed feelings about them. Frankly, I don't trust them. But I have very little contact with the German population except for those two people I mentioned earlier in our discussion. I have no further acquaintances, so I am not going to seek out people. But, as I say, when I go over there, I don't let them know that I was born there. I am an American citizen traveling in Germany.

Do you think there is a possibility to forgive?

That's a hard thing to say. Some people say you can forgive but not forget. The people who really did all the dirty work, most of them are no longer alive now or are old people and they should have been punished at the time. Now, when you look at it, let's say they find some Nazi who is by now maybe eighty-five, ninety years old. He's probably sick and decrepit. What can I tell you? This makes no sense at this point. Forty years ago it would have made sense, yes. Now, these people are so old, they don't care. So what are you going to do? Put them in jail for the rest of their lives when they're that old? But mostly they should have all been punished.

How do you think the German people reacted to the persecution of the Jews?

They did nothing, period. They did nothing. They did nothing to stop it. Guilt by omission is as bad as guilt by commission. You can be just as guilty by not doing something as you are guilty of doing something.

And yet, you can't say all Germans. I don't know if you have seen the movie *Schindler's List*. There you have a man who bribed people. He did everything he could to save twelve or thirteen hundred people. He went through all kinds of little misdeeds in order to save people. If you had more people who stood up like that, things wouldn't have happened. And he was a Nazi in the beginning. But he saw what was wrong, and he changed it.

ELISE AND HERMANN GOTTFRIED

The common people, they were watching you. They were all detectives in civilian clothing.

Hermann was born the son of a Berlin law professor in 1923, and Elise was born the daughter of a Berlin widow in 1924. They left Germany in 1939 on a children's transport to Great Britain.

Elise: My mother was a widow from 1936 onward with two young children. A man we knew always promised my mother he would take her out of Germany. He wasn't born in Germany—he came from either Romania or I don't know where. He was a watchmaker, a non-Jew, and he was very friendly with us, and he was supportive. On the night of *Kristallnacht* he went to our business and said to the people, "Look, this is a poor widow with two children. Leave the business alone." But they didn't. They smashed the windows and robbed whatever they could get. So he wasn't very successful in that. But he was the one person I remember that would support us. [Still] many people were friendly to us. We didn't feel the anti-Semitism directly. They didn't do anything against us. But maybe I was too young to notice, and I was in a Jewish school.

Hermann: I was in Berlin and I was nearly fifteen at the time of *Kristallnacht*. As a matter of fact, a few months before I left I was hiding out. I left Germany in April 1939 and my father was still in Berlin. He was a professor of law. He was given forty-eight hours to leave or otherwise he would be sent to a concentration camp. There were many people who tried to go over the border illegally. My mother, my sister, and my brother were in Berlin, and he went probably with a group of people to try to get across the border. But he was caught in Aachen, terribly beaten, and sent home with the idea that he would be collected and sent to Sachsenhausen concentration camp. I don't believe he ever went to Sachsenhausen, but he came back [to Berlin] and he died shortly afterward. I was not there anymore when he died.

It was illegal [to try to cross the border]. They would not let anybody through. You had to have papers—papers were a lifeline. If you had no papers to go to Holland or Belgium, you were caught on the border. We had an affidavit to go to America, but there was a waiting list for about ten years ahead.

Elise: A religious Jewish organization that sent children to Palestine after a certain training gave us an opportunity to go to Scotland in order to do our training there. Everybody tried to save themselves; it was not a question of age. What mattered was which opportunities one had to leave. We were all supposed to go to Palestine, but the British had set up a certain quota system, so we couldn't go there.

Before we left Germany, we had received letters from people who had left earlier which said that Lord Balfour had donated a castle to house Jewish children and that there were two hundred children there. The glorious letters that we received said that it was a castle with beautiful rooms, so my mother told me that everything was beautiful and everything was nice there and she tried to make it sound as nice as possible. So we thought we were going on vacation somewhere. I didn't realize it was really for good. I was fifteen years old.

Hermann: I was already quite mature [by the time of] *Kristallnacht* and also had seen the treatment of Jews being hunted and beaten up by other young kids our age. So I remember what was going on. We were Zionists and we were thinking about having a Jewish state and we saw that Jews were being treated as outcasts. We were some of the lucky ones to be able to go to England. There were ten thousand children who were saved by the British to go to England. We were two of the ten thousand.

Elise: I knew that some of my friends that had left earlier were in that castle, but that's all I knew. I thought I would go to somebody I would know. I knew one or two people who had written back and they were very happy there. So I thought, "Okay, I'm going to see a friend of mine." I didn't realize that I would never see my mother again or my sister. I knew that they were very quiet when I left, but I couldn't understand why. My parents told me it was so beautiful there and they packed everything up and put in some of the books of my father—we had a large library and my mother wanted to save certain books. It didn't really sink in. I didn't realize this was final; I thought it would be temporary. It didn't bother me at the time to leave Germany because everybody tried to leave. Some people went to Shanghai, some people went to Palestine. Everybody tried to save themselves somewhere. I was glad to get out.

Hermann: When we left Germany, I was politically quite up-to-date. I knew what communism meant; I knew what fascism meant. I knew what Hitler was doing to the Jews. I became convinced that we had no future in Germany and we were trying to get out of the place. I knew we would end up in concentration camps—my teachers and parents and other people. I was also present in 1938 when my grandfather was deported to Poland—I was at the railway station. I had seen what was going on and I knew there was no future for any of us. I hated the Germans and I wanted to have it out with them and show them how I hated them. I wanted to have the most dangerous assignment in the British army. I was accepted in the tank corps of the British army and became a tank commander, and I stayed in the British army for a considerable time. After the war, I was stationed in Berlin and I was one of the first Jewish soldiers who came to Bergen-Belsen.

Do you continue to hate Germans?

Hermann: Yes. I make no distinction among Germans from my generation. Anybody born before 1945 is detested and hated by me. There were a few exceptions, but I've never met them. My blood pressure rises anytime I see any German of my age because I imagine him wearing a Nazi uniform. Even so, I have to draw a line. The line is 1945.

Elise: I don't feel that way. I feel definitely that I would not like to associate with the older generation, but I feel that the younger generation we have met are very friendly, very nice, and different than their parents were.

What were your school years like in Nazi Germany?

Elise: We didn't associate with non-Jews. In 1933, I was nine years old. You felt already at that time that you were different from the rest of the Germans. The Germans didn't want anything to do with us either. I was in a public elementary school, and there the Jewish children were always the better students, and, whenever it came to Saturday, the teacher would say to us that it was *Judenfeiertag* [a day off for Jews]. They were always friendly. But there came a time when they couldn't give good marks to Jewish students anymore. That didn't happen to me because I left before that. But I had a cousin who was told that she should find another school because they were afraid to give her always the best marks in class. They were afraid because she was Jewish. In *Gymnasium* I went to a Jewish school. Our friends were all Jewish. At that time, Jews were already looked at as something second-class. Still I knew I was a Jew, and I was in a way very proud to be a Jew.

Hermann: You must understand that you are talking to two people who had a very religious upbringing. We were not assimilated. We had a Jewish education. We were conscious of being Jews. Of course, like my father, we were also very proud that we were German, which, of course, I lost after Hitler came. But the Jewishness and its self-consciousness were instilled in us. People who came from assimilated backgrounds couldn't understand why all of a sudden they were called Jews and had a much harder time coming to grips with the matter. I knew Jewish history; I knew how we were persecuted. But I've had German Jewish teachers who were more German than the Germans and these people I detested, because after a while I saw what was going on.

Ninety-nine percent of the German population either were anti-Jewish or they were *Mitläufer* [fellow travelers] and continued going along with it. They saw us getting beaten up in the middle of the street. They saw us being sent away. You were treated in a most cold manner. I've seen truckloads of people being taken away to concentration camps. I've seen people come back from concentration camps with their hair completely shorn off. I had a teacher who gave us a report about what happened in Sachsenhausen. I was one of the lucky people who was in a Jewish school. My brother was thrown out of a Christian school. He couldn't go there after 1937. Jewish children couldn't go to any school, so we had our own. We could not go to theaters or movies or anything, so everyone concentrated on emigration, wherever they could go. Unfortunately, America did not do what they should have done. Many other countries did not do what they should have done. They could have saved many of our people but didn't. That's the end of the story.

As children, fifteen years old, we were thrown out into a world where we could not speak the language. But we adjusted very quickly. I didn't speak a single word of English when I came to Britain and I learned it very fast. We also had the idea of going to Palestine, but then the war broke out and we were restricted.

I was then interned as a German, together with German seamen. We were sent to a German camp outside London. We were a group of forty boys from that place in Scotland, all German or Austrian and all Jewish boys. We marched into this camp and we had to stand at attention. We stood guard. We wanted to protect ourselves from the Germans. At night the British soldiers moved out. We went on a hunger strike because we wanted kosher food even though about half of us were not interested in kosher food. But after a while we just wanted food. In the meantime, we had people working on the outside to get us out of the camp because we were not really Germans. We were then sent to Liverpool, where ships were going to Canada.

There was a famous boat called the *Andover Star*, a British boat that transported German and Italian prisoners and civilians to Canada. Just a few hours before we were to board this boat, a telegram came saying that we had certificates to go to Palestine and we were taken off that transport. As it turned out, that boat was torpedoed and I think 80 percent died. We were released after that because the British understood that we were not really enemy aliens and we were sent back to Scotland to work.

How do you feel about the Jews who remained in Germany and survived or returned to Germany to live after the war?

Hermann: Many of the survivors are not always good people. Quite often the scum survived. Why? Because they were strong enough to go over other people's dead bodies. Those German Jews who live in Germany, I call the scum of the earth. You can repeat it to them. They are people who have no honor. After they have been thrown out of the country, to go back, to stick there because they get a pension!

Elise: They said they didn't want to learn a new language. They didn't want to start from scratch. You can't judge. They couldn't start again.

Hermann: I would not allow my children ever to set foot in Germany if I can help it. You would say I must be very hateful to them, very vicious. I am not. I understand German culture. I was brought up in Germany. I know Schiller and Goethe and Heine. All these people I've studied. But it has nothing to do with me anymore.

Elise: Our children aren't interested. But, if they wanted to go, I would let them.

Hermann: I told them I don't want any of my children or grandchildren ever to set foot there. You forget one thing. When Jews were taken out of their apartments and deported, who were the first ones in the apartment? The neighbors! When I was a soldier, I came back to Berlin after the war in 1945. I went to the house where my parents lived. I went into our neighbor's apartment and I saw my parents' candelabra. I didn't ask them any more questions.

Didn't the Jews have to turn over their property to the government when they left?

Hermann: The procedure used to be that the Gestapo sealed the apartment and took the stuff out. Where they put it, I don't know. But on *Kristallnacht*, which was a complete organized plundering, who came? You think the police came to get it? It was the neighbors who came into the apartment and smashed the glass and smashed the china and took whatever they wanted. It was a mixture of SS guys and neighbors. People saw an opportunity to get things that they didn't have. That's it! Do you think they asked our permission to take something?

Did you ever feel that your family was being watched?

Hermann: Yes, of course. You just had to be careful in everything you did. Being a Jew, you were marked. The common people, they were watching you. They were all detectives in civilian clothes, like the FBI in a corner watching you. The Gestapo only came in after you were handed to them. That was before the war. After the war started, the Gestapo had organized razzias.

I'll tell you a funny story, a true story. Many Polish Jews were peddlers. Some of them also tried to get people together to marry. So we had one particular old Jewish man who always had a pocket of photographs of young girls, Jewish girls. And when he came to somebody, he said, "Look here, would you like to meet this girl and make a wedding?" Well, they picked this guy up outside our house. He was a harmless little guy who was trying to bring people together and they accused him of *Mädchen* handling, a kind of white slavery, and the poor guy was taken away and never heard of again. This just shows you how the mentality was; how they were thinking of every conceivable way of prosecuting a person, a harmless person. He was trying to make a living. Because many Jewish young men could not go out and meet other girls, we tried to meet them in other ways. He was a matchmaker. They did everything possible to make our life a misery in every possible way. They wanted us to disappear.

Did you ever wish that you were not Jewish at that time?

Hermann: Correct. I had a very bad experience. There were people going around getting people to join the Hitler Youth. I saw these young people in uniforms, playing the drums like in the Middle Ages. There was one guy who came up to me and said, "Why don't you want to join?" They wanted to enroll me. I didn't tell them I was Jewish—I disappeared. I thought many times to myself, "I wish I was them," because who wants to be persecuted? You don't want to stick out.

Elise: You want to belong.

How do you feel about being Americans?

Hermann: I'll give you an answer that I think many people would give you. I have been German, I have been stateless, and I have been British. I am now American. But I was always a Jew, and always will remain a Jew.

Elise: A Jew first. Because we found out that if you were a German Jew, you ended up in the alley. If you were an English Jew, they were very nice to your face. But behind your back, you were a refugee and you could never really be English. But I'll never forget that we are thankful to the English people that they saved us. But I'm foremost a Jew, and then English. I'm foremost a Jew, and then American.

Hermann: Ninety-nine percent of all Germans were Nazis or followers of Nazis. My wife may feel different, but I don't. And to that 1 percent, I give the benefit of the doubt. There were some exceptions, but it's so minute.

REBECCA WEISNER

Every few weeks they rounded up people and shot them.

Born in 1926 and raised in a Berlin working-class family of Polish extrac-tion, Rebecca Weisner was forced to go to Poland in July 1939, was deport-ed to Auschwitz in October 1942, and escaped from one of the death marches near the end of the war.

I was born in 1926. My first memory is from 1932 or 1933, when I used to go to the park to play with my friends. It was different in Europe in those days. You could go in the street and nobody harmed you. But I did see the Socialist and the Nazi Party fighting and shooting in the streets. This was how we grew up there.

At that time, we lived in a working-class neighborhood in East Berlin, a few blocks away from Alexanderplatz. Both of my parents were from Poland. My parents were religious; they were Orthodox. Near to where we lived there was a police station. I remember they were barricading it every night and there was shooting going on just below our window. We were on the first floor. My mom kept my brother and me under the window in case a bullet came through.

Anyway this was my first experience as a Jewish kid. In 1933 I entered a German school, a little German Protestant school, because we lived at the time in a working-class Gentile neighborhood. I remember having Hebrew lessons three times a week in the first few months in the first grade. The teacher came in to teach us Hebrew in the German school. I was one of about seven Jewish kids there. I remember with Germans I had a lot of fights because they called me "Jew, dirty Jew" and things like this.

When I was six, Hitler came to power. I started school in April 1933, just at the same time. I remember that we were the only Jewish people in that apartment house and there were some German girls I was friends with—we grew up together—and, all of a sudden, one day I come down and they call me "dirty Jew." My friends, the friends I grew up with!

I couldn't comprehend it. I would say to my mother, "Why do they call me dirty? I am not dirty." And she said, "You had better get used to it. You're Jewish, and that is what you have to learn. So just take it." But I didn't want to take it. I fought. I fought in school in the first grade and I remember my aunt told me that I once locked up a girl. I don't know how I locked her up in the bathroom at school, but she missed her whole hour and they were looking for her and I didn't say anything. Well, during the pause they went into the bathroom and they heard her scream and so they found out it was me. They then kind of punished me. They put me in the corner and they gave me a note for my mother to sign. She kept saying, "Hey, listen. If you are going to be like this, you are going to cause us a lot of trouble." I said, "Why? Why is it different for me?" I couldn't comprehend why I should be different. It was me.

After the first grade was finished my mother sent me to a Jewish school. These were all private, but those who couldn't afford them were supplemented by the Jewish *Gemeinde*. It was a regular school like the German one, but it wasn't German. Every day we had one hour of Hebrew. But everything else was like any other school. And we had other languages too, like English, because we were being prepared. It was 1934 when everybody was thinking about emigration.

Did you have Gentile friends after you went to the Jewish school?

No, they were never allowed to play with me. They wouldn't talk to me. They called me names like "dirty Jew" and probably some other things.

I was very upset and I caused a lot of trouble for my parents. Luckily they were Polish citizens. Because of me my mother was arrested twice that year and had to stay overnight at the Gestapo. The teachers called the Gestapo and said that I was not well behaved, that I reacted too violently. So my father said, "Look, you have to keep quiet. You cannot do anything. You cannot say anything." And I couldn't accept that; there was no way I could accept that. And then it happened a second time, and, if she would have been a German citizen, she would have been already somewhere else. But, because of the Polish passport, they had to release her. At that time you were still protected by Poland. And so after this I learned to keep quiet more.

Then we moved into a Jewish neighborhood in the Lothringer Strasse. We were close to that famous religious, Jewish street, the Grenadier Strasse. That is where you had all the kosher stores and you had all kinds of Jewish things that you couldn't get in other stores. There, where we lived in Berlin, each city or town of Poland had their own little synagogue.

So I started the Jewish school and then things went better for me. But we had a German school across the street and we had a lot of trouble with German Jewish kids. They were always taught that they were better than the Eastern Europeans and they looked at us like we were from Eastern Europe even when we were born in Berlin. So there was a lot of fighting between the two sides. There was a lot of resentment from the German Jewish people.

There are so many incidents. We weren't allowed to go swimming anymore [in the swimming pools]. Jewish kids were not allowed to mix, so we never learned to swim really. But we used to go outside of Berlin with the subway and the train and we, by ourselves, went bathing in the Wannsee. And we had only one Jewish sports stadium left. I belonged to a Zionist Jewish organization and we were very into sports; sports kept me going. We had competitions every few months, and in school we had a lot of sports too, indoors and outdoors. So we were always into sports and we had a lot of friends, all Jewish friends, but all from Eastern European backgrounds.

Do you remember seeing many signs and symbols of anti-Semitism?

Oh, I do. I saw the *Stürmer* newspaper. It was all over the place; it was on every corner, you couldn't miss it. There were the Jews with the big noses and all that. I could not understand that anybody could imagine that Jewish people could look like this. I guess you could say I was a little angry with that; there was a lot of anger that came out later.

Also I remember that there were Christmas displays in one of the big department stores. I used to love it. In '37 I said to my mother that I wanted to go to see the display. Now my mother was dark blond—she didn't look Jewish. But I was very dark like my father. So she said to me, "You can't go there. You look too Jewish." And this gave me another complex—I looked Jewish. I said, "Now how am I supposed to look?" She said, "Well, you are a Jewish kid and you look Jewish, so you can't go there." And then there were the Germans who gave us a lot of trouble. There were so many minor incidents. But, all and all, I must say that with all this anti-Semitism, me and my Jewish friends, we had a pretty good childhood. We belonged to Jewish organizations, belonged to Jewish schools. We knew we had to accept it and that was it.

What did you think when you saw Hitler Youth walking around?

Very, very afraid. Now, I used to see Hitler sometimes. He used to come by in an open car especially on Unter den Linden by the Brandenburg Gate. One Saturday my mom and I were out walking on Unter den Linden because that was the thing to do and we could still go to one Jewish café [near there], but no Jews were allowed on the left side of Unter den Linden because Hitler lived in the

Kaiser Wilhelm Strasse and we couldn't walk there. On Unter den Linden we saw Hitler come by in an open car with his arm raised up and everybody had to raise his arm back. So my mom said, "You better raise your arm. If not, everyone will realize that you're Jewish." And I said, "No, I can't do that." She said, "Do you want to get me arrested again?" So I had to do it. But I always rebelled against it.

Now I will give you an incident that happened in 1936. There was one café in West Berlin that was called Café Dobrin. I was too young but my brother went there. Many young Jewish people in their later teens went there to meet somebody—it was a hangout—and the Gestapo used to come by every few weeks, unannounced, naturally, and just take everybody in. Among them there was a cousin of mine who was maybe eighteen or nineteen. He was born in Berlin, but his parents were stateless—they were from Poland. Anyway, he had no country and he just disappeared. His name was David Adler. It didn't take six weeks until the postman came and gave my aunt a box and she had to pay twenty-five marks. She opened it and it was his ashes from Buchenwald. This was an incident that I had witnessed in 1936. He was taken from that restaurant, that café, where they were hanging out. He didn't do anything. They just came and took you.

That wasn't the only incident. How do you think so many Jewish people from Germany wound up in Buchenwald way before 1938?

What do you remember of *Kristallnacht*?

On October 28, 1938, they took my father out of the apartment. All the Polish Jews were rounded up and it took something like twenty-four hours to round them up. My father was taken and my brother was taken (he was just sixteen) and my grandfather was taken; my mom and I and my grandmother were left behind. They took them to Poland, but we didn't know that for three days. Now my mother's sister lived in Stralsund, which is near Stettin and Rostock by the Baltic Sea, and I had just been there that summer helping my aunt with her little baby girl. In that little city lived about twenty Jewish families, all immigrants from Poland, but all related. I remember well how my mother then put me on the train and my aunt took me off the train and how, at age twelve, I went there and they all were beaten up. They were already beaten up on the streets by the Germans. I don't know how they knew they were Jewish, but being that it wasn't such a big place, maybe they knew that. They didn't arrest them, but they were beaten up. This happened in every small town in Germany except in Berlin.

Now, what happened to my father was that he somehow got out of that internment camp on the Polish side of the German border and went to the town where he was born, where he still had sisters and brothers who remained there. And then he called us from there and said that everything would be okay and that we shouldn't worry.

When did you leave Germany?

I went to Poland because we had to leave in July 1939. We got from the Jewish committee an apartment with a room and a kitchen in a small town in Silesia near Krakow, about half an hour away from Auschwitz by car. I was there when the German army marched in. It was six in the morning when we heard on the radio that the Germans had marched into Poland. By nine o'clock they were in the town. My father's brother was like a big shot [in that town]. I think it wasn't more than two days that the Germans were there before they arrested him. But he ran away and they sent the dogs after him and they killed him. Every few weeks they rounded up people and shot them. That was before they even had camps [in Poland]. In 1939 I was just thirteen, August 11 was my birthday. I never went to school after that; I had finished just barely the sixth grade in Berlin.

Did you know about any other shootings of Jews?

There was no way of getting any news. But, yes, we did hear some things from some people who traveled, from the ones who didn't look Jewish. Some of them had Gentile papers, if they were blond and spoke a good Polish without a Jewish accent. My uncle from Berlin from my mother's family wound up in the Warsaw ghetto, but I didn't know much about it until after the war. Near the end of the war, I myself escaped from the death march. That was a tough thing.

Anyway Auschwitz wasn't ready yet. One day I was walking down the street with a friend and two German officers from the Nazis stopped their car and said, "I take you with me. You come here." Like a kid with a big mouth, I then said to them in German, "You can't take me. I am too young to go." He gave me right away a slap on the face, a big hard one, and said, "You come with me." And then they took me and the girl who had walked with me into the school. Later on they rounded up a lot of Jewish girls from that town, I think about forty, and we were sent to a *Durchgangslager* [a transport camp]. We were there a few days. It was hard for me there; it was like I couldn't cope with it. It was in January or February 1942.

[Then we were sent] to a women's camp near Breslau in eastern Germany. At the beginning, we were not too bad off. But sometime in September or October 1942, my brother, my parents, my grandparents, and my cousins were all taken to Auschwitz and nobody ever saw them again. Then they came at the same time to my camp; maybe it was a few days later [and we were sent to Auschwitz].

Did you know about Auschwitz already, about the gassing of Jews?

We already knew by late July, August. One came from this camp, one came from that camp. Somehow we knew those things were more or less going on—that there was Auschwitz and that they had gas ovens to gas all the people, children and so. We knew that.

I cried for maybe two days because I knew that I was all alone. I only had one brother and I really didn't want to live at that point. I never cried again after that time. Until today, I still cannot cry and I have had a lot of emotional problems because of all those things. I can't cry; I choke, but I can't cry.

You know, they were young—my mother was forty; my father was forty-four; my brother was just barely twenty—and this was something that I had to live with.

What was it like in concentration camp?

They took away whatever we had—our watches, clothes, and everything. They shaved our hair. It was tragic. You know, you're a young girl and they shave your head. We didn't get any food anymore. If you asked me what was the worst in the camp for me personally, it was hunger. It was also cold; we didn't have much warmth. We slept in an old factory hall, in bunk beds, up and down in wooden bunks and straw. It was like an outdoor, not an indoor, house, with little holes in the middle.

All my life I had to run around in the middle of the night. I still do. Over there, where you were walking, you had people screaming, and people crying, and people praying. It was so weird! It was so frightening! I'm still trying to figure out today how they cleaned it all up. There was no water, no paper. In '44 it went from bad to worse for us in the camps. We were exhausted. Once I was beaten in the lower back, and I have had to have surgery from that. Twelve years ago I was paralyzed. It was a long story. Also I have had psychological difficulties. I've had psychiatry on and off for twenty years now. I finally gave it up because it didn't help me. They were not qualified to help a survivor.

How do you feel about Germany today?

I have a big problem with that. I blocked the German language completely. Until recently, I practically didn't remember a word. I just didn't want to hear about Germany.

In 1977 I got an invitation from Berlin to come for a visit with my husband. If I would have gone much earlier, I would have gotten all this restitution money, but I just didn't want to hear or know about it. When we went there in '77, I said to my husband, "They're paying. This isn't our money. Maybe we should go." I felt that maybe I would get over it if I went there.

I met two school friends on the plane and we landed in Berlin. They gave us a hotel and a few marks. One day we decided to visit our old home in East Berlin. We took the subway and got out on the Alexanderplatz. Then we walked to where we used to live, and what do you think happened when I came to the house where we lived? It was gone. The house I had lived in was leveled to the ground. Apparently it had burned. This was the instant that I acted like a maniac. I felt like I don't come from anyplace—no background, no home, like out of the thin air, nothing to look back at. It was a very weird feeling. You come to collect something from your childhood and this is gone.

Going back to your life in Nazi Germany, how did you get out of the concentration camp?

I liberated myself I guess. I ran away from the transport in January or February after New Year's in 1945. It was the coldest winter in Europe in 1945. We didn't have much clothes or shoes. We had to walk in that cold weather and we had no food after the first few days. If they were in a good mood, they put us in a barn. It wasn't warm, but it was better than the snow. But most of the nights we were outside sitting or whatever—it was so cold! Then I said to myself, "I'm not going to make it." I was near the end. We were Auschwitz girls; there were like three and a half thousand girls. I remember that when the girls sat down, they were shot. They couldn't walk; they would sit down and were shot. So I said to myself, "What can I do? I am not going to make it either way, so I'll take a chance." And when we walked by a certain woods, somehow I had the chance to run into the woods. Some girls followed me and they were shooting at us. But instinct told us to hide behind the trees and I guess they gave up on us.

That was a lucky thing because the Germans were evacuating east Germany already. They were going west, so we went east. At night we were walking and in the daytime hiding. Then we said, "We have to get some food." So we took a chance, and a farmer found us in a barn sleeping. He was nice and gave us food. We had prison clothes on—girls from Auschwitz completely in prison clothes. There was no way we could take our clothes off; it was too cold. Anyway, he gave us some food and said, "You can sleep here. But, in the morning, you had better go." Our only hope was to get to the Russians. It took us two weeks, and then we got to the Russians.

JOSEPH WEINBERG

We did not feel, especially in Stuttgart, the anti-Semitism.

Born in 1914 and raised in Stuttgart, Joseph Weinberg emigrated to the United States in June 1940 and returned to Germany at the end of the war as an interrogator for the American army.

My parents originally came from Austria. In 1928 my parents separated and my mother had her own little business in the *Städtische Markthalle* [city market hall] in Stuttgart. I went to school in Stuttgart—to a *Realschule* [secondary school] and then to a *Handelsschule* [business school]. When I was finished, I became an apprentice in a Jewish firm.

While I was in school, I didn't notice very much anti-Semitism, except that, of course, I was always with Jewish men. We had religion in school, but I had this along with everybody and did not have much trouble. I joined a German sports club in 1934 where I did running. I liked long-distance running, 1,500 and 3,000 meters. In 1936, I think it was, I was told that I couldn't stay in the club anymore because I was Jewish. Then I joined the Reichsbund Jüdischer Frontsoldaten [Reich Association of Jewish Frontline Soldiers], which had a sports club. We, the Jewish people, had our own Jewish Olympiad in Berlin. I was elected to go there because of my talent as a sprinter. I also belonged to another youth organization called the Bund deutsch-jüdischer Jugend [Association of German Jewish Youth].

I grew up in Germany. I tried to connect with people. We had good friends who were German people and who were very nice. We did not feel, especially in Stuttgart, the anti-Semitism. It was not so bad in Stuttgart as in other towns further north. After the apprenticeship, I was kept in that firm, a Jewish firm, and stayed there until 1937. When they closed, a German man came and said, "Jew, we cannot keep you because we will not get any orders from the government." So I had to leave the firm. There was no problem, except that I was Jewish. So they were very sorry about it.

Do you really think they were very sorry about it, or did they just say they were?

No, they were. There was one fellow who actually brought me in as an apprentice. I stayed in touch with him after the war. Then, of course, I had no job and I got these little jobs. My mother had a stand in the *Städtische Markthalle* and she was very well liked. She was always called Mama Winterchen. Strangely enough, there were only two Jewish people in the *Markthalle*.

In 1938, when November 9 came, I came home from a job I had temporarily. I heard on the radio that the synagogue was burning. It was around six o'clock. I took my bicycle and went over to the synagogue. We lived in the center of the town, so it wasn't very far from there. I drove over there and saw people standing in front of the synagogue. There were two fire engines and screams of "Fire!" The left and the right sides of the synagogue were burning. The people were just standing there and just looked. I don't know whether they were sorry. It was so quiet. I went home and told my mother what happened there.

In the meantime, we found out that was the *Kristallnacht*. The next morning I went to the *Markthalle* with my mother and sister. When we walked upstairs, all the doors were ripped out; all the food was smashed together and lying in the center of the store and the money and everything was taken away. All we had—butter, flour, herring, everything—was piled up there. My mother, of course, cried, and we also cried. There was nothing we could do. We just walked away and never could come back to the place to see it. It was the end of my mother's place and she had no more work to do there.

We had an apartment in the center of Stuttgart until 1938. After *Kristallnacht*, we had to move out. We had to go into a Jewish house where only Jews lived. We got an apartment on the third floor; it was a five-room apartment. My mother then started to rent rooms to make a living.

At that time, I looked around at what I could do. I was connected with the *Jüdische Gemeinde*, which organized things for the Jewish people to do, and there was a choir I belonged to. The man in charge was called Director Adler. He was originally in the Stuttgart school of music. Of course, he lost his job and that's why he started that group. So I joined that choir and we were singing. It was wonderful—we were all Jewish people together there. But, after a while, they closed up that group too and we were not allowed to sing anymore.

Then he opened up an office where he helped Jewish people. When they had a visa to organize, he saw to it that they got the proper visa. He had connections with the American consulate. The American consulate spoke to him and said, "What you can do is screen the papers." Before anybody came to the U.S. you needed a visa. You needed certain papers and they all had to be put together. Soon after that, he asked me to come and help him in that office to screen the people. We advertised that whoever needed papers should come to us and we'd tell them what they needed.

When you wanted to emigrate, you needed permission from the Gestapo to get out of Stuttgart. So the Gestapo opened up an office next to us in the same building. That means there were two offices. We had an office with a door to the Gestapo. When the papers were finished, we went into the office of the

Gestapo, showed them the papers, and they gave the okay that the people could emigrate. It was a complicated situation because the Jews and the Gestapo were sitting there together. We also helped after 1938 when some Jews were taken to concentration camp and came out with a permission that they had to leave the country within two weeks. We helped these people get papers as soon as possible from the higher-ups in New York who could get them to the U.S. It was a complicated thing, but Director Adler had wonderful connections.

Wasn't it already difficult at that time to get a visa to go to the United States?

That's right. He organized it wonderfully and we all helped together. We had nobody in the U.S., but he said to us, "Stay here. If the time becomes bad, I'll help you to get out. Don't worry about it." I lived with my mother and my sister. We tried to write some people in the U.S. to help us, but there was no way. So I stayed right where I was.

I, otherwise, had people in Stuttgart like an English teacher. She was German; she helped me learn the English language. She was seventy-five years old and she wanted to drive a car. As a Jewish man, I couldn't drive, but she asked me to show her how to drive anyway. She said to me, "Help me learn how to drive the car and I will help you with the food." It was difficult for Jewish people to get food because you had a ration card and you only could buy food in Jewish places and that was very short sometimes. So she gave us food sometimes. What I want to say is, there were people who went out of their way to help us.

I was also fortunate in that my mother came from Bukovina and was considered a Romanian citizen at that time. Also I personally had a special document which said I could go out and go wherever I wanted. The Jewish people could not go into the city after eight o'clock. They had to stay home. But I was authorized because of my job to go out after eight o'clock. The SS gave me a special permit that said that I had permission to stay in the street after 8:00 P.M.

Did the Germans you knew stop having contact with you because of their anti-Semitism?

No. It was the fear of others seeing that I had been in touch with them. Of course we noticed that more people all of a sudden were gone and that the group of Jewish people was getting smaller and smaller.

The war broke out in 1939 and we didn't know what was going on. My uncle, in the meantime, was in the United States and wrote to us about what we could do. But he had no money and there was no way he could help us in the United States. I then spoke to Director Adler and he told me not to worry about it. [But then,] in May 1940, the Germans conquered Holland and there was no way of getting out over Holland to the U.S. and Director Adler then said to me that it was the last time for me to leave. Soon after that he went to the American consulate and within two weeks I had my American visa.

That was the last time I saw my mother. I went to the station and I said farewell to her there. I left at the end of May from Genoa. I went to Genoa with ten marks and with two other people who were also in the office where I worked. We arrived on June 1 in the U.S.

What happened to you in the United States?

My uncle picked me up and I started off with a job in a bakery where I cleaned plates at night. Then I went to a fur place where I worked for $12 a week. After that a friend of mine who was a baker in Jersey said that there was a job there and that he would make me a baker. So, in January 1941, I went to Jersey and started to become a baker. At that time, there was a draft and everybody here in the U.S. who wanted to become a citizen had to sign up for the army. So, in March 1941, I got a letter from the army that I would be drafted in three months.

After I was trained in the U.S., I was brought in 1944 to a camp which is today called Camp David where they took German-speaking people and trained them to interrogate prisoners of war. Then I was sent to Belfast, and, after D-day, to Paris. I got a jeep and was assigned to different divisions that were in front to get the prisoners of war. I was caught in the Battle of the Bulge when the Germans encircled us. But it was just for a short time because we were so strong. Eventually we got out of that and continued on further toward the Rhine. While we were at the Remagen bridgehead, I interrogated the man who was in charge of exploding the bridgehead, but never did. That man gave himself up. He didn't want to do it. He said he would rather be a prisoner. I myself crossed the bridge while the bridge was still standing there. It was destroyed, but we could walk on it. The next day twenty-four of our boys crossed that bridge and at that moment the bridge collapsed and they were killed there. German flyers came over and bombed it several times; they never got a direct hit. But, of course, they came pretty close, so the bridge eventually just collapsed.

What was it like to interrogate these German prisoners of war?

I personally asked questions like: "How do you like Hitler?" Strange enough, I found that most of the prisoners were all pro-Hitler. They believed in Hitler. There was one guy I still remember. He was a nice guy. I said to him, "Look, you see what's happening. Why are you still so pro-Hitler?" "Well, we believe he did the right thing," he answered. That night he tried to grab the gun of one of the guards, but the man was aware of it and shot him. The next day he was dead and I never had a chance to continue talking to him.

Did you ever get back to Stuttgart?

At the end of the war I found out that Stuttgart was liberated by the French army and I said I'd like to go down to Stuttgart and see whether my mother was still alive. I hadn't heard anything. I took a jeep and it was quite a trip from Leipzig to Stuttgart. I went to Stuttgart three days after Stuttgart was liberated. The house where my mother lived was completely destroyed. It was in the center of town and there was nobody around I could ask. But I had some names of people I could ask. I found the street where they lived in an address book and then went to that street outside Stuttgart, which was still standing there. The man was Jewish and his wife was Christian, so their daughter was half Jewish. I had my uniform on. So when the wife heard somebody outside, she looked and she yelled, "Go away, soldier!" They were afraid that we wanted to rape her. I took off my helmet and said, "I'm Sepp from Stuttgart." She couldn't believe it. The daughter was in the basement hiding. Then they recognized me.

That's how I found out that my mother was taken away in 1943. They didn't know where to. They said it was to a Czech camp and I only was told later that she went to Auschwitz. My sister was taken too, but they were not sure where they really went. That person who had taught me English was also still alive. She was now about eighty years old.

Could you explain more about the Gestapo officers you once worked with in Stuttgart?

In Stuttgart, the Gestapo was much more lenient than the SS, which was more strict. That's why my mother got away with a lot of things; they left her alone. When I went back to Stuttgart, I found out that the Gestapo and the SS were sent to Ludwigsburg by the army and by military intelligence. I went there and somebody told me that the man who was in charge of the office where I had been was there. I went there and asked whether I could speak to him and I was allowed to because I was in military intelligence. When I asked him questions, he said he could not remember all these things anymore. I said to him, "You know, it would be very easy for me just to shoot you down." Anyhow, he didn't answer very much and there was not much I could do. It was a very strange situation. I didn't really know what I should ask him. We talked about fifteen minutes. It was hard for me to ask him questions.

Had he been in charge of the deportation of Jews in Stuttgart?

I'm not really aware who was in charge, because I really had nothing to do with it when they were taken away. But always the SS were the bad people. The

Gestapo more or less just did their job. That was in Stuttgart. I know the Schwaben were much more lenient than further north in Prussia and Hessen. They were more anti-Jewish there than in Stuttgart. I must say that the situation in Stuttgart wasn't so bad. They just obeyed orders more or less. I knew many people who didn't do the Hitler salute, who just held back.

I had no other contact in that respect with the Gestapo. You stayed away. Also they didn't want to have any contact with the Jewish people.

+3+

JEWS WHO WERE DEPORTED FROM GERMANY DURING THE WAR

MAX LIFFMANN

Fear was not something I knew.

Born in 1921 and raised in Mannheim as the son of a salesman, Max Liffman was deported to Gurs concentration camp in France in October 1940. In September 1942, with the help of the French Huguenot population of Le Chambon-sur-Lignon, he escaped to Switzerland.

Those who were in the camps distinguish between those who left before the outbreak of the war—survivors—and those who left but were in camps—Holocaust survivors. The distinction is very small. Until 1983, my wife and I did not consider ourselves Holocaust survivors because we were not in the eastern camps. But I was twenty-one months and my wife was thirteen months in Gurs concentration camp.

Let's start from earlier. The *Gauleiter* [Nazi regional leader] in Baden decided, "We are going to get rid of our Jews." Now, you must understand that when this was done, the Nazis were still talking about Madagascar and the term "Final Solution" didn't exist yet. So they decided, and they got the blessing from Hitler, to get rid of us simply by putting us onto trains and shoving us across the demarcation line into the so-called non-occupied French zone. This was done on October 22, 1940.

There was a total of 6,548 people from Baden, Pfalz, and the Saarland. We were picked up at home by the Gestapo. At that time I was working at what was called the *Hilfsverein*, which helped Jews in emigration matters.

How did the emigration work for Jews who wanted to go to the United States?

The United States had two consulates in Germany. One was in Stuttgart and one was in Berlin. These were the only two, to my knowledge, which had visa departments.

The Americans erected artificial hurdles from one minute to the next to slow down the emigration to America. The Stuttgart vice consul, Taylor, who was lord over the visa, was infamous. In fact, his secretary was a girlfriend of my wife's uncle. She was a Swiss and she quit eventually in disgust because she couldn't take any more of the crap that was going on there. It was outrageous. You see, for Germany there was a quota of, I think, 26,000 a year. When my parents finally decided that they wanted to get a quota number, we had number 41,000. That meant at the time that we had two years to wait before we would ever be able to get out. You had to wait. But there were some people desperate enough to get out who had the money to bribe people so that they would be given a lower number. The people who were bribed were the Americans.

Could you explain more about how your own deportation worked?

We were taken to the main railway station in Mannheim. When they came to get us in our apartments, they were very polite. They came in and told us that we were under arrest and had an hour to pack and that we could take blankets along and some food and no more than one hundred marks. We had no warning, nothing. But, because I worked at the *Hilfsverein* and the head of my office was also the contact between the Mannheim Jewish Community and the Gestapo, I had known the day before.

I lived at this time with just my mother in my grandmother's apartment. We were the only Jews in the apartment building. There must have been twenty or twenty-five people in the house besides us. We had a big apartment with six rooms plus a kitchen. My grandmother was not there because she had to leave Germany at the beginning of the war, on September 1, 1939, in a big hurry; she was an alien, a French citizen.

My dad had left Germany before *Kristallnacht* and had originally gone to Greece. He had once been very well considered by his firm, in which he worked as a *Vertreter* [sales representative], but they dumped him in late 1936 or early 1937 and he left Germany in March 1938. He had planned to try to establish himself in Greece and then bring the rest of the family there. But he was expelled from Greece because the competition found out who he was, what he was up to, and they prevailed with bribes. Then he went to Italy, and from Italy he eventually crossed illegally into France.

My mother had once met him in Italy in August of 1939, and they were so convinced that there would be no war that they didn't call for me. All they had to do was pick up the phone, call me, tell me to pack a suitcase and come down, and I would have been gone, because we all had passports. But my mother came back and the war broke out half a month later.

When the war broke out, there was a general mobilization from which we were not excluded at first. So we had to present ourselves. But we were immediately demobilized because we were not fit to serve in the German army, which was fine. The only thing was that three or four weeks later I found myself on the train going to the eastern part of Germany to harvest potatoes and sugar beets. We were all Jewish boys and were just sent there to work and we stayed in the ballroom of a *Gastwirtschaft* [inn] that was not even guarded or anything. I was lucky because they let me go home when the harvest was over. I had a close friend there who was not permitted to come home anymore and ended up in Auschwitz.

After I got home my mother managed to get me into the *Hilfsverein*, which was controlled by the Reichsvertretung der Juden in Deutschland, where I worked as a secretary. Then, on the afternoon of October 20, 1940, my boss was told that tomorrow we would be deported to France, and we were sent home. At first my mother did not want to believe it when I told this to her.

When we left the apartment with whatever we could carry, we locked it, gave the key to the police, and they put a seal on it. We were then walked by two Gestapo officers dressed in civilian clothes to the main train station in Mannheim. Many people saw us when we walked through the street. We remained at the train station for probably two, three hours, until they had enough people. Eventually there were three and a half thousand people at the train station. Among them were children and old people—my wife's grandmother was ninety-two years old. They were all so stunned. Nobody knew what was coming next. But I said to whomever I saw that to my knowledge we were going to France. That was a positive, yes, but we didn't know what was going to happen tomorrow.

We were then put on a regular passenger train—old cars, fourth class, which didn't exist anymore in those day. We didn't have policemen with us when we traveled; we had an SS contingent that came through the train to make sure we had no more than one hundred marks with us. "If we find more than a hundred marks, you will be shot," they said.

Were you happy to leave Germany?

No, you weren't happy to leave. My parents had grown up in normal times, and until 1933 had a good life. We didn't really know what was going on. You didn't know what was going to happen tomorrow, so you coped from one day to the next. German Jews of my generation had gotten the whole shit from January of 1933 onward. Don't think it was easy. We had to fight in school for survival, and eventually we didn't even talk about it at home because our parents had other worries. It was not a nice life.

But a lot of people who left in the '30s voluntarily, or involuntarily, were crying for German culture. I'm sure I didn't feel that way. The German Jew was supposed to be fully integrated in Germany. Yet, when I think back, my parents had no Gentile friends in their social intercourse at all. Even though my parents weren't religious, and I'm not religious, all of our friends were Jewish before 1933, and, of course, after 1933. But we knew we were Jews. My father in Germany had been an elected official of the *Gemeinderat* [Jewish community council] in Mannheim.

How had you been treated by the German population, by your schoolmates?

Well, in school in 1933 through 1934, they started to taunt us, you know. Unbeknownst to me, I took care of this when I beat somebody up. At my school there was a custom that the class would go every other year for three days to a youth hostel during the summer months before the big vacations. We would go there and walk and play soccer and have a good time. And then somebody started again with something. It was very innocent—you know how boys are. I picked a fight with somebody I figured I could beat up, and he really got beaten up quite badly. From then on, nobody ever bothered us again.

I went to non-Jewish schools all the way until I left school. Because my father was a frontline veteran, I left school only when I decided there was no more sense in my going there anymore. The children of frontline veterans were only removed from public schools after November 1938. I went to the public school until December 1937 and then I went to a private commercial school where I was the only Jewish student.

Did you feel a lot of fear when you lived in Nazi Germany?

No. Fear was not something I knew. You know, you were apprehensive, but I didn't have fear.

What about *Kristallnacht*?

On the morning of November 10, 1938, my mother called me at school, at maybe ten minutes past nine, and told me very abruptly, "You go now to Heidelberg. You're going to meet your cousin in Heidelberg and then you stay in the woods and call me at 5:00 P.M." The synagogue in Mannheim was burning already, but I wasn't there and I didn't know about it and nobody bothered me. I then went directly—this was only a ten-minute walk—from my school to the main railroad station. On the way there I passed the place where we used to live with my grandmother and I saw an apartment building being destroyed. At the railroad station I then bought a ticket and went to Heidelberg. In Heidelberg I met my cousin and we went up into the woods. We didn't hide; we just walked around all day in the woods. By the time I called my mother just after five, Goebbels had already been on the radio to call it off. So when I talked to my mother, she said, "Oh, I think you can come home. I think the worst is over." In Heidelberg I hadn't been in any great danger because nobody knew me and I didn't look Jewish. But if they would have arrested me, I would have ended up in a concentration camp.

What had happened to your mother and to your apartment when you got home?

My mother was very cool, calm, and collected. You have to understand that my grandfather's house was two houses. There was a loft in the back, a three-story loft. It wasn't very big, but it was a three-story loft and there were all kinds of things there that you could smash up. So, when these people came, they went into the loft and started to smash things up. But then my mother picked up the telephone and called the French consulate, as, after all, my grandmother was a French citizen. And in less then ten minutes, an SA man appeared in front of our house, went into the loft, and yelled, "Jeder raus" [everyone get out]. After this he was guarding the house because it was French property, and so nothing happened to our apartment.

Let's return to your deportation. What happened when you took the train to France?

First in Mulhouse the SS went through the train with cigar boxes in which they had French money and gave us two thousand francs for our one hundred marks, which they collected. From Mulhouse we chugged along through the occupied zone until we came to where the demarcation line started and the SS dismounted the train. The train then continued on until we came to the main station at Lyons, where we were fed. On the train there had been some French gendarmes, but nothing else. We could've jumped off, but we were too German to do that.

We were now in Vichy territory. Altogether we were three days on the train before we arrived at Gurs, where we remained until July 1942. Now, understand this. The French are very strange people. The French permitted the operation of some social services within the camp there. Among these was a Jewish organization that took care of needy children. They considered it their task to get as many of the young generation out of the camp as they could, and so my wife [who was then my girlfriend] and later I were taken out of the camp. I was taken out of the camp on July 24 or 25, 1942. Had I been in the camp on August 1, I would have been deported [like my mother and mother-in-law].

Where did you go when you left the camp?

When I left the camp, I was taken to a farm run by the Jewish Boy Scouts of France outside of Lyons. There I was supposed to help with the farmwork. This is a very sad chapter. My bad luck was that this was a completely Orthodox operation. The director of this farm was an Alsatian Orthodox Jew who was assisted by two German rabbis. But then, in August, the raids came in France and they started sending the Jews to Auschwitz.

One evening during dinner on a Friday night there was a short announcement that we on the farm would be raided in two and a half weeks and that they would come to arrest us. "But don't worry," we were told, "We will take care of it. You will be dispersed and you will be hidden."

In this period, my wife had come to see me—she hadn't seen me since she had left Gurs—and to tell me about what had happened in Gurs, that the deportations had started. We had no illusions about this. My generation, even my wife who was three years younger, was very streetwise. We had no illusions where these trains would go. We knew the trains would go east. I didn't know exactly what this meant at the time, but I knew it meant that I would never see my mother again.

With my wife I arranged that if something should happen and I was getting into trouble, I would try to go to Le Chambon, where she was staying. Little did I know that three weeks later I was on my way to Le Chambon. Because right after this the leadership [of the organization that had been helping me] dispersed and then together with three others—one who had come with me from Gurs and two somewhat older fellows from Poland who were not religious—I was on my own, as it had been decided that we didn't deserve to be hidden. I would say this was the typical attitude of anything ultra-Orthodox. They helped forty or fifty Jews, but the four of us were not helped. They told us, "You're on your own."

The fellow who came with me from the camp and I then left and went to Le Chambon. My wife had explained to me how to get there. We got there in the middle of the night and we camped in a little woods. And then by sheer chance—or if you believe in angels, maybe a guardian angel—the next morning at 5:30 a group of girls walked by that had slipped out, because they knew that also in this village there were raids, and among these girls was my wife.

My wife then took me to the wife of a man who later became the first finance minister of France under de Gaulle, André Philip. Philip was a university professor who had joined de Gaulle in London already in 1940. They were Huguenots and his wife lived in Le Chambon. She took me on that day to a villa and I slept there one night and I was fed. The next night I was taken on foot to a farm about an hour and a half away, where I stayed for three and a half or four weeks. That was a very nice farm. But, since these farmhouses were very small and there was a daughter, I had to stay in the barn and I only got out of the farm every evening for dinner, which I ate with them in their kitchen.

The people in Le Chambon then helped me escape to Switzerland. This was around September 20, 1942. But I was caught first by the Swiss army on the border, inside Switzerland, and returned the next day with forty others who were collected in the twenty-four hour period when I was caught. This was also a very sad story. We were told in Le Chambon to bury our false papers when we got onto Swiss territory—we had false papers; I had a false French identification. So, like a good German, I buried my false papers somewhere high up in the mountains, about 4,000 meters high. The only paper I had left was my German-Jewish *Kennkarte* [identity card], which was stupid, but I wanted to make sure the Swiss understood who I was. So we were in the group of forty that was shoved back. But I didn't go back to France. The Swiss left us in what was called no-man's-land, up in the mountains, and they told all forty of us, "You see that village down there? Don't go into that village. Go around to the next village, because in that village is the French gendarmerie who will arrest you."

When I got to the village, I went to the Jewish congregation, who turned me over to the Swiss after they assured me that I would not be returned. What happened in Switzerland was this. I was first a few weeks in the quarantine camp. After that I was transferred to a labor camp on December 23 or 24, 1942, in the French part of Switzerland. From this camp, I was eventually transferred to so-called refugee homes and I ran the office in these. We were not free to move around in the labor camps. But we were free to go to the village on Saturday and Sunday, and every six or eight weeks we would get three days off. The only thing you worried about, if you worried about anything, was that the Germans might invade Switzerland. But, by the end of 1943 or the beginning of 1944, it was a foregone conclusion that Germany was going to lose the war.

HERTA ROSENTHAL

All the Jews were leaving Leipzig, and they [the Germans] were happy, a lot of them. They were standing there laughing.

Born in 1925 and raised the daughter of a businessman in Leipzig, Herta Rosenthal was deported to Riga in January 1942.

I went first to a public school, a *Volksschule*. For three and a half years I went to this public school and then they started bothering me—nobody really in particular, but students in the class during recess. You know, "Jude, Jude"! I didn't like this anymore, so I said to my mother that I wanted to get out. That must have been in 1934–1935. It was after Hitler came to power, because, otherwise, I wouldn't remember that. And then my mother put me into the Jewish school in Leipzig and I stayed there until we were deported. I couldn't stand those kids, but the teacher was all right—he didn't bother me too much. But the children were very nasty, especially a few.

Outside the school I wasn't bothered. I didn't look Jewish. I played with our neighbors who were Jews. The people downstairs were not Jewish, but they were very nice people. So we were all friends together. I didn't feel the anti-Semitism much. My father was still in business. Later on my mother had more problems, but that was after this time.

Where did you live in Leipzig?

Until about 1940 we lived in the Gustav-Albert-Strasse and then we had to move to a *Judenhaus* and we lived there until deportation. It was a very good apartment, a house of about ten rooms and ten families lived there. Each of us had one room. We were lucky. We had a bathroom and a kitchen across the hall. So we had one room and the kitchen across and other families lived in the other rooms. The whole house plus the *Hinterhaus* in the back was also for Jews. We had already then the bombardments and alarms, when we had to go in the back of the coal cellar. We were not allowed to go to the *Luftschutzkeller* [air raid shelter].

Did you experience much anti-Semitism at that time?

I used to go to a *Fischgeschäft* to buy fish. I brought the fish to my mother. They didn't give fish to my mother because she looked Jewish, but to me they gave it. She looked more Jewish. To her they said, "Kein Fisch mehr" [there is no more fish]. Then I stood in line behind her and I got fish. So I didn't look Jewish. That was in 1940 to 1941, during the war already. But then we had to start wearing the star and it was different. But nobody noticed me. I was a young girl. I will never forget that I was told that: "You don't look at all Jewish. You don't have to put that on." But it was a law. You had to, you know. But I didn't. A friend of mine and I went to a restaurant at the railway station, the *Hauptbahnhof*, and had dinner there, the two of us. But they didn't bother me because we didn't look Jewish. You took chances.

Did you have problems with the Gestapo?

We personally didn't have any problem with the Gestapo. We had to report once a year. My father had become German years and years ago. Then Hitler took his citizenship away—he was of Russian background. So I remember that we had to report to the police. I didn't even know about the Gestapo. You saw more the SA and the SS walking around in the city. But I had really nothing to do with the Gestapo.

Were there people in the neighborhood you had to be especially cautious around?

We knew there were Nazis like the superintendent or the *Hausfrau* downstairs. You had to be very careful there and in some of the stores where we knew we shouldn't say anything. Where we lived later on was in a real Jewish neighborhood, so we didn't worry too much about it. We didn't have contact with non-Jewish people later on.

When you lived in that house for Jews, were you still going to school?

At that time my father had to do forced labor. He worked first in some chemical factory and then he worked in landscaping. He had never done landscaping before in his life. My mother and I didn't work. I went to school part-time. We had some classes in the school building for some time, almost until the end. That's when they brought all the people from the other towns and we were all together.

When the deportations started, how were they arranged?

First we heard about deportations from other cities. That was already in 1940–1941 and Leipzig wasn't touched. Finally, in December 1941 or the beginning of January 1942, we got the letter that we had to report to the

Sammellager [assembly camp] on January 19. We took along whatever we could carry. My father was very upset. But my mother packed, sewed, put coffee on, and everything else. And then, on January 19, 1941, we reported to the *Sammellager*, where we stayed until January 21. Then we were put on trains and sent to Riga.

I don't know exactly how many people were in the *Sammellager*, perhaps a couple hundred. Most people were Leipzigers and some were from the other smaller towns around Leipzig. It was in a school building. There were guards outside and we couldn't go out, but we could look through the window. When aunt Marta came to bring us sandwiches, they chased her away. I saw her again after the war when I came back. From the *Sammellager* they took us on trucks to the Bayrischer Bahnhof. It's in the back [of the city] and that's where they took us and sent us away. They took us during the day, in the morning.

Could this be seen by many people?

Everybody saw it, and they were screaming bloody murder. All the Jews were leaving Leipzig, and they [the Germans] were happy, a lot of them. They were standing there laughing. They brought us during the day, not at night. There were both SA and ordinary citizens there. A lot of them were ordinary citizens. There was also army there; it was during the war already. But most of them were ordinary citizens.

Where did you think they would take you and what would happen to you?

My father said that if they send us to Poland we're lost. We didn't know what was going on. We didn't know about Auschwitz. We knew about Buchenwald, Sachsenhausen, but the other we didn't know. We thought of Poland, because you heard from people who were deported in 1938 and came back that there was a big problem with the food and the cold. So I didn't know anything. I was so numb. Then they said that we're going east and my father said they're going to send us to Russia. Then we were on the train and we went to Königsberg. In Königsberg we stopped. But they didn't send us to Russia.

On January 24, 1942, we arrived in Riga. There were already people there from other places. They came in November–December 1941 from Cologne, Bielefeld, Kassel, and from all of southern Germany. I think we were one of the last, Dresden and Leipzig. They took us into one of those buildings there and my father was taken away. My mother saw him only three or four weeks later.

The first thing we had to do was to shovel snow. It was a very, very bad winter. Since I was a young girl, a young man from Leipzig and myself had to get water because everything was frozen. There was a very big ghetto and they killed all the Latvian Jews there, an awful lot, in order to make room for the German Jews. Outside of that ghetto there was a big Jewish hospital, so we had to clean this up. I used to go every day, me and my mother, to clean there.

After that we had to start working. I had to work for the *Luftflotte* [air force] outside the ghetto. We went there with guards. We were picked up in the ghetto and we were not allowed to walk on the sidewalk and we were marched to wherever we were going. In 1943 we were sent to cut peat, the whole group of young people. I stayed there for about six months. After that they sent us back again and then they liquidated the ghetto. Then I met my mother in the concentration camp in Riga.

The Latvians were worse than the Germans. They are terrible. Once in a blue moon an old man who spoke Russian and Latvian used to bring me a sandwich. But he was the only one. The Latvians wanted to storm the ghetto. They wanted to kill the Jews. So the Germans had to protect us—the German army or SS or whatever it was. It is paradoxical.

In November 1943 we were sent to other camps. We had to stand for roll call a few times and people were selected and sent away never to be seen again. My mother was already in Kaiserwald—they made a camp there outside the ghetto—and I met my mother there. Then they sent us to another place also in Riga. There I stayed until they put us on a ship and sent us to Stutthof near Danzig. My mother died there in Riga. Twice every day we had to stand for roll call. In the morning and at night. On one roll call we were ten in a row and one of those SS men started counting: "One, two, three, four, five, six." I was sixth. He pulled me out and then I went to one side. In the next row came a girl from Hamburg. She was very short. Then came a Latvian old lady. I thought that this is absolutely no good, there's something wrong, and I noticed that all of my friends were not going. We were sent to labor camps.

When I was in a small labor camp of five hundred women, we had a very nice SS man there. His name was Müller. As a young man he used to work for Jewish people in a shoe store. He was with us during the winter of 1944. He said that his people were not going to work until they sent them some warmer clothing. It was very nice of him. He didn't have to do it.

Then I got sick. I had some kind of a cold. The Jewish doctor said, "You stay in bed." All of a sudden they were calling us. All the girls who were not well were going to be sent away. It was no good. One evening I was standing and crying outside of the barracks and the *Oberstabführer* asked why I was crying. I told him that I was going to be sent away, but that I was not sick and hoped that he might just come and watch me work so I could prove that to him. So three days in a row he came and watched me. And one day before they were sent away, he came over and said to us that we were going to be sent to Bromberg to a *Stickerei-Fabrik* [embroidery factory]. I replied to him, "You could say that to your own grandmother!" He could have shot me. But he looked at me and started smiling and didn't say one word. When I came back from work the next day, the group was gone, but I was still there. I had got myself out of it. He was a very decent man. He was very decent to us, as decent as possible. You had to try and get yourself out of those situations. Then [after being marched back to an old army camp in Germany,] we were liberated by the Russian army. It was on March 10, 1945.

What had you heard about mass executions or mass murder of Jews?

I knew only about our people in Riga. They had no gas chambers there, but they shot people. When I came back from working for a while with sugar beets, they had a Jewish police force in the ghetto, all Latvian Jewish boys. They were all taken into the woods and shot.

When the last selection was made before we were sent back to Germany, we were about 2,500 people in that camp. When we were sent away, we were 500. All [the rest] got shot because they had no gas chambers. Auschwitz, I only heard about after the war. I never knew about it. I knew about ghettos in Poland, but I didn't know about this.

ERNST LEVIN

I don't care that they say today that "we didn't know about it." Bullshit!

Born in 1925 and raised by his grandmother in Breslau, Ernst Levin was deported to Auschwitz in January 1943.

I shut it out of my mind. My kids really knew almost nothing about my background other than I had come from Germany. I had an accent; they're American kids. It was only in the past four to five years that I was even willing to talk about it. In general I wasn't going to talk about Auschwitz, for example, because anybody who really wanted to learn about Auschwitz didn't need my description. It's been described I don't know how many times. There are deniers of the Holocaust. There'll always be some. There are people living in this world who'll swear the earth is flat and not round.

I was in Auschwitz III. That was a camp that was built as an *Arbeitslager* [work camp]. We furnished the raw material for the construction of a huge factory built by IG Farben. I don't know if it ever produced anything, but, in addition to the inmates themselves, we had a huge number of civilians working there: Germans who had come from IG Farben; forced laborers from France, Belgium, Italy, Czechoslovakia, Poland, you name it; volunteer workers from these countries; and English prisoners of war. In this particular Auschwitz, the survival rate was, of course, very low. At least it was not an extermination camp in the sense that Birkenau was.

I was born in Breslau in 1925. My family initially was quite well-off. My father left my mother before Hitler came to power in 1929. I have no recollection of him. He left for South Africa and we never really heard from him again. I know that he died in 1936. My mother died rather young in 1932, also before Hitler came to power. I have a sister and we were raised by my grandmother in Breslau. Eventually we wound up in the Jewish orphanage in Breslau.

How were you treated by your classmates and others in your school?

We were kicked out of the German public schools rather early, probably in 1934. In my home, politics were not discussed very much. I was eight years old when Hitler came to power. I remember the day that Hitler was elected chancellor in 1933. I was in the *Volksschule* and all my classmates were walking around in the aisles of the classroom saying "Heil Hitler, Heil Hitler, Heil Hitler!"—kids eight years old! That was something they had heard at home; they couldn't possibly have known what this was all about. Their parents probably were quite enthusiastic. Of course "Heil Hitler" had never been mentioned in my home so I was completely floored and, in response, I went and said, "*Freiheit!*" [Freedom], a slogan of the Socialist Party. They pounced on me.

I have very little other recollection of my early school years in the *Volksschule*, but I think it was in 1934 that the Jewish students were told to leave the German schools and that they established Jewish schools. The one in Breslau was the *Israelitische Volksschule* on Am Anger 8. It presumably had the entire range of students from six to whatever. But actually my formative school years were among Jews who came from rather well-to-do families by and large.

Until the outbreak of the war in September 1939, I went to a kibbutz. Very few people actually know that there were kibbutzim in Germany in the late 1930s allowed by the Nazis. I went to one that was in the Niederlausitz, and there were others in Paderborn and there were others—there were quite a few. These had originally been founded by the emerging Zionist movement in Germany.

I spent a couple of years there until the late 1930s, and then I went back to Breslau to live with my aging grandmother. By that time everybody was going to be incorporated into the German war effort. All Jews who were able to work had to register. This was about 1941; I was sixteen. I was assigned to work in a small automobile tire–retreading factory outside of Breslau. This was run by a man named Otto Glück who was a German capitalist. He had four or five of these. His business was, of course, booming with the war. He was under contract to retread the automobile tires of the Wehrmacht. He was not an anti-Semite. Somehow he must have had close contacts with many Jews prior to all this. He was a decent guy without exposing himself.

Even if you were not an anti-Nazi, everybody was scared to make any move. Everybody already knew about the concentration camps and the Nazis somehow furthered that. Everybody said, "Stay calm or else you will end up in KZ [concentration camp]!" They didn't know the details, but they all knew "KZ." They all knew there was something going on.

Glück had six or seven Jews assigned to him. He wasn't cruel to me or anything, but we were deeply restricted in what we could do. We were paid the standard minimum wage for laborers at that time. With the Teutonic passion for exactitude, we were integrated into the German medical and social system. I always felt that maybe I should make some claim because I worked there for two years and I contributed into that social security system.

Where were you living at that time?

With my grandmother in Breslau. She had a very small apartment, basically a two-room apartment. One room was occupied by her son, one by me and my grandmother. In 1942, by edict, Jews couldn't ride bicycles anymore. I had no transportation to my place of work; I was supposed to walk. It was at least ten kilometers each way, a rather long walk. Then the boss of this company said, "I'm going to buy you a bicycle for the firm. You can use it to go to and from work." He was rather decent. It was a typical German workplace. It was the glory days of the Third Reich. France had been defeated, the troops were occupying half of Europe or more, and the war with Russia had already started, but the initial success had been spectacular. The average German worker was confident that the end of the war was near. Some were very anti-Semitic: "Get out of my way, Jews!" Others really couldn't care less. The young ones, the apprentices, were all indoctrinated Hitler Youth. Eventually, I guess, they were all drafted into the army and perished in Russia.

The deportations in Germany had started. The deportation of the Jews from Germany took place over a rather extended period of time; it wasn't at all that all Jews were picked up at once. There were various transports. Nobody ever knew where they went to at that time, but word filtered out from German troops coming back from Poland, returning on leave. And, of course, they were talking about what was happening to the Polish Jews. I was told by people that it was quite well known in Germany at that time already. Many Jews in

Germany had at least one Aryan with whom they had contact. Either these were their former mates or had been people who had been married to a Jew or had been close friends before Hitler came to power. Not all connections were broken between Jews and non-Jews; many of these relationships still existed. We had a woman [working with us] who had been married to a Jewish man who had died. We were told what was going on with the Polish Jews. Frightening!

Did you hear about mass shootings or about concentration camps?

Word was filtering out. It was also filtering out that transports were leaving for the east from the ghettos. It was known at that time that these transports went directly to Treblinka or Auschwitz. Terrible, terrible! But people didn't want to talk about it. When the German Jews learned about it, they really refused to believe a lot of it. The German Jews themselves would say, "This is atrocity propaganda. That can't be so. After all, it's the twentieth century and we're German." Many of them still considered themselves German. They didn't believe it primarily because they didn't want to believe it. Who can blame them?

In Breslau the transports started in 1941. My grandmother had sisters, all of whom were sent on these transports. These people were taken away and they had nothing but their baggage. They left behind all their belongings, apartments, rooms, whatever they had. There were some vague rumors that they were going to the east to work. My grandmother's sisters at that time were in their sixties. How were they going to work in the east? There were sick people. "What is happening to them?" they wondered. It was very disturbing, yet nothing was known for certain. Nobody knew of the gas chamber in Auschwitz at that time. Breslau had a very large Jewish community, the second or third largest in Germany. The only Jews left in Breslau at the end of 1942 were those who were integrated in the German war effort.

How were you treated when you went to the shops?

It varied. You had many stores with the big signs: *Juden unerwünscht* [Jews not wanted]. At least 40 percent of them had these signs. In my particular case, there was a grocery store run by an old man and his wife. By that time he was already in his late sixties. He knew my family, my grandmother. I would make it a point to go to his store just before he closed. He would sneak me all kinds of things. When nobody was in the store, he would whisper, "How is your grandmother?" He was a very decent man, always looking around making sure that nobody was there. But, if I was alone in the store, he always gave me a little something, a little extra bread, or kerosene for the Bunsen burner since we couldn't use electricity or gas. He certainly was very helpful. The same was true for some other stores in my immediate neighborhood where my family had been known. By and large these people—there were some exceptions—wanted to be left alone. They had no particular animosity against the Jews, notwithstanding the fact that they had been exposed to a constant spate of anti-Semitic propaganda. I don't think the *Stürmer* was read by them.

I cannot particularly say that I was treated cruelly by the German population as such during these years. This was from 1940 to 1942, when I was fifteen to seventeen. But by some people, yes, I was treated cruelly. By that time you already wore the star. There were people on the street that would make an effort to spit at you, but it was not the norm.

I had two cousins who were *Halbarier* [half Aryans]. My mother's brother had married a woman who was not Jewish and these were the two offspring. After the Nazis came to power, her brother was active in the Nazi Party. The blot on his record was that his sister had married a Jew. So the wife divorced my uncle and petitioned to be allowed to take back her maiden name. They were transformed into a typical Nazi environment because her mother and her brother were very active. The cousins became little Nazis, even if the Germans never recognized them as true Aryans, since they were *Halbarier* in this crazy world. They eventually were drafted in the Organisation Todt and did road building or whatever for the Wehrmacht.

Right after the war, when I was in Paris—they had somehow heard through an uncle of mine who lived in England that I was alive—I got a letter from them. All of a sudden, they had taken back their original [Jewish sounding] name because that was now fashionable. This was in 1945. They wanted food packages like nothing had ever happened. I think I was unduly harsh really. Their father had been killed in Dachau in 1938. All of a sudden, they were victims like their father who had been killed by the Nazis. During the regime, they were spouting the ideology. I don't want to have anything to do with them. They're probably still alive in Germany.

How much did you already know about the concentration camps when you were deported?

I was on the last transport when Breslau decided to become *judenfrei* [Jew free]. I think it was in January 1943. This German guy I was working with—he was actually a *Meister*, but he had not been drafted because he was already too old—then gleefully said: "Na ja, jetzt geht Ihr mal Steine kloppen in Russland!" [Oh yeah, now you are going to go break rocks in Russia!] I figured that this was going to be our fate. In general it was said that we were going to be relocated to the east—to work in the east.

Just about four weeks before I went on my transport, there was one transport before mine and a friend of mine named Helmut went on that transport. That transport wound up in Treblinka. In a place near Treblinka, there was also a contingent of Germans working, one of whom we had known. Helmut wrote a letter and gave it to this man and said: "Send it to my Ernst." I got this letter. I never knew who sent it or how they got it out. He told me in this letter that he was near Treblinka and "hier ist ein Lager, wo die Menschen chemisch behandelt werden." [Here is a camp where the people are being treated with chemicals.] It is amazing that even at that time he wouldn't say that they were gassed. Isn't that amazing? I was thinking, "What the heck does he mean?" I guess he eventually was gassed. He certainly didn't survive. Therefore I would have known four weeks before I was arrested that something was going wrong.

The Israelis today say, "How could you just walk into it like sheep to a slaughter? Where was the resistance? If you have a knife or a club or whatever, try to take at least one with you." That's one of the great debates and it's very true. I've asked myself that very same question. Where would one have gone? Where were you going to flee to? We were in Breslau, everybody had an ID, everybody was catalogued. There was no way you could get on a train and just take off. The trains were all patrolled constantly because travel even for the Germans was restricted. You had to have some reason to go somewhere. You couldn't just in 1942 decide anymore that you were going to travel to Berlin. Where were you going to get your food ration cards in Berlin? Where were you going to stay? That was all naturally impossible. I must admit that I put it out of my mind despite [having heard] that "Menschen werden hier chemisch behandelt." I wound up in Auschwitz, as this particular transport wound up in Auschwitz.

The list of who was going on the transport was left to the Jews. The Jewish *Gemeinde* would be told that "1,500 Jews are to be assembled, and please do it." The Jewish *Gemeinde* would then notify those people who had been selected to go on the transport.

Did you get any information about the aim of the transport?

They didn't know themselves. The reason why the Nazis could annihilate this number of people was the fact that it was a very secret operation. Obviously the Germans knew that these Jews were being transported away. Some of them benefited by going into the apartments that were sealed and stealing whatever they could steal. No questions were ever asked. What had happened to all these Jews? Where did they go to? Trains would take off and come back empty. Where are these people? This question was not asked by the Germans. The Germans knew in a way that something was happening.

I don't care that they say today that "wir haben es nicht gewußt" [we didn't know about it]. Bullshit! We didn't know in detail what was happening. They probably didn't know that there were gas chambers in Auschwitz or in

Treblinka, but they knew that the Jews were vanishing. The German cities were *judenrein* [Jew free]. Cities celebrated weekend articles like: "Berlin *judenrein!* Breslau now *judenrein.*" One had to ask the question: "There lived 45,000 Jews in Breslau. What had happened to these 45,000 people?" This question was never asked, just like the question what are these concentration camps? What is happening there? Of course the Nazis forced that by whispering campaigns: "If you don't toe the line, that's where you're going to go too. If you're listening to enemy radio broadcasts, then you are making atrocity propaganda and you're going to go there."

Did you ever listen to foreign radio broadcasts?

One woman who was a friend of my family and an Aryan had this Telefunken radio. Breslau is about as far away from the English BBC as one could be and the Germans were jamming the transmissions. But at night you could try to receive the BBC from London, and, although you got the constant "brrrr," you could in fact hear the German broadcast from London if you put your ear to the radio. There were many others who somehow had access through Aryans to the BBC, which was listened to because it was already quite obvious that you never got the true story [from the Nazis]. The Germans knew very well that Goebbels was lying to them all the time. I remember at the time that we were quite well informed about Stalingrad way before the German broadcast started admitting that something was going wrong with the Sixth Army. The BBC was broadcasting that.

One more question about the period before you left. What about the Gestapo? Was one always living in fear of the Gestapo?

Oh yes. Uniformly the Jews were in dread of the Gestapo. So were the Germans. Gestapo never meant anything good, for Jews or non-Jews. After all, it was the Geheime Staatspolizei [secret state police]. There was terror in the hearts of the Jews as well as the Germans. The only intercourse with the Gestapo that I had was when they came to arrest me. I already knew I was going on the transport. I was told to be ready. I have forgotten what the date was. I was to go on a transport and take with me things that would be used for work in the east. They did come, two of them, in their traditional leather coats. They said, "Are you ready?" I said yes and my grandmother started to cry. A terrible, terrible scene. I don't want to think about it. They had a truck downstairs and there were already some twenty to thirty Jews on it. I was just told to get on it. Then they picked up all the other Jews and eventually took us to a building owned by the Jewish *Gemeinde*. There was a policeman outside. We were all so neat. Nobody thought of escaping. We stayed there for three to four days until they had a train ready with freight cars. We were the last German Jews [in Breslau], maybe two thousand.

The amazing thing is that in front of that building there were also a lot of Germans who had congregated together trying to pass things through. [They were] not policemen. They were coming and saying, "Can you get this package through to Mr. and Mrs. So-and-so?" The situation changed completely once the train left and arrived in Auschwitz. Even the loading into this *Güterwagen*, our transport, was relatively doable, Breslau being very close to Auschwitz.

The Nazis liked to say, "A Jew is a Jew is a Jew is a Jew." In reality the schism between the Polish Jews and the German Jews was enormous. The German Jews who had been living in Germany for generations and had been fully integrated in the German society regarded themselves as Germans. In fact there was total surprise to learn that they were Jews. After Hitler came to power, they would think that this was a passing folly of some deranged madman who could not possibly survive as a chancellor in Germany—that it was something that was going to pass. The Polish Jews had never been assimilated into Polish society by and large. They had their own language. They spoke Yiddish.

The Polish Jews have always regarded the German Jews with some sort of contempt because the German Jews had lost their Jewishness as far as they were concerned. They would go to pray on the high holy days and that was it. Word had filtered out of Poland. I'm sure it was a cause of a lot of dismay. There must have been many German Jews asking, "Is this going to be our fate [too]?"

By that time it had become quite obvious through Hitler's speeches that what was planned was, if not the total annihilation, at least the total subjugation of the Jews as such. Yet maybe it's a sort of fatalism in the Jewish nature altogether. They have been persecuted throughout history. Primarily I think it was something that the Jews just couldn't believe—that a country in the twentieth century that had produced Goethe and Schiller and Mozart would engage in behavior that was absolutely foreign to German culture.

Many really [first] woke up when they disembarked in Auschwitz. All of a sudden, whoever still harbored any illusions had them destroyed, were brutally beaten, and herded like cattle into groups with their children—indescribable scenes at Auschwitz at two in the morning. The vast majority never saw the camp from the inside anyhow. They were gassed immediately.

I have always maintained that Hitler, the Nazi regime, actively encouraged the emigration of the German Jews. After all, many German Jews arrived in America in the early '30s and they took all their belongings, not their money necessarily, but at least their furniture. Certainly the Nazis did not discourage emigration. The German Jews were relatively slow to respond. If you think about it today, these were people who had established a career in Germany whether they were merchants or doctors or lawyers or what have you. The only language they spoke was German; the only culture they knew all their life was

Goethe's Germany. It's very, very difficult to emigrate without any funds into the unknown, where you don't speak the language and you have to compete with the native population. To be reluctant to do that is totally understandable. Still quite a number of German Jews emigrated in the '30s to any country that would have them or they had connection or could transfer funds to. America was one of them. Others went to many countries in South America, or to a lesser extent to Asia, until the *Kristallnacht*. That was the wake-up call in a sense to the German Jews that this man was going to stay in power.

The U.S. didn't open their doors as wide as they should have. The German Jews were relegated to leave for a place like Shanghai, one of the few places you could go without anything but a ticket on a boat, or to Colombia, Central America, England. My sister got out on a *Kindertransport* [children's transport], in which English families took in German Jews' children. There were a few children saved that way. The rest remained in Germany after the outbreak of the war because they had no funds—not all German Jews were wealthy. In America you had to have someone who would vouch for you that you wouldn't become a public burden.

Hitler always said, "Hey, it's not us that prevents the Jews from leaving. But look how right we are. Nobody wants them!" After the outbreak of the war the Polish, Hungarian, Greek Jews could not have been saved. But the German Jews could have been saved. It's a very sad commentary. I can really only speak for German Jewry. In all the transports that came from all the other countries, I don't know how many died, how many survived. Very few survived. From the people I had known in this kibbutz, of 120 people, I only know of a few survivors. These were people in the prime of their lives.

To survive in Auschwitz, rule number one was youth. If you had any chance at all, you had to be young. Rule number two was you had to have an awful lot of luck. For me, getting to Auschwitz III was another stroke of luck. Where you worked, what you worked on [were also of prime importance]. If you were assigned to one of the innumerable commandos, you didn't last very long, not on the ration. In rain, snow, cold, and with no clothing, you could last maybe two to three months. No way you could survive. If you were given a broom in one of those vast factory halls to just push around, you could look around to see if anybody was coming and lean on the broomstick. Even if you did this for ten to twelve hours a day, it was a hell of a lot better than carrying sacks of cement.

**Could you explain more about this "different Auschwitz camp,"
Auschwitz III?**

It was run by civilians, mostly recruited from IG Farben. Workers, master craftsmen, foremen, they were the ones who in fact ran it. They saw these living corpses marching daily into their territory in commandos as slave workers—some of them were nothing more than skin and bones—under the most deplorable conditions. I was extremely lucky that in 1944 my capo came to me and said, "How much schooling did you have?" He was not a communist. In Auschwitz capos were either Polish or people with green triangles (criminals).

The capos wore the triangle either up or down—up was for *Schwerverbrecher* [serious criminals]; down was for petty criminals—anyway losers, "asocial elements." You could have been a German who was involved in the black market and you were dubbed a criminal. Or you might even just have rubbed a Nazi Party boss the wrong way and made some remarks against the regime and you found yourself with the green rather than with the red triangle that was for political inmates. There were some Jews who were capos, usually those who had been in the camp for quite a while. Somebody named *Judenfranz* never returned from work without bringing at least four dead Jews along—he personally murdered them. But most were just trying to survive. You can only talk about individuals.

What about the German guards?

They were Waffen-SS. It was a complex many miles long and wide, and every fifty feet there stood a guard. The guards had the most boring job of all. Many didn't even speak German and had no particular relation with the inmates. The average guard was like a private in the army. I can say very little about them. I had very little contact with them.

My very first commando when I came to Auschwitz hadn't completely been fenced in. We were digging a foundation—all Jews from Breslau, about sixty, with spades. None of us knew how to dig. Four guards surrounded the hole. It was bitter cold, January 1943. This one guard was looking at me. I think I was crying. I was a blond, blue-eyed kid; actually I was very Aryan looking. He said to me, "You! Where do you come from?" "From Breslau," I replied. "Well, now you are going to pay for what your parents have done." That's how he, I guess, eventually rationalized that. This was one of the very few contacts I had with the guards.

There was another group of SS men who were not guards but sergeants in the SS (*Scharführer, Unterscharführer*). They were all young. They were in charge of five or six blocks. Each block had two hundred people. Basically, they would very rarely show their faces. The one thing about the SS, their most distinct quality, was laziness. This was not really surprising. By the time these men volunteered for service in the SS, the unemployment in Germany had largely been eliminated. These men had to fit in somewhere. They really didn't want to work, to go out and get a job. Enrolling in the SS was one way of beating the system, so to speak, from their point of view. If they could get away with doing nothing and having someone doing it for them, usually the inmates, they were certainly not going out of their way. Some were incredibly cruel. But many of them were just trying to stay out of the Russian front. For them, this was a soft cushion. Here they were sitting [pretty] and had an opportunity to enrich themselves. In fact, some could become very, very wealthy.

There was enormous wealth accumulating in Auschwitz. If I told you that you were going to be transported away from your place of residence in Cologne to some unknown destination to work without ever coming back to your home, what are you going to pack?—all your valuables—your money, your gold, your watch, your rings—that'll come in handy. That's what these Jews did from Poland, from Hungary, from Greece. Since you knew it might be taken from you, you were trying to hide it by sewing it into the seams of your clothing, into your suitcases. Then these transports arrived and you dumped everything. The SS knew well that in this huge pile of abandoned things, clothing and suitcases, there was a tremendous wealth in gold, diamonds, money, German marks, American dollars, Greek drachmas, you name it. They established a separate commando; it was called Canada by the inmates. It was the function of Canada to find it by opening the seams. If they found it, they turned it over to the SS. These were men who had no strong political connections anyhow. "Even if we lose the war," [they thought to themselves] "if I can get my hands on this money and these diamonds, I'm going to sit pretty for the rest of my life." That was the philosophy. So everybody stole. There was certainly great opportunity to enrich themselves.

When I got there, we were told to undress. Someone said, "Can we go to the toilet?" They said, "All right, you can go to the latrine." What was thrown into that latrine? I know I threw my watch in there—that was all I had. I didn't have any riches. By that time even the strongest believers in German civilization had come to realize what was happening. They parted with the things they hadn't parted with before. There must have been millions of rings and what have you. Wedding rings had been thrown into that latrine. It gets me upset to think that even today many of these former SS guards are probably living in Germany in *Wohlstand* [comfort and prosperity], maybe even with loot gotten from the Jews of Auschwitz.

What about the German civilians in the camp?

I was told that there was an office upstairs and they needed somebody who could count well and also spoke fluent German. So I was brought up there and there was a German sitting there. He must have been in his early sixties and was wearing a Nazi Party pin. There was also a young man who had been rejected by the Wehrmacht—he had a heart condition—and a third one who also had been a reject from the army. I was assigned to that guy. They conducted *Arbeitsstudien* [production studies].

These people talked among themselves a lot. I would never open my mouth.

The man who was running this office was very proud to announce to anybody willing to listen that he had joined the Nazi Party in 1928 and had number 8,000 or something. In other words, he was Nazi number 1. The other two were considerably more subdued. To them he was a convinced Nazi. The way he would talk to me was clearly that I was the slave and he was the master. He did not mistreat me, but I understood that I was his slave. If he would tell me to wipe his ass, I would have wiped his ass. One of the others was an Austrian, who at one time when we were sitting alone in the office (by that time in 1944 you have to realize that there was a very distinct possibility that Germany was going to be on the losing side) asked me, "What's going on over there in Auschwitz? This smell and these chimneys; what are they doing there?" After all, when the wind was right, you smelled the corpses burning. I said to him, "Well, those are crematoriums." And he said, "What are they burning?" That was only twelve kilometers from Birkenau.

Another time he said to me, "If we lose the war, Austria will be independent again." I didn't say a word of course. By that time we all knew that Germany was going to lose the war. The big question was, Are we going to survive it? Nobody had any doubt about what was happening. They were talking and they had their *Oberschlesische Beobachter* [newspaper]. You could gather from that what was happening. There were other sources of information. With Czechs and Poles and Italians and French and Ukrainians all working usually in separate camps, there was a certain amount of interchange between these civilians and these ten thousand inmates working all over the place.

Later on it was claimed that nobody knew, that nobody was guilty of anything, that there were just a few [who knew]—Hitler and Goebbels and Göring and Himmler—that were all hanged in Nuremberg. This was impossible. The scope of the annihilation was such that it involved hundreds of thousands of people. The German Reichsbahn transported people in trains that were stuffed full of humanity being unloaded in Treblinka or Auschwitz and then left empty.

Auschwitz was never really liberated as such. It was evacuated. There were a few thousand people left who had really thought they would all be killed. But Auschwitz was evacuated by forced marches to Gleiwitz, a march of sixty kilometers in the winter, in January 1945. It took a terrible, terrible toll. I was in one of these marches.

From Gleiwitz they had trains. That was a time when every railroad engine was needed to transport raw material, but the Nazis were using them to transport corpses, so to speak. The transport I found myself on went from Gleiwitz into Austria to Mauthausen. The cars on these trains by that time were cattle cars. When people looked down on these trains from overpasses, they saw what must have been the most indescribable sight. Car after car passed by in which there were strange creatures in striped things, packed together like animals. As we were traveling through Austria, we could of course look up and see those people. I found no recognition, no sign of absolute amazement about what was happening. To me, it was almost a sign of collective guilt. They were unmoved by what must have been the most terrible sight.

As I got to Mauthausen, which is not too far from Vienna, the train was stopped and we got into contact with all kinds of German railroad personnel. There were cries of "water, water!" At least in my cattle car we had a tin can and a string. As the train was moving, that can was bouncing out in the snow and was picking up some snow and then we hauled it in.

Mauthausen was completely filled up and they said they could not possibly accommodate us. The decision was then made to go to Czechoslovakia. It was quite amazing. Almost the moment you crossed the border from Austria to Czechoslovakia there was the same sight. But this time it was the Czechs who were seeing it. There were people from these overpasses that cried when we arrived on the train. Don't ask me how, but obviously the Czechs knew what was in these trains—Poles, Czechs, Jews, what have you. In any event, the train left Czechoslovakia and went on to Germany, to the same stoic silence and non-comprehension as in Austria.

The question of how the Germans behaved during the war and before the war cannot be answered in black and white. They behaved like Germans. There were good ones, and there were bad ones. There was a vast mass of indifferent ones. The vast majority were, if not indifferent, collaborators.

RUTH MENDEL

I wouldn't be alive if not for my mother.

Ruth Mendel was born in Frankfurt in 1929 and deported to Auschwitz in April 1943.

We were among the last Jews in 1943 to leave. My parents didn't have to wear the star in the beginning because my father was a Czechoslovakian citizen. So, at that time, when others were wearing the star, we did not wear it for a short time. But, by 1942 or so, we had to wear the star too. At any rate, after the Anschluss, my parents helped a lot of people, mostly young men, escape from Vienna or Austria and make their way through Frankfurt, where there was a fairly large Jewish community, to somewhere in the west, probably Holland, but hopefully to England because Holland was invaded and the Jews there had the same fate as anyone else.

We lived on top of a Nazi; he had a hardware store in Frankfurt. We lived on the second floor and he lived on the first floor. There were five floors and there were two families on each floor. When we were children, we'd run up the stairs, or we'd move a chair, and every time we did something that bothered him he would knock on the ceiling. We knew he was a Nazi because for parades he was always wearing a uniform, a black uniform. Maybe half of the people in this apartment house were Nazis.

In 1942 we were told that we had to leave the apartment. We were taken down to what had been the old Jewish orphanage. It was like living in a ghetto because we were not allowed to go out. There was communal cooking. It wasn't like the ghetto in Warsaw, which was absolutely terrible, but we were not allowed to leave. Only my father was allowed to go out. That was pretty late, because by 1942 most of the Jews had been taken away and they were not in Frankfurt anymore. So then they started picking on the ones that were left and they found us—we were thirty-seven in a crowd that were sent to Auschwitz. We had been at that orphanage from the fall of 1942, because I remember Hanukkah there. My father was lighting candles and I started crying as if I had some premonition of what would be the next Hanukkah. You know, we wouldn't be there.

How aware were you at the time about the deportations?

Oh, we were aware. Every few days, every few weeks, my friends were taken away. What they told us was resettlement. My parents must have known [what this meant], but they didn't tell me. They didn't tell us, you know. We were children; we didn't know what resettlement meant. At first, the people were taken to Lodz. Once in a while from the ghetto somebody did get a postcard back, but very few, and then you didn't hear from them anymore.

Of course, no information was given to Jews. Whatever you heard was through the grapevine and through supposition, except for one time, and I don't know how it got through to us. This was when we were still living in our apartment. My parents got in the mail—and we didn't know who even mailed it, and it was written on a brown piece of paper, like from a paper bag—a letter from two of my young cousins. They were a few years older than I was at the time. I don't know how it got mailed. I don't know how it found its way to our apartment with our address on it. They were from Poland and they wrote to us that their parents had been taken away and that they were probably dead, and that they expected to be taken away also in a few days. That was the end. I don't know if my parents intended for us to know it, but we found out about it. That was one of the communications we had.

Did you have fear all the time even as a little girl?

Yes, in a sense. For one thing, I always had this feeling that my father would be able to protect me, protect us. When you're a child, you feel your parents are almighty. But I realized then that your parents cannot. There always was this fear. There was this fear when we started going to school that we would get beaten up.

I was run over by a bicycle in 1933 when I was only four years old. I was walking at the edge of the park with my parents and a Hitler Youth boy on a bicycle drove right into me and drove over my knee, on purpose of course. He knocked me over, but luckily nothing was broken so my parents didn't say anything. They didn't go to the police to complain because if you went to the police and complained it only meant that you would be beaten up. The police wouldn't do anything about it anyway.

Did you feel humiliated as a Jew?

I think I was able to separate material things from the real values. But when we came to Auschwitz, every time an SS man or SS woman started howling *Schweinjude* or whatever else went with it, I looked around me, saw what was happening, and tried to keep in mind who the real *Schweine* were, they or us? I mean look at what was happening! They were killing people, in horrible ways.

I had that feeling right along. I had a real disdain for them. I did not feel that I was less important. I didn't feel that I was inferior. I felt that I had a superior morality. I mean I didn't express it in such terms at the time. But I felt, "Look at these people. Look what they're doing."

Before you were deported, what do you remember about the climate of anti-Semitism?

My parents would send me to go to the bakery in the morning, because a child would not be thrown out or whatever, and every so often, as long as we were not wearing the star, my mother was able to stand in the line and get some potatoes. Also my father had some pocketbooks left from his business—he manufactured pocketbooks and belts—and he was able to trade them for some food.

Of course we were afraid. We always wanted to be inconspicuous. We didn't want to awaken anything or anyone. In the house where we lived, there were about ten or so tenants. They were not Jewish people. Some were quite friendly, but they stopped talking to us after awhile.

Also I remember Streicher's newspaper *Der Stürmer*—that was everywhere. My father didn't buy it obviously. I saw it on newsstands, on the kiosks, but I didn't pay attention. What I remember very vividly is Hitler's speeches almost every Sunday morning, because everybody had their windows open and I guess they wanted to show how patriotic they were. He screeched away like "Oooh, oooh"—you know how he speaks when you see the newsreels of it. I remember every Sunday morning the church bells going on one side and him just screaming on the other side. It was very strange. When I came here Harry Truman was running for president and I saw him on television and in the movies and I couldn't believe that here was a man running for a political office and talking calmly. He didn't pound on the table, didn't pound on the chairs, and he behaved himself like a human being. I had thought the only way you could conduct a political anything was to scream and shout and pound tables and all that.

Also what I saw a lot were these posters that were advertising the BDM [League of German Girls] and the Hitler Youth. They had these cute little girls with these blond pigtails and a couple of freckles on their noses and that was the ideal German girl. And they had these cute boys for the Hitler Youth. They were plastered all over.

My parents told me not to play with non-Jewish children because kids will fight over a toy, or whatever, and the parents will get involved and a Jewish parent could not win out against a non-Jewish parent. For example, I was sitting one Sunday morning on the stoop in front of our house and a little girl walked up. This had to be in 1934 or the beginning of 1935. I was five years old and she was maybe older. The little girl walked up to me and said that she wanted to play with me and I said, "No, I can't play with you because you're not Jewish." I do, though, remember playing with one Jewish girl, and we stayed friends. In 1942, she lived diagonally across the street from us. She was always hanging out at my house and I was always at her house and there were other friends there at times. In the summer of 1942, early summer, she was taken away. I saw her from our apartment window in a group of Jews that was being marched to one of the railroad stations. There were about maybe fifty people. They were able to take with them two weeks' supply of clothing and some food. I saw her walking through the street, a forlorn little girl, and that was the last I saw of her.

We did not associate with Germans. We really didn't. But my father had a friend and it's a very strange story. He was a very strict Catholic, as far as we knew. His daughters walked around with big crosses and he was a builder of churches. He was not a poor man. He had a dark red Mercedes and he lived in a mansion, a very large house with orchards around it, and they had apples and peaches. Well this man always told my father whenever he saw him, "Oh, don't pay attention to the Nazis. You see how crazy Hitler is. This is going to be over very soon. Look at how he carries on; he's such a maniac. Do you think the other countries in the world are going to pay attention to such a maniac? It's going to be over before you know it." This went on and on and on, and then he used to come and trade a pound of cheese for a pocketbook, which you couldn't buy anymore. His daughters got pocketbooks and things.

When we packed up and had to leave our house, my parents packed a big steamer trunk with paintings and my mother's silver and a couple of other things. They put them into the steamer trunk and he said he would put it in his garage and then we were taken away. When we came back to Frankfurt after the war, we met him in the street one day and he was crying. He said the American authorities needed his big house for army quarters and that they were living there, and that he was thrown out of his house, and his wife was sick, and one of his daughters had been killed in an air raid. We really felt sorry for this poor man; he was always so nice to us. He then asked if we would be able to intercede with the American authorities and help him get his house back. We didn't know anything better, so we went from one authority to another until we were finally at the right place where we could speak about getting him his house back. And the American officer said, "What's his name? Oh sure, that's fine." Then he came back with a folder about two inches thick. The man had been a member of the Nazi Party since 1931 before Hitler came to power and that was how he was able to buy up houses and make a fortune. He had never told my father anything like that. He had kept on talking as though he was our best friend and had our best interests at heart.

He must have known that we would never come back because he had started using our things. He had emptied out our trunk and two paintings of ours were hanging in the hallway. When my mother went in with all these American soldiers, she was taking them off the wall and the soldiers said to her, "What are you doing?" She said, "They're mine," and she walked out with them and with the trunk. My mother also mentioned that he was with his other daughter when she had met him and that she was wearing a little black onyx ring that my mother had packed away. So he knew what was going on, but he didn't tell us. He knew, so he took all the things that were important to him.

So they were friendly to us, but I think only in the sense where they could find a profit or something. When my parents had to leave the apartment, when we had to go to the orphanage, different Nazis came up to buy my parents' furniture for three marks or whatever, a sensible bargain. It was really disgusting. They fingered everything and they were so anxious and so eager to get anything. Their eyes would open up. They wanted this and they wanted that and they were grabbing everything.

What do you remember about being deported to Auschwitz?

One morning we were marched to the train station. It was for Hitler's birthday on April 20, but we were leaving on April 19, 1943. He had already suffered a defeat in Stalingrad and also in El Alamein, and I think he was in a bad mood. To make him feel better for his birthday—that's what we were probably told later on—they tried to give him a birthday present and make Germany *juden-*

rein [Jew free]. I don't remember if we left Frankfurt on the nineteenth or if we arrived in Auschwitz on the nineteenth, but it took about six days to get us there. We were the thirty-seven people from the orphanage in Frankfurt. On the way we picked up a lot of Polish women who had been brought to Germany as slave laborers and had probably complained that maybe the food wasn't good or that the fourteen hours or whatever they had to work wasn't good. As we went from station to station, they picked up more people who ended up in Auschwitz with us.

When we left the orphanage, we had to walk through the streets to the train station, one of the commercial stations. It was early in the morning. If people were watching, I didn't notice. When we got to the station, it was a beautiful, bright day and my father was separated from us—from my mother and me and my brother who was four years younger than me—and we were put on the train. There were only thirty-seven of us. These were people who had been married to non-Jewish partners; two people who were from Romania were going also who had been protected for a while. We were put on one third-class car with windows and all. I don't remember if they had them closed or open, but I didn't see anything particular, except that there had been a lot of air raids on the night before.

At any rate, when we were on the train, we were taken off every night and brought to a jail or some kind of collection place. This went on for seven or so days because they didn't want the train to move at night. This was probably because the air forces of the allies would have been able to bomb a moving train. They would have recognized the light and the smoke and they would have been able to bomb this train. So they took us off of the train and put us into all these different places at night, and, in the morning, they put us on the train again. It took about six days until we got to Auschwitz.

The whole trip I was trying desperately to get just one sight of my father. I never saw him again. When we got on and off the train, he was in a different car. Men were separated but my brother stayed with us. Women and children stayed in one car. I would have thought, "Oh, look how nice they are." As it turned out, women and children arriving in Auschwitz were gassed. But we were not. We were taken into Auschwitz and the other prisoners that had been there already knew their way around and said to us that the reason we weren't gassed was that they thought, "Well they'll die soon anyway, so it doesn't pay to run gas into the trains for just a few people."

When we arrived, the SS was there with the dogs and the white gloves and the whips in their hands and beautifully pressed uniforms. At the time there were no selections. We were taken to the women's camps. My brother was also taken into the camp with us, into the women's camp, he and his pal from Frankfurt. A few weeks after that time, they said that it wasn't moral that my brother should be with all these women who would obviously be in the nude changing and everything. It wasn't moral, so they took him and the other boy into the men's camp, which was separated from the women's camp by a wide road with electric wires on both sides. We couldn't go over there. Once in a while, if he happened to be outside and we were looking, we could see him. At least his mother knew that he was alive.

The first thing they did was shave our hair, take our clothes off, and put the tattoo on with the number. One of the women on our transport was a nurse and we saw someone being carried on a very primitive sort of litter and her hands were dangling. She obviously was dead. I had never seen this before, and I turned to this nurse and she said, "Oh, she's probably just sick." They still wanted to protect us as children. But, of course, once we got into the camp, we saw this every morning—ten people, at least ten, dead, being dragged out and dying and all this.

Did you have to work when you were there?

Yes, in a day or two. One of the first things we did was dig ditches. They were little moats outside the barracks, about three feet deep where the wastewater ran. Next to it there were roads and we were digging ditches and they told us to smoothen the road. And there was this humongous road grader, but it wasn't motorized. They filled that with water, and they had hundreds of prisoners pushing it so that the roads would get smooth. That, together with the two hundred or so calories that they gave us in Auschwitz, was designed to break our spirit and to break us right away down into a state of malnutrition.

That whole summer the crematorium was going day and night. During the day it was all smoke and at night you could see flames coming up. You could really see it. You could see it from miles away. In Birkenau I stayed with my mother the whole time in a big barracks, sleeping on boards with three pieces of straw or whatever that were infested with lice and fleas. I wouldn't be alive if not for my mother. The crematorium was going and the flames were coming out. At night you would see it red. During the day it was black because of the smoke. There were little pieces, chips of bone, flying all over the place.

Did you expect to survive?

Yes and no. Strange answer. I had typhus. My mother dressed me in the morning. I was out of it. I really am not aware of many things that happened to me. She dragged me to the work that we had to go to. She put me back into bed at night. She had nothing to give me, except holding my hand. And in the morning the same thing routinely happened again. What just recently came back into my memory was that while I was sort of semiconscious and having this typhus and being dehydrated and running with diarrhea and all these things, I was sitting there and I was looking at my mother and she was holding my hand—the only medication—and I was thinking I cannot die because I cannot do this to my mother. She lost her husband, she lost her home, she lost her business, she had lost everything, and even my brother wasn't with us. The situation was not good and I could not let myself die because that would be one more thing that would add to her grief. I think that was one of the things that got me through.

My mother, when she went to Auschwitz, was forty-two. She was a tremendous source of strength to the other young women who were there. They had lost their families. They had lost their mothers—their mothers were probably a little bit older because I was the youngest one in the group—and she would talk to them. She knew that their families were destroyed, but she would tell them that the war would be over soon and that they should keep courageous. One of the chief occupations at the time was talking about the food you would make when you would get out: about the chicken soup they were going to cook, the fish they were going to cook, and the meats, and how they would keep the holidays again.

Everybody called my mother Mutti. It was like she was a friend to everyone and she was that way through the whole war, through the whole time in the concentration camps. Everybody liked her. Everybody came for advice and anything. And when she came out and we came back to Frankfurt, it was as if someone had placed a large hand over her throat, enough air could go through for her to exist, but she could not live. She was really a victim of the Nazis, as if she had been killed in 1944 or 1945 or whatever, because her life was just nothing after the war. She didn't want to enjoy herself; she didn't want to do anything for herself. And yet she had a tremendous desire to live. In the last few years, she was totally paralyzed.

When did you get out of Auschwitz?

They put us on a train on November 1, 1944. We had no idea how we were picked to go on this train. Someone told us it was not to go anywhere—at the end of the tracks was the crematorium, a few yards or so away. But someone else told us, "No, you are supposed to go to Germany as laborers." Of course you couldn't trust this, but it turned out to be true. We stayed at the railroad station a whole day and then they finally moved us. We traveled for a few days and we arrived in Ravensbrück. There they opened up a big tent for us to go in. There were no beds or anything. There were a couple of barrels on the side for toilet use. They didn't give us any food. They didn't give us any drink. What I remember about Ravensbrück mostly was that it was raining and we were so parched that we stuck out our spoons—we had these ugly little rusty spoons— under the tent and we were waiting for the drops of rainwater to accumulate so that we would have something to drink. The problem was that we were so parched that we didn't have the patience for the spoons to fill up. So, every time we had a few drops in our spoon, we sucked it up. We were there for several days, I don't remember how long. Finally they distributed us into the barracks where the other women were. There were mostly German prisoners: prostitutes, "asocials" of all kinds, and maybe prisoners who had complained about the German system or something like that. We stayed in the barracks. I only remember the rainwater thing and that it seemed a little cleaner and the food seemed a little bit better than what was in Auschwitz.

I don't remember how long we stayed there, just a few days, and we were then taken by train to what was known as a slave labor camp. They had Polish women in this camp working as slave laborers. It was a camp for a thousand women. When we got there, there was no one there and it even had signs of civilization. In the middle of the barracks there was a fountain with maybe twenty-four water spigots like they have in dormitories or something like that. The water wasn't working, but it was a sign of civilization. When they put us into the bunks, next to the beds there was a makeshift closet for clothes. We didn't have any clothes to put in it, but the closet was there. It was amazing that we were away from civilization like three years or so and here we saw signs of civilization. We were like, "Oh my gosh, there's a whole other world out there that we had forgot had existed." I mean these were very primitive things that you wouldn't even keep by today's standard. But that's what we had.

In the morning we had to get up, say our prayers, eat breakfast. There were actual seats, long seats, and long benches and tables where we were given whatever breakfast there was. It was slightly better than Auschwitz. We were walked out of the camp with SS men all over the place along the road. When we got to the woods, there weren't many trees; there were camouflaged nets and branches of trees and things on top. And then we would walk up to a little mound, and the mound was overgrown with moss, or grass and weeds and whatever and in that mound was a door and they opened that door.

It was actually a factory. Our section manufactured bullets and another section was working on hand grenades. We sat at a long table and they gave us something like a hinged instrument that was similar to a hamburger press that you have now. There were 144 little holes in it and there were half capsules that you had to fill with gray powder, I suppose it was gunpowder. Then we had to fill up the other half also with 144 of these little things and pull it over. Now, the reason the SS women were sitting on both sides was so that we would not maybe miss putting the powder in or miss-set these little halves so that these bullets wouldn't work. They were very carefully watching us so that we were calibrating it properly. Sometimes I was able to scooch it over a little bit, thinking that maybe if I moved it over a couple of millimeters it might not work right. I considered that my effort in helping the war.

Do you think the Germans were mostly indifferent to the fate of the Jews or were they more hostile to the Jews than that?

My brother said that a few days after *Kristallnacht*, my father and he went downtown to see the different stores that had been destroyed and there were Germans standing around and they looked glum and they were shaking their heads as if they couldn't believe that such a thing was possible. People tell me that some Germans hid Jews. I didn't know of anyone of course. During the war it seemed that, yes, they were indifferent. But, if given a chance, they would be against us. As I said, my brother saw this, but I didn't see it. He told me about it, but I never perceived them as friends. I considered them all as enemies. Some would beat up on Jews and were worse than others.

How do you feel about Germany and Germans today?

At one time I said that there were two Germanys and too bad there weren't a hundred of them, broken up into little pieces. That's how I felt. I have been back in Frankfurt, I think three times, since we left in 1947. When I went to Frankfurt, I went back because I wanted to look at the cemeteries, at my grandparents' graves. I had my grandfather's stone restored, because in 1936, when he died, my father wasn't able to get him a granite stone and it was pressed sand and it washed away. I also went to my grandmother's grave a few times. I stood in front of my best friend's house. I stand there and I'm looking for her with her grandmother coming out with her apron and a tray of cookies and begging me to come into the house and have a cup of coffee with her. So when I go to Germany I'm looking at the people walking by and I'm saying, "Oh, these are all the people that turned from these beautiful posters, these blond, blue-eyed posters. They're turning into these old decrepit people. They're nothing. They're not superpeople like they wanted us to believe. They're really just humans like anybody else."

When I came back to Frankfurt in 1945, it was toward the winter and the houses were all ruined. There were just houses standing there with the gates as sort of an abstract thing sitting on top of the rubble, and I was thinking to myself, "I'm sure there must be dead people under there from when they were bombed." I have not forgiven myself for this feeling because I said to myself, "Oh my gosh. These poor people buried under there—burned by the bombs and killed by the bombs." Why should I feel sorry for the Germans when I had all these friends that they killed? They brought this all on themselves. My friends never did anything to provoke this.

HELMUT GRUNEWALD

I know that I'll be sent to Auschwitz and be gassed anyway.

Born in 1918 to a Jewish father and a Catholic mother and raised in Cologne, Helmut discusses in his interview how he and others knew about Jews being gassed in Auschwitz before he was sent there in March 1943. A trained architect, he returned to Cologne after the war and oversaw the rebuilding of many of Germany's synagogues.

In the Third Reich, my father was denounced by his best friend, who wasn't a Jew. I don't know anymore exactly why this guy denounced him. That was already in 1933. What made it particularly dangerous, though, was that the SA then came to search our home and found a revolver that they had planted somewhere and then took my father under arrest. But, since he was physically disabled from what they thought was a war wound, and because he was, of course, a great talker, they finally let the matter go.

Even after the war, when someone was needed to give a talk or the speaker wasn't able to show up, they would always call upon my father. "You have to speak like Goebbels," he would say. "You have to speak for an hour about whatever stupid stuff, it doesn't matter what. But the last five minutes have to stick because that is what the people remember. Everything else is forgotten. The last five minutes are important, and they have to stick."

That was certainly not stupid, and that's what happened. He was a great speaker. It didn't matter if it was about the dedication of a monument, a political issue, or what. He could speak about anything. It was unbelievable.

How was it with your mother? Did she convert to Judaism?

No, she didn't convert. My grandparents came from the Eifel [region]. And, since we had very strict Catholic relatives, there were even some difficulties with the wedding. Her father was a police officer in Cologne, right up until his death in 1949. Even the apartment that we had on the Siebengebirgsalle, as Jews were not allowed to have apartments, was listed under my grandfather's name.

As a policeman, was he able to help you during the Third Reich?

No, no. He couldn't at all. The only thing he could do was help my father rent the apartment. It was kept in his name, and we lived in my grandfather's apartment. That way, the apartment was safe after the death of my grandmother. Otherwise, he couldn't help me, although he certainly did know people who had left the police and gone to the Gestapo and so on. There were many who left the normal police for the Gestapo.

When and why were you arrested?

[I was arrested on] December 1, 1942, as a *Mischling* [half Jew]. We had a Jewish friend by the name of Helmut Berg and he was living here illegally. His parents and all of his relatives had been taken away and he was still living in Cologne illegally, and, of course, they were always searching for him. So then they went after his entire circle—who were mostly *Mischlinge*—and, in one stroke, they were all arrested. I was one of them.

When they came to our house, it was on a Friday evening. My grandfather was at home, but my parents and I were out. We were in town and weren't there when they had come to get us, so they then said that we had to report to the Gestapo on Saturday morning.

My father went there first to hear what these people wanted, and, of course, they arrested him immediately. Then they sent my mother back home, where I still was, and the Gestapo called up and said, "You have to come here immediately; otherwise we'll come and get you." So I then went to the Gestapo as well to hear what it was all about. In any event, I then got arrested along with my father.

Were you working before you were arrested?

I was working. I mean, working is an exaggeration. I played music for a while in a bar, and, parenthetically, this Helmut Berg was also there playing music with us. The other two who played with us in the bar were regular musicians. I [almost] only played American pieces, of course; I couldn't do otherwise. I played the piano. That was sensational back then to have a bar where such music was played. Today, it's called Chez Nous. It's on the Grosse Budengasse, which is a side street running from the high street to the hay market. And then, if some higher-up in uniform would drop by—they also frequented this bar— we'd get a signal, and I would immediately start playing a German hit.

Did you wear the Jewish star when you were playing?

No, I didn't. I never wore the "Jewish star," never. As a *Geltungsjude* [a person of mixed parentage whom the Nazis literally "considered to be a Jew"], I was supposed to do this. But I never wore one. I simply had no desire to do that. I had almost only Christian friends at the time, mostly university students and so on. One of my best friends was the son of a Gestapo officer named Trierweiler. He worked in the market hall for an Italian company, and every day, he would bring fruits and vegetables and I don't know what all to our house. He didn't even know that I was a Jew. No, he didn't even know it.

I was always being asked, "Why haven't you been drafted yet?" [And I would answer], "I'm employed in a factory as an architect. They get Wehrmacht contracts, and I'm indispensable." So that's how it went for a long time.

But your father, as a Jew, had to wear the Jewish star, right?

Also not. Never. He simply didn't wear it.

Wasn't that dangerous?

Yes of course it was dangerous. But nobody noticed, never. And then came the interrogation by the Gestapo. They kept asking what I knew about Helmut Berg and what was going on and so on.

Were the Gestapo officers mean or friendly? Did they call you "Du" or "Sie?"

They called us "Du" [which is an insult], and they also spoke in Cologne dialect a bit. They certainly weren't friendly, but I was neither beaten nor tortured or anything like that. I was just interrogated, and I was only at the Gestapo for three weeks.

How many people were in your cell?

Ten to twelve people certainly. One could hardly lie down there. I sat on the floor and also slept sitting up. There wasn't any more space. I was the only German. The others were Russians and Poles and so on.

You said that you knew the son of a Gestapo officer named Trierweiler. Couldn't he or his father be of help to you in some way?

No, they didn't bother themselves with that. For example, I'll tell you a story. While I was playing in this bar, they would never control us, even though they had those military and Gestapo controls every evening. Because we were musicians, they thought that we had to have been registered and had to have been under contract and were okay. But they controlled everyone else. I did that for a month. That was in June to July 1942.

Wasn't that just the time when all the Jews were being deported?

Yes indeed. They were already gone. Berg was already living here illegally. But because we were playing music there, they assumed that everything was okay.

Around this time there were also some people from Mönchengladbach who were opening a huge bar and were hot to hire us. I couldn't say that I wasn't able to do that, so I went there and played at the opening in Mönchengladbach with four people and a female singer. Since all kinds of bigwigs from the Nazi Party were there, we had to play things like "Im Leben geht alles vorüber" and "Lili Marlene" and other nonsense like that. But, when they left, the real music started. I only did this for one evening, though, and then I went back to Cologne.

Trierweiler's son liked to play jazz as much as I did. So, when I told him that he should go there if he wanted to but that I couldn't go with him, he went there to play again on another evening. That same night at twelve o'clock, Trierweiler's father called us at home—since I was already in bed, my mother went to the phone—and said, "Is your son at home?" "Yes," my mother answered, "but he's already asleep." "Well, then ask him where my son is," [he replied,] because he knew that his son and I were nearly always together. But, when my mother told him that she couldn't confirm that, he said, "Then I'll have to have all of those youngsters taken to a concentration camp, including my son. That is just no way to behave."

This had all happened half a year before my arrest. But [when I was finally arrested,] my father was already there. While he was being interrogated [at Gestapo headquarters] by Büttner and two other officers, he said to them, "I don't know why you want to interrogate me? I know that I'll be sent to Auschwitz and be gassed anyway."

He knew that?

Yes. He said that, "I'm going to be killed there."

Thus one already knew in December 1942 that they were killing the Jews?

Oh, yes. One knew that. But then they said to him, "What kind of atrocity story is this that you are telling us? What makes you think that they are killing people there? How do you get that idea?" "Ah, you don't have to tell me that," my father said. "I know that. I know exactly what's going on there."

That is a very important point. How did he know that?

My father was extremely well connected, also in non-Jewish circles. That people were being murdered in Auschwitz and in Poland in general was evident anyway. And it was also already known that Auschwitz was very clearly an extermination camp.

That was already known?

That was already known. Yes.

And had you also heard that?

Yes, I also knew it. [Proof of this can be found] in the postcard [I wrote], which is in the exhibition at the National Socialist Documentation Center [in Cologne]. On it is written, "I'm now being sent to Auschwitz. I don't believe that we will ever see each other again." I had placed this into the hands of someone I didn't know and he actually dropped it in the mailbox.

How did the people know about Auschwitz?

One already knew about that. Something like that gets around quickly. It gets around very quickly.

Even about Auschwitz?

Yes.

Did you listen to the BBC at home at that time?

Yes. Everyone did that—the men who were at home, the younger men who had not yet been drafted, or the older men who were not going to be drafted or were on leave or even on the front.

Aryans and Jews as well? Both?

Yes, of course. When the Gestapo came for us, my grandfather was at home and they were listening to the news on the English station in our apartment. As I said earlier, we were in town, and he was at home listening to the news from the BBC at 7:00 P.M. And then the Gestapo came by looking for us. When they entered the room, he had forgotten to turn off the radio—he was, of course, over seventy already. Nevertheless, even though the news program from the BBC was on, this didn't interest the Gestapo at all. They merely looked around to see whether we were there or not, and then they left again. Later on, my grandfather told us that the radio had been on when they came.

Why did so many people listen to the BBC even though it was extremely illegal? Could you receive the BBC with a normal radio?

Yes, we only had a *Volksempfänger* [people's radio set] at home. People wanted to know what the other side was saying. Everyone knew anyway that they were telling lies to us here.

But was that a daily occurrence, like the way people watch the evening news today?

Yes. We listened to it every day. The news came on at noon, in the afternoon, and in the evening. It always lasted for six or seven minutes, with military reports and so on.

But how did one know about the mass murder operations?

One knew that already. In Jewish circles, one already knew that about the Polish Jews. One knew that already.

But didn't you consider that to be a rumor?

We believed it. We knew that it was true. It was just as my father had said to them when they had asked him, "What makes you say that? What's with this nonsense?" He replied to them, "You don't have to tell me anything. I know that. So why do you want to interrogate me for so long?" After this, they sent him back home to demonstrate that all of that was not true, and then my father went immediately into hiding. He went to the Eifel, to my grandfather's birthplace, and was hidden there.

You spent some time in the Klingelpütz [prison in Cologne]. Was it worse in Klingelpütz or in the cells at the Gestapo headquarters?

I was there from the end of December 1942 until the end of March 1943. That was certainly better. One knew that people weren't tortured there or things like that. That wasn't done there.

We were held in so-called investigative detention. The food was awful, but one could still get some things from home. I even had visits from my mother, once a week, I believe. Once she tried to bring me some cake but it was confiscated. So one didn't starve. It wasn't like in Auschwitz, but it was bad enough.

At first, there were five of us [in my cell]. Of the five, only one was a political prisoner, and the other three were criminals. Then there was me. After a while, I somehow managed to get put alone into a single cell, and that was better. Otherwise, however, it was certainly awful. I was in that single cell for over two months until I was deported.

When you were in Klingelpütz, did they continue to interrogate you now and then?

Yes, every now and then. There were always two or three officers. I was never interrogated alone. It was like this: I was not an interesting prisoner. I was neither a political prisoner nor anything of the sort. Political prisoners were something else altogether. They were interrogated in a totally different way. But I actually had done nothing except that I was not an Aryan. Nevertheless, you were a second- or third-class human being. We weren't at all interesting for them. We had simply been arrested and were to be sent away.

Before you were arrested, did you experience a lot of anti-Semitism from your non-Jewish friends and acquaintances?

None of my friends knew that I was a Jew. As a result, the topic never came up. I don't know what would have happened if I had said, "I'm a Jew." It never came up as a topic. Our topic was music or sports, completely nonpolitical [things].

But you certainly had a good antenna. Did you really experience very little anti-Semitism?

Not from my friends. Otherwise, yes. Otherwise, anti-Semitism was everywhere. Yes, it was. Even in my own family, from my grandfather's brothers, for example. One of them was a civil servant in the city, and the other was a school principal. They were anti-Semitic. They were my mother's uncles, and they were really anti-Semitic—ever since Hitler [had come to power], but not previously. But, after Hitler, yes.

You were deported from Klingelpütz to Auschwitz in March 1943. Is that correct?

Yes, to Auschwitz, in a prison car. The transport took about ten days. We made stops all over the place. There was always something being added on to the train. Then I was placed in quarantine when I got to Auschwitz. I was in the main [camp at] Auschwitz, not in Birkenau. Birkenau was the extermination camp. Auschwitz was the labor camp.

What were you thinking when you were on the way there? Did you think this is the end?

Yes, of course. Everybody thought that.

Did you think about escape?

No. That was impossible. That was impossible from such a camp. That was impossible.

How long were you in Auschwitz?

Three months. After that I was transferred to Buchenwald. I have to say honestly that although I was in Auschwitz for only three months, I weighed only thirty-six kilograms. I couldn't have lasted much longer.

The difference between Auschwitz and Buchenwald was incredible. When I arrived, I had to go to the Gestapo again, where they said, "Ah! That's Grunewald. He's an architect and we have to put him in the construction office." First, however, I was put in quarantine again. So I was in such a block again and I remained there for fourteen days. Then I went directly to the construction office, and that actually saved me. I mean, people died there just like in Auschwitz, whether they worked in a stone quarry or were shot for some reason or other. But one could not compare that with Auschwitz, because it was not an extermination camp in that sense. There was clearly a bit of a difference.

In Buchenwald, a Czech man founded a jazz orchestra. I played piano in it, and, because there weren't any notes, wrote all the arrangements for the ten or twelve musicians that we had there—all American pieces, only American pieces. I wrote 138 arrangements in those two years. Every month we gave a concert, or every six weeks a jazz concert. So it went . . .

We were liberated in April 1945. The war wasn't over yet, but the Americans were already on the Elbe. Then my father came out of hiding and came and got me and we went to the Eifel where my father had been previously.

When did you come back to Cologne?

I first went back to Cologne in 1949, or nearly 1950, when I was commissioned to build a hospital, which was a huge project for me. Since then, I have remained in Cologne.

What was it like after the war to be a Jew or a half Jew in Germany?

Since I was a Cologner, or am one, I could get used to living here more quickly, but you were cautious in choosing your friends of course. But, the eastern Jews, for example, who came here had it really bad. They didn't know whether they should remain here or emigrate or what. Then came the founding of Israel, and many of them decided to go to Israel.

Yes, I was alone back then. I built the synagogues in Cologne, Bonn, Dortmund, Münster, Mönchengladbach, Koblenz, and Wuppertal. I also built all kinds of other things, of course. I built over two thousand apartments. I had plenty to do, so much that I wasn't able to think about Auschwitz or Buchenwald anymore. I had no time for it. That first started to come back to me recently after I stopped working. Fifty years had passed and then the television and the press and all these people started coming to me. Only then did it get stirred up in me again. Before that, I didn't have time to think about it.

There is one thing I would like to say to you. The Nazi period and especially the school as well gave one a complex, an inferiority complex, as a young person. I haven't ever really lost it. After the war, I have dreamed again and again about the concentration camps. No doubt, I have dreamed about the concentration camps every other night, right up until today. But I have never dreamed that anyone was doing something to me. Rather, only that I was confined, that I wasn't free. That's what I have always dreamed about. "Why in fact aren't you free? The war has been over for a long time. Why are you still here?"

HERBERT KLEIN

We were the last ones deported in 1943.

Born in 1922, Herbert Klein was the son of the head of Nuremberg's Jewish community and was deported to Theresienstadt in June 1943.

My father was the secretary or what you would call the general director of the Jewish community in Nuremberg. For that reason he had almost daily contact with the Gestapo, because the Gestapo kept on telling him what had to be done, what the Jews had to do, and what the Jews could not do. During the later part of the Nazi time, the Jewish community was affiliated with the Reich Association of German Jews, so all the local Jewish communities were actually part of this bigger organization. My father obviously had no say in the religious part of the community; because that was the rabbi's job. He also had nothing to do with the schools, the Hebrew schools, except maybe by being involved with hiring the teachers. Officials of the community were all paid by the government.

My father was first hired in 1923 to organize the taxation of the Jewish people for the religious taxes. He remained working for the Jewish community in Nuremberg until 1943, when we were deported, and he worked for it again after the war from 1945 to August 1946 when we went to Munich before we emigrated.

Altogether six of us were deported: me, my parents, my sister, my brother-in-law, and my brother-in-law's mother.

There were almost no survivors from Nuremberg after the war. As far as I know, from Theresienstadt, where I was liberated, there were only thirty-five people [from Nuremberg]. A few more people who were deported in the earliest transport to Izbica also came back and the rest of the Jewish community were some Jews from mixed marriages who had stayed in Nuremberg and not been deported.

The Nazi Party in Nuremberg was almost the strongest in all of Germany. The anti-Semitism and so on was so especially strong because of Streicher. After the *Kristallnacht* pogrom, however, the party did not have the power that they had before that time because Streicher had taken some of the money from the Jews without the party being involved. On the ninth of November, in almost all the cities in Germany, the demonstrators, or the pogromists, were in civilian clothes. But in Nuremberg they were all in uniform, and, for that reason, they embarrassed even the propaganda ministry in that they wanted it to be seen as a spontaneous uprising.

What was the Gestapo like in Nuremberg?

The Gestapo in Nuremberg after the 1938 pogrom were actually more liberal than in most places in Germany. In Berlin, for instance, they just grabbed people on the street, put them into trucks, and deported them indiscriminately. In Nuremberg no families were separated; the families were deported together. Whether this was good or bad, I don't want to say, because entire families were destroyed. There were no survivors of very many families. My relatives, for instance, were all deported together, but there were no survivors.

My father, like I said, had almost daily contact with the Gestapo and he would be called in to Gestapo headquarters for certain things. The Gestapo, for example, would tell him, "We know that this Jew doesn't wear his star or doesn't work," or something like that. But they were not going to do anything about it until one of the Germans denounced them. Before someone was denounced, they did not have to react officially.

When I say Gestapo, I mean the organization. I don't mean that each particular Gestapo agent had any kind of liberal type of feeling. There was one there, in particular, named Worth who was very good, but the rest of them were Nazis through and through. He was a higher official who you could say saved a lot of the people because of his not reacting. He was an older man, about the age of my father, born around 1882.

I'll tell you about one or two particular cases. You know about the blackout law. My sister's mother-in-law, who was an older lady, went into a room one night and not realizing that the shades weren't down switched on the light. But even though she immediately shut the light off as soon as she noticed that the shades weren't down, somebody immediately denounced her. It was always like that. These Germans could not wait to get a feather in their cap. Anyway the case came to the Gestapo and it came in front of this particular man. In most cases, when it would have gone any farther, it would have been concentration camp immediately for her. But he made the case into a fine. It was, you know, deadened.

In another case where we actually were involved, it might have been in 1940 or 1941, my father and I and a couple of younger cousins went bicycling out in the countryside to see if we could find some eggs or something. I was seventeen or eighteen at the time. We got some eggs and some butter and on the way back for some reason or another my father, who was out ahead of us quite a bit, suddenly came back to us and said, "Keep on going." So we went on riding to the control station and said we didn't know anything about it all, but immediately the eggs and the butter were confiscated. The Gestapo officer in this case also saved the neck of my father as well as ours in that it didn't go any farther, even though it was completely forbidden to get any kind of food outside the ration. But he [Worth] kept it from becoming a big issue.

Your father must have had an enormously difficult job. Did he have to prepare the lists of people to be deported?

No. As far as I know, the Gestapo had told him that this or that section of the city had to be cleared of Jews and these kinds of things, and my father knew the names before they became public. But it was the Gestapo who actually wrote these lists. My father's brother was deported as well as other members of the family on March 25, 1942, and they died, everybody. Where they died is something that I would really like to know. I know they were all deported to Izbica, but I'm not sure where they died. I've been trying to find it out for the past fifty years.

The crazy part of the whole system is that you can't figure it out by any kind of norm.

For instance, I worked from 1941 on as a labor slave in Germany and the foreman saved my life, even though he was a Nazi with a gold medal. At this time during the war, you could only work in a place where the Jews were separated from the Germans. But I was lucky in that I was hired in a bookbindery where Jewish men and women were binding books in a separate room, and not in an ammunition factory or on the railroad track, where most of the Jewish people were working. After all the Jews working at this company had been deported, except for myself and another older man who lived in a mixed marriage, it didn't pay for this company to have a Jewish department anymore, and for one reason or another I had to carry some of the big linen rolls used in bookbinding linen to the elevator and there were women sitting nearby on a machine stapling a magazine together. One of them, who by no means had been unfriendly to me, asked me as I walked by, "What are you going to do with this linen?" I then made a kind of joke and said to her, "I plan to have a suit made out of it so that my yellow star will shine up better." She then immediately reported me to the master, who was an *alte Kämpfer* [longtime Nazi]. It could have cost me my life as he normally would have had to report me to the Nazi labor organization. But that evening he called me and said, "What kind of a stupid remark did you make? Do you know what could happen to you?" Luckily for me, it didn't go any farther than to him.

Where did you live in Nuremberg before you were deported?

I lived in a small apartment on the southwest side of the city from 1941 to 1943. This was not a Jewish area.

What happened to your apartment when you were deported?

When you were deported, and this happened with every apartment in Nuremberg, the Gestapo would seal outside the door and after that they would open it only when they would auction the stuff off. Or they would steal it themselves; that happened all the time. Before the deportation, when people were still living there in my apartment building, one of the Gestapo officers came into one of the apartments and told the Jewish man who lived there, "This carpet is to be brought tomorrow morning at eight o'clock to my office. The chairs too." This was not an unusual case.

When I returned to Nuremberg after I got out of concentration camp in 1945, all the Jewish apartments that I saw were utterly destroyed. That means you did not have a chair to sit on, a table to eat on, or a bed to sleep on, and you had no cup to drink out of and so on. What happened is that they came into the apartment and more or less ruined everything they could see. It didn't matter if it was an original Rembrandt: They went at it with knives; they took hammers and hit it against the wall. Everything was destroyed. I saw the apartments of at least three of my aunts which looked like that.

Did the same kind of things happen to your apartment during *Kristallnacht?*

Before 1938 my parents had lived in a different place. One of the SA officers had wanted to get this apartment of my parents, but there was still at that time a certain amount of legality and they couldn't throw you out; it was like tenant protection. But, on the ninth of November, my father had a very hard day having to be at Gestapo headquarters and having to bring back orders for the Jews and so on. He had a lot of mental anguish because of what happened at the Gestapo and he couldn't sleep. He usually never took sleeping pills, but on this particular night he took a sleeping pill, and then, at four o'clock in the morning, the bells rang to our apartment building. My mother didn't want to wake him up, but they kept on ringing and ringing until she did wake him. In the meantime, a woman in the house woke up too. She was a non-Jewish woman who had not been unfriendly to us even though we knew she was a Nazi. She then went downstairs and opened the door for these guys. They then came up to our apartment, rang the bell, and kicked and screamed, "Open the door, Jew!" My father then said that he would only open the door to the police, and they then said, "It's the SA and we're as good as police." My father then went to the telephone and dialed the police department and said to them that there was a break-in going on at our apartment. Meanwhile, my father tried to fight back against the SA men, but it was not much of a challenge for them to beat him down and they went around and smashed everything, breaking the glass and so on. When the police finally came, they took my father into what was called protective custody. At police headquarters he met a lot of other Jews who had been arrested and were going to Dachau, but, because the police had come to our apartment, the SA didn't take anything.

What do you remember about your deportation?

Around June 13 or 14, 1943, we had the Jewish holiday celebrating the giving of the Ten Commandments. Synagogues were then forbidden in Germany, but in Nuremberg we were allowed to use one room of the synagogue for Jewish services, which used to be the schoolroom. Anyway, we had almost no Jews left at the time; the only remaining Jews from Nuremberg were in mixed marriage besides our family. The Jews from Nuremberg who had still not been deported all had to move to Fürth, the next city closest to us. So there was just one room there and my brother-in-law, who used to be a teacher, was doing the job of the rabbi.

At this time I'm telling you about, two Gestapo men then came to the office and told my father that the Reich Association of German Jews had just been dissolved, that all Jewish activities were now forbidden, and that they were really supposed to arrest him. But, since they had known him for so many years, they said that they would allow him to remain only on house arrest. After that we went home.

Sometime that afternoon, however, the two Gestapo agents then came back and said that it was denied that he be on house arrest and that they had to arrest him. My father must have had extremely good nerves and self-control because two non-Jewish women were in the apartment with us at the time and this would not have been too good because non-Jewish people were not supposed to be around Jews. But, when the Gestapo came to the door, these two women went into my parents' bedroom and my father went to the bedroom door and closed it. These two women were in there and the Gestapo were in the living room and never noticed them.

When the Gestapo officers arrested him, my father asked whether it was permissible to have his own food brought to him and whether he could take along his little briefcase because he didn't know how long he'd be there. Around noon the next day, I was allowed to bring food to him that my mother had prepared. When I was there, they brought me his briefcase to bring home with me and I noticed that my father had written something on the back of the tag on the briefcase. While he was in jail, he wrote that he had learned that we were to be deported in three days and that we should get ready. In jail he had met the business executive from the Jewish community in Fürth, and all over Germany these Jewish community leaders were being arrested at this particular time. Before the Reich Association of German Jews was dissolved, the Gestapo needed these men to work [for them] and these men had not been deported.

By the seventeenth of June we were deported. After being taken to the assembly center in Fürth on a furniture truck, we were deported. Two trainloads of people were made up. One of them went to Theresienstadt [which we were on], and the other went to Auschwitz on the same day. We knew that we were going to a different place than them and we were in a different train car.

How did you feel toward Germany and the Germans after the war?

How did I feel about the Germans? Not in a particularly pleasing way. It is very difficult for me to have actual contact with Germans. With younger Germans it is possible. With older Germans it is hard.

My father grew up in a different Germany than I did and for that reason I think he had a certain kind of a German feeling that I never had. I mean, I never was accepted as German and so I have absolutely no German feeling. Nuremberg was supposed to be a very beautiful city but it never did anything for me. When I came back to Nuremberg after the war, the whole city was on the street you could say. I was happy it was bombed. To trust the older Germans, you would have to really know them, know how they were before. Now with a younger one, it's very similar. I think the poison is still in a lot of them, replicated. So I don't trust them. A liberal view would be that 90 percent of the Germans were for the Nazis. I would say the percentage is even higher.

Germans tell you lies like, "Oh! We never knew anything about it. We were no Nazis." After the war I had to go to the office of *Der Stürmer* to pick up the books of the Jewish community. There were lots of papers and letters left all over the floor there and these were very incriminating types of letters, like about people who had shot Jews, or from people who had said, "Kill them all." For example, one of these letters was from a woman who had written to Streicher: "Why don't you put all the Jews in one room? I myself would kill them." She was sixty-nine years old!

In the beginning, I was the only younger survivor in Nuremberg, as the other people were [mostly older Jews] from Theresienstadt. Afterward some of the people returned who had been deported to Riga in 1941. One of them was a young fellow who was about eighteen or nineteen. He had been very involved in the Jewish sports club and he still had some of the little emblems plus a tiny white little button with a blue Star of David on it. So we put these stars on and went to the address of this woman. It was not far away from where we lived in Nuremberg. We went there and rang the bell and an old woman opened the door and said, "Ah, two young gentlemen from the Social Democratic Party. What can I do for you?" And I said, "We are two Jews and we want to be liquidated." Now, you can imagine that this woman got a little bit of a shock. "I don't understand," she said. So I said to her, "I have a letter from you here that you wrote to a good friend of yours and said that if the Jews were brought into a room, you yourself would liquidate them." "Oh, I never did that, I never did that," [she insisted]. "But," I replied to her, "who else would write this with your signature?"

Do you think the Germans knew the Jews were being killed?

A lot of them did. A lot of them didn't. Look, how many people do you think were involved with the killing? It wasn't just Hitler who killed them. Don't you think that some of them must have talked about it and so on?

What did the Jewish community know?

Actually we did not know. We knew that in concentration camps like Dachau people got killed. My father sometimes had to open caskets and identify people with wounds [that indicated] they had been shot from close distance. I mean, one knew that. And one knew about all kinds of accusations and things like that. But nobody knew that [the Jews were being systematically murdered]. Nobody knew that because when my sister was deported from Theresienstadt to Auschwitz, first of all, we didn't know it was Auschwitz.

Still I'm sure certain things must have been known. When the Germans say they never heard anything, that's a lie. One knew Dachau was a concentration camp. One knew they killed people. One knew that Sachsenhausen was a concentration camp. One knew about Buchenwald and about quite a lot of them. So, if someone said they didn't know anything about it, that's a lie. But if they say they did not particularly know that the Jews were murdered by the millions in Poland, that I accept. Even so, it is very difficult to accept. After all, we were the last ones deported in 1943. There were another two years of war. And how many of these concentration camps existed? Now, in each one of them were guards. With six hundred concentration camps, how many guards were in each one of them—ten, fifty, one hundred? So multiply it. I know it's a lot more than that.

When I was deported, I was in a train in one of the Czech stations someplace and a woman reached into the car and gave us some bread. How did she know about us? I have no idea. She didn't say a word; she just reached in and disappeared.

There was also a man, a Quaker. I met him before friends of mine at their house were deported, and he came to us after they were deported. This was a man of my father's generation; he was very religious and absolutely fearless. I have told you already that we still had Jewish services in that one room. He came to my father and said, "I want a yellow star from you." My father replied, "For what?" And he said, "I want to come to the services." My father said, "Are you out of your mind?" He said, "Don't worry about me. Just give me one." My father said, "I won't give you a yellow star. I won't." So what did the man do? He went to Woolworth's or somewhere and bought himself a yellow handkerchief, stuck it into his pocket, and then came to the Jewish services every Friday night. Nothing ever happened to him. Like I said, this was somebody who helped. He didn't help you by trying to hide you or something like that. He just wanted to show his cooperation, or his sympathy.

WERNER HOLZ

I was blond, blond.

Born in 1924 and raised in Krefeld as the son of a Jewish butcher and a partly Jewish mother, Werner Holz was arrested in April 1943 while illegally riding on a train. After spending several months in local jails, he was deported to Theresienstadt and later to Auschwitz. After surviving a death march in which only eighteen out of nearly four thousand prisoners survived, he returned to Krefeld after the war. In 1947, he emigrated to Chile.

My parents were artisans. My father was a butcher, a sausage maker. My family had been in the same business for generations. My father spoke French and of course German. He was born to a Jewish family that had lived for several generations in the same city [Krefeld].

My father had a brother, Federico (Fritz in German), three years younger. He lived in Belgium and was able to leave (Europe). In 1940 he came to Chile on a ship called the *Simón Bolívar*. The boat hit a mine in the canal de la Mancha and it sunk. But my uncle was saved and went to England and then they set off again. My uncle came to live in Chile and bought a small parcel of land in San Bernardo. He brought me to live with him in 1947.

My father died very young in 1937. I lived with my Catholic grandmother, my sister from my mother's first marriage (also Catholic), my mother, an aunt, and my brother Kurt. In 1938, he went to China because he was very violent. He didn't know how to handle the Nazi oppression and hit anyone who insulted him. He wouldn't allow them to treat him like that for being half Jewish, but they ended up treating him like a Jew. Before he left, he told me never to let anyone insult me. "The second they start to insult you, hit them in the mouth," he said. Anyway, he left when I was only fourteen.

I continued on in Germany, studying a bit. Afterward I went to Cologne, sixty kilometers from where we lived. I studied precision mechanics and then stayed in Krefeld working in a machinery firm. They treated me very well and the boss was a good person. My coworkers also considered me a good kid.

And one day [in April 1943], as fate would have it, I was arrested while taking the train. I was traveling in the direction of the Dutch border to meet a classmate when the border police entered. I thought that the Gestapo had arrived to inspect the passports, ID cards. I was taken prisoner. They took me to a city on the border called Kleve. I was there for two months in a very inhumane jail; a cell of pure cement. There was nothing, nowhere to sit, no bed. I suffered a great deal because there was nowhere to sleep. I had to sleep on the cement in the cold weather. Spring had just begun, but it's very cold in Germany at that time of year. I was nineteen years old. I suffered a lot during those months. I lost the concept of time. The food was scarce and horrible.

Later they sent me to another jail in Krefeld for fifteen days. There I had a blanket and a wooden slat to sleep on, but no mattress. While I was there, my relatives found out I was being held prisoner. My sister came to visit me, but they wouldn't let her see me. They brought clothes so I could change. The clothes I had were so full of blood from the beatings I received, my mother fainted when she saw them.

From there they sent me to a third cell. [This was better.] There was a cot with a straw mattress to sleep on. It was clean and I was able to bathe. They gave me envelopes to write letters. I was extremely thin; I had lost at least twenty kilograms. My sister was able to visit me, giving me courage and helping to revive me, because really one loses all sense of reality.

From there they sent me to Czechoslovakia, to Theresienstadt. I was there for about a year and a half. I was able to recuperate quite a bit because my family could send me half-kilogram packages, twice a week. Even if it was just two potatoes and an onion, I was able to recuperate.

And from there they sent me to Auschwitz with a group of about four thousand prisoners in cargo trains, directly without any food. I arrived at Auschwitz, and all that one knows and all that has been written [about it], I experienced— the crematoriums, the red skies, the ash that fell as if it were snow.

I was lucky because I had joined up with four other guys. And all of a sudden they sent us to work in a railroad cafeteria in a concentration camp. They sent us to a camp in a German city on the frontier with Poland. Since I played the piano and the accordion, I formed part of the camp's band. In the morning we played marches as the prisoners marched off to work and at night we played for the [camp personnel] in their cafeterias and lounges. I played the accordion with other prisoners and played jazz. And during the day they had us working in the kitchen, which made things a lot better in terms of food, because, more than anything, people died of starvation.

Then on January 18, 1945, they took us on a death march. We were 3,800 prisoners. We walked three days and three nights. There was snow and it was very cold. It is very cold in that part of Poland. The majority of the prisoners were left behind. Those who couldn't go on were machine-gunned. All five of us friends ended up being wounded. I wasn't wounded badly, but some of my friends were—one got a bullet in the lung, another in his neck, but I had better luck.

We ended up surviving. Out of thirty-eight hundred prisoners, eighteen of us survived. We were lost for about a month in the forest, with the Germans on one side and the Russians on the other. We were between two fronts until, final-ly, we decided to march in the direction in which we thought were the Russians. We turned ourselves in to them. Being Germans ourselves, we didn't want to say that we were persecuted by the Germans. So we told them we were Czechoslovakians. I had learned a bit of the language in Theresienstadt, which helped. In total we were five Germans who, according to them, had been per-secuted for racial issues. But I can't see what difference in race you could find between me and any other German, because I have never felt myself to be any different in terms of my physical condition, my education, and things like that. Finally, the Russians believed us and we arrived at the border with Russia.

[After the war ended,] I returned to Germany. In the beginning of June 1945, I arrived in the city where I was born. It had been completely destroyed by the bombings. My sister was there with her eighteen-month-old child and other relatives, but, unfortunately, my mother had passed away. They had killed her also. About a year and a half later, I was able to obtain passage to Chile, where my uncle Federico (Fritz) lived. He welcomed me and we worked together.

So, I began my life again here. I have very good friends, and I feel loved and welcomed, and even sometimes admired, because with the force of my hands—that are now all crooked—I was able to make a clean, healthy life for myself. But I have never been able to forget the terrible past that has marked my life.

How much time did you spend in jails and prisons and camps?

Two and a half years. I didn't have permission to leave the radius of the city and I left [to visit my friend near the Dutch border]. I wasn't allowed to leave, but it wasn't a crime that would warrant the kind of punishment I received.

The Nazis pretended to be a superior race. This is an absurdity because as you can see in the photographs of those who made the laws—beginning with the great murderer Hitler and all of those who surrounded him like Goering and Goebbels—they had figures, were ugly. They didn't have any of this mus-cular stature, blond hair, blue eyes, and so on. Absolutely nothing. The absurd thing is that they pretended to form a pure race from the old Nordic races when they themselves didn't have any of these aspects.

With me being part Jewish, I had more of a German face than they did. I was blond, blond. This seems stupid to me—the ridiculousness of their pretensions to be superior when they themselves actually didn't have anything of this phys-ically. You enter the world with what your parents, your family, the world gives you. If you disapprove of certain people who are different from what you like, you can't go against them.

I don't want to forget the past. I am not going to forget the horrors that I have lived that truly have no comparison with anything. Perhaps in another world there are things just as horrible. I recently read a book about the Russian advance into Germany. Many Germans died, Germans who were victims of the same Nazi system. But the difference was that a big part of them looked for it. They voted for what was then their government. I am not going to say that I would not have also voted for them if I had been given the chance. Perhaps I too would have had my swastika.

What can you remember about the first years of Hitler's rule?

I was nine years old when Hitler came to power. In our case, we were a mixed family, and we had, of course, friends and family who were not Jewish and supported us a great deal. My parents were well liked, but they died young. My father died in 1937, when the government had been in power for four years, but they had not yet begun the most violent acts.

For me, as a child, it was like being expelled from the community. Playing with other children, all of a sudden I would be told, "Don't come to my house anymore. I don't want you to come play with my child anymore." So you start to be isolated. I think that blacks in the United States felt this same kind of great discrimination, with the difference that the Jews in Germany were Germans like all of the other Germans. They weren't part of another category, they were the same patriots and nationals. My father, who was Jewish, was a fanatical nationalist. He was always talking about the war, the patrols. So, it was absurd, all of this. It was a violent shock for a nine-year-old child to hear all of a sudden, "Don't come to my house anymore."

Would you say that there was much anti-Semitism before this time in Germany?

I could not say that I noted any anti-Semitism previously. Never. It was more of a religious thing. It was never about race, like they said. How could they speak of a race, when the people have moved from place to place and have intermixed? In my case, even more so, because I have relatives on both sides. It also supposedly had to do with the hate of Christianity toward Judaism. But that's also absurd; Jesus was also Jewish and started Christianity. The rules of Jesus were rules that he had learned while being a Jew. I have never practiced Judaism. I would much rather say that I belong to the entire Jewish community, where I am welcome and nothing else matters. But I can't really say the entire community, because I don't belong to even half of it. But I can say that I have very good Jewish friends. When I began working in this country, many of my clients were German Jewish immigrants. We made everything like what you could buy in Germany, and we sold to all of the Jewish immigrants.

Besides the change in the behavior of your friends and their parents, what other changes did you notice at the time?

Above all I noticed that my mother, my sister (who was from my mother's first marriage and wasn't persecuted), and my Catholic grandmother (my Jewish grandparents had died long before I could meet them) were preoccupied that something would happen to me, as you could imagine since I was the only one left after my brother had gone. So my family protected me. I had an advantage because I played an instrument. Because I played the piano and accordion well, the neighbors and other kids loved me. I played at the parties we had.

The city where we lived was maybe too small for there to be much of a [Nazi] movement in the beginning. The other cities like Munich, Berlin, Nuremberg, and Frankfurt were much more important in the Nazi movement. All of the terror, I really felt more secondhand and not from my own experience.

I was a child in the beginning, but I did know that there was the "Crystal Night" when they destroyed all of the houses. I lived through that. Friends called our house telling my mother, "Go out with the boy into the streets because they are going to the houses. No one knows what they are capable of doing. Perhaps in the streets they aren't going to do anything." My mother and I walked around in the city all night long. We saw many horrible things. We saw them burning the synagogue, destroying Jewish houses, breaking crystals and porcelain. They threw a piano through the window onto the street. They were all drunk. The windows in Jewish shops were all broken.

The following day, they found out that they had taken all of the Jewish men to concentration camps. But it wasn't so horrible yet because the women and the other relatives still had the option of showing that they were preparing to leave Germany for other countries. Once they had the immigration ready, they gave them permission to leave and they were saved. But they went with a miserable sum of money in their pockets; they couldn't take hardly anything. Beforehand, they had to get rid of anything of value like jewelry, fine porcelain [and so on].

What experiences did you have with the Gestapo?

They summoned me several times. The Gestapo I knew was that of Krefeld. And in Krefeld, there was a certain person in the Gestapo who had been my brother-in-law's classmate and he did something so that I would be sent to Czechoslovakia, rather than somewhere else. Perhaps because of that my life was saved. But I know that my mother followed me when I went to the Gestapo. The head of the Gestapo's [Jewish desk] was named Schulenburg. My mother begged him: "Please, dear Mr. Schulenburg, don't deport my son." And she took his arm. He didn't push her, but he shook her off and my mother fell to her knees. This left a very bad impression on me, this memory of Schulenburg.

I could never give a testimony to cleanse the terrible image of the Gestapo. I would have them strangled. Because if you have a mother and you love her, you know that they killed her and you have to think that it was thanks to a certain group of people that were in favor of this kind of thing. I don't believe that any-one in the Gestapo was forced to be in the Gestapo. They all knew what they were doing. I am not one to hate, but I can [hate] in this case. I have learned to forgive many human conditions—practically all of them. I can forgive robbery, maybe bad treatment, but murder cannot be forgiven. I cannot forgive a person who plans a murder.

When did you find out that there were concentration camps?

It was known. People talked about it secretly. A man who sold some forbidden things on the black market, because there wasn't much butter, sold a pound of butter for an exorbitant price and they sent him to a concentration camp. And they said that they had already sent the ashes to his wife. Everyone knew that they existed, they knew and they were afraid. But no one imagined that they were gas chambers or crematoriums. And I swear I saw them, I saw them.

Was there an atmosphere of fear in Germany?

Yes. There was, in reality, also a time of euphoria. When the first advances were made in the blitzkrieg, the German soldiers took things out of all of the coun-tries they occupied. Women of bad reputation, fine liquors came out of France, specialty chocolates. There was the appearance of a bonanza all of a sudden: "We are conquerors. The führer has made us rich. He is conquering every-thing." And they sang, "Today Germany is ours and tomorrow the world." And of course, all of this is contagious, above all with young people, to see them-selves so powerful. So, as I say, if they would have let us, we would have prob-ably participated because we were Germans like the rest. But because of the stupid laws, they didn't let us participate in these barbarous acts. So there was the euphoria but, at the same time, there was fear to say something, to listen to the radio in London, to do whatever thing went against the desire of the gov-ernment. This was dangerous to the point of risking one's life. You were afraid.

What do you think of Germany and Germans today?

What do I feel after being in Chile for fifty-five years? I still feel nostalgia for the memories of my childhood. The music makes me cry. Memorial poetry gives me goose bumps. I play the piano and I play melodies that are German romantic songs. They're in my memory. I never forget them, and I sing them from time to time while I work in the field, when I'm working on the tractor. I don't have a very good voice, but I find strength in the songs and they are all

German songs. So, the feelings are something that you can't change. The pain you can erase for a time, but finally something emerges that is inside of you and you can't change it. It's in the nostalgia. You feel something toward the United States, like you belong to that country. Do you sometimes feel sad to be far away? When I go to Germany, I have been there five times, not for very long, but after fifteen days, I am ready to come back to Chile. It's not that I get excited and would go back to live in Germany. I couldn't with the character of the Germans, not with my own sister whom I love very much. I could not live there. There have been Germans in my house whom I have to admire because they are 100 percent in my favor. They have supported me like everyone else. I don't know if it is that I have a pain that is special. . . .

I am very pleased with life, with the people with whom I have lived, with those who are still with me. The life here hasn't been very easy, milking cows at four in the morning. I didn't have much of a life of dances or entertainment during the first thirty or forty years. Animals are demanding. You always have to be giving them food to eat, water, milking them, cleaning everything. I was always fanatic about cleanliness. This was all a ruin when I bought this. It was a ruin. The roof was sunken, the house was full of mouse holes. I was lucky. My grandmother always told me, "Take care of your hands." I can't take much care of them now. Look, they're all crooked, and I play the piano really badly, but I am going to play you one of the German songs that I like.

HANNELORE MAHLER

We didn't want to believe it
because we could have been next.

Born in 1921 in Krefeld to a Catholic father and a Jewish mother, Hannelore Mahler was among the last Krefeld Jews to be deported in September 1944. After the war, she returned to Krefeld and raised a family.

Until I got married, I worked in the office of a tie factory that was under a military contract. Before that I had been on a farm doing forced labor. Of course, I had female colleagues there [at the tie factory] whose brothers were soldiers and so on, and [they would come on to me] and that was held against me. That is to say that I was then denounced [for race defilement] by one of the girls from my school in the class below me. I know very well where she worked, but I have never talked about it before. That took place in the winter of 1940.

[Actually] I had always held to the Nuremberg Laws [which outlawed sexual relations between Jews and non-Jews], and that turned out to be the reason why my husband and I got together. Both of us were [considered by the Nazis to be] first-degree *Mischlinge*—a horrible, horrible word.

When you were arrested, what was the Gestapo officer like who interrogated you?

Well, if he hadn't perchance been with the Gestapo, I would describe him as a jovial person. Had he not been with the Gestapo, I could have well imagined him at his table of regulars in a pub. On the other hand, how could such a person who made such an impression on me, for example, have performed such a job? That's also a question that I have.

Can you remember how he acted during your interrogation?

Like a government official. He was a civil servant. Those above him told him what to do and he did it. Think about it. I was still just a child. How old was I then in 1940? I was eighteen years old. So, by jovial, I don't want to say that he wouldn't hurt a flea, absolutely not. Because he did have a function, and I don't know whether he was forced to take this post, or whether it had been his choice to go to the Gestapo.

But what I'd like to tell you about is what bothers me terribly in the first place. After the war, they all said, "We didn't know anything about it." [But, in September 1944,] when we were arrested, we were marched past the main church [in Krefeld], the Dionysiuskirche, with our Jewish stars and backpacks, and I was pushing a baby carriage with my little son inside of it. And, exactly then, the mass let out, and, yes, they all saw [us]!

We had been assembled at the police station on the Hubertus Strasse in a former school. And then, on Sunday morning, the twenty to twenty-five of us were led on foot through the middle of the street to the courtyard of the Hansa-Haus, and there I met my mother. We had walked through the city along the Westwall [boulevard] and crossed the Dionysius-Strasse just as the people got out of mass and were leaving the church. Indeed, they had to have seen us.

Was it clear to them what was then going to happen?

Yes, but of course. They certainly didn't believe that we were going to a sana-torium. Their fellow classmates, their colleagues, the people they had done business with were all gone. Their fellow tenants, their neighbors, all of them. Certainly they must have thought, "Where have they gone?"

That had been on the same day that the paratroopers landed at Arnheim, and then we were put onto an open truck going to Düsseldorf, where there was a collecting point at a slaughterhouse. Before this we had been told that since we were going on a transport for workers, they would have no use for any children. I was pregnant at the time, but I had on a large coat, and you couldn't tell it. Anyway we ended up staying one night at the slaughterhouse.

Now comes something really strange. My husband and I were the only mar-ried couple, and the only *Mischlinge*, and I was the only woman on the trans-port. [The first] stop we made was at the train station of a place somewhere in the vicinity of Lippstadt and then we were taken to a farm, where we slept on the ground in a cow shed. Our baggage was put into the troughs. Every morn-ing we had roll call. There was no toilet or anything like that, so we had to slip off to relieve ourselves in a field somewhere. For cooking, there was a large container that the farmers used for boiling animal feed; previously it had been used for laundry.

We were there for perhaps ten days. Then we were sent on in stages to Berlin. We had to make some stops along the way to decouple the train cars and because of the constant air raids. We were in a passenger car, not in a closed cat-tle car, and then we [finally] reached Berlin.

[In Berlin we stayed at] a school on the grounds of the Jewish hospital that had been turned into a jail. But, at the very beginning, we were put up in the hospital, and my husband was some other place than I was where he was put to work shoveling coal or something. Then we were told to hand over everything we had, like our savings account books that we still had with us. While we were doing this, I found out that my mother-in-law was also there at the same place where I was, and I remember that before we parted I gave her my wedding ring and my watch. Then we were moved from the hospital to the school that had been transformed [into a jail], where I was put in a single room with a lot of other people. At any rate, that was a catastrophe. But, I have to say, those who were there with us in Berlin knew considerably more [than we did]. After they had taken all of our cash and everything from us, one guy then came to me and said, "Here's twenty marks. You'll be able to use this when you get to Theresienstadt."

How did the people in Berlin know considerably more?

I also don't know why this was exactly, but they knew. They said, "If you have money, you can buy something." Then somebody gave me the twenty marks.

At the station before we were put into the Theresienstadt concentration camp, there were SS standing there all over the place on the running boards of the train. Then we were told that we were not allowed to keep anything with us—no money, no jewelry, nothing at all. But I still had my twenty marks, and my husband still had his driver's license, which we had sewn into the lining of his jacket while we were still in Berlin. Then we were forced to undress and I stood there in front of a young SS man, perhaps eighteen years old, and what do you think I did? I held the twenty marks very finely in my hand and acted as if I had a cold. I now wonder why I had taken such a huge risk on account of only twenty marks, for which I was only able to get something like a piece of bread later on. Anyway, we spent the first night in Theresienstadt in the Dresden barracks, in the morgue on the stone floor. That was on the thirteenth of October.

So this was the time frame between my arrest and my arrival in Theresienstadt. At the time there were still transports heading to the east, and I then found out that my cousin and her eight-year-old son had been sent on to Auschwitz on the previous day, on the twelfth of October.

You also might want to know about my mother's tragedy. In February, my mother arrived in Theresienstadt with several other Krefelders. She was standing next to me when we were liberated. But just after this came the typhus epidemic and my mother told me that she had volunteered to help care for the ill. Even though the Russians had given immunization shots to her entire nursing staff, she still got infected [and died].

When did you first hear about the mass murder of the Jews?

That was actually more or less in the camp. In Berlin, one had whispered about it, and one was always questioning whether it was true or not. But nobody had dared to say anything openly about it, so it was still only a kind of assumption. That is the way that it is when you yourself are in a situation where you can be sent away on a transport at any time. You don't want to believe it.

How did you see yourself back then? Did you consider yourself to be Jewish?

Yes. I did not consider myself to be Christian. My parents also sensed that, and for that reason, in 1931, when I entered middle school, they said, "Without our going to court to change it, if they ask you, you are Mosaic," which is what they used to call it earlier. And, at the time, I also had taken lessons about Judaism and I had Jewish friends and everything. We knew who we were.

Look here. I am now, of course, also the only one who is still remaining here [in Krefeld], and I hold myself back somewhat, perhaps a bit too isolated. I am part of the Jewish community and have my plot in the Jewish cemetery here. I can't do anything different. Today, the situation is that there are only five or six members of the Jewish community in Krefeld, and they're all from Russia.

Okay, back in the Nazi period, what was the anti-Semitism in Krefeld like?

My parents took me out of school in 1935. I was so isolated. Nobody could come over to visit anymore. The parents of my classmates didn't want that. And in school, I had been put in the front row, and there were no classmates next to me or behind me. It was as if I had the plague.

Were you the only Jewish girl in the school?

In my class, yes. But in the other classes, there were some. That's the way it was in the last weeks of 1935 before I left. But I would like to say something more positive. When I went around in Krefeld with my star, say in 1942, I always tried to carry a bag in front of me [to conceal it]. But when one person knew you were wearing a star, most everyone knew. Still a [former] classmate of mine crossed the street in the center of the city and came over to me and gave me her hand and said, "You are and will always remain Lore for me, and for me nothing has changed." That is to say that things like that also happened.

But there was also the other side?

Yes. That was larger. We weren't allowed to ride on the trains. We weren't allowed to ride on the street cars.

Those were official things. What about the normal citizens?

They just looked the other away. They looked the other way.

I would like to ask once more whether you really hadn't known about the mass murder of the Jews back then.

In effect, we knew nothing. Sure, we said, "Where are they? What's happened to them? And so on." But this was among ourselves, and afterward there wasn't anybody left whom one could talk to.

Yes, we suspected that those who had been sent away had not been sent to a sanatorium. But, since we ourselves could have been the next ones, or were— we were practically on the list to be mowed down—we didn't want to believe it, because we could have been next. Do you understand what I am trying to say? We talked a lot about this afterward in retrospect. In retrospect, we said that we had suspected it and left it unspoken during the war. Everyone knew it. Everyone had thought that it was so. But we did not want to talk about it, because you could be there yourself.

When one suspects that those, who had been arrested and taken away and had never been heard from again, had not been sent to a sanatorium, you can almost compare that with someone who is about to be tested for cancer. One just doesn't talk about it, even though everyone knows that it is so. Do you understand? One just doesn't talk about it.

✦4✦

JEWS WHO WENT INTO HIDING

ILSE LANDAU

I had been caught and sent to Auschwitz
. . . I jumped out of the train!

Born in 1910 to a Jewish department store owner from Düren, a small city outside of Cologne, Ilse Landau moved to Berlin in the late 1930s and went into hiding in January 1943.

We were very much loved. We didn't have any enemies there in Düren at all, nobody. As a matter of fact, among my intimate friends were a family who had a *Gastwirtschaft* [restaurant]. When they had Easter or Communion or any religious things, we were invited and so on. And they would come to my parents' place too. The father of the family always used to say, "Ilse is my ninth daughter." Only when the Hitler time came did we notice that people began to change. The elderly people naturally didn't want to have anything to do with it because it was against their inner beliefs as they were either good Catholics or Protestants. In my father's *Kaufhaus* [department store] there were many

Catholics and Protestants who didn't change, for whom there was never a difference. You didn't notice that there was anything anti-Semitic.

Then, in 1938, the Nazis came to Düren and they were interested in buying the store. So my father and my uncle sold it. When they were talking about things at that time, an interested young man who was with his father-in-law said to my father, "If you don't give me the store the way I want, you are going to be shot." So he had no other choice but to give the store away. Then we moved to Berlin.

Where should we move to? There was no work. But in Berlin there was still opportunity and one could try. My father was so German; he served four years in World War I. His life was German. His great-great grandparents were all, since 1700, in Germany.

So we moved to Berlin, but I wanted to get out of Germany. I didn't want to stay there. I tried to go with my sister, but she didn't want to leave without my parents. We had no visa. My in-laws wanted me to come to Brazil. So I applied for Brazil. I had already packed to go, but then I was warned that two cousins of my father-in-law had been caught at the border of Switzerland and shot on the German side. So my father said, "No, you are not going." We then applied to come here [to the United States].

In the meantime, I did war work in Berlin. I had to work for Siemens. I was quite well liked because I did very good work, they always told me. That was in 1941. The people I worked with were all Jewish. Only the foremen and foreladies were German people. They were marvelous to me. As a matter of fact, I can honestly tell you that my forelady invited me to her house to give me some good food because we didn't have much to eat except potatoes and vegetables. She even wanted me to stay with them, but I didn't want to bring them in danger. They had a little girl, and I didn't want that.

I lived by myself in the Nymphenburger Strasse. My parents lived in the Innsbrucker Strasse. The foreman, who was in his fifties, liked me very much. He said that he had never seen anyone do such work as I did; I had to do welding for submarines.

I was so very much liked that one day the forelady even said to me, and I've never told this to anybody, "Ilse, I'm afraid that one day they'll take all the Jews away. When you go home this afternoon and I'm ahead of you, I will drop my passport, my work passport, and at least you will be able to live with it. Maybe it will help you in your illegal times." And she did it. She dropped her work passport with the picture in it and everything and she applied later for a new one. I never did use it, but I carried it with me because I had to go illegal. We looked a little bit alike. I had blond curly hair like she had. And she was not afraid. She said, "You always can say you found it."

What do you mean by saying that you had to go illegal?

With my late husband, who was shot in Oranienburg-Sachsenhausen [concentration camp] on March 16, 1945, I worked in the underground against Hitler. I helped distributing the fliers. I went underground in January 1943. I lived with the family Bn. until I was exposed by a Jewish girl. She had also been living underground but ran out of money and was caught by the Nazis stealing something from a department store. They promised her that they would let her live if she became a spy for them.

We went underground in January 1943, because we heard from the brother-in-law of my late husband that all the people living on the Bayrischer Platz would be picked up. He was working for the Jewish *Gemeinde* in the Oranienburger Strasse as an electrician and heard somebody mention this. The Oranienburger Strasse was the registration station for the Jews who were staying in Berlin. He had a friend working there for the Jewish *Gemeinde*. She had the *Kartothek* [registration catalog] and knew that everybody would be picked up. But the Gestapo also had their *Spitzel* [spies] there and they knew exactly where the [Jewish] people were living. They knew exactly that we were five different families living in five rooms—we had already been disqualified from living in our own apartment.

So I went to the family Bn. He had worked for my very best friends when they were still in Berlin and before they went to Brazil. They had a big outfit in Berlin making blouses and dresses for ladies.

Did you stay with this family or did you change the places where you were hiding?

Yes, I changed hiding places. I had friends. My late husband was a manufacturer of leather belts and buttons. He had people working for him and they offered that we could stay with them. A family named Schröder took us in. Also Elisabeth B. helped us. She worked as a salesgirl in the Nymphenburger Strasse in the same street where my parents lived and was married to a Jewish boy. Altogether—not at the same time, little by little, one recommended somebody else—we stayed in eleven different places.

Some thought that we were bombed out and that I was a Gentile and that my husband was too. First of all, my [husband's] name was very German and I had big long curls then. Elisabeth B. recommended us to her parents. They lived in Niederschönhausen. They had a little bit of land and were such poor people, very poor people. But they took us in for one or two nights and then when we found other places. My friends, the family Bn., recommended me to Mrs. S. Her husband was in a Russian prison camp. Then we went on our own to Fürstenwalde and tried to get a home there and told a lady who had her own house that we were bombed out and that we didn't want to go back and sleep in Berlin.

You also distributed leaflets. Did you do it for some political party? How dangerous was it?

For whom? Against Hitler. They were not at all communist. A *Justizinspektor* [justice official] and his friends produced the leaflets. I didn't know everything; they didn't tell me either. They were very discreet so nobody who would be caught should give away the name of the other. I distributed the leaflets in Berlin. The people didn't know I was a Jew. Sure it was dangerous. I went by train every night.

Actually I did not distribute them myself, my husband did. He placed them on the walls of buildings. I do remember [that they had phrases like] *Frieden für den Aufbau* [peace for (re)-construction]. They wanted *Aufbau*, rather than war like Hitler—very intelligently done.

I got caught because I had gone back to the Bornsteins and the superintendent [of their apartment building] had seen me there all by myself. He had been somewhere out in the street and had seen me dressed with a hat and sunglasses in the neighborhood of the Klosterstrasse, near the police presidium. He recognized me and gave that information to the police. But he also went to the Bornsteins and told them that I had been seen in the neighborhood and that I must be hidden somewhere. So, from then on, the police, the Gestapo, overheard all of our telephone calls—something we didn't expect. This was the end of our time, so to speak. It didn't take long before I had been caught and shipped to Auschwitz.

What happened after you were caught and sent to Auschwitz?

I jumped out of the train! Near Kattowitz they opened up the cattle train. When we had to make our business, we had to go into the corner where there was a pail and a bedcover on a line. They wanted to throw out the excrement, so they opened the door. The man with a bayonet and the other one with a gun were sitting next to the door and talking to the people. It was cold, high snow. So I left my handbag there on the straw and went after the pail, and, when they opened the door, I jumped. The train was going fifty miles an hour and I didn't know if I'd be alive or dead. I didn't care, I just wanted to escape. I wanted to get out. I didn't want to go to Auschwitz.

I then had to walk to the outhouse of the train station. When I got in there, I thought I was getting crazy. I started laughing, crying. I didn't know what I should do. I was all alone. I couldn't talk to anybody.

Didn't the men guarding the train notice that you had jumped off?

They didn't notice me. They noticed only when they were counting the people at the gate in Auschwitz. That I was told from a girl who survived. Because her mother was Swedish and father was German, they let her live but they didn't send her back before Auschwitz was closed. She told me that on her return. I don't know how she found my address; I think she called up the Jewish *Gemeinde* and found out that I was a survivor. She had given me some zwieback, a little packet, and I lived on these two or three cookies. On my way back I took the first train [that I could get].

I had money hidden in a button of my overcoat. I hid the money in the button, *ganz feingefaltet* [minutely folded up]. My husband had done this. It was a miracle. The twenty marks were not larger than what a dollar is here. When I got the next train that went in the other direction, the girl [conductor] asked me why I didn't take a ticket at the *Schalter*, at the ticket service. I said that I didn't have time and when I heard the train coming, I ran because I wanted to make the train. She said, "Okay, I will write you a ticket, but not as far as Fürstenwalde/Oder," and that's what she did. That was only the first ticket that I got. That was from there to Kattowitz. From Kattowitz I then got a ticket by local train to Fürstenwalde/Oder and from there I telephoned Mrs. Schalkschmidt, who then picked me up in the night at about twelve.

[After a few days] my husband joined me. Because of the way I looked, he passed out from horror. He thought that I was a ghost. He had not known that I was still alive. On the next morning we traveled back to Berlin. We stayed there overnight and I remained there, but my husband then went back to Fürstenwalde. After that, since we knew we could not stay in our old hiding place because the porter had seen me there, my husband called his cousin and asked if we could stay for a night with her until we could find another place to stay. That conversation was overheard.

When we came to the door of the house at nine o'clock and rang the bell like we had made out with them, the SS were already hiding in the bushes. While we were ringing the doorbell, the cousin of my husband asked her husband if we could stay overnight for one night. To this he said, "You would not leave your cousin standing in the street during a bombing attack, would you? Let him come in for one night." For saying that, he was shot in Plötzensee [prison]. But my husband's cousin was not shot. She, as a Jew, was allowed to live. He, although he was not Jewish, was a delightful man. I was so sad about him. I couldn't imagine that he would be shot in Plötzensee at just about the same time as my husband.

I and my husband were then arrested in late October 1944 and he and I were delivered to the Alexanderplatz *Polizeipräsidium*. He was interviewed separately. I only saw him once standing in line there. Then I saw my girlfriend, Mrs. Schalkschmidt. She was also there at the Alexanderplatz. On December 16, we were taken to Schulstrassee/Iranische Strasse. I wasn't transported again from there, but my husband was brought to Oranienburg. I stayed in Schulstrasse/Iranische Strasse and was hired so to speak as a dressmaker and had to make dresses from silk that the Nazis had stolen in Belgium and France; I had to make elegant dresses for them. I sometimes got one half of or an entire *Brötchen*, a little roll, with a little bit of margarine on it. But I didn't eat it. I took it into the room where the little girls were and distributed it to them. I said I'd rather die than eat in front of them. I never ate it. They kept me there until the Russians came.

When did you first hear about the mass murder of the Jews? Was it before you were put on the train to Auschwitz or after that?

We had heard already that the other people were murdered in those other, nearer by, concentration camps like Bergen-Belsen and Sachsenhausen. There was a lot we had heard about.

When you were on the train going to Auschwitz, did you know that you'd go to Auschwitz?

Yes.

What did you know about Auschwitz at that time?

That they all would be gassed. Only a few who could work [might survive]. They were to dig the graves, cook for them, clean the toilets, or whatever there was to be done as work. That was the same as in Theresienstadt. My father died in Theresienstadt, and my aunt saw it with her own eyes that they had nothing to eat.

When did you first hear about the gassing of Jews and from whom?

That I can't tell you.

Was it from other Jews, or from Gentiles, or from the radio?

From radio maybe. But I didn't listen to the radio, my husband did. I went to sleep. I had to sleep. I wasn't able to listen. A man is still stronger, you know.

Where did you get your food when you were in hiding?

We went to the vegetarian restaurant, but not each day. They gave us food and some food stamps. There were a few other people who knew that we were illegal. So, naturally, we went to restaurants where you could have dinner. It wasn't so hard if you didn't want to eat meat. We didn't eat *kulinarisch* [high cuisine]. We had potatoes with sauce and salad. We didn't eat meat because we naturally couldn't afford that. And, as I said, this friend Mrs. Bredig still gave us food stamps, carrots, potatoes, or sometimes a can of sardines.

How much did you live in fear of the Gestapo?

Always. Always. There was never a moment where we saw that we were secure, never.

You mentioned spies, even some Jewish people?

Yes, I even have a book here about [a Jewish spy named] Stella. Naturally, I know her. Her parents were killed in the concentration camp where my father was. And there was this girl who had given me away when they picked me up at the Bornsteins. One day I saw her going again on the *Jagd* [hunt], so to speak, to look for victims. Like always, she had an SS man on her right and on her left. I jumped up and gave her a slap while she was speaking to the two men. I don't know if I knocked her teeth out or whatever, but I came in solitary confinement because of it. I couldn't even go to the toilet alone anymore, but I had to do that. That was before I went on the transport to Auschwitz.

Finally, how did you get to the United States?

I just came on the Truman directive after the war. I didn't want to stay in Germany and then whom did I have there? Few friends survived with me. To whom could I turn? In Germany they didn't want any refugees, no foreigners. A lot of countries didn't want any because you take the work away, the food and the work.

I loved Germany, but I wouldn't be happy to live there anymore. They took my life away. They took everything away. There are some people who went back home because it is very hard here when you get older. But I don't see the point. I would rather die here than go there. There are only a few people left. Who do we have there? A few in the cemetery to visit, that's all.

LORE SCHWARTZ

In any case, I came out of the war a virgin.

Born to a shoe store owner in a small German town in East Germany in 1921, Lore Schwartz went into hiding during the war but was caught in June 1944.

My parents lived in a small town. We had a shoe store. In 1938 my father was arrested and carted off to Buchenwald. On the second of December he got out because he was an injured war veteran. On the seventh of December he died. In 1943 my mother was deported to Poland.

I was not a very good student and I had what you might say was a boyfriend. He was a Christian boy, as we had few Jews in our town, only a few families. And then he was told, of course, that he wasn't allowed to do that. I mean, we were only taking a walk together on the promenade. We were so very young.

I was not in school very long during the Hitler period. When I was fifteen years old, I went to a home economics school in Munich for one year where we learned to cook and wash. There were forty students, twenty children whose parents had already emigrated and had left their children there, and twenty teachers. There was no anti-Semitism.

After this I went back home in 1938 and went to Leipzig in order to learn dietary cooking in a Jewish hospital. Of course, that was a terrible year. That year my father died after the ninth of November. My brother was in school in Leipzig too, in a Jewish school. After the hospital closed, I went to Berlin. There, again, I was [working] in a Jewish hospital run by Jewish doctors. I was only allowed to take care of non-Aryan patients. After that, I was on the road.

[During the war] the Gestapo was in that hospital. In fact, Eichmann had us come down to the Jewish hospital. He wanted to select people. For everyone who escaped, ten people were shot. But I escaped from the hospital with an ambulance. They were putting the transports for the concentration camp together. Every time a doctor and a few nurses had to go to one of those centers *(Sammellager)* where they sent them away from. It was during what they called the *Fabrikaktion* [factory operation of February–March 1943], when people from the factories were immediately called and sent to the concentration camp. I was supposed to be in one of those transports.

They were looking for me at the hospital. The hospital in Berlin was concentrated with all the Jews who were left. The big shot in the hospital was Dr. Lustig. After the war the Russians caught him and got rid of him, because, even though he was Jewish, he was a terrible, terrible, terrible man. He worked with the Gestapo. He was looking for me, all right?

Did you know that he was working with the Gestapo at that time?

Sure. The Gestapo was right in the hospital, in the laboratories in the back. Dr. Lustig was looking for me because I didn't show up to go on the transport. I had left with the ambulance through the gates and I was gone. I went at first with my fiancé's sister to a farmhouse near Danzig. She had connections there. I didn't know where to go and I had nothing. It was a big farm and we stayed with the gardener from that farm.

Did they know that the Gestapo was looking for you?

Not at this point. They asked who we were, and friends of my fiancé's sister said that we were friends of theirs from Berlin who were bombed out. On Sunday mornings we went to the church there. One thing I could never do was to kneel down. I just could not. I just bent my head. I'm not a religious Jew, but I just could not kneel down. The farmer there wasn't very happy about that, so we left.

My fiancé's sister then went to a sister in Gleiwitz who was married to a non-Jew. Her brother, my fiancé, and her husband had been sent away and were in the concentration camp already. I [went back with her on the train as far as Berlin] and then I stayed in Berlin for a while, [while she went on to Gleiwitz where] she stayed throughout the war with her sister. Of course we were in touch, and I was there in Gleiwitz after that at one time or another. But I stayed mostly in Berlin. I stayed away from her most of the time. We never got on anyhow. Even at that time, we didn't get on.

Where did you hide in Berlin?

You wouldn't believe it. Above all, my friend in Troisdorf helped us with everything possible, with all kinds of food coupons and things. She was half Jewish. Her father was non-Jewish, her mother was a Russian Jew, and her sister was Aryan and was with me in Berlin at the hospital. But later she went home to Troisdorf.

When I came back to Berlin, I met somebody on the street who was apparently a communist and I went with him to his house and stayed with him for a while. But I had to work because I had no money. At one time I worked in a restaurant on the outskirts of Berlin cutting spinach. Sometimes I slept there too, but I couldn't remain there because people started asking questions. Others worked there as well, like a woman from Ukraine who was an *Ostarbeiter* [Eastern European forced laborer].

The boss was in love with the owner and she was pregnant from him. She thought that I was in love with him too. Even though he was the ugliest thing you could ever see, she was suspicious. This restaurant was in an apartment house and he was the *Luftschutzwart* [person in the building responsible for enforcing the blackout during bombing attacks]. He asked who I was, and I told him that I was just working there. He wanted to know where I lived. So I gave him the address of my fiancé who wasn't there anymore. He then [made inquiries to find out if in fact] I was registered there—in Germany you had to be registered with the police—and found out that I wasn't and he was suspicious. So I told the boss lady who was pregnant, very highly pregnant, that he had got me in trouble.

I then left and I went to Cologne, where I stood in front of the cathedral and called my friend in Troisdorf. After that I went there and she put me up in a hotel in Bonn and paid for it.

Didn't you have to register with the police?

No. For women, it wasn't that hard because you didn't have to go to the army. I said that I lived in Berlin and that I was bombed out—the more bombs that fell, the better I felt about it—and after that I was able to get ration coupons and money. I lived in the Sternstrasse in Bonn and I was registered there under the name of Hertha Berger. Whatever name I used always had the initials HB. [While I was in hiding,] they called me by four different names. I had to survive. That's the way it was.

After staying there for a while I couldn't overstay my welcome, so I went to Gleiwitz to visit the other side of the family, to the one who was hidden there and the one who was living there. I stayed in Gleiwitz in her apartment because she had to go to do forced labor. The sister who was hidden there was hiding behind the piano.

When I was in Gleiwitz, I knew that my fiancé was in Auschwitz-Birkenau. You will think I'm crazy, but I went by train to Birkenau, which is only a jump from Gleiwitz. I went into the concentration camp and said that I had promised a lady in Berlin to look for her son. I had noodle soup with the SS there, with the guards, and they said to me that they didn't think that he was there, but why don't I come back tomorrow. I gave the guards cigarettes and schnaps and then I left. But I went back again the next day—I could see women without hair carrying stones—and told them the same story again. The next day there were, of course, completely different men there.

Which year was that? I didn't know that it was possible to visit people in Auschwitz.

It was between 1943 and 1944. I just played dumb. If I tell the story to someone, they think I'm absolutely crazy. I was just in the guardhouse; I wasn't in contact with the prisoners at all. Then I went home to Gleiwitz and that was the end of the story.

After that I went back to Berlin and stayed with a woman whose husband was apparently an SS man and also a pimp in the Lothringer Strasse in Berlin—the worst. If you asked me today how I got to them, I don't know, but I stayed there. I had met this woman on the Kurfürstendamm who also was in hiding and she told me about a woman who had a massage parlor and she protected me. She had a little doggie and a massage parlor. The things I did there, I don't regret today because I had to live. In any case, I came out of the war a virgin. But it was terrible, absolutely terrible what was going on. She had a sign saying "massage, health massage." The men came there just to, very crassly stated, get a hand job. The real thing, I had no idea about whatsoever. Anyhow, I stayed with her for quite a while. She had a young housekeeper there, the other masseuse, who really was licensed, but she also did the same things.

Somebody then came from Gera "to satisfy a special patient," and she knew who I was. But nothing was ever said about it, never, never. In fact, we were going to the movies together to see Marika Rökk, but we never made it. It was the worst bombing attack there ever was. From there, I don't know how I got to the Lothringer Strasse to the pimp, a huge pig. He got me a job in a laundry with some very nice people, who also knew who I was. That was the way it always was, either they threw me out or they kept me. Anyway I slept there and I learned how to eat horse meat. The woman there was very good to me and that was in June 1944.

I just wonder how it was possible to find people who would hide you.

They were afraid, most of them. Thank God, except in that one case I mentioned, nobody checked up on me.

[Anyway, when the woman with whom I was staying went on vacation,] I met a friend at the beauty parlor on June 16. At that time, we were six people in constant contact. Five of the people were hidden not far from the beauty parlor near the Anhalterbahnhof. You had to make a certain *Klingelzeichen* [signal with the outside doorbell] in order to be let in. Somebody from upstairs then screamed out the window, "Didn't you know Frau Krause had Jews and they were nabbed yesterday?"

I then met a friend at a hotel not far from Anhalterbahnhof whom I had met in the massage parlor. I didn't do anything with him. He just gave me money and left. There was also another one like this who also gave me money and who also knew who I was. I said to him, "Look, the older people from Frau Krause got caught. I'm afraid it's now my turn, too, because I have a terrible feeling." My clothes were all in a locker in the Bahnhof Zoo. He said, "Look, the invasion has just started. Do you think that in all this commotion that they will take such big trouble to look for a little girl like you?"

[What had happened was that another Jewish man had been caught and he turned the five Jews in to the Gestapo.] He was caught and then he mentioned the five people—two dentists, an old lady, a young lady, and a child. He got caught and he was told [by the Gestapo], "If you tell us about more Jewish people who are hidden, you'll go to Theresienstadt. Otherwise, we'll send you to Auschwitz."

Was it known at that time what Theresienstadt and Auschwitz meant?

We did know, because we had worked before in those transport camps. The old people and the war wounded and the Jewish community employees went to Theresienstadt, so you knew that there was a preference, that there must have been something special about it. Auschwitz, I was there, so I knew. I was there as a visitor. I also knew that my father was in Buchenwald and that he died a few days after he was released. We knew that it was no picnic whatever was there. How much the Germans knew, I don't know. But I can tell you that later on when I was in a work camp that you marched there in the wintertime without hair and without clothes. So they must have known, too. Definitely! If anybody tells me they didn't, they did.

How was it that you had to go to the work camp?

I went to the Ku'damm and I met a neighbor of my aunt who had already lost an arm in the war. Too bad he didn't lose the other one. We went out for dinner to Café Kranzler and then I went to the Bahnhof Zoo to call Troisdorf. When I came out, he had called the Gestapo. That was it—I was caught. I never found him again after the war. Maybe he was killed in the bombing—I hope so. I was caught and I was put into Oranienburger Strasse where all the *Ostarbeiter* were. They had got caught because they didn't want to work.

I was picked up by an SS *Scharführer* who was working in the *Sammellager* for the Gestapo. His name was Gustav. He knew me from there. So I was where I started off from. They then sent me to Theresienstadt. I was in Theresienstadt until October. Then I was sent to Auschwitz like everybody else. But I was only three days in Auschwitz because the Russians were already not far from there. And so I was sent to an *Arbeitslager* [work camp] in Kurzbach near Breslau. We had to carry trees. It was winter, bitter cold.

The commandant was very reasonable. He got us some warm clothes. From there we were marched toward the middle of Germany. First, we stopped in Gross-Rosen, in one of those other camps, and stayed there for I don't remember how long. We marched and marched. Finally we ended up in Bergen-Belsen, where I was liberated on April 15, 1945. That's it.

Apparently there were a lot of people hiding in Berlin. Had you known a lot of other Jews who were in hiding?

Quite a few. I don't know where they were hiding, except for one or two. One was named Gabriele. I don't even know if she survived. There was an apartment in Charlottenburg in the middle of the city. I never could make head nor toe out of what happened there, but I know that there were Jews hidden there.

You must have lived in fear all the time.

No, not at all. Nothing would have happened really, except that they sent you away. I knew that I couldn't live through the war through what I did. I had the feeling—I don't know how to tell you this—that I had nothing to lose but myself. I was all alone. My mother was away, my father was dead, my brother was in England, what else could have happened?

What did you know about Gestapo spies while you were in hiding?

There was a whole group in Berlin. You had to watch out. I don't know if you've read the books about them, [like about] Stella; she was in Berlin. Yes, we knew about them, about Stella and her friend Jakobson, something like this. And there were some in the Jewish hospital. I mean, they weren't giving out their names in the hospital, but you had to be careful. Lustig was married but he had two nurses who were his girlfriends and they were spies. They also collaborated with the Gestapo.

It's amazing that you had lived in hiding, but you still were walking around and going out to cafés.

Too many times actually, because I got caught at Kranzler's. Otherwise, I really lived a free life. I was bombed out several times, but I had money at all times, and food ration coupons, and I was called by four different names.

ROSA HIRSCH

There were some people who tried to help.
But they were such a minority.

Born to a tobacco store owner in Magdeburg in 1924, Rosa Hirsch sur-
vived the Holocaust in hiding with her parents.

In 1933 my parents had a wholesale tobacco store in Magdeburg. The SA
brown shirts were standing in front of it and said, "Don't go in. Don't buy from
Jews." So my father decided that this was not a life to live here, and, in early
1934, we emigrated to Paris. Unfortunately he lost most of his money there and
his two sisters from Berlin wrote to us: "This man [Hitler] cannot last. This
man cannot last. It's not so bad. Why don't you come back?" Even though he
originally wanted to go to America, they persuaded him to return to Germany.
Also my grandfather was still alive. So we went back, unfortunately, in 1935,
and we were never able to get out again.

When we came back in 1935, we went to Berlin, not to Magdeburg, and I
had to go to a Jewish elementary school. It had already started: You could not
sit on benches; you could not go into these stores anymore; there were these
signs. And then, of course, we had the *Kristallnacht*. That was the beginning of
the end.

Shortly thereafter they closed all the Jewish schools and I went to work for a
dressmaker. Quietly, so that nobody should know, she showed me how to cut
dresses and how to sew. At least in this way I was occupied during the day. She
certainly was not a Nazi, and neither were the other people that were working
there. But then it started. It would have been 1938 when men were deported to
the concentration camps, right? Luckily my father was never picked up, but my
uncle was. Since he lived in a small town in southern Germany, he went to
Dachau along with the rabbi of the town. The rabbi died in the concentration
camp, therefore you knew already then what was happening. My uncle, however, was able to get to America in 1939. But we got stuck in Berlin.

Then the war broke out in 1939. Before that already I had some girlfriends
whose fathers were from Poland and they were sent back to Poland—first the
men and then the families followed—and I never heard from them again. Even
after the war, I tried to find them. But I couldn't. They probably perished somewhere. Then, little by little, we knew that people had got picked up—in 1941,
if I remember correctly. We knew somehow through word of mouth who was
going to be picked up. Somehow things leaked out and all of a sudden we found

out. My father worked at an ammunition factory and I did some slave labor. My mother didn't work, she was ill. And then we found out that we were on the list, that we would be picked up. I honestly don't remember how, but somehow we found out.

We lived at that time together with some other people, including a cousin of ours who was already in hiding. One day the doorbell rang and we didn't open the door. They kept knocking, and, all of a sudden, we saw them go back to the super and then come back with a key. So my mother had no choice. My cousin and I went to the back of the apartment and my mother must have looked like this wall. Luckily, however, they had only come for the furniture of the owner of the apartment who was also a Jew. But he wasn't there. I think he had died earlier or something. Anyway, I had met actually a Nazi who wanted to help me and I told him that if he wanted to help me, he had to help the whole family. It was either all or none. So we went into hiding, at first in the basement of our own building. The super, who certainly was not a Nazi, provided us with the cellar actually.

One day at six o'clock in the morning or earlier, even before we had gone into hiding (you know, you had to wear the yellow star), I was at the subway and we were not allowed to sit down. But there was a sort of fire extinguisher there and I was sort of leaning on it. All of a sudden—I must have fallen asleep—someone yelled, "Get up, you Jew." Nobody said anything. They could have defended me in that I wasn't really sitting down or anything. But people really didn't come to your defense. Naturally, there are always some people that try to help and be nice and kind, but, as a whole, they believed Hitler when he said, "Listen, if this Jew doctor doesn't have a practice, you will get it." So it was to their advantage.

There was a musical here in America many years ago called *South Pacific*. In it there is a song that says you have to be taught to hate. And that's what he did. He really taught people to hate and to be nasty. Because, by and large I think, before Hitler there were not that many anti-Jewish feelings. People lived very happily together. I was a small child, but I had non-Jewish friends. My parent had non-Jewish friends. But then, all of a sudden, they disappeared. They were gone.

But we were very fortunate, my parents and I. In Berlin, through the help of one man, we met the manager of a shoe outlet, who was a White Russian. He had grown up as an anti-Semite. You know, his parents had told him never to sit by a Jewish child, that they smell differently and so on. But then he found out that they were not any different from other people and most of the friends in his life ended up being Jewish people, because he really appreciated them. So he made up his mind to try to help as many people as he could and he helped my parents and myself and hid us in his house. Unfortunately, while we lived in his house during the war, he died at the age of fifty from a heart attack. But his wife continued [to hide us]. They were definitely communists and they definitely helped and supported us, so we ended up being saved by the Russians. And, even before we got to their house, we had stayed with a poor woman who was a communist and she fed us and so on.

Since you had blond hair, could you have not worn the yellow star when you went out?

Well, you could and you couldn't. You were afraid. Because once they catch you, they shoot you right away. As a matter of fact, it had to be sewn on. The stitches had to be so close that you couldn't put a pencil between them. They checked that you could not put a pencil between the stitches, because some people tried to sew them on very loosely and then at one point pull out the thread. You sort of tried, but somehow you were afraid. The consequences of being caught were too great. If they asked for identification, you were then caught.

The indignities that we had to live through. You were not allowed to own any jewelry, except the wedding bands of wives and husbands. You were not allowed to have any pets: no birds, no fish, no cats, no dogs. You were not allowed to have a phonograph or to play records. I think, also, no radio. But some people, you know, kept the radio. All these little things, little by little, lowered your self-esteem, like you were not a human being anymore.

Do you feel a sense of hatred toward the Germans?

Let me put it this way. When we came to the U.S., even though my parents never spoke English too well, we certainly didn't speak German at home. I mean, certain phrases you can't help. Even today, you use certain phrases, certain expressions. But the thing is, you really made an effort not to; you didn't want to have any connection. Even today, to be very truthful, I am not a lover of Germans or Germany. I do not trust them. I always feel there are anti-Semites everywhere in this world. People have prejudice everywhere. But nowhere in the world were 6 million people killed systematically just because they have a different religion. And nobody did anything about it. So they all accepted it, silently. Maybe they made a fist in their pocket, and so I wish, but nobody really did anything. There are a few exceptions. Quite a few people were hidden. Maybe a thousand. What is a thousand? It's nothing, right? So there were some people that tried to help. But they were such a minority. But I really don't trust them and I really have to say today that every child is a product of their parents. There are very few exceptions where children think differently than the way their parents are. So it's inherent.

I once went back to Germany myself when my son was thirteen years old. We took a trip instead of making a big celebration here for his bar mitzvah. My husband was from Mannheim and he wanted to go back, but I didn't. For two days we stayed in Mannheim and we met some old school friends. One of them had become a banker. In the course of the conversation, he said that he had been several times to America already. And this was our first trip overseas. Here I am struggling, scratching money together to make this trip with my family, and here's this guy who became a banker, who has been several times to America. You know, it got my gong. I couldn't wait until I left Germany. It was like hot coals under my feet. I wouldn't want to go back for anything. They could invite me. They could do anything and I wouldn't go back. I just don't want to have any part of it. My parents, my grandparents, and generations back, they have all been from Germany. But I don't even want to eat cake in Germany. I want to have dry bread in America or anywhere else. I don't want any part of it. I have no friends and I have no family there. Whatever family I had in Germany got killed in the concentration camps.

Can you remember having non-Jewish friends when you were still in Germany?

Before we emigrated to France, I had non-Jewish friends. But I had no contact with them afterward anymore. I didn't have any non-Jewish friends in Berlin. It depends what year you are talking about. If you talk about 1935 or 1936, we only had Jewish friends. At that point you could still walk around and go any-where, but you really didn't have many non-Jewish friends. You may have had one or two, you know, and some of the neighbors were okay at that time.

In the 1940s, did your relations with your neighbors change or did they remain okay?

Well, they were afraid. But some of them stayed [cordial to us] and gave us some ration cards and helped us out with some kind of food. For instance, there was a neighbor in our building who was always very friendly. He also used to like to drink and he came home very late. One time when my father came back early in the morning from the night shift, this man came home with a big sala-mi under his arm. My father's eyes popped out and he took it and paid him for it. A few weeks later he saw him again and said, "Listen, if you ever have anoth-er salami . . ." Even though it was horse meat, it tasted very good. Only when we knew it was horse meat, it wasn't so good anymore.

Was this really important help that you received from the Germans?

Yes, it was. Yes, because we only got a minimum of food. I mean, you could only shop at certain hours, late in the afternoon, and then we had to be off the street again. It's the indignities that one had to suffer—they were really terrible.

It is a little bit of what one person could do. People were really afraid at that point, because they could wind up in a concentration camp just as easily as anybody else if they would get caught. So at least at that point they were afraid. In the early years, they could have done something. They could have protested or something.

Why do you think that they didn't protest or do something in the early years?

Because they really believed it; they really believed what they were taught. If they lived by the law, they didn't have to be afraid. They were taught that a Jew is not a human being, a parasite, so you leave it alone. They had nothing to be afraid of. But if they had been thinking that these people used to be my neighbors and we were friends, well, maybe not close friends, but we were acquaintances, and all of a sudden they are parasites, they are not worth anything anymore, then something isn't right. But, as a whole, the Germans do not think for themselves. They are followers. They are not leaders. You see the difference here for instance in America. Somebody comes along like a McCarthy and all of a sudden people get mixed up. But then they come back to themselves and they say, "That man is crazy." They think for themselves. They are not followers. They are not like sheep like the Germans are. The Germans follow anybody.

Did Jews in Germany know about the mass murders during the Holocaust?

In the beginning, you really thought they were going to work camps. I guess they didn't want to admit it to themselves. Nobody knew for sure. I mean, at least nobody of the people I knew. We knew that it was something horrible. When the mail came back from my aunt's with address unknown, we knew they were not alive anymore. But nobody knew about gassing. I don't think anybody knew that. I mean, maybe they thought they died of hunger or maybe they died of something else. We didn't know.

Did you know about any spying being done on you?

No. I'll tell you something. You always were afraid. You didn't talk to other people. Even among yourselves, you only whispered because they say walls have ears.

Do you think 1945 came as a liberation for the non-Jewish Germans?

No. If somebody was not a Nazi, okay, for them it was a liberation. But for the rest, they were happy when Hitler was invading left and right on the western front or on the eastern front. But when Stalingrad happened, it then hit home all of a sudden. Before that point they were happy. They were winning.

But when the bombs were falling in Berlin, I was happy even though they could have hit me just the same as anybody else. I didn't care at that point. I rather felt, "Let them destroy it." If they would have wiped out all of Germany, I wouldn't have cared.

When I came back to Berlin [at the end of the war from being in hiding] thirty-five miles outside of Berlin, I felt like a stranger, like an alien dropped onto this earth. They were not my people anymore. I spoke the same language, but I had no more connections to them. It was only two and a half years that I was in hiding. But in those two and a half years, I wasn't part of it anymore. I couldn't talk to them. I couldn't. If I would have been in the Amazon, I couldn't have felt stranger. After the war ended, we got in touch with the American army and we were on the first liberty ship that came to America. I couldn't wait.

Part TWO

"Ordinary Germans'" Testimonies

✦5✦

EVERYDAY LIFE AND KNOWING LITTLE
ABOUT MASS MURDER

HUBERT LUTZ

**In my ten years in the Hitler Youth, I never heard
anybody suggest that you spy on your parents
or that you spy on anybody else.**

*Born in 1928 and raised as the son of a midlevel Nazi Party functionary
and former truck driver in Cologne, Hubert Lutz was a member of the
Hitler Youth from the age of seven to seventeen. A physicist by profession,
he emigrated to the United States in 1959.*

I was born on April 29, 1928. My father at that time was a delivery driver for a
coffee company. My mother was working as a saleslady in a textile store in
Cologne. Both were low-income type of positions. There was a lot of unemployment in Germany at that time and they were happy to have some money
coming in. At the time we lived in the southern part of Cologne, near the

southern railroad station. Since my parents' income was not overwhelming, we lived in a mixed neighborhood with an interesting division of stations in life. One part of the street was where mostly engineers and office workers and policemen lived. In our house there was a bakery and we shared the same floor with my maternal grandfather and his wife. In the house next door, the people were even worse off. Most of them were unemployed construction workers— very low income—and the next house after that was where some people lived who had family members in jail and there was also some illegal activity going on, like trading stolen goods.

We went through some pretty bad times. My father for a while was looking for a job and he had to report to the unemployment office. I don't know how often, but it seemed to be very often. Since there was no supervision for me, my dad took me along to the unemployment office. I remember that distinctly because it was very exciting. People were waiting in line to get their little stamp for employment money while they were looking for jobs. There was a lot of discussion going on, and I remember that quite often there were fights. The interesting part is that from that time, it always seemed to me that the fights, so people said, were started by the communists, and often times they got into fistfights.

So very early on I was scared of communists, because to me they were the evil people. Sometimes when we went out for a walk on Sundays, there were street fights going on and you'd ask who it was: "The communists, the communists, the communists!" There were some communists in the area where we lived, but, strangely enough, there were also Nazis in the area too, and they seemed to get along rather well together.

So then we were living on what little money my parents brought in. And my grandfather, who had started a small company of his own, also supported us with a little bit of extra money so we could make ends meet. There were no luxuries, but it was okay.

Then came 1933. In January 1933, when the Nazis took over, I was not yet five years old. I remember very clearly all the writings on the sidewalks with swastikas and the hammer and sickle and people yelling and marching and all that. Then came a big commotion and people said that the Nazis won. A short while after that, when my father again was at the unemployment office, he ran into his company commander from WWI. It was sort of a big surprise. This company commander then invited my father to come to a meeting of some party. I don't know whether he was an official or officer or whatever, but it turned out to be the Nazi Party. So he went to one of the gatherings, was very impressed, and came back as a member of the Nazi Party wearing a brown uniform. Up to this day I don't know where the money came from. We sure didn't have any money to buy that, so there must have been somebody who furnished uniforms for people.

That would have been in 1933, and from then on my father was gone most of the time working for the Nazi Party. My father was born in 1900, so he was thirty-three years old at the time. What exactly he did, I don't know. He was not paid; he was still on unemployment. But then his new party friends found him a job. I don't know the exact date when this happened. This was when the unions were closed down. The Nazis established what they considered a replacement for the former socialist unions. Dad did office work, clerical work, and that was when he got paid. It was not a high-paying job, and there was a problem, by the way, in that the Nazis demanded that any man who was working should not permit his wife to work also. My mother was not supposed to have a job; they had to keep that a little bit quiet. On the money that he was making at the NSBO [National Socialist Shop Cell Organization], we just couldn't live.

Because of their slightly improved income, my parents moved into a modern housing project in the suburb of Zollstock, where, at the age of seven, I joined the Hitler Youth. I remember this very distinctly. We used to play on the street, all the kids. Then one day my friends said, "We have to go to a meeting." I asked about the meeting and they said, "Why don't you come along? Why don't you come and join us?" They were all members of the Hitler Youth, which up to that time I hadn't even realized.

So this was when you joined the Hitler Youth. What was it like?

Yes, it was the Jungvolk, the Pimpfen. So I went with them and I remember that the guy in charge of the group, who was maybe three years older than I was, said, "What do you know about drills and such?" My father and I had played soldiers at home, so I showed him what I knew, like about-face and all these commands. He was impressed and said, "Fine, join." It was something that, to us kids, did not have any political content whatever. I remained a member of the Hitler Youth from seven to seventeen.

Whenever you have kids at that age, around ten years, or twelve years and younger, you have to maintain discipline. The discipline in the Hitler Youth was maintained simply by having certain punishments. For instance, if you talked out of turn, you were punished by not being allowed to wear your scarf for three weeks. That was not for really severe crimes; it was for clowning around or whatever. The other punishment was a more severe punishment. Part of our uniform was a dagger. Can you imagine a ten-year-old carrying a dagger? It was an honor to be allowed to wear that. If you did something really nasty, you were not allowed to wear your scarf and your dagger and that meant that you were like an outcast. If something worse happened, they would send you home and you had to work it out with your parents. That worked really well.

Were children in the Hitler Youth encouraged to become spies for the Nazi Party or to spy on their parents?

In my ten years as a member of the Hitler Youth, I never heard anybody suggest that you spy on your parents or that you spy on anybody else. Here is an example of how we felt about "finking" on somebody. One day while we were in school during the war years, we decided that, "Hey, we need a day off, so why don't we simply stay out of school tomorrow, and then, when we come back, we will simply lie in unison and say somebody came and said there was no school." All right, that was stupid, but we did it. What happened was the son of the chief of police of Cologne was in my class and he went to school on that day and finked on us. So the next day, we all came back to school and the teacher asked, "Why didn't you show up?" I was the class speaker and I was just about to open my mouth, when, wham, he hit me in the mouth! And then I thought, "If this is going to go on, I think I better tell the truth." So I said, "Well, I don't know." And he asked, "Whose idea was it?" That's when we immediately pulled together and said, "We don't remember. It was a general discussion and we don't remember who said it first. It was just one of those things." We knew exactly who had come up with the idea, but we wouldn't tell. And then the police chief's son told on us again, but we denied that it was true. That was the way we were brought up. You did not fink on your friends.

Now comes the interesting part. We were all punished, except for the police chief's son. The punishment was we had to come to school on Saturday afternoon and spend six hours doing all kinds of extra homework, which, thinking back, was a good idea. I mean, we learned something. But, from that day on, this son of the police chief was shunned by every teacher. They wouldn't ask him questions; they wouldn't even talk to him. You just didn't fink on someone. It was considered the lowest thing you could do.

But when your father became an *Ortsgruppenleiter* [Nazi Party local branch leader], didn't he receive denunciations from the civilian population?

Yes. It was his job to take a look at them, but he never handed them on. He had to look into it. That was the job. He'd call these people to his office and find out what really happened. For example, a Jewish lady who on the way to the air raid shelter shouted, "I wish this war was over." Some neighbor interpreted this to mean that she wished we would lose the war. You know, it was interpreted as a derogatory remark against the Nazi government and it was reported as a treasonous remark. So my father had to look into this. But, after hearing the facts, he said, "No, this is nonsense," and the whole matter was dropped.

There were some people in our society who denounced others because they liked the power and liked to make other people feel that they had this power. On the other hand, there were also people who just liked to help out. They thought it was their patriotic duty to help out and do things for no pay. And then there were yet some other people who simply enjoyed the limelight.

Did your teachers ever encourage denunciations?

I have to say that most of our schoolteachers in Cologne were anti-Nazi. There was never anything discussed of that nature in school. My Latin teacher was Jewish. Around 1943 he committed suicide. My favorite teacher was my math teacher. I remember that one day he asked me a question. I was wearing my uniform, and I stood up, clicked my heels, and he blew up. He said, "I don't want you to do this. I want you to act like a human being. I don't want machines. You're not a robot." I stood there and I thought that I was doing the right thing, so what was he yelling about? Then, after the class, he called me to his office and said, "Look, I'm sorry I blew up. It's not against you." And he kind of apologized, which made me feel very awkward because I had a high respect for the man. Here was this man apologizing to me, a punk kid. Only later on did I understand what was behind it. He was probably afraid that I might report him to the Gestapo. By the way, during World War I he was a frontline officer, with decorations. A super gentlemen, his speech, his behavior, was flawless.

Denunciations weren't even talked about. It was so taboo, you didn't do that. From little on, you did not fink on your friends. What was expected was that somebody who did something wrong turned himself in and said, "Yes I did that."

Was there a great climate of fear for ordinary people during the Nazi years in which people were constantly afraid of being arrested by the Gestapo or the regular police?

No, absolutely not. In the apartment we lived in between 1937 and 1943, we even had a Gestapo officer living in the house, Hubert Nordstern. . . . After all, I didn't do anything they could denounce me for.

During the middle of the war years, weren't there things you were scared of?

We were scared of the bombing raids. Every night since 1942, after every bombing raid, I was out there putting out fires, rescuing people, moving furniture, and helping people get shelter. So we were very busy. That was a strange situation. During a bombing raid, I don't think there was anybody who wasn't scared with the ground shaking and the walls moving, dust flying all over the place, and homes crumbling on top of you. But we were kids then. We would crawl out of this, go to work, and tell jokes. The jokes, I think, were a necessity, a means to overcome the pressure and the fears, like a release valve. And there was also this feeling of togetherness. My friends and I stuck together; we helped each other. Fear from the inside, no. Fear of the Gestapo or the police, absolutely not. In June 1943, we were bombed out. . . .

What was the Gestapo officer like who lived in your building between 1937 and 1943?

We lived on the ground floor and he lived on the floor above us. He was very friendly to me, to everybody. But there was one person in the house, and this was the guy that lived on the same ground floor as we lived on, who was deadly afraid of Nordstern just because Nordstern was a Gestapo officer. The rest of the people in our house felt at ease with him.

Nordstern was, I would say, in his beginning thirties. He was younger than my father and had two boys. He talked to me rather often. One of the things I had was a tendency to walk slumped over, and he would say to me, "Walk straight, or I'll kick you in the ass." He liked me and he felt because of this he had some parental authority or so. My dad would be the same way. It was not as harsh as it may sound; it was a friendly reminder.

Did he ever relate anything to you or your family about the murder of the Jews?

Yes, that was in 1943 after a bombing raid. After the bombing raids we had received special rations. Part of the special rations for adults was coffee, real coffee, so my mother had some coffee. We were all shaken up because of the raid, and I had been out firefighting. I came back early in the morning to take a nap and I heard my mother talking to Mrs. Nordstern in the kitchen. Her husband had been visiting for a few days [on leave from the eastern front], and then had to move on. And then she said to my mother, "Mrs. Lutz, do you know where my husband is?" My mother said, "No." And she said, "Well, he is in the hospital. He had a nervous breakdown. The nervous breakdown was because they are killing people, women and children, in Poland and in Russia." And my mother said, "I can't believe that." And she said, "Yes, he told me a story where somebody shot a woman, took her baby, hit the baby, and grabbed the baby by the legs and bashed its head against a wall." My mother said, "I cannot believe this. There is nobody who would do that."

My mother was in total denial, there is no doubt about that. But it was about so-called partisan cleanup actions. They supposedly wiped out partisans, which were a big problem for the German army. The partisans were really effective at blowing up trains and so on. So the German approach was, if they knew there were partisans in the village itself, to wipe out the village. And that's what they did. It was not mentioned in the reports that those were Jewish people. Just imagine: they shot a woman and they took the baby. Somebody took the baby and killed the baby by smashing its brains out!

The reports we heard were always presented as antipartisan activities. Now that doesn't make the killing of women and children acceptable by any means. But there is a slight difference here between fighting partisans, who were actually attacking you and fighting you, and rounding up Jews and killing people who were not really doing a damn thing to you and so on. But you also have to see that Russia had refused to obey the Geneva conventions. And, in addition, the British had made it very clear that they bombed women and children to weaken the home front. So I think a lot of people thought, "Okay, if that's what you want, that's what you get."

But did you not hear specifically about the murder of Jews?

We heard about a transport of people going out. There were rumors that people were killed, but there was never any mention of gas chambers. There were rumors that said people were squeezed together in these camps and most died of typhoid fever. And that was in essence the execution style. Now, about shootings, that was in connection with the partisans. Nevertheless, I am sure that they rounded up Jewish people and executed them along with the other partisans. I didn't really give it any thought. I was fifteen, sixteen years old. We heard this on the periphery. That was not, to kids of my age at the time, our primary interest.

When Jewish people were disappearing on these transports, what did you think?

We didn't think about it. No, we didn't even think about it. They were out of sight. I'm talking about people who are fifteen years old. And there were the bombing raids and there were questions about food.

There weren't very many Jews, first of all. Even at the time when all the Jews were still in Cologne, you hardly ever saw any Jewish people where we lived in the Cologne suburbs of Sülz and Klettenberg. There were very few Jews who lived out there. For us kids there was no reason to talk about that, because we didn't see them disappear. So we didn't see these roundups that they talk about, where the people were put in streetcar loads and sent to the Messegelände [Cologne Congress Hall] from where the Cologne Jews were deported to the east. I never saw that. Very few people did see that. Still, there are a number of people, more than two or three or ten, that did see it. But compared to the 750,000 people who lived in Cologne, they were a small minority, that's all.

What about what happened on *Kristallnacht*? Did you see that?

Yes, I did. There was only one Jewish store in my neighborhood. And when I went to school in the morning, I didn't even go by that toy store, because that wasn't on my route to school. Other kids came and said, "There are toys all over the place, all over the place!" But, first of all, once we came to school, our teachers told us not to go, not to look at that. And, when they could, they informed the parents that they should take their kids and keep them away from that stuff for safety reasons. Anyway, they made an effort to make sure that the kids didn't see it. I think I saw it only a couple of days later.

I did see the burned-out synagogue, the one on the Horst Wessel Platz on the Roonstrasse. That was the big synagogue for us. That was around for a long time throughout the war. Yes, I did see that. But did it impress me? No, because there were so many burned-out houses all over what used to be the Horst Wessel Platz.

What do you remember about anti-Semitic propaganda?

Well, for one, there was the *Stürmer* magazine. Nobody in my family would ever touch that thing. It was, some people called it, pornographic. I mean, it was real, heavy-duty anti-Semitism, usually purchased by members of the SS. But I don't know anybody in my circle, among my friends, social democrats or Nazis or whatever, who ever read this. The *Stürmer* was displayed more publicly. They started out, by the way, placing it in glass window boxes and they ended up covering these boxes with mesh wire because the glass windows were often shattered. So that shows you there were some people who were not very happy with that. We kids used to go and look at it, because it was wild stuff. It was pornographic, not in the sense of showing nudity or girls or something, but it was real low-grade type of propaganda given to the people. I would say it was the *National Enquirer* equivalent in the Nazi Party. Truth didn't mean anything; distortion was enormous. It was almost like reading dirty fairy tales. So that was one example of propaganda. During the war there were also a number of propaganda movies.

Mostly we felt, however, that we were being propagandized in terms of the allegedly positive aspects of the Nazi program. That was pounded into us. But it was on such a theoretical level that somebody in his early teens was turned off. We didn't want to hear political education.

What did you think about Hitler? What did the people around you think about him?

He was admired, very much admired. We all really loved him. We felt that he could do no wrong. Whenever something went wrong or was obviously wrong, people tended to blame it on the underlings. I'd only seen him twice, and the length of time was for ten seconds each time. So I can't base any opinion on that. I do remember that there were lots of pictures of him, though. As a matter of fact, in our office at the *Ortsgruppe* party headquarters, there was a picture of a little girl handing him a bouquet of flowers. Also we had this image of him feeding a little deer and being seen with his Blondie, his German shepherd dog. And you saw him breaking ground for the Autobahn, shoveling dirt and so on. He had the image of a savior, and he was looking for that. He was idolized to the point that when I was eight years old I asked myself, "What happens if he dies? He does everything."

What did you do when Hitler died on April 30, 1945, a day after your birthday? Were you sad?

I ate my birthday cake. No, it wasn't a sad birthday. I remember when they said the German army surrendered, my mother said, "Thank God! This stuff is over." But, for my father, the world collapsed.

In general, what was it like for you to live in the Third Reich?

To us, it was the most exciting time of our lives. As a Hitler Youth, you liked action, you liked to show what a tough guy you are. You know, like fighting fires and dragging people out from under the rubble; wearing your steel helmet and having a cigarette in the corner of your mouth. We didn't know any better. You see, when the Nazis came to power, I was five years old. I grew up in this, so it was a normal way of life to me.

So it just seemed normal to you?

Yes. Sometimes when we had Hitler Youth meetings in the early days we did these so-called military drills. I found them boring. I had done that a thousand times, and we went again and I'd find that boring. Then again, I learned to circumvent certain inconveniences by, for instance, volunteering for training in the signal corps. I learned Morse code. To them it was cheap military training. When we were drafted eventually, some of us knew how to fly an airplane, some of us knew how to run radio equipment. But, to us kids, working with real military transmitters and using Morse code and being up there right with the big shots in the military made us feel good. It made us feel important.

When did you first hear that Jews were being murdered in great numbers?

In great numbers, I would say 1948, 1949. We knew about concentration camps. In 1945 after the war there were a lot of people running around and showing their numbers, their tattoo numbers. There were some pictures that were shown right at the end of the war, like when they liberated Dachau, Buchenwald. But that to us was almost understandable because the pictures they showed were of people that had obviously died from starvation. You could see their skeletons. We had not been through that kind of a starvation, but we knew how quickly you lose your weight. And there was also the word that most of these people had died from typhoid fever. And there were many other typhoid cases, for instance, in France and in Buchenwald. So, yes, that was not excusable. On the other hand, there were times at the end of the war when a lot of our people didn't have anything to eat.

What about the gassing and the shootings?

We tried not to believe it. We simply said, "No, that's too brutal, too gruesome, too organized." Quite frankly, I began to read more and study more about it when I was in this country after 1959. A lot of people asked me, "How come you guys didn't know this? You claim you didn't know anything about it." And, I asked myself, "Well, how come you didn't know this?" So I started reading a lot and I started, well, maybe reading with a biased mind, hoping that I would find reason to believe that it was not true. But the evidence piled up. This became more convincing by the day. So I also asked myself, "Could we have done anything different? Where did the responsibility lie?" My conclusion was the responsibility lies in the fact that people didn't do anything about it. They just stood by and closed their eyes and ears. And I think that is true. People just didn't want to believe it. They didn't.

MARTA HESSLER

They came and arrested my brother.

Born in 1910 and raised in a working-class section of Stettin (today Szczecin, Poland), Marta Hessler describes how her brother was arrested in 1933 for conspiring against the Nazis and the social constraints of everyday life for those who opposed National Socialism.

Because of our political views, we were appalled that Hitler had come to power. My brother was completely against the Nazis and he was arrested in 1933. He was left-wing politically, a communist. He had friends who corresponded [with comrades] in Pomerania and were against Hitler. They wanted to stage a major affair, possibly even a revolt, against Hitler in Pomerania, and they used my brother as an intermediary. The mail would be sent to him and he would forward it. They didn't say what it was directly about. But they were friends, and so he knew more or less what it was about.

Then [one day] they came and arrested my brother. Two or three men came late in the evening between nine and ten, knocked on our door, and searched the house. My brother-in-law had also just arrived there and they grabbed him and my brother as well. The next day they released my brother-in-law, since he had nothing at all to do with the entire affair, but my brother remained in jail for three months.

He experienced horrible things, like how they were beaten. But he also always had a bit of luck and so he was able to get out again. After three months, he was released because they couldn't prove anything against him. He had been working at the *Stettiner Abendpost* [newspaper] and the mail had been sent there and he had forwarded it. So he was able to say afterward that he had never known what it was all about. His friends, colleagues, [and comrades] all testified that he had nothing at all to do with it and didn't even know what it was about. And, as a consequence, he was eventually released.

They [those who were involved in the resistance] then stopped. Some of them were sent to concentration camps. For many years, though, we were kept under surveillance. Someone from the police would come by, albeit in civilian clothes, and make inquiries to see if we were doing things like greeting one another with "Heil Hitler." They even went to our landlord, who owned the building, and asked her, "What kind of impression do you have?"

Were there also pogroms against Jews in Stettin in which the shops were destroyed and things like that?

Yes. That was completely awful. I saw the shops where the windowpanes had been smashed in. We had been walking in a busy shopping street and my mother started talking with somebody. Suddenly there was this crowd of people stating their opinions. My mother was actually a rather quiet person, but she joined into this conversation about politics. And then she almost got arrested. This was because a group of Hitler troops had just come down the street with the [swastika] flag and we didn't salute them. So they then grabbed somebody out of the crowd, my mother, to take her away. But then my brother showed up and made a big fuss and said, "What's going on here? Come, Mother." And then he left with her.

We lived in a distinctly working-class section [of Stettin]. The atmosphere there was more against [the Nazis] than for them. Naturally, there were some who said, "Oh, that's really great!" Otherwise, things would not have gone as far as they did. But they never actually said things like that to us. We also knew who was absolutely against [the Nazis]. Since we had been living there for more than thirty years, we knew these things, and we knew the people there and what their political opinions were and how they stood. We also always expressed what our viewpoint was too.

[Later, however, it was different.] The building in which we lived was completely destroyed in the bombing. Because of this, we were provided emergency housing in the city and then we had completely different neighbors with whom we had to be cautious. It was not like where we had previously lived.

One day, a neighbor suddenly came up the stairs in a brown uniform. My mother had enjoyed good relations with his wife and they held the same opinions about many things. And now here he was coming up the stairs in a brown uniform. My mother turned completely pale. We felt completely terrible. We both thought that this was the end, that they'd be coming to get us: "If he tells them what we think . . . "

But then his wife came by and said, "You don't need to worry. We won't say anything." And my mother answered, "I'm glad to hear that. Otherwise, I would have said that you had bought the entire trousseau for your daughter from Jews." [She said this] so as to eliminate [the possibility of our being denounced]. Otherwise, it would have gone badly for us if he had passed on things that my mother had discussed with her. My mother had spoken very freely with her against the war and against the Nazis.

Yes, we did have to march along with the others. If [we didn't do so,] we would have had to be sick in bed or have a doctor's excuse. Like on May 1, we would have to march along with the others in those huge parades where they were singing Nazi songs. But we would get out of there as quickly as possible, out of the parade, if it were somehow possible. [We'd say,] "I don't feel very well," and the like.

Did others do that also?

No, not very many. They were fearful. Those who openly admitted that they were against [the Nazis] would be led through the city. Their hair would be cut off. I didn't see this myself because I was at work. But a lot of people who had seen it talked about it. Everybody was [therefore] very cautious. That was severely punished.

ROLF HEBERER

For 60 million Germans, that was what the people really wanted.

Born in 1927, Rolf Heberer grew up in Freithal, a midsize city in Saxony near Dresden. In his interview he discusses the broad support the Nazis received from the German people and his father's activity as a Nazi Party block leader.

As a child, one was, of course, ecstatic [about the Nazis] at first. There was always something going on. The Hitler Youth were always making trips somewhere. One felt like part of a community. Mostly it was the case that those you went to school with or who were in your class were all involved. I mean to say that the Nazis understood well how to fill people with enthusiasm for certain things.

My father was a civil servant back then, and, as a civil servant, he was more or less obliged by the Federation of Civil Servants to be a member of the Nazi Party. This was not because he was trying to get ahead in his career. That wasn't his intention. He was not an enthusiastic supporter [of the Nazis], rather, as one used to say, a fellow traveler.

Until 1933 there was the period of unemployment. And then Adolf basically got the unemployed off the streets with the measures he took, like building the Autobahn. The people were content. They had a job, but what they did, well, that's another question. Nevertheless, they had a job. [Back then also] the so-called Winter Relief Organization was founded. They organized local collections, such as you have today, for example, of old clothes. In those days these things were organized by the party. The Nazi Party members in the individual residential districts had the task of realizing the measures set for them. So clothes were collected, and food as well, from those who had more than they needed. That was the kind of thing which led people to say, "Hitler helps the little people." That he had ulterior motives was not something one experienced at first or saw either.

We didn't have it bad. We actually had a carefree childhood and youth, at least until the war. I certainly can't complain. A civil servant's earnings were not exactly high back then, but one could live well. I mean, one basically had everything until 1939. The public assistance worked well. That anything was missing was not the case.

Then the war came and the whole thing looked somewhat different. On September 1, 1939, the war broke out with the invasion of Poland. And then there were the ration cards. Most people experienced the rationing of food-stuffs, but not just foodstuffs. Practically everything was rationed, whether clothes or even cars or motorcycles. They even rationed gasoline. The only thing that always continued to burn during the war were the lights.

Criticism of the regime? Not in my vicinity, and not among my relatives either. Our landlord's sons were in the army, in the Wehrmacht. Of course, there was indeed criticism there. In those circles there was a lot of criticism. But otherwise? The only criticism [worth mentioning] was something we actually heard about only later.

My father had a cousin who was married to a Jew who was later killed in Theresienstadt. That was a truly unusual affair. Her husband had been, as a Jew, an officer in World War I, and until 1943 they had left him alone. It was only at the end of 1944 or the beginning of 1945 that we first found out that they had picked him up.

Did you know any other Jews?

No. Back then Freithal had about 50,000 inhabitants. But in the city of Dresden with its 1 million inhabitants, everything was a bit more concentrated. Although we did not go to the city often, when we did, we would see them going around wearing their Jewish stars and then one would think about it.

Nevertheless, one has to take into consideration what the propaganda was like back then, what they hammered into people's heads. Over and over again, the same thing. And then the people also believed that it was right to mark them [with the Star of David], that they were bad people or bad human beings who were harmful to National Socialism, and that we had to eradicate them, and so on. That was the propaganda that was spread, and most, at least 75 percent [of the population], believed it. Because if they hadn't believed it, they would have gone to the barricades. But nobody went to the barricades. That is to say that they believed it. Such is life.

What was it like with the shops? Did they have signs such as "Don't buy from Jews?"

That was at the beginning [of the Nazi period]. I can't remember very much about that anymore. Oh, yes, there was that large department store Eckstein. That was a Jew. It was a large department store and it offered good value. I can still remember that quite well, how they smashed in the shop windows and then posted signs: "Don't buy from Jews" or "This is a Jewish shop" or what have you. I can still remember that. One talked about that, of course. He had never done anything to anybody. He just ran his business, sold his wares, and at a fair price.

Nevertheless, your father was still a member of the Nazi Party? What was that like?

He was a dues-paying member, and he also served as a block leader. The people who lived [in the area assigned to him and who knew him well] and had problems or desires, or I don't know what all, would come to my father and say, "Listen, Rudi, can't you help me out?" He was a civil servant, and so he helped people with the tax authorities. And then there was the matter with the Winter Relief Organization. [In all of these cases, it was the other way around as my father sought these people out.] It was the case that almost every month there was a list of things to be collected. My father drew it up conscientiously. Every now and then I would help out, and then I or my mother, depending on who had the time, would have to march out [to do the collecting]. We would go door-to-door and make a note of who had donated. Things like that were the function he had back then within his residential district or down in Freithal.

Did you ever listen to enemy radio stations?

We had only short wave, but our landlord built radios as a hobby. He tuned in every now and then. Then he'd say, "Today I heard this and that."

Did he take precautions? He apparently wasn't very afraid.

No, because everybody knew one another. On the main street where I lived, everybody knew each other. The houses were all single-family homes. People had been living there forever and a day. Most had known each other since adolescence. In a big city, it's different than in a smaller city.

At the beginning of this interview, you said that most grown-ups welcomed Hitler's measures.

Yes, clearly. One has to remember that in 1923 we had the inflation. As my father told me, it went so far that people were paid every day and evening, but when they went shopping, their money was already worthless. By the end, the mark had inflated a trillion times. That was crazy, but that's the way it was. Everybody was unhappy. Whoever had money could get by, but normal citizens couldn't and were naturally angry. Before the Nazis came to power, all kinds of people had taken their own life.

   Then Adolf came to power with his new idea. For most that was indeed better. People who hadn't had a job for years had a job. And then the people were all for the system. When someone helps you get out of an emergency situation and into a better life, then you're going to give them your support. Do you think people would then say, "This is all such nonsense. I'm against that"? No. That doesn't happen. How things were done later on is something else. But the people at that time were happy, even full of enthusiasm, and they all joined in.

   You have to understand the people. They were from another time than today. First they experienced this unemployment. Nobody had anything. Everything was expensive. And suddenly everything was different. The sun was shining for everybody. Okay, there were some who were completely against the regime, and they were locked up. They ended up in a concentration camp or I don't know where. But, for the common masses, let's say for 60 million Germans, that was what the people really wanted.

What did people think about Germany taking over other countries?

At meetings and rallies, it was maintained that since we Germans could not maintain ourselves any longer, we therefore had to take over countries like Russia and the Ukraine, or the breadbasket as one always said. And then in addition to that, in 1918 Germany had no colonies anymore after the lost world war. Before that we had several colonies in Africa and overseas. Now they were gone and Hitler had, of course, exploited this: "We don't have any more colonies. In order to continue to maintain ourselves and to proliferate, we need more land." The propaganda had prepared the people so that when the war broke out they were in favor of it. First came Czechoslovakia, when the Sudetenland was brought "home" into the Reich. That was another argument the Nazis used: "Wherever there are Germans, they have to come back into the Reich." Therefore, since there were Germans living there, one had a reason to invade.

The people were ecstatic over this. I can still remember that we were in the Erz mountains in 1938 and preparations were already under way. There were already troop movements. While we were up there with a car of some of our friends, we noticed that something was going on in the woods. And then they closed all the borders to the Czechs. Three or four weeks after that, we then heard on the radio that the Germans had marched into Czechoslovakia and the people were all for it. There was nobody who said this was wrong.

That's just the way things were done back then, and the great majority of the population had been prepared for it. Goebbels was the best propagandist there ever was. When he spoke, people were ecstatic. The population that eventually lost house and home were later no longer ecstatic. That was at the end of the war. But in 1934, 1935, 1936, it was completely different. At that time they were all ecstatic.

GERTRUD SOMBART

Most people were, of course, for Hitler.

Born in 1918, Gertrud Sombart was raised as the daughter of a former policeman in a small town outside of Dresden before moving to Dresden during the Nazi period. She describes how her father was once arrested for being politically unreliable, and how she had heard about Jews being shot in Poland.

My father was not at all enthusiastic [when Hitler came to power], not in the least, because he said from the start, "Whoever votes for Hitler is voting for war." Well, that came back to haunt him. But my father was, nevertheless, fortunate inasmuch as we lived in Torgau, which was a small city, and that he was a supervisor at the DKW, [which produced motorcycles] and was the biggest company in Torgau.

To keep the peace in the factory politically, it was ordered that nobody could wear a party badge. Previously my father had been a policeman and had acted fairly with everyone no matter whether they were communists or what have you. But the order was given and that's what he did. But, because of that, he made himself some enemies. They never forgave him for telling them to get rid of [those badges] and they just went on wearing them under their lapels.

One couldn't really say that my father was politically engaged. He wasn't in any party but he did have something against the Nazis because he would say, "They are going to cause a war." And he would always say, "Why do we have to have that Austrian, Comrade Schnürshuh," which was an expression used for Austrians in World War I. "It's not as if we don't have any Germans who could govern here."

My brother, on the other hand, was for Hitler. He had first studied music and then he joined the 100,000-man army. [But my father did not have to be worried about my brother though.] Not at all. My brother would never have betrayed my father the way those others did.

Do you know of cases where that happened?

My father had a colleague. His son was in the SA and sold Hitler's book *Mein Kampf*, and his father was against it. The two of them, father and son, kept poking into each other's business and then the son said that he was going to denounce him to the authorities. [Soon afterward] the father shot himself.

Indeed the son would have done that. When I once ran into him after the war, I said to him, "And you're still going free?" He was really nasty, one could say. A guy who was going to turn in his own father and his father had then gone and shot himself!

How was it that your father ended up being arrested?

My father had gotten word through one of his coworkers or someone else that they had something on him. At the time we would travel to Dresden every weekend and, when we were gone, they would come to our place but nobody would be there. So they arrested him at work and locked him up and placed him in investigative detention at the police station in Torgau. Whenever they nabbed someone, he ended up there.

[My father had attracted unfavorable attention from the Nazis on several occasions] and that was a reason for his arrest. They had wanted my father to become an SA instructor because he had been a policeman. But he told them that this was absolutely out of the question.

And then there was also the matter of the Russian Jewish technical director, Herr Dorin. At least a year prior to this time, it had been announced that he was coming [to work at my father's factory] and people were already saying bad things about him even though nobody knew him. And then, when he arrived, he turned out to be a wonderful man. He looked a lot like my father. He was blond, nothing like a Jew. Although his wife and his daughter did look Jewish, he didn't. He was an absolutely wonderful person.

When they decided they wanted to arrest him, the Dorins called my father and he immediately went over there. [When he arrived,] the SA were already there with all of their bayonets and they were about to knock down the door. My father had already known these guys, one of whom was a man with a criminal record. And to them he said, "You cowards. Now you are going after defenseless human beings with fixed bayonets, and with an ex-convict on top of it all." That didn't win him any friends.

My father then called the owner of the company. He still had a say in matters in town, and he intervened on Dorin's behalf so that they then didn't take him away. [Dorin] soon left and went to work at the Skoda Works in Czechoslovakia. And when the Nazis came into Czechoslovakia, he went to England with his family and he died in England.

Anyway, my father didn't make a lot of friends and therefore they came to arrest him. Luckily for him, the owner of his firm also intervened on my father's behalf and demanded that my father be released. I don't remember how long he sat in jail there, but it wasn't all that bad. [He even was allowed out on occasion,] but only to see the family.

When my father was released, we went to Dresden and opened our own shop. But not long after this the shop was boycotted and nobody came anymore. I assume this had been done in a similar fashion to the boycott of the Jewish shops. At one of their party gatherings, the Nazis had probably said, "You can't shop there anymore." And so the people just stopped coming.

Whatever the case may have been, we had to give up the shop because we were accumulating debts. My father then looked for work and got a job at the Kuchen-Palma [company]. But this didn't last very long and then he looked around and looked around and then he went for an interview at an insurance company. When he got there he said to the boss, "I want to point out right off the bat that I had to give up my job again because the party determines everything." But the boss responded, "That's of absolutely no interest to me. They don't concern me at all." That was really a stroke of luck.

Back then, did you listen to enemy radio broadcasts?

Yes, to the English, only to the English. Back then, you had to set the volume really low, and it was best to cover it with something. And you were not supposed to tell anyone about this, because there was a guy who had listened to an enemy radio station and it had been overheard and they killed him. Most people were, of course, for Hitler.

The fanaticism was really extreme. [For example,] the wife of my boss when I was working back then at a construction company had once sat out the entire night on the Schlossplatz because Hitler was at the Hotel Bellevue and she had hoped to get a glimpse of him. Before this she had called me up and said, "We want to see our führer." [So I went over there myself] and, when I got to the Postplatz, he had just gone into Café Weber and I thought to myself, "Okay, wait a few minutes and see if he really is so fascinating." People were screaming, "We want to see our führer!" But it took too long for me and I eventually said, "You can have him."

And then, at the time when they tried to kill Hitler, I was with my husband and said to him, "Oh, that was such bad luck." To this he responded, "For heaven's sake, don't say that. There's an SS man over there." But a woman who was there with us then said in the course of our conversation, "I'd kill that Hitler with my own hands." You see how varied the people were.

My boss [at the bank where I worked at later] was also really great and he was also completely against the persecution of the Jews. He said that some Jews had offered to give him a building, but he had declined. He said that the Jews were poor wretches and that it would bring us no blessing that they were being carted away. And the poor fellow, such a decent person that he was, ended up having his house be destroyed and being wounded in the next air raid . . . and he died shortly thereafter. I cried over this. He was such an upstanding person. But then there were also so many fanatic people: "We want to see our führer!" To think that when Goebbels said, "Do you want total war?" they screamed, "Yes! Yes!"

After your father was arrested, did you live in constant fear that something like this would happen again?

You always had to be afraid because my father was somewhat careless. My mother had the most fear and she would say, "Keep your mouth shut and be quiet. Don't say anything about it." My father liked to talk. But when he knew that someone could be dangerous to him, then he wouldn't say anything. You could notice by a person's general behavior if you had to somehow be cautious around him.

We had this one man working with us who was only the head of a very small department, but he had some kind of function in the SA. This guy was dangerous. He would send young men from the bank to the military who had not joined the SA and weren't so enthusiastic about the Nazis. He made sure they went to the front and not many of them survived, perhaps only one or two from ten managed to return. He whored around and lived it up out in Freital where there was a soap factory. They would hold never-ending parties. There were so many people dying every hour and every day at the time and these characters were boozing it up and partying.

After the big air raid on Dresden, people started to become critical, but this was dangerous. One wants to save a sinking ship if it is possible. One day, however, when I was walking down the Kesselsdorferstrasse, I saw a guy who had lost everything in the air raid and he was yelling, "We need to give thanks to our führer! We need to give thanks to our führer!" He did this with such obvious mockery. Still, nobody did anything to him at the time, but I don't know if anything happened to him later. All I could think about this was, "Mensch Meier!" [Author's note: This was a derisive name people sometimes used for the Luftwaffe head Goering.]

Did you know anything about the mass murder of the Jews?

Not about the mass murder. We heard from my mother, who had heard from a female patient at the hospital, that there were such camps. But we thought they were labor camps because one had put them to work in the war industry. Nevertheless, she had provided some hints about that, but not anything specific. We did, however, get some more specific information from an acquaintance of ours. He had been working at a large power plant in Poland. He wore the Order of Blood decoration, which was for those who had been with the Nazis from the very beginning. Nevertheless, he was basically a good man, hardworking and industrious. We were friends with him and he knew what our views were. He would never trick us. While he was over there in Poland, he had seen how Jews were forced to shovel out ditches and were then shot. After that he said to himself that he was not going to go along with that, and then he returned [to Dresden] and talked about this.

But you apparently didn't know until after the war that people were being killed in those camps?

Yes. There was, however, the time when I did see this one group. They were Jews and had probably been in such a camp. That was here in Dresden. Nevertheless, there were around fifty of them at least. They looked like starving wretches, haggard, and were merely able to shuffle themselves along. The population thought they were criminals. They looked like criminals.

ERWIN HAMMEL

They felt like members of the master race.

Born in 1924 and raised in a Catholic family as the son of a Cologne salesman, Erwin Hammel discusses the attractiveness of the Hitler Youth and soldiers' attitudes during the war.

In 1933, we were eight or nine years old and understood practically nothing about political events. I only remember the rallies and marches. At that time we were still members of the Catholic Youth Organization, and sometimes the Hitler Youth would come by with their flags and so on and try to provoke us and start a brawl. But usually it ended up peacefully.

I entered elementary school in 1931. In 1938, I then went to a monastery school in Steinfeld in the Eifel region. This was basically a boarding school, and it was more or less cut off from the outside world. So, in effect, we knew little about what was happening on the outside.

I came here to the Three Kings *Gymnasium* in 1940. That's when it began to get serious. Soon I was given a choice either to join the Hitler Youth or to leave school. There were only two boys in the whole class who were not in the Hitler Youth—Thomas, who also came from the monastery school, and I.

At home we talked relatively seldom about politics and the Nazi state. My father was not in the party; he was a salesman and he had a printing press and basically stayed out of [politics]. My mother was very religious and was certainly not in favor of National Socialism. Therefore, at home, we never really discussed politics. Partly this was because we had a certain amount of fear. One had to be cautious. The next-door neighbor could be someone who was deeply involved in the party and might pass on what he heard. The danger was always there—just don't say too much so that nobody got into trouble.

The Three Kings *Gymnasium* was known to be not exactly in line with the party and we basically had rather decent teachers there. We didn't experience any reprimands or anything of the kind if someone was not in the party. Nobody paid attention to that. I know now that the rector must have been a party member, but we weren't really aware of it then. On Saturdays the Hitler Youth had to report for duty and thus they didn't have to go to school. But those who weren't in the Hitler Youth had to go to school and on Saturdays we had shop classes. It is interesting that sometimes the Hitler Youth leader had to come to the school to fetch his Hitler Youth members because they suddenly preferred school to the Hitler Youth.

As children, we didn't have the opportunity to travel, so we didn't get to know Germany from another point of view. We didn't have that at all. This made the propaganda that we were exposed to seem very plausible. We heard and saw nothing else. People today can't imagine this at all. Freedom was whittled away one slice at a time, so that in effect there was no real possibility of a serious revolt. Everything was forced into line. We didn't have the opportunity to hear about the world abroad. There were no foreign newspapers, and so on. Today you can go to any kiosk and buy an American or English newspaper, or a Polish one or whatever, and you can read what others think about us. But back then we didn't have any such opportunity.

The Catholic youth organizations, schools, and so on were all forced into line. All of a sudden, they were all taken over by the Hitler Youth and National Socialism. They didn't even resist. The free scout movement remained against this for the longest time. But they were slowly nabbed as well. And then the special youth groups were founded—for example, the Hitler Youth Flyers— when boys showed interest in them. And if you wanted to fly, you didn't ask, "Is that a [political] party? Is that National Socialist?" As a boy, you more likely said, "Man, I have the opportunity to fly a glider." Also there was the NSKK, the National Socialist Motor Vehicle Operators Corps, which drove motorcycles. However, only those who were 100 percent National Socialist got to join them. You could only get into such units if you were in the Hitler Youth early enough and toed the line. So I didn't get in.

Had I been in the Hitler Youth for at least three years, I then could have been transferred to the navy. Fortunately, I had a schoolmate in the house next door who was a *Fähnleinführer* or something like that. And I went to him and he said, "Okay, pay the membership dues for three years, backdate them, and then you'll have allegedly been with us in the Hitler Youth from this or that time and you'll be able to get in with them." So that's what I did. That cost fifty marks back then.

So I then got into the Naval Hitler Youth, and that was basically more interesting to us because we could cruise the Rhine and didn't have to march along the streets and bellow songs and such things like the regular Hitler Youth had to do. That's why a lot of boys eventually joined the Hitler Youth. Whoever was interested in something—be it water sports, airplanes, or motor vehicles—had to join the Hitler Youth. Otherwise there were no other organizations.

Therefore, it was really easy to pull in the youth. If some guy had an [official] post, was a civil servant, he had to become a party member. Otherwise, he lost that post. All the teachers had to become party members. All the postal officials had to join the party. Otherwise they were out of a job. So okay, everything was pulled in eventually. And once one was a party member, he wasn't allowed to say much. Otherwise he would have to leave and then he'd also lose his job.

Did you have Jewish classmates when you were in school?

We had one. I knew him very well. That was Max Berkowitz. He was also with me at the monastery school in Steinfeld. Luckily the monastery school was able to send him off to Belgium at the right time and he survived the war and was later ordained as a priest.

I still remember how the persecution of the Jews started way back at the start of the Nazi regime. The Jews weren't allowed to enter restaurants and so on. I still remember how my father had soon got into trouble, because he had gone into a bar with Herr Berkowitz, the father of my schoolmate Max. My father's view was: "This is my guest and nobody has anything to say about that."

I also remember how the SA were suddenly standing out in front of the department stores like Tietz, which is now Kaufhof: "Germans! Don't buy from Jews!" and so on. Before that, we hadn't even known that Tietz was a Jew. That only came out later. You barely picked up on this as a child. As a child, you hardly had given it any thought. . . .

When the war began, I joined the 116th Armored Division under the command of Lieutenant General Graf von Schwerin and we had more or less decent officers as well. I was first in Russia. Later, after the second deployment, I went over to the west. I was in a unit where one respected his opponent as a soldier. This was the case even as far as the officer corps was concerned. We didn't follow the principle of take no prisoners and the like. To the contrary. I still remember one incident when we captured a wounded American. He had a bullet lodged in his body. I went with him to the first aid station, and the medic there didn't want to bandage him. For the medic, he was the enemy. I then made a real fuss about this. In our unit, we didn't stand that kind of behavior.

There were a lot of concentration camps in the east. Did you know about them?

You knew there were concentration camps. What they looked like from the inside, you didn't know. The first thing I halfway knew about, once I started to perk up my ears, was in Bielitz [today Bielsko, Poland], where I was in a military hospital. Bielitz-Schielitz had originally been German territory, but it became part of Poland after World War I. In our room, we had a guy of whom it was said, "That guy was in a concentration camp." He then said to us, "Don't ever ask me about how it was there. I don't want to go back there again, and I'm not allowed to say anything about it." I then basically said to myself, "Don't ask. Don't get him into any kind of trouble. He has his reasons for not wanting to go back there. That must have been awful for him." That was the impression I had.

That was the first I ever heard about that and the first time I realized that not everything was in order in that regard. On another occasion back then, another guy said to me, "Hey, it's stinking here of smoke again. They're burning people again." But it didn't occur to anybody that those who were being burned had been killed in large numbers. Instead, you had thought, "Oh well, they must have died of an illness or something like that." Of course, malnutrition and disease were all over the place.

I later grew critical when we were here in the Ruhr region and we saw trucks full of corpses that had been shot up during an air raid. This was practically during the last days of the war. That's when I started to take notice. Those couldn't have simply been sick people. What bothered me most was that all the bodies were naked. That something like that had happened, I saw for the first time here in the Ruhr region. In four or five places, independent of one another, truck trailers had been driven into ditches and so on. The corpses just lay on top of one another in layers. They just lay there in piles. That was the first time I ever saw something like that, and then you heard things like, "Man, all sorts of things must have gone on."

And had you heard anything about the shootings?

You certainly heard that the SS took rather drastic action whenever anything happened because of the partisans. Whenever somebody from the SS was shot somewhere behind the lines by underground fighters or partisans, and so on, then the SS went out and executed whole city blocks of people. Obviously for them a human life hardly mattered, especially when they were enemies. As I was saying, we hadn't seen ourselves how the SS treated people, but the information was passed along by word of mouth that they acted rigorously.

What were the soldiers' attitudes toward the Nazi regime?

In the first years there was considerable enthusiasm among the population whenever the radio announced special reports on military successes. "We showed the English!" it was said whenever ships were sunk, and so on. In general, we had the feeling that we had been attacked and we had to defend ourselves. We even thought that, as Germans, we were invincible. That was the feeling back then.

At the beginning everybody was happy to be a soldier. They felt like members of the master race. "I'm a soldier. Nobody can do anything to me!" And so on. Whenever soldiers were on leave, they strutted around as if they were terribly important. . . . It was indeed rather pleasant in the first couple of years. But afterward, when people were badly off and so on, nobody wanted to be a soldier. It wasn't so nice anymore.

When did the mood turn?

That was more or less in Russia, after Stalingrad, or sometimes after the first winter there when there were freezing temperatures to the point that legs froze off and so on. When you saw the comrades you'd just been drinking with, how they had been maimed and so on. Nobody wants to admit today how it was, how you trembled, above all before an attack. Afterward it was even worse. People actually cried and wet their pants.

ANNA RUDOLF

You, good girl!

*Born in Bavaria in 1923, Anna Rudolf worked during the war in Berlin at
a film duplication agency alongside several young Russian forced laborers.*

I studied stenography with the goal of becoming a secretary and that is what I was.
I was a secretary at the German State Library and I worked there for many years.

In 1937, when we came to Berlin, it was already in turmoil. Even at fourteen
you are still aware of some things. At that time, you would hear things like,
"Hitler deserves to have his head cut off," and "Who knows what is yet to come
and what is going to happen? This place is seething!"

I had a friend whose father was a communist, an old communist and he would
say, "Watch out, something's going to happen." And, when I was called up for
service during the war, there were two colleagues of mine who were learning
Russian, and I asked them why they needed to know Russian. Their answer to
me was, "Watch out, they'll be here soon." So that's how it went.

During the war, every hand was needed and I was called up for service. I
could choose between working at a cable factory or working as a uniform seam-
stress or working at a film duplication agency. Of course I chose the latter, but
that turned out to be rather foolish. I ended up in the short film department and
there I had to make copies of the films. I also copied feature films, but mostly I
worked on film shorts. For example, if Hitler looked in bad shape in one of
those film shorts, I would have to excise those strips. For this we had a closed
box with a small slit in it and we had to throw away the strips so that nobody
could somehow get hold of them.

Who determined what was to be cut out and what was to be kept?

The bosses certainly. Down below where the films were screened, we had a
room for short films and also one for cinema films. After the films had been
played, one then had to decide [which parts of the films were to be cut out], but
the political filmstrips were always reviewed by the boss as well. Once this had
been done, the films were then sent to the front. My job was to make copies of
the films.

All at once we got a number of Russian girls who had been brought to
Germany [to work as forced laborers], and there were many nice ones among
them. Our overseer was a guy who was walking around all the time in his SA
uniform making the rounds through all of the various departments. He would
say to us that we were not allowed to talk with these women. "And why not?"

I'd ask, "They are people just like us. They can't help it that they have to be here." So I often was at loggerheads with him. When I told my mother about this, she would always say, "Just you be careful or else he will have you taken away."

Those girls were always hungry; they hardly would get anything to eat. Sometimes I would give one of them a slice of bread and butter, and they would say over and over again, "You, good girl! You, good girl!" There was one time that I was standing around talking with one of the girls who had the same first name as mine, Anna: "What's your name?" "Anna." "I also Anna!" And, as we were talking like this, our overseer came by and saw that I was talking with her—he was always sneaking around like a cat—and he showed such a face. "What did I forbid you to do?" he said. And I said, "She's just as much of a human being as I am and as you are too." This made him mad and furious and he then sent me upstairs to the boss's office. But the boss actually was quite understanding. When I asked him why I shouldn't talk with these girls since we couldn't have any big conversations anyway as they couldn't understand much German and about all we could do was communicate through sign language, he understood me. "But take care," [he said]. "Watch out whenever that guy is nearby." Yes, indeed, he was a decent guy, a really decent guy.

Did you know where and how the Russians lived and how they were treated?

They all had plank beds to sleep on and they only got food to eat once a day. Nobody was allowed to speak to them. They had to work like dogs and they had to carry those heavy reels. And that overseer we had was a great big piece of crap. One time he even kicked one of the girls. Both my male and female coworkers were much more kindhearted, but they just looked away and said nothing about it as they were all afraid. Still, what I mean to say is that they were mostly generous to the girls, although you could easily notice that there were still some of them who hated those Russians.

Because he could no longer hear properly, my father was put to work as a supervisor in a Russian work camp. This had a fence around it and there were about thirty men working there. They all lived in filth, really in filth, in the open air. My father later told me, "This is something I can't bear to look at anymore." My father then saw to it that they cut down some trees and had those thirty men make a roof for themselves. And he also got hold of some roofing paper so that it didn't rain on them. Despite this, they still froze and shivered. I can still remember how that my mother and we two girls had gone over there twice, it was in Krampnitz, and how my mom couldn't bear to look at it all. And then she said, "Oh my word, how can we help these people?" So then what she did was gather up the cigarettes that she and my father got from the ration coupons and handed them [to the Russians] through the fence. They only just looked at her in amazement that they would get something from the Germans.

Then there was Christmas. This was to be the last Christmas before my father was taken to prison camp. Mom had baked cookies and she took a whole bucket full of them out there. At the time my father was a sergeant major and they treated him like an officer. And he had a young fifteen-year-old Russian boy who cleaned for him and shined and polished his boots. My father always acted humanely. He never pestered anyone or beat on him. And my mom gave the boy a big, beautiful plate full of cookies. Tears rolled down his face and we girls cried too. Then he stammered out to us, "Comrades too! Comrades too!" I've never seen anything like how they tackled those cookies. Despite everything, they shared with one another. And over and over again, they said, "You good woman. You good girl."

What about the persecution of the Jews? Did you, for example, experience the events of 1938?

That was really awful. When that happened I was walking down the street on the way to do some shopping and I thought to myself, "What is going on here?" We lived just around the corner from the synagogue near the Friedrichstrasse and so I could follow the whole thing. [In October] they brought all the Jews out of the synagogue and forced the men onto trucks. The women and children ran after them, screaming and yelling. Then they went away, and three days later the women and children were also picked up. I said, "Mom, what's going on?" And she said, "It's about the Jews. Who knows where they're going to?" [And then I replied to her], "But they are human beings just like us. Why are they being taken away? They haven't done anything wrong." Nevertheless, you had to keep your mouth shut.

And then [one day in November] when my mother and I were walking down the Neue Königsstrasse, it got really terrible. I had just wanted to buy myself a new pair of shoes, and then [we saw how] they were smashing in all of the shop windows and taping up Jewish stars everywhere and stealing like crazy. I could only stand there; I was devastated. Then my mom said to me, "Come on! Come on! Otherwise, we'll also be in trouble." It was awful. All the way down the street, one shop after another was destroyed, everything was smashed to pieces. They were in a rage, and what a rage, I tell you. One man continued to hit another man across the back with a truncheon. It was probably a Jew who could not get out [of a shop] fast enough or something like that. It was awful. Then I said, "Mom, I can't go on any farther. We have to go home, we have to turn back."

Earlier you said that there were all kinds of rumors going around in Berlin. Did you have a lot of fear of the Gestapo?

Well, yes, you knew people who even in the earlier days were wearing their party badges. And, since my mom often collected for the Winter Relief Organization, she knew a whole lot of people, and she would always tell us to be careful. And you knew yourself about how you had to be careful around this guy or that guy. It was always talked around about whom one had to watch out for.

We were always somewhat reserved and cautious because one basically had fear that one would be the next. And afterward, at the end of the war, it got really awful. Then there were soldiers hanging from the streetlights. They would have signs around their necks, saying "traitor" and nonsense like that. When some people were found trying to find a safe place for themselves, they would then be labeled as traitors.

Did you know before the end of the war about the concentration camps?

No. You would often hear things like, "He has been taken to a labor camp. He did something and he's been taken to a labor camp." But everything was covered up and kept concealed. Nobody knew anything specific. And then we'd hear again, "They packed that guy off to Dachau." My parents had thought that Dachau was a labor camp until it got around what kind of camp it really was. After that, everybody was afraid and nobody dared say to anything.

Did you know from rumors before the end of the war about what had happened to the Jews?

Yes, even already during the war. That was all certainly talked about. But, as I was saying, it was always just said, "They are going to a labor camp." That they were gassed, and so forth, nobody had thought that. Nobody had thought that. Afterward, after the war, I worked with a Jewish woman whose father was a tailor. Her entire family had been taken away and her father had been forced to make and mend clothes in a concentration camp. But her brothers and her sister and her mother were all gassed. She herself had been hidden and so both she and her father survived. Anyway, she told me all about what went on there, how they were beaten, and how they had to do all that work. That was certainly horrible.

My father had hidden a Jew. He was from our homeland [in Bavaria] and they had come here to Berlin. They had wanted to get out of here, and, by chance, they had run into my father on the Friedrichstrasse. At the time, my father had a brief leave from the military and so he ran into my father and my father hid him. My father never talked about where and how and what he did so that nobody could ever find out about this and so that we girls wouldn't blab or something.

PETER REINKE

Why should I have been afraid? We just sat there in detention.

Born in 1925 and raised in Cologne as the son of a plasterer, Peter Reinke describes how he got in trouble because he didn't want to go along with the Hitler Youth and some scenes from the aftermath of Kristallnacht in Cologne.

I experienced the origins of National Socialism as a small child. I can still just barely remember the demonstrations before 1933, mostly by the National Socialists and the communists. They always ended up in brawls or worse [with the result] that the police had to intervene. As far as I was concerned personally, I was from a home [that had opposed Nazism]. My parents were very Catholic, and my father had nothing at all to do with them. He would always say, "I'm a Christian. I cannot be a communist or National Socialist, certainly not an atheist [like them]." That was the way he would talk. As a Christian, [he] wasn't exactly the kind of person who was married to the church. He went to church and that was it, nothing else. But he did continue to value Christianity, because that was what he had learned at home, and he couldn't stand it when they began to persecute and mobilize the people against the Jews. He would always say, "I participated in World War I, and they fought right next to us just like the others."

In the area where we lived, my parents wanted to keep me off the streets, so I ended up with the Jesuits. It was like this: When I got out of school, I would go home and eat, and then I would go back to the Jesuits, to the Jesuit cloister on the Stolzestrasse in Cologne. There, I could do my homework under supervision, and there we could play or otherwise preoccupy ourselves. This resulted in my eventually becoming an altar boy, and after that I remained with them until I began my apprenticeship.

When I started my apprenticeship in 1940, the war had already started. The pressure, especially on the Catholic youth organizations, was great. Our freedom was constantly being curtailed. In the summer, we would often go to the forest after church on Sundays. But we couldn't travel there together on the tram. We would have to go there individually or, at most, maybe two of us at a time. The Hitler Youth was after us and wanted to prevent us [from forming independent groups]. More or less everything was forbidden. All of the youth organizations were forbidden, except the Hitler Youth, and we didn't want to join up with them.

This led to the emergence of passive resistance among the youth and to some brawls. I think it was in '36 or '37, or it could have been in '38. Anyway, one morning a sermon was held by a young priest, and when we got out of church the Hitler Youth was everywhere and also the SA. Soon a huge brawl broke out.

[Nevertheless we] eventually had to join the Hitler Youth. There was no getting around it. One was basically forced to join up, and everything was already directed toward premilitary training. There was absolutely nothing else. From childhood on you were in training.

Wasn't there also pressure from the teachers in school to join the Hitler Youth?

That depended on the teacher. In elementary school, it was less the case. Anyway, I joined up with the Hitler Youth when I began my apprenticeship. Until the end of elementary school, when we were about fourteen, we were in the Young People (Jungvolk). After that you then came into the Hitler Youth. This was all done with a big celebration and to-do, and my father was then supposed to buy me a uniform, which was something he would never have done.

Then there was the problem with my training as a bricklayer. At that time I was working at a construction site in Wesseling and had to ride there on my bicycle. This meant that I was always on the go. And then, on Sunday morning at 7:00 A.M., I was supposed to show up at the Hitler Youth. This made me incredibly angry. It wouldn't be until two or three on Saturday afternoon that I would get back home, and then I would have to do my homework, because on Monday I had classes. So, I didn't go to the Hitler Youth. My father would say to me, "No, you're not going today. You're completely exhausted. That doesn't even come into question." So, in the end, I was punished. The police summoned me and told me that I had to report for duty [with the Hitler Youth]. And, after that, I ended up sitting in detention from Saturday until Sunday evenings.

Didn't this all make you afraid somehow?

Afraid? Why should I have been afraid? We just sat there in detention. There were justice officials who were watching over us. We'd get something to drink and eat. We had to be in our bunks at such and such a time. We had to go to sleep and get up early at such and such a time and wash up. And you couldn't walk around either. But, it wasn't all that bad. We were practically still kids, fourteen, fifteen years old. I got special rations, juvenile rations. At the end of 1942, when I turned seventeen, I joined the navy.

For me personally, I would say, the worst thing that turned me against the Nazis was November 9, 1938, this indiscriminate destruction of the Jewish shops. Not only that, they enriched themselves from this in the process. I saw that with my own eyes.

After my father came back from work [that day], he then had me walk with him through the town because he thought it was important to do this. First, he wanted to see what had happened himself. And, second, he wanted to make clear to me what this meant. I was twelve years old at the time, almost thirteen. But the most important thing for me came early that morning when I went to school. When I was on my way to school in the Stolzestrasse, I passed by a Jewish bakery and the entire bakery was destroyed. The windows had been smashed in, all the bread and other things like cakes, pies, and so on were all lying there in the street, unsold, and being trampled over. And nobody was allowed to take anything. On the other side of the street there were kids from large families who went to school with me who were living there and they hardly had enough to eat. So I then thought to myself, "How is this possible? How can they do this?" After all, in the Catholic Church, we were told that one should never throw away bread!

While walking through the streets with your father, you must have asked your father what happened and why. Was it clear to you what was happening?

An official at the German embassy in Paris had been murdered, and [the assassin] was supposed to have been a Jew. That was more or less the apparent cause. The whole thing with the Jews had already started years before this. The Jewish shops had that Jewish star on them, and sometimes there were SS or SA men standing in front of them and no one was allowed to go in or shop there. A good German [it was said] didn't buy from Jews and so on.

You said at the outset that the persecution of the Jews began in early 1933. Did you witness that too?

In the building next door to ours, but living on the same floor as us, there lived a skilled worker and his wife and two kids, who were somewhat older than I. I think the husband worked in a big company here in Cologne as a foreman. For quite a long time, they had already been contending with taunts and insults. Often it was the case, and it had been so since even earlier, that when we would see a Jew go by we would mock them and yell out things like: "Jüdd, Jüdd, Jüdd, hepp, hepp, hepp, hät en Nas wie en Wasserschepp!" (Jew, Jew, Jew, hop, hop,

hop, you've got a nose like a water pot!") That had all been nonsense. But later it got serious when a lot of [the boys] were in the Hitler Youth, or the Young People, and they then did it considerably harsher. You have to consider that the Jews had Sabbath, and Saturday was their day of rest, while for us Christians it was Sunday. That was yet again another cause for rebukes: "The Jews aren't doing any work. They're not doing anything!"

My father was a plasterer. When he needed something for his work such as overalls, he went to this Jewish secondhand store and bought them there. If you were the first to enter this store on Monday morning, you could bargain with the Jew forever because it would have been a great misfortune for him if you left the store without buying anything. That's the way it was with the Jews, and my father knew it and used it to his advantage.

Did he shop at Jewish stores even when those [anti-Semitic] signs stood in the windows?

Even then. That didn't bother him. But I don't think that he would have gone in if an SS or SA man was standing out front. He wouldn't have done that even though he couldn't stand them and the entire system. He wouldn't have directly provoked them. But the Nazis were not standing in front of every shop.

I left school in 1940 and had to take up a profession, either in a construction trade or in a related trade. I couldn't do anything else. At the beginning of the war, guidelines were issued from Berlin that the children who came from these families [like mine] would have to enter the same profession as their parents in order to curb the shortage in skilled laborers. That's what they wanted and I had to accept it. So then I learned to be a bricklayer here in Cologne at a company with a good reputation. I then took my examination and became a journeyman—I also had good grades from my trade school—and eight or ten or fourteen days later, I was then drafted by the Labor Service.

In early 1942, I volunteered for the navy. Already earlier when I was an apprentice, I had wanted to become a seaman for my profession. So I signed myself up and went off to the Labor Service. That was located down there somewhere on the right side of the Rhine. After three or four weeks of training, you then swore an oath to the führer, as was usual in the military. [Sometime] after this some Waffen-SS troops showed up. There was an officer and several lower-ranking types, about ten men. Everybody who was over 1.68 meters was supposed to go to the Waffen-SS.

We then came under a lot of pressure. We weren't able to leave. We weren't allowed to go outside during the break, absolutely nothing. Only the small ones could get out of this. But then I got lucky. They needed more personnel for the navy and the authorities from above, either from the admiralty or from the personnel office, arranged it all. Two or three days later, a car arrived and a navy officer with a medal around his neck got out and he got us out of there. First, though, he gave them all kinds of shit. It was a show to beat hell. He told them, "These people are to be released at once." And then we were immediately given civilian clothes and marched back home. At the same time, I got my marching orders. I was at home for a day, and the next evening I had to depart for training with the navy. I entered a course, and after two months, I had the training in Husum [Schleswig-Holstein] behind me and became a mate.

While you were in the military, did you hear anything about the concentration camps or the deportations?

No, no. Not much. Not much. It was said that the Jews who hadn't been deported had been made to work. That was what the [Nazis] had publicly told the people. What was done there, nobody knew. But we did indeed see how concentration camp prisoners had been forced to work, such as, for example, the Hiwis. These were Russians, White Russians, or Ukrainians who had to carry out all sorts of functions. They had to work. They had to load and unload and perform all the menial tasks that needed to be done anywhere in the Wehrmacht, in any unit.

Did you ever hear any rumors or other things about mass executions?

No, no. I didn't know about that. During the war we didn't hear anything about that. We were seldom on land, only for loading up supplies. [But there was this one time] when we were in Libau [Latvia]. The naval base lay outside the city— at the point where the open territory began—and there was a lot of shooting. Then a rumor went around that they were shooting Russians. But then, we knew that the Waffen-SS didn't take any prisoners when they were dealing with the Russians. On the other hand, Waffen-SS men were shot by the Russians. There was so much shooting going on in the area—the front was only fifteen kilometers away—that you couldn't really tell who was shooting whom and where the shooting came from.

HELGA SCHMIDT

There was never any particular sympathy for the Jews.

Born in 1921 and raised in Dresden, Helga Schmidt discusses Hitler's popularity and people's attitudes toward Jews in general.

I was only twelve years old at the time Hitler came to power, and at that age you don't pick up as much as an adult. But I would say that people took a wait-and-see attitude. They were curious, but also full of expectation: "Is what he has promised really the case?"

Can you remember if and when attitudes toward Hitler changed?

They changed in the course of the next few years when he could point to successes. He got rid of unemployment. Just about everybody had a job. He helped poor families with lots of children. Families with lots of children got preferential coupons for foodstuffs, for clothing. They could buy them for less. Security for the population was restored. Crime disappeared completely. And, finally, the cultural amenities [also contributed to Hitler's popularity], like the Strength through Joy Program, inexpensive visits to the theater, and things contributing to the population's cultural life in general. That won a lot of support for him.

Workers were given a greater say in matters in the factories. The boss no longer decided things alone. The eight-hour-day was introduced throughout the country. I know that we at first worked on Saturdays like any other day. Then came the regulation stating that the work week would end at midday on Saturday afternoon.

Did you know anything about the negative aspects of the Hitler era?

As older children, we were at first wild with enthusiasm about the Nazi regime. There was, of course, the Hitler Youth, which my father was against. Therefore, even though the school exerted a bit of pressure [on us to join], I was among those who were not in the League of German Girls [BDM]. And it was not pleasant for an older child to have to stand on the sidelines, because that is not one's inclination.

What I considered negative were the street collections, which were held for one reason or another nearly every week. Collections were held for this and that—and in a rather pushy way. And house wardens were assigned to go around from house to house with lists for collections. And this was also pushed on you. The notion was that, "Whoever doesn't donate is the enemy."

Among our relatives we had one who was a convinced communist. Whenever we got together, there was always an argument. He was actually the only active communist in the family, while the other relatives, like my father, were mostly social democrats. Still, my father did not display his opposition openly. In public he remained rather quiet about this. He only let it be known among friends and relatives when he knew exactly whom he was dealing with. And we already knew at the time that a good number of people had already been picked up who had shown themselves in public to have been active communists or active social democrats.

Were there people in your building you could not trust?

There was a disabled soldier. As far as I can remember, he had never worked. He lived only from benefits. Then we had one fellow in our building who belonged to the SA. We were all careful around him. The others were all rather moderate. We did not feel that we were somehow in any danger or that we were put under any pressure.

Were you aware of the discrimination and persecution of the Jews?

In the area where we lived, here in Leptau, near the Freiburgerstrasse and St. Anthoniastrasse, there weren't any Jews. There were, however, Jews at school. I went to school with a Jewish girl. She was highly intelligent, pretty as a picture. She never let herself get mad. From the start, she kind of set the tone in class. One time during a physical fitness period when we had to let ourselves be timed with a stopwatch, she got angry with the teacher for some reason and said, "Let's all run really slow and make him mad." And we all did it too!

She had friends in school. She was good-natured. She was only protective about her private life. She never spoke about private matters. She never told us about her family life. There were other Jewish girls at school—not in my class, but in other classes—with whom she mostly hung around. They spoke Hebrew among themselves. When I left this school in 1935, she was still in that class. I don't know any details about what happened later to her.

Did you know about the *Kristallnacht* pogrom in Dresden?

We didn't experience it ourselves, but news got around that in the night they had set the synagogue on fire and smashed in the Jews' shop windows.

What did people say about it? Were they okay with what happened?

Well, there had been a tendency over several years to present the Jews as exploiters. And when that has always been pounded into people's heads, people will also believe it. There was, however, a large part of the population who didn't think that was quite right and who said, "They're fleecing us. They're making money from us, and so on." Certainly there was something of a negative attitude toward the Jews, but before Hitler it did not exist to the same extent. One tolerated them. One let them live. There was never any particular sympathy for the Jews. But to directly label them as our enemies and exploiters, that came from Hitler.

Did you shop in Jewish shops?

At first, we shopped in Jewish stores, probably because they were less expensive than other stores. But then they closed little by little and eventually there weren't any more of them. They had been taken over by others. We went shopping in the Kaiserwerther Strasse. The larger shops there were all owned by Jews. That was well-known. Also it was well-known that department stores and larger shops in the city center were Jewish. Signs were taped on the windows and doors of the Jewish shops and department stores saying "Jew" and so on, and we didn't trust ourselves anymore to shop there because it was said that we were being watched. And we believed that.

Can you remember the first time you became aware that Jews were being rounded up?

Oh, that came very late. It was toward the end of the war that we found out about that. I can't say exactly when that was. You had not personally experienced it. You didn't know anybody. It was [only] talked about.
We did experience one thing though. A half-Jewish woman lived in my in-laws' building. She was married to a German. She didn't receive her food ration cards from her distributor. She had to pick them up at a certain office. Her mother lived with her. I don't know what was going on with the food ration cards. Her mother stayed there for the rest of her life. She was already old. They didn't take her away. She died at her daughter's place.

Did people's opinion of Hitler change after Dresden was bombed?

Some people's opinion of Hitler fell already at the start of the war. Already at that time my father and his buddies said, "He's crazy. What does he want?" And as one country after another was taken over, they said, "This is absurd. How does he intend to keep this under control?" As the defeats piled up, public opinion against Hitler grew, but a large part of the population still trusted him, "He'll pull it off! The wonder weapons will come along! He'll defeat them yet!" Nobody thought any further about what things would be like then. The soldiers sent things home from the occupied countries, wonderful things. And that had helped the people in their duress. We had practically nothing left to eat and nothing to put on.

WERNER HASSEL

A large number of people really didn't know anything.

Born in 1920 as the son of a Center Party politician, Werner Hassel grew up in Leobschütz, a small town in Upper Silesia. Even though he listened to BBC broadcasts both at home and in the military during the war and was stationed in Poland, he says he did not know about the mass murder of Jews.

I come from a family that had always been involved in Center Party politics, that was a Catholic party. My father was highly involved. In addition to this, he was a city council member. He gave speeches to the party and before elections. My father's [main profession] was rector of a large school. At that time he had been the head of a school of continuing education for apprentices in Upper Silesia. He was a very well-known figure. They didn't always deal with such figures in a very relaxed way back then, but [this status] also offered a certain degree of protection.

We lived at the time in Upper Silesia, in a county seat with 15,000 inhabitants. It was a very interesting town, a prosperous and attractive town. [After the Nazis came to power,] the times were rather difficult for all those who were of a different opinion. My father was the only one in the entire town who never said "Heil Hitler." The words never left his mouth. But he was also so well-known that one couldn't give him a whole lot of trouble. He was no do-gooder, but he had done a lot for the town.

Nevertheless, he had been involved in a lot. [He was constantly under surveillance.] You never knew who it might be when the doorbell rang. The maid would go to the door first. If there was a march, for example, we children were not allowed to touch the curtains [to look out on the street]. There was always somebody with a leather trench coat standing there in the hallway. And, especially when there were two or three people at our place, there would be several people standing outside in front of our house [from the Gestapo]. We children had to go to bed early, but we knew that those guys in the leather trench coats were still standing there. That was how the surveillance of my family began.

Although I had a sheltered childhood, there was always something of a feeling of fear, because one knew that if you were picked up you would never come back. And then we heard for the first time about the concentration camps. I had already known about them for a long time, but knew nothing [in specific]. For us they were jails where they sent people. What actually happened there was something we didn't know. [The Nazis] also observed who went to church and who didn't go to church. They made note of this, but it wasn't ever used negatively against them somehow.

We also had a lawyer [among our acquaintances], who was a Jew, Dr. Luft. He had been slipped into a factory where they made submarine parts as a supposed non-Jew. I only learned about this later on. Because one heard at the time that he had left town and wouldn't come back again. In reality, he was still here but working in the factory, and there wasn't a soul who knew this except for my father and a couple of other people who were protecting him. Later, [after the war,] Luft became a justice official in Hesse.

Basically, this was a difficult time, and also for us boys. But as a youth, you don't take things so seriously that you only go around with your head down. It wasn't like that. We still played outside. We had bikes and rode around on them like crazy. We had wonderful surroundings. There was a fear there, an uncertain future, but it was an interesting time that I wouldn't have wanted to miss.

[When I was drafted into the army,] I was in Görlitz [today divided between Germany and Poland] for four weeks of basic training, and after that I was transferred to Poland. It was bitterly cold. While we were standing around outside, the sergeant came out and yelled to us, "Who can type?" There were a whole lot of us who could do that. "Who can take stenography?" There were also a few who could. "Who can do both?" I was the only one. That day marked the start of a string of luck for me. I got an office job. From that day on, I neither held a weapon nor anything like that in my hands. I wrote. I began with weekly reports and duty rosters, which I did well enough. After that I was given some special tasks.

What did people know about the mass murder of the Jews?

The soldiers out there on the front knew effectively nothing about the concentration camps and the mass murder of the Jews. I cannot imagine that [they had known]. I would have been aware of that. Especially since I came from a very different political past, I would have heard about that. A large number of people really didn't know anything. I myself didn't know where Sachsenhausen was or Auschwitz. That really was only known by people with inside information. When we were in Poland, we heard absolutely nothing [about the murder of the Jews], no rumors, absolutely nothing.

There was only one single incident. After the first two or three days that I had been in the office, [which I had been transferred to], I was then sent over to another building. The place was full of mud. There were no cobblestone roads. It was all muck. When it rained, everything turned to muck. And it was there that I had my only experience. I saw how a sergeant was abusing and swearing at a man: "You bastard, you Jewish pig, lay down there on your belly." The poor man was then forced to get covered from top to bottom in the muck and grovel along and so on. That didn't sit well with me. I stood there like I was in shock, like I was petrified, [and I thought], "What the heck is happening here? He just can't do a thing like that."

So I then went back and told the master sergeant about this, how that sergeant so-and-so had just forced a man to grovel in the muck. "He can't do that!" he said. "It's a good thing that you have told me this, but otherwise [keep your mouth shut about this]."

There were perhaps a few people in the Wehrmacht who were Nazis and hated the Jews, but that was the only incident I personally experienced. I felt sorry for the man, without knowing that he was a Jew.

In regard to the invasion of Russia, there were loads of Jews there in the areas we went through, except that we didn't know it. We only noticed that there were incredibly beautiful women there and well-dressed people. The villages in Poland were something unusual, all made up of wooden cottages, which sometimes were very attractive. All the people there were Jews who had been forced to move out of the cities. At the time, we soldiers didn't give it much thought. [We merely wondered,] "Why do they make the Jews leave the cities and stick them here in these villages along the Bug?" The real soldiers didn't know about this madness.

Weren't there any rumors?

No, there weren't any rumors either. I would have heard them. Everybody was shit scared that we were heading into Russia and who knew what was going to happen then. What I heard from the officers and the generals was, "Kids, this will never end well." Those were the officers I knew, and with some of them I had very close personal contact. None of them were Nazis. They all would say only, "My God, this isn't going to end well." These were the officers, the majors, and a lieutenant colonel who belonged to the general staff, because in my job on the Bug I was attached to the general staff.

What did you know about the *Kristallnacht* pogrom in 1938?

On that day when the synagogues went up in flames, we were able to look out over the trees and the gardens and see the steeples from our window on the second floor. There was a fire alarm and the steeples were burning. You felt like you were caught in a cloud of fog, uncertain, fearful.

Something has just occurred to me. My father was not supposed to leave the apartment. But why this was the case was not explained. Our building had a garden and on the right side was a rustic fence. Next to that was a large apartment building with several families. And there was a Nazi who lived there who had passed a slip of paper under the bushes to my mother with a cross on it, which meant, "Don't go out." I don't know about all the things he had his fingers into, but, nevertheless, he would always warn my mother like that with these slips of paper.

Who participated in the pogrom?

They were all people in uniforms. There was a large store on the corner that sold clothes and all their stuff was lying in the streets and there were people standing there and watching. But, otherwise, that had all been done by people in uniforms. And then trucks arrived and the things were all loaded onto them. I don't know where they were taken. That was something that nobody could know. But, as far as I can remember, no civilians had participated in it.

Did you listen to British broadcasts during the war?

Yes, of course. We only listened to London when we listened to radio in the military. I had a "detector." Do you know what a detector is? It was this little thing. It was really, really difficult. But with care and the help of various wires, like the underwires from the bed and so on, you could get lucky and pick up a broadcast. And when you got it, you didn't touch the thing again, so that you could keep tuned into the station.

Did most people also listen to these broadcasts?

A lot of the others did, but nobody came right out and said so. There were two medical students who lived across from me. One of them listened [to these broadcasts], the other didn't. One of them was "colored brown" [a Nazi], the other wasn't. To pick up London, that was an experience. That was great with those little detectors. All of a sudden it was there. You could also get Cologne. That was no problem. But to receive London, that was only possible with those wires from the bed. Across the street, the idiots set up large loudspeakers and let Adolf blather. It was a crazy time, a sad time.

+6+

Everyday Life and Hearing About Mass Murder

HILTRUD KÜHNEL
That was his hobby, measuring skulls.

Born in 1920 and raised in Frankfurt as the daughter of a school principal and Center Party politician, Hiltrud Kühnel studied dentistry during the war at the University of Frankfurt. Her anatomy professor told her class about his research on the skulls of Jews who had been killed in concentration camps. She also heard about the gassing of Jews in concentration camps from Catholic clergymen and other friends who visited her family's home.

My father was a Center Party deputy in the state parliament and was very much opposed to National Socialism. In school, as long as he was in charge, "The Horst Wessel Song" [the Nazi Party anthem] was never sung, the hand was never raised in the Nazi salute, rather only the "Deutschlandslied" [the German national anthem]. In September 1933, my father was fired as principal for being politically unreliable, and we actually had it rather rough.

185

My parents tried to keep me from hearing too much about it, but you still noticed a great deal. My mother continued to have a good deal of contact with the wives of Jewish chemists. We had a big circle of acquaintances. And Mrs. H., who was Jewish, wore her Star of David and that didn't bother Mom at all. My mother still went to visit her across the street. And Mrs. H. would say, "For heaven's sake, Mrs. E., you'll get into trouble!" And to that my mother would respond, "We already are." So Mom kept right on doing that.

My father had it very, very hard. He received almost no money. He had to do tutoring work in order to feed us. And we were always being watched. At night, the SS or the Gestapo would sneak around outside our house in order to see if anything was going on. Evenings, when we thought now we can go to bed, we would hear them snooping around. They were a loud bunch. Every four weeks, the SA would come to us on those so-called "stew Sundays" and ring the doorbell and look in our kitchen to see whether we were also cooking stew as we were supposed to do.

We were always afraid that my father would be taken away. And if it was to become critical, my father and mother agreed that whenever they would come by—for example, they often came by in the evening to check on whether a secret gathering was taking place at our house—that my mom would leave the light for the entrance door on if my father wasn't there. And, therefore, my father would know that at the time it was better for him not to come home and that he should stay away for a while longer until those characters left.

And, if you wanted to study at the university, you had to join the Labor Service. Otherwise, you weren't allowed to study. When I was in the Labor Service, one was supposed to show up and salute the flag. But I never saluted the flag. In fact, I never raised my hand [in the Hitler salute]. The female Labor Service leader would then punish me by having me clean the latrines. It was disgusting. She would constantly be calling me in and asking me about my views.

And then, when I began to study at the university, I would always have to pass a special test before I would be allowed to progress on to the next semester. We were the only seven dentistry students in Frankfurt.

What kind of political views did people have in your neighborhood?

We didn't have much contact with them. The good acquaintances we had stood by us. But, as for the others, we no longer had any contact with them. We were somewhat isolated. We did, though, still continue to have some really good old friends who shared our political views and we would get together with them. And, for that reason, the Gestapo would keep coming by and roam around through our house because they wanted to see whether they could find something so as to arrest my father.

Did you ever listen to foreign radio broadcasts at home?

Always. We were always doing that. That was the English radio station, the BBC. We did that secretively, that is to say very quietly. That was another reason why the Gestapo and the SS were always checking out our house; that they might perhaps hear something and then pin something on us. I only remember that we were very afraid that my father would be sent off to a concentration camp.

Back then, what did you imagine concentration camps to be?

Extermination camps. That's what I imagined concentration camps to be.

You didn't simply think of something like a labor camp?

No, no. Extermination camps! You knew that was what they were. Hence, if someone says today that he had never known that, it is absolutely not true.

Do you mean to say that not only you knew about that but others did as well?

That was known by others as well.

How did one know that?

From the circle of acquaintances that you had, from the clergy and from good friends who shared our political views. It was talked around about what they were doing there. Those were indeed real extermination camps.

When did you hear about extermination camps for the first time? Can you give an exact date?

That must have been 1938 to 1939 at the time of *Kristallnacht*. That was in November 1938. We were sent home from school. That morning our school principal said to us, "Please go home immediately, all of you. Horrible things have happened." I had to go back home with my schoolmate, from Frankfurt to where I lived in Höchst. Anyway, that was horrible for me. They had taken the cakes from Jewish pastry shops and thrown them onto the street. They cut open the Jewish families' down blankets. There were a lot of Jews in Frankfurt. You could see the feathers floating around in the street. The cigars, the pipes from the tobacco shops, everything was lying in the street. The windowpanes were smashed in. I came home crying. We really could only cry. And then we said, "Those are beasts. Human beings don't do things like that."

But that isn't exactly the extermination of human beings.

No, but that was the beginning of the disregard of a race. They classified them as inferior. I would say that is when one started to know about it all. But, for heaven's sake, you weren't allowed to talk about it.

But how did one hear about it then, if one wasn't allowed to talk about it?

For example, from a clergyman who was often at our place and from some others, whose names I can't recall, who said, "We heard that . . ." That's how.

But what had they heard exactly?

That the Jews were being gassed, and the foreigners. Indeed, one knew about the gassing.

One heard this expression exactly?

Gassing. Yes.

That they were being gassed, you heard this from clergymen? In your own home?

Yes, in our home. I already said that this was a kind of meeting place that the Nazis were aware of. They were aware that anti-Nazi groups were still meeting with my father.

Did you hear about this from the clergymen yourself?

Yes. Politics was the only thing they discussed at our place, whether it was over lunch or otherwise. I can really only recall political conversations at our home.

That's how I grew up. The clergymen knew that at our place they would never be named as a traitor or anything like that because of what they had made known there.

I wonder how the clergymen got their information. Did they say how they found out?

No, they didn't tell us that. It only came up in the course of conversation as yet another atrocity that was known.

Did you also hear about it during the war as well, say in 1942 or 1943?

We heard about it then as well, only then in 1942 to 1943 in greater detail. But when it started, after the *Kristallnacht*, everyone knew that something horrible was to come. Perhaps "everyone" is an exaggeration, but at least all of those we frequently met with.

It also made the rounds at the university. I attended lectures on anatomy by Professor August Hirt, who later went to Strasbourg. He was a repulsive man. He told us that he went to concentration camps and picked out the skulls of Jews that he wanted to measure. That was his hobby, measuring skulls. When he found skulls that interested him, the Jews were killed.

And he openly mentioned this during lecture?

He openly mentioned this during lecture. There were people, students, who applauded. They thought it was wonderful.

When was it that he mentioned this during his lectures?

When did he mention this? I began studying at the university in 1940. So it must have been around 1940, 1941, 1942. He needed the skulls; that was his hobby, measuring skulls. So he went to the concentration camps and picked out skulls, even among the living. He didn't say that they had then been killed, but that was what one was given to understand. Well, if he was picking out the skulls he wanted from living people, it was clear what was up because one knows that only the skulls of dead people can be measured correctly.

Did the students talk about it?

Not all of the female students. But Waltrud and I did, and we talked about it with those who were our friends and who also held the same political views.

Did you believe all of this?

Yes. I have to say that I had never raised my hand [in the Hitler salute]. I had never said "Heil Hitler." Not even in the large May Day demonstrations when we as pupils all had to go there and the "Horst Wessel Song" was being sung. I never raised my hand and my school friends didn't either. Whenever some SA man came up to us and said, "Heil Hitler," we then turned our heads. For the times, that was rather brave, wasn't it?

RUTH HILDEBRAND
The soldiers on leave . . . did a lot of talking.

Born in 1909 and raised as the daughter of a civil servant in Berlin, Ruth Hildebrand discusses the rise of the Nazis, the treatment of Polish forced workers during the war, and how she heard about the murder of the Jews from soldiers on leave.

My father was a civil servant, a low-ranking civil servant. After World War I was over, he was in the Free Corps [until December 1920] and then went to work at the district court in Schöneberg.

I took a year of sewing lessons and a year of cooking classes here near Berlin at an estate that no longer exists. Then I worked in a flower shop. After that, I became a saleswoman and I got married in 1929.

The first time that I noticed [the Nazis] was in the winter of 1924 or the spring of 1925, when I was fifteen. I can still remember that the trees were bare when they drove through our street in a large, open truck. That's when I saw the flag for the first time. They had on those brown shirts and the swastika flag was enormous. I then asked my father [who they were]—he was a staunch German nationalist—and he said, "Those are fanatics and they will never manage to take over power."

What do you think contributed to Hitler's later success?

Above all, it was the huge unemployment—I also was unemployed. Back then the unemployed would be standing from the steps of the labor office down to the street just to collect a couple of pfennigs. But I never went there; I never collected any money. But afterward, once Hitler came to power, it was wonderful. Everybody had a job and there weren't any more unemployed people. They were happy to have a job and the foodstuffs were cheaper and the wages were raised a bit.

Somehow things were going better in the first years. It was nice that there weren't any unemployed people. But, after a while, it slowly became clear to me that Hitler was aiming at something. And then in 1938 the bomber planes of the German army flew over us and we immediately knew that sooner or later war would break out. And then it came.

What did the people around you think about Hitler and the National Socialists?

Many of them were in the party. My mother-in-law and her husband were 500 percent [Nazis]. Whenever my husband and I went over to their place and they opened the door, we would already hear Hitler and other leading Nazis giving speeches on the radio before we even came in. We would just pull the door back shut from the outside. Why should we sit down and listen to that? We were communists. My sister was one of Blomberg's secretaries. Do you know who Blomberg was? General [Werner von] Blomberg here in Berlin? He was fired by Hitler because he had married a prostitute. That came out and he was forced to go. My sister also had Nazi leanings, but not my brother-in-law.

One time, I did see Hitler very close up. My daughter was still very small. She was born in 1937, so it must have been in 1938 or it could have been in 1939. Anyway, the war hadn't started yet. [Foreign Minister Joachim von] Ribbentrop lived here in Dahlem and he had a large house and it was his birthday. I think it was April 30. I was taking a walk with my daughter and kept hearing "Heil! Heil!" And I thought, "Huh?" As I drew nearer, I saw a couple of people standing in front of a driveway and I said, "What's going on here?" "The führer is in there," [was their answer]. I got curious and remained standing there for a while, and then I saw him driving out in an open car. He had beautiful blue eyes and a suntan. Of course, the people then [cried out, "Heil Hitler!"] You had to do that, you know, because if you didn't, you would get into trouble. That was a kind of oppression from the very beginning.

One day when my husband and I were still quite young, there was a parade passing by with march music. We had been standing on the sidewalk and we wanted to get through. Then one of the men jumped out of the ranks and started toward us because we hadn't raised our hand. When the flag passed you by, you were supposed to raise your hand in the Hitler salute, but we hadn't done that. From that point on, whenever we heard marching music, we ducked into the next entryway. We avoided that "Heil Hitler" stuff whenever we could.

Then there were the demonstrations that took place on May 1, 1933. I can still remember that glorious day in May with brilliant sunshine and everybody going into the streets full of enthusiasm. But, in the years that followed, we were forced to join in and everyone would try to slink away when they could. [For example,] I remember how I was once there when [Labor Minister Robert] Ley was preaching and one person after the other was going away.

On May 23–24, 1943, when my son was just three months old, we were bombed out. Because of that, we were forced to leave Berlin as I didn't have a home anymore. We spent the first four months in East Prussia, where, from my window, I could even see the road that led to Hitler's headquarters in East Prussia. After this we were supposed to get a new apartment in Berlin, but then came the heavy attacks [on Berlin] when the Kurfürstendamm and everything were in flames and we had to leave Berlin again. Since we couldn't get another apartment because the working people who were bombed out got them first, I then joined a transport of young women and their children that went to [the town of] Guben.

But, in Guben, the air raid alarms turned out to be just like they had been in Berlin. I didn't want any more of that, so I then left the town and [found a place to stay at a farm]. There were two Polish men with us at this farm, the youngest of whom was seventeen. Like so many other Poles, they had been grabbed up by the Nazis from the streets of Poland and carted away. And [at a neighbor's place] near us there was a female Polish student who possessed nothing at all except for the dress she wore every day.

The farmers treated the Poles badly, very badly. Our farmer had once beaten another Pole with a stick because the Pole hadn't milked all of the cows and hadn't explained why. He beat him so badly that his whole arm was mangled. I heard about this from the other Poles. The older of the two Poles also told me that the very first person that he would like to kill was that farmer.

Returning to the years when you were in Berlin, what can you remember about the *Kristallnacht* pogrom of November 1938?

We had a lot of Jews living here. Certainly a number of shops were destroyed here in the Rheinstrasse since they were all in Jewish hands. The Jews were disliked because, how should I say it, everything was in Jewish hands: the large stores, the large companies, the apartment buildings. That was all in Jewish hands. [In one case there was a building] that was remodeled, with larger apartments being converted into many smaller ones. The Jew who owned the building acted in such a shameless manner that one of the neighbors took him and placed him in a bathtub full of water. Those Jews had taken a lot for themselves, although not all of them.

I knew two Jewish families. I pretty much grew up with their children. The family S. lived here on the Rheinstrasse, and the family H. lived in the same building as the mother of one of my schoolmates. My mother was very good with her hands. She knitted sweaters for the H. business. We had very friendly relations with these people.

You always had to be cautious because they [the Nazis] had informants all over the place. [For example,] there was a man living in our apartment house on the Taunusstrasse who was a civil servant but also a "golden rooster" [a party functionary] and wore a uniform. After work, he would go to the party's local headquarters as he was also our local *Blockleiter*. During air raids he would sit in the cellar with his hat pulled down so far that we couldn't see his eyes, but he was watching everybody.

Also, the people who lived above us were always giving that Jewish woman, Frau K., a hard time. One could hear through the open windows when they were cursing at her and so on. My father-in-law did this too. One time, when I said to him, "What they are doing to the Jews just isn't right," he responded, "There should be a Jew hanging from every tree."

I also saw the Jews being picked up. Nobody was allowed to go out into the streets as they were all cordoned off from one corner to the next and there were trucks waiting there [to take the Jews away]. Nobody dared to say anything. We were all standing out on the balcony; that is, all of us women, since our men were not there.

Frau K. lived in the apartment building just in front of us and she was also picked up. Her husband was a Christian and she was a Jew. When they took her away, we were all standing there on the balcony and we were all crying. Her husband could not help her and he just stood there in front of his car with his arms hanging down. After a few days, she was back again because he was a Christian.

We also had a Jew in our building who was supposed to be deported to Theresienstadt, a simple, modest man. But he took his own life by turning on the gas faucet. When the Jews who lived on our street were taken away, their midday meals were still lying on the table. After that, their apartments remained empty for months before they were rented again. They never came back.

I also knew very early on that the Jews were sent off to whatever camps. My husband was stationed at the Luftwaffe's front control center here in Berlin and the Wehrmacht was located close by. And then the soldiers on leave would go there, and of course they did a lot of talking. My husband also told me about this, but I wasn't allowed to tell anybody else. Had I done this, my husband would have been put up against the wall, I would have been sent to concentration camp, and I never would have seen the children again. One had to keep quiet.

What did you know about all of this?

Only that the Jews were being sent there. That the Jews were being gassed, they didn't say. They didn't go as far as that. The soldiers who had escorted the trains with the Jews had to get off just before the gates [of the camps], and then they rode back again with the train that was now empty. That's what they said, and my husband told me about this late one evening. It depressed him so. It weighed heavily on him, and also, of course, on me. That they were gassed came out later. It did leak out slowly, however, that they had somehow met their death there. But one did not hear anything specific.

Did you believe the rumors you heard?

That that was possible, yes. With [the Nazis], yes, most certainly. Because they, above all the SS, were rather brutal with everyone.

EKKEHARD FALTER

Rat-a-tat-tat, dead.

Born in 1925 and raised in Dresden in a middle-class family, Ekkehard Falter describes how his father spent six months in jail after being denounced by a friend for making a critical remark about the war effort, how he himself got into trouble when he was in the Hitler Youth, and how he heard from an SS man about atrocities the SS committed in Poland.

When I was sixteen [in 1942], the SS held a recruitment drive one evening in my school's gym. Since I was a blond youth, the two SS officers there worked on me to get me to make a commitment to sign up for the SS even though I was still a minor. They first tried to do this with finesse. They said it was an elite force, and that I would get a decoration if I accepted their offer to commit at that point already. But I told them, "I'll pass. I am a horse rider and I would only like to join a mounted unit." That turned out to be my salvation. Because they then said to me that I was disowning the state, but they didn't follow up on this indirect threat.

Anyway, at the beginning of 1943 when I was seventeen, my cousin and I and two of our friends decided to stop going along with the Hitler Youth. We stopped wearing our uniforms when we reported to duty; we would turn right when the section leader would tell us to turn left. He then soon reported us and we were placed before a Hitler Youth court. Although I ended up being demoted and lost my leadership position, I didn't care.

Nevertheless, legal proceedings were then filed against us with the public prosecutor's office. Altogether there were five of us in this episode with the Hitler Youth when we demonstrated officially that we were no longer going to toe the line. But we ended up talking our way out of it all by claiming that we were only playing a practical joke on our Hitler Youth leader. Had we presented it as political opposition, it would have turned out worse for us. Fortunately, I was soon drafted into the army. I got my high school diploma on an emergency basis, was inducted, and never heard anything about the matter again.

Why had you done all that? Had it been just for fun or for some other reason?

Out of opposition. We simply didn't want to go along. We didn't put on our uniforms anymore. We didn't want to submit to this regime anymore. You can well imagine that by that time one was starting to have a different point of view.

And, whatever the case was, we were soon going to have to die a "hero's death" anyway.

My father was terrified over the situation. In 1941, while he was playing cards one evening at a local bar here in Dresden, he had made a critical remark when a man came by with a collection box asking for donations for the Mothers Relief Organization. What my old man had said was, "Please excuse me. That will all be going just to support the war anyway." That very night at four o'clock my father was arrested and he was then held in custody for six months while awaiting trial.

It was touching to see how my aunt went about trying to secure his release. She was the proprietor of a well-known wine bar in Dresden and she had a lot of connections. So it ended up that my father got a merciful judge and was acquitted. It was all worked out over connections. There was a large table of regulars in her bar. So she told them all about her brother-in-law's fate and then some of these people from that table intervened on his behalf. The mayor of Dresden himself even frequented this bar.

And then came my affair, which naturally upset my father terribly.

How was your father's arrest carried out?

They came early in the morning, at four. He had arrived home at half past ten, and by four o'clock the police were here, the regular police, and took him under arrest. He was allowed to get dressed, and then they disappeared. I was already sound asleep, but then my mother came and told me that my father had just been arrested. At the time, it wasn't at all clear to us why. He had not told us what had happened earlier. He had only been a bit tipsy and had wondered what that guy had wanted with that box anyway. After all, it was just going to the war effort anyway and not to people who were in need.

We were never allowed to visit my father. He was held in investigative detention and sat in a cell with other people. One had deserted and the other had somehow knocked a weapon out of the hands of a noncommissioned officer who was threatening him. That was a very serious offense against his superior. Both had been condemned to death. And so my father sat in the jail on the Münchner Platz until, half a year later, he was acquitted by this older gentleman, a normally trained judge who had no special connections to the party.

The man who had blown the whistle on him had been playing cards with him at his table and had known him for years. The people who had come along with the collection box hadn't known who he was. Thus it had to have been a friend. And we know in fact who he was. We found this out while the war was still going on. When my father got out of jail, he took him to task and the man apologized.

He had been a civil servant himself and had thought that since others had also heard what my father had said, he had needed to cover himself.

What was it like in school? Were the teachers strong supporters of National Socialism?

There were some nazified teachers. In 1933, when I was eight years old, I was standing around during recess and yelled out, "Red Front!" Nobody in my family was in the Communist Party or the Social Democratic Party. It was just a gag. But then the teacher came by [and heard what I said]. I knew that he was super brown [i.e., a huge Nazi supporter]. So that very afternoon he went to my father and said, "Take better care of your son. He did this and that." For him, it wasn't just a foolish, boyish prank.

So one knew already in 1933 which teachers were more inclined to National Socialism?

One knew that. There was this one teacher, an English teacher, a young man. We were eleven or twelve at the time and already at the Gymnasium. Thus it had to have been about 1937 or so. There were still Jews here. And if one of them at our school would say that he didn't know something, this teacher would say, "A typical representative of your race." Given the way boys are, that was then reason enough to beat him up. The weaker ones are victimized.

I noticed how Jewish classmates were gradually withdrawn [from the school] or pulled out by their relatives, but the disappearance of the Jews is not something we took note of officially. I have to tell you honestly that I really didn't know that the Jews were deported. I only came to know that first in 1943 when I was drafted into the Labor Service. What happened was that we were called on to dig out an excavation pit for an airplane hangar. Jewish men were working nearby and the camp where they were interned was located near our Labor Service barracks. Using our shovels, we acted as the guards for the Jewish workers. They were confined, but they would receive something to eat. They were conspicuously isolated from us and we weren't allowed to talk to them. They also had Jewish supervisory personnel. We were under a certain amount of pressure. We had to fulfill a certain amount of work, and so did the Jews.

That was when it first came to my attention that Jews were being incarcerated for racial reasons. It then became clear to me. After half a year I left the place. I don't know what happened to the Jews after the excavation pit was finished, whether they were sent back to a concentration camp or whatever else.

Did the general population know about the concentration camps? Were there rumors?

One knew that there were concentration camps. The Dresden members of the Communist Party were incarcerated at the Hohenstein Castle. In 1933, after the Nazis took power, they were collected there, and the population of Dresden knew that there was a concentration camp where members of the Communist Party were incarcerated. At that time there weren't any concentration camps where Jews were being held, unless they were politicians. Only in 1943 did it become clear to me that Jews were being incarcerated in large numbers. They disappeared without any ado, picked up one by one. I knew that there was a special stratum of Jews here in Dresden that was richer than others who had pensions or had emigrated. But, in the inner city, there were also poorer Jews from sections of the city where less affluent people lived because rents were cheaper. They didn't have the money to emigrate.

Were there rumors about concentration camps where Jews were held under poor conditions?

That is a very complicated question. We boys didn't know about it. Whether some fathers knew about it is to be assumed, but they didn't talk about it. They [probably thought] that young people shouldn't be burdened by it as much as possible.

Here in our area we had a lot of prominent people from the arts and industry who frequented the local spas. A large proportion of the spa guests were Jewish. Many people who worked in the spas like the Weisser Hirsch became affluent due to the spa guests, and they opposed these Nazi policies. I can remember that the local Nazi Party headquarters had a lot of difficulties here.

My grandfather had a lot to do with Jewish spa guests, and that is something I will never forget. In 1935, a grocery store where we often shopped displayed a huge sign that read, "Jews are not wanted [here]." And then my grandfather said, "International Jewry won't like that. That'll have dire consequences." So here at the Weisser Hirsch, where people earned a living from the Jews, from the spa guests, one did not have much sympathy for this policy of persecuting the Jews.

When did you first hear about the concentration camps and the mass murder of the Jews?

We've come back to this question. I've wondered about that often myself. I was in Pilsen [now in the Czech Republic] with a wounded knee that I sustained at the front and it had to be operated on. This was when the war was ending and the Russians were coming ever closer to Pilsen. Lying next to me was an SS sergeant. He had been shot in the leg and was getting ever more uncomfortable. "I've got to get out of here," he would say to me.

At night he would tell me about things they had done. Because it was all so horrible I couldn't sleep anymore. It would be a chapter in and of itself, and I don't now want to talk about what he and his combat unit did to the population, like hoisting them up into the air with their feet and then shooting them.

He told me that he didn't understand how that could have happened. He said that there had been people with them who had passed their university qualification exams and had come from solid middle-class homes, but in only half a year they had been reeducated to the point that they no longer were bothered by what they were doing. [For example,] they had rounded up all the people in a Polish village, women and children, locked them up in a church, and then shot at them from the church's gallery before setting the church on fire. "We then lay around the church in radiant sunshine while the church burned. Those who had not gotten out were screaming, and then the door suddenly opened and a small child came out. One guy then got up, rat-a-tat-tat, dead. [Having been involved in all of this,] can you imagine that I am now going to remain here?"

And then, with the pin that had been just implanted in his leg and in a cast, he got up and took off. He even told me about things that were still worse. I don't want to talk about them here. They are that dreadful.

STEFAN REUTER

One heard in communist circles that numbers of Jews were being gassed.

Born in 1920 and raised in a working-class family in Berlin, Stefan Reuter describes the communist resistance in Berlin and his Jewish wife, who went into hiding.

I come from a relatively simple family. My father was a worker who helped construct the Berlin subway and then went to work for the Reichsbahn [the national railway]. He was a lineman. After the war he worked in an office at the Bundesbahn [the West German railway] and he ended his career with a red cap as a supervisor at the Zoo Train Station. That is to say, he reached civil service status. My mother came to Berlin from Pomerania as a young girl at the age of seventeen. For fifteen years she worked as a maid, mainly in Jewish households.

I had only an elementary school education, but I continued to go to school until I was nearly thirty. I attended mainly evening courses and furthered my education until I was able to open my own carpenter's workshop in 1949. I then built it up until it had more than thirty employees and it was rather successful.

I wasn't quite thirteen when the Nazis took power. I experienced myself how the SA marched through the area, from the Brandenburg Gate down into the Zillestrasse. And they put a tank in the street where I lived because there were so many communists living there. I then cried bitter tears because I knew that another era had begun.

As a twelve- or thirteen-year-old, I had belonged to a sports club. I was in the VfL Charlottenburg in the Berlin Gymnasts Association and also in Die Fichte, which was a communist youth sports association. Through my involvement with these organizations I experienced and was aware of what was going on against the Nazis.

When I began my apprenticeship in 1936, the journeyman working with me was a communist who had been in a jail in Brandenburg. The Nazis had arrested him because he was a communist. He died about ten years ago and always remained a communist. Whoever went through this school remained a communist his entire life. He really looked after me and influenced my life to a great extent as well. I was never in the party. I was never in the Hitler Youth. I wasn't in anything and I still got through it all.

When I had to stop working at my original firm, I immediately got a new position. To do this I first went to an office located on our street here in Grunewald to introduce myself. When I entered the room, a big Nazi clad in brown was sitting there. He was a real big shot. When I said to him, "I'm not in the party," he responded, "it doesn't interest me at all whether you're in the party or not. I'd like to hire you. I have the impression that you're capable."

Do you remember anything about the deportations of the Jews in Berlin?

I remember the deportations because the company where I did my apprenticeship was on Korunen Strasse in Charlottenburg, and a whole lot of Jews lived in the Korunen Strasse. They were dealers of old furniture and the like. There I experienced, as an apprentice, how a big truck drove up with soldiers and took the Jews out of the buildings and carted them away. That was something I saw myself. In fact, I saw it happen twice. But I had no idea what then happened to them.

Did you then talk about this with other people?

Only in passing. [We said things like:] "Some people just came here and took away the Jews. But what's going to happen to them, and where are they taking them?" It was said that they were taken off to a concentration camp. But what was a concentration camp? Actually, it wasn't discussed very much. I think a whole lot of people were afraid and didn't want to talk about it. I myself was rather indifferent and didn't think about it very much. My mother was a cleaning lady and worked for Jews, but otherwise we didn't have much contact with them. It was only later through my wife that I had a lot more contact with Jews.

My first wife was a Jew. I got to know her in February 1942 when I was a soldier and had returned from Königsberg to a hospital in Berlin. She was living illegally in Berlin. [Prior to this,] when she was living with her aunt and a cousin, she had received a notice from the police telling her that she should pack a suitcase and go to the police station. She put a note on her suitcase saying that she was going to take her life and left the suitcase behind and took off. Then she walked up the Kaiserdamm to the Witzleben Bridge, tore off her star, and let it fall on the railway tracks below. Having done that, she was now illegal.

I got to know her ten days after that through old communist connections. A female friend of mine got in touch with me and said, "We have here with us a certain Lotte, and she's now illegal. She has a German boyfriend who has just been killed in Russia"—it was strictly forbidden for a Jewish girl to have a German boyfriend—"and she would like to talk to you because you were also in Russia. Would that be possible? His parents have just got his belongings back, but she still can't believe it."

After that I met with her in my friend's apartment, and she told me about everything. She asked me whether this was possible. I told her that, of course, it was possible, and that there was no point in her hoping that he would come back. She was extremely sad about this, and so I said to her, "Maybe you will meet a man in your life who you'll love just as much." And, after this, I was together with this woman for over thirty years.

While she was living illegally [in Berlin], I met her every now and then. I was a decorated soldier. I had the Iron Cross, the silver Wounded Badge, and the [infantry] Assault Badge, which you got when you had been severely wounded. That all provided a certain amount of protection for me when I met with her. She was living and working illegally in Berlin at the time, working for the Communist Party as a Jew.

What was she doing with this illegal work?

She had connections with Czechoslovakia. She distributed fliers and things like that. She continued working with all those people. Above all, and what was extremely important, was that she pulled her cousin and her aunt through it all as they were also living in hiding. They all survived; all three survived.

How was that organized so that nobody caught on?

That was very difficult for my former wife back then because she looked very Jewish. I would say at the time to her, "You look like Rosa Luxemburg." But she made it through. She put on glasses and had her hair colored blond. She had to change her looks somewhat. She was very attentive and took care that she didn't run into anybody who knew her. After the war was over, we moved into an apartment and finally got married several years later in 1953. After that, I learned everything about how she had gone into hiding and how she had done all that.

She had lived here for a while and then there for a while. For example, she had lived for three weeks at an opera singer's place. He was in the party. During the denazification after the war, she denazified him by telling them that she was a Jew and that he had helped to pull her through. At the time, she had to pay for a lot with her body where she lived. It was a very, very hard time. She was extremely strong and clever and also had the support of communists who were still in Berlin at the time.

It was also a difficult time because there were Jewish spies for the Gestapo, among them Helen Kübler. Helen Kübler was a Jew who ran around Berlin trying to find Jews and then blew the whistle on them. While she was living illegally [in Berlin], my wife had been afraid that Kübler would come and notice her because she looked so Jewish.

During the war did you hear about what was happening to the Jews either from your wife or from your other contacts?

No, as crazy as it is. Sure, it was talked about, but I didn't have any solid proof. At the time when my wife was to be picked up, one heard in communist circles that numbers of Jews were being gassed. There were these rumors, but there was no direct proof. After all, one can talk a lot. My thoughts leaned more toward the view that it could really have been possible.

Did you yourself have ties to the communists?

I had connections through my journeyman. I was once in Czechoslovakia and picked up some fliers. I was still an apprentice at the time, still a young fellow, and didn't think much about it. A communist took me over the border on his motorcycle. He had a BMW with a sidecar, which I sat in. We were there one day and the next day we came back. After that, I didn't have anything more to do with the distribution of the fliers.

I have to be honest with you. Even though I had been involved in this and had worked for the communists, I was, nevertheless, not very interested in politics. For me, my work and my advancement were more important.

ERNST WALTERS

Gassed. They were killed and soap was made from the bones.

Born in 1911 and raised in a family of miners, Ernst Walters became a Nazi Party cell leader in 1937 in Schwalbach, a small town in the Saar region.

I was born and raised in the Saar region. I was the tenth child in a family of twelve children. After World War I, my father, who was a Center Party man, gave an address to five hundred workers at a mine and got into a quarrel with a priest [over what he had told them]. For this reason my father left the Center Party and joined the Social Democratic Party. SPD [members] were excommunicated [by the Catholic Church], my father among them. This caused me enormous difficulties in school, but I still managed to leave with a good diploma.

I got to know the mines, even though I had wanted to become something totally different. In mining, men were beneath livestock. There was such exploitation and hazardous conditions, and the number of unemployed [in Germany] was around 8–9 million. And it was really tough even for those who were working. If they weren't productive enough, they landed on the street. Anyway, all of this injustice that I experienced in my training and in my experiences in mining had an effect on me politically.

In 1935 the Saarland was to take a vote to determine if they wanted to merge with Germany. That was the referendum, a yes or no question. You know how the population voted. The election went 98 percent for merging with Germany. This was not really because they were voting for Hitler. Rather, at the time, it was about getting out of this slavery and exploitation. My father, who was already political, told me, "Keep your hands out of politics. If Hitler comes to power, there'll be a war." He knew more than I did. But, as a young man, I hadn't seen much of politics. I had only seen that Germany was in a better situation, that the people there were less exploited, especially economically.

At the time, I was in the SPD's paramilitary organization, the Reichsbanner, which was the counterpart to the SA of the NSDAP. So I was politically active. And because of this, I was also in danger of being sent to a concentration camp. An old school friend who was working at the time in the mayor's office—he had sat next to me on the school bench for eight years and I had sometimes helped him out physically because he had polio—then came to me and said, "Ernst, listen to me. The party is opening up. Ernst, it's your turn. Join the party." He was [the party's local] business leader and he was the right hand man of the local *Ortsgruppenleiter* [branch leader] of the Nazi Party. So I then became a member of the party. [But] I wasn't there with all my heart. That will be seen later. Anyway, in 1936, he had me appointed block leader [of my town].

What was the name of the town?

Schwalbach. It had 10,000–12,000 inhabitants. It's near Saarlouis and there were five cell leaders. A cell leader had about four block leaders under him. The block leaders were local authorities. We wore the same uniforms as Dr. Goebbels. And then, in 1937, I became a cell leader. That was a big honor to be able to go to the party congress in Nuremberg for free.

What kind of functions did the block leaders and cell leaders have?

The block leader was lower down than the cell leader. The block leader was more of an assistant to the cell leader, who had more authority. If newlyweds wanted a marriage loan, they had to get a certificate stating that they had a clean political record, and that was something the cell leader did. He had the power to say yes or no. I said yes to everybody. But later I did some things for which I would have been shot had I been found out.

There were a lot of denunciations in the Third Reich. Were these handled by the party or by the Gestapo and the police?

That was all done by the party, not the police. No, no. The police were friends and helpers. Here, in the entire town, there was just one policeman. [There were] no Gestapo men.

If one wanted to denounce someone, how did that work? Who would one go to? To the cell leader or the *Ortsgruppenleiter* or to the block leader?

That was during the war. I'm talking about the time before that. I busied myself with marriage loans. Or, when people wanted to join the party, I would be asked, "Who do we have here? Is he reliable?" [An applicant] couldn't have a criminal record. If somebody had been in jail because he had committed a theft or had beaten somebody nearly to death, he wouldn't be accepted into the party.

Did you make it to *Ortsgruppenleiter?*

No. Then came the war, and it had been expected already that this would start. Near to us on the Saar they were building the "Western Wall" [line of fortifications] That all had to be organized from Saarlouis to Saarbrücken in three days. And that then became the function we had.

Hitler had been given a blank check from all of Germany for the war because he had said, "Give me five years and you won't recognize Germany anymore." And that's the way it was with the building up [of Germany]. There had been 8–9 million unemployed people and that was all done away with quickly. They were all called up for the Reich Labor Service. Everybody was busy. Nobody was unemployed anymore. People who had gone hungry found work. But nobody had thought that this would lead to war. My father knew better, but not the masses. The masses had seen that they were better off economically, and that was the main thing. And then, later on, they even had fun in this: the Young People, the dispatching of people to the countryside [to help with the harvest], the Strength through Joy program, the vacation trips. The little guy was able to get something for himself, later on even the Volkswagen. The people were at work. It was all a lot of fun. I myself had a motorcycle and I earned a lot of money. When the war broke out, I was still a member of the National Socialist Motor Vehicle Corps.

Were you drafted immediately?

No. I first became a soldier in 1940 after the western campaign was already over. Everything had gone quickly until 1940, and then I became a soldier. At first I was in the infantry in Wiesbaden, and then I attended a special training course for infantry engineers because they needed people who knew something about mining. From there, when it was finished, I was transferred to Bucharest because of [my ability] in the French language. I was the only person in the entire battalion who could speak French. Under Hitler, foreign languages were forbidden—there had been no foreign languages in the Gymnasiums. As they told me, "If you know how to speak French, you'll learn Romanian quickly as well."

When exactly was that?

That was in 1942. All the things I experienced in Bucharest! There had been a roundup and the whole street was full of people: older women, older men, and children with tiny bags. But they didn't have any baggage and there weren't any twenty- or thirty-year-old men with them. And then they were loaded onto a freight train. That was at the gara du nord, which was the train station [in Bucharest]. And then I passed by and I asked myself, "What's going on here?" The people were being guarded by the SS. They were Jews. One saw that because of their noses. Wherever the German troops went, the first thing they did was pick up Jews. It was like that everywhere. Wherever they were spread out throughout all of Europe, the Jews were picked up.

Anyway, I was working at the Wehrmacht transport control, and since I am not blind, I was worried [about what I had seen]. At that time, however, I still didn't know where they were being taken. But I found this out later on.

[After I had been in Romania for a while,] I was transferred to the military command at Saarbrücken, to the Reich Rail Service Directorate at Saarbrücken. That could have been in May 1942. Just to explain, everything that was transported went over the Wehrmacht. It was our job to give instructions to the Reich Rail Service Directorate concerning things like the train wagons and other things related to the train transports. That's why it was called the command. I was in [department] 4B, which was primarily for the hospital trains, unloading them, distributing the wounded to the military hospitals. We dealt with the area here from the Eifel: Bitburg, Mayen, Trier, Koblenz.

Were there also Jewish transport trains?

Yes. Those were [called] Stalag. Have you ever heard the word Stalag? The concentration camps were also called Stalags. The trains were also called this. These trains of Jews were loaded, for example, in France. I have to explain this so you know how this worked in technical railway terms.

You now have twelve states in Germany, or however many altogether. That's how it was with the Reich Rail Service Directorates. There were also, I believe, twelve of those, such as Cologne, Saarbrücken, or Frankfurt. Every Reich Rail Service Directorate involved a handover. When train no. 3 passed through the different directorates according to its schedule, the personnel would then be changed. This means that they didn't travel from Kiev to here with the same personnel. They don't do that today either. So when they went through another district, another directorate, they would then change the personnel.

Let's say there was a Stalag train coming from France. . . . When it reached Saarbrücken, it was then handed over. We always got a copy of [its schedule]. So when I had such a train, I would know about it in advance and I would then make the necessary arrangements, for example, provisions and so on.

Where were these trains going? Auschwitz?

With the destination of Auschwitz? I didn't know that. I didn't even know the destination for the other types of transports.

When did you first become aware about the fate of the Jews?

That was already in 1935, at the time the Saar region was annexed to Germany.

When you were working with these trains in Saarbrücken in 1942, 1943, did you have any thoughts about what would happen to the Jews?

I now have to tell you something here. [During the war] my parents [were evacuated and] were in Hameln and I somehow got the news that they were there. Since I had my motorcycle, I decided to drive there—I even had somebody riding on the back of the motorcycle with me. And then on the way back, we drove through Thuringia. I don't know what town it was, as I didn't take notice of it. But, anyway, we made a stop there and the place was stinking: "What is that smell?" "Over there is a concentration camp, that's where the corpses are being burned, where soap is being made from the Jews."

In the concentration camps, [there were] Jews, and not only Jews. There were also communists. And there were also some in our town who disappeared. There were some who disappeared who were sick. That [all] was managed by the party. The party had them disappear.

You mean the handicapped?

Yes, and epileptics and the like. Those kinds of sick people. They were all [gone]. That was well-known. Today nobody wants to admit to having known about it. But they did know about it.

What was it that they knew about?

That they were being sent to concentration camps.

The Jews or the handicapped or both?

Yes, all of them. The Jews were also arrested in the exact same way. They were gone. I was in a town where one knew everybody. There were two Jewish families. They were also suddenly gone. Did they flee? I was also in the soccer club and we had a Jew there, a soccer player. He was a baker by profession. He came from a neighboring town, and then he came to our town. He was then exposed, and then he was also arrested, because he was a Jew. But where was he sent to? The people also knew about that.

You said that everybody knew about it but later denied this and said, "No, we didn't know about it." Was it discussed among the population that the Jews were being annihilated?

One knew about it.

Did they somehow hear about it or see it?

Let's say not just Jews. Others were arrested too.

Right, but the Jews were not just arrested, they were also annihilated.

There was an only son in our town. He was a proud young man who had been called up into the SS, and he was in a concentration camp. The young man simply didn't go along, and he was shot as an SS man. And that was also known to us in our town.

But where the Jews were concerned, did they talk about that? Many people say that nobody talked about it.

They're lying.

You said that everybody knew about it?

Yes, everybody.

How was that? Did people talk about it?

Yes, of course. People were arrested and sent to concentration camps. The handicapped, the sick . . .

And you said that they knew that the Jews, the bones, were being made into soap?

That was talked about among the soldiers, that they were being gassed.

They said that they were gassed? They had also said that?

Gassed. They were killed, and soap was made from the bones. The people were nothing more than that.

Wasn't it especially dangerous to talk about that?

It wasn't dangerous.

It wasn't dangerous?

No.

Weren't people afraid that Gestapo officers would be there?

They weren't there with us in our town. There was no Gestapo there.

EFFIE ENGEL

[The BBC] also confirmed it, and with rather exact information.

Born in 1921 and raised in a working-class family with communist leanings in Dresden, Effie Engel describes how her cousin was arrested and sent to a concentration camp and the way that she learned about the mass murder of the Jews near the end of the war.

In 1933, I was twelve years old. I noticed that something had changed when my father came back from a large metal workers demonstration directed against the Nazis. Like many of the demonstrators, he was horribly beaten up by the SA. The metal workers association had called the demonstration to protest Hitler's seizure of power. I can still remember that when he came home all black and blue, my mother cursed up a storm because he had gone there in the first place. At the time she was very nonpolitical. So that was actually my first impression [of the new era].

What was it like in your school? Did anything change there?

The progressive teachers in our school all left and we got a number of new teachers. In my last two years of school, we got some teachers who had already been reprimanded. The fascists allowed them to be reinstated if they thought they were no longer compromised by anything else. But I also knew two teachers who never got a job again in the entire Hitler period. They had to sell postcards to get by. I still know these people. As children, we had actually liked those two teachers who were never reinstated very much. They had taught us a lot and their biology classes had been very interesting.

Our homeroom teacher was one who had been reprimanded and reinstated. He was a former Gymnasium teacher who had been transferred to an elementary school against his will. This was a demotion and a kind of punishment for him.

What about the other teachers, the National Socialist teachers?

Well, I only had one of those. He was in the SA and came to school in his uniform. I couldn't stand him. In part, we couldn't stand him because he was so loud and crude.

Did you have any Jewish classmates?

No, there weren't any. I lived in the Dresden working-class suburb of Übiger. Most of the Jews were shopkeepers and salesmen and few were workers. So we didn't have any of them with us because of their position in society. I didn't know any [Jews] there.

Did you know any workers who were arrested or interrogated?

Yes, certainly. I knew many from our suburb. Among others was my cousin, whom I got along with very well. He was in the SAB, which had splintered off from the SPD [Social Democratic Party] because the SPD was too reconciliatory and, in their opinion, had helped Hitler come to power. He got arrested. In '33, a whole lot of the members of this working-class party from our suburb were arrested, above all those who had held some kind of leadership function in the party.

At first, my cousin hid out at a friend's place. They already knew that it was dangerous for them, because the SA had been marching around grabbing up people from their homes and hauling them off. So my cousin went into hiding, and then the Nazis took his mother into custody, the so-called *Sippenhaft* [a kind of special arrest for family members]. I can still remember this as a child. Then the Nazis loaded all the people they had arrested in two large, open trucks and carted them off to an old castle in Überberg. My aunt, his mother, was one of them, and she remained there for two days.

I can still remember that my mother became incensed about this and said, "That's outrageous. They're keeping them there and they're not getting anything to eat. They can't even go to the toilet." It was absolutely awful.

My aunt had a weak heart and she was extremely worked up. Her son then worried that she wouldn't be able to cope with this and he turned himself in voluntarily. We thought this was a mistake. In the end they would have certainly let the old woman go because she didn't have anything to do with it. Anyway, he turned himself in and consequently ended up at the concentration camp in the Hohenstein castle. Already before this he had been badly mistreated here in Dresden. My aunt couldn't bear it all and she didn't even go to visit him. My mother had always done that. She would go to visit him and try to bring him something to eat or some fresh underwear.

[During his interrogation,] he was supposed to testify about who his comrades were, but he only told them that they wouldn't get anything from him. And so, among other things, the Nazis broke all of his fingers. Afterward, his fingers were bent and his joints were damaged. At any rate, they beat him up terribly. After this they sent him to Hohenstein, to that concentration camp, and he was held there for about a year and a half. Things didn't go very well for him there either. All kinds of harassment and beatings went on there too. He was my favorite cousin, and so, as a child, we said, "The [Nazis] can only be bad people."

Did you hear anything about parties and organizations that went underground and continued to exist after 1933?

Yes. I had heard about that. They all knew one another from their work and they continued to meet together. But I only know specifically about the efforts of the SAB, because of my cousin's involvement. And what I know is that this group also produced [anti-Nazi] pamphlets. My mother had told them that they could produce some of them at our place, and so they came to us and wrote their pamphlets and leaflets on a typewriter. Even though my mother was not very active politically, she was outraged by what they had done to my cousin. Then one day, she said, "No, it's too dangerous. They'll lock everybody up. Get your typewriter out of here. You can't do that anymore. You're all in danger." That was understandable because one might hear them banging away on the typewriter in our apartment when previously this had not been the case.

For example, there were some people living below us who were in the Nazi Party. Although they never would have turned us in, as they were very loyal to us, there were some who would have done that. So then the [members of the group] picked up their typewriter and buried it somewhere. I don't know where they took it. And that was actually the end of this, above all because several members of the group, including all of the leaders, had just been arrested and locked up.

Was your cousin still active in the SAB or the underground when he came back?

No, he was under surveillance. Back then the Nazi Party would always put someone in place to be observing those people. And everyone knew this, so they had to be cautious. Despite this, they continued to meet but did not carry out any political agitation. They only met to discuss how they viewed the situation.

"We can't meet anywhere," [my cousin said,] "because we are under surveillance. We can't even spend time together as friends, because they'll simply always assume we're up to something." So, they decided to take French lessons at the Technical University of Dresden and formed a group for a language class.

Our ancestors were French, including those of my cousin, but that was a rather long time ago. They had probably left because of the French Revolution. Anyway, he convinced all of his friends to take the French course and we went there once a week to our French lessons. Immediately after class, we would meet in a bar and exchange views about the situation. I was then actually a bit of an alibi, so that when he went home, he wasn't going alone. He was always under surveillance.

The lessons lasted from 1936 to 1937. Students who were in their later semesters and would soon be finished did the teaching. They had a very good knowledge of the language. It turned out that our teacher was a Jew. His name was Israel, and one fine day, he disappeared. When we got to class, we found out that he had been picked up for some reason. With that the class was canceled, and that made us furious once again.

Where did you think they sent him?

We had no idea. Our view was that he had been sent to a concentration camp somewhere. Although he was completely nonpolitical, he was a Jew. We hadn't known that was the case previously, although we should have, since his name was Israel. So it only occurred to us after they had taken him away. Oh well, we were rather naive at the beginning. I was still half a child.

A bar is a public place. Wasn't it dangerous to meet there?

There were never any guests where we sat. They had probably sought out a bar where we could be alone. Maybe the bar owner was a leftist. I don't know. Anyway, I never followed the discussions much, and I wasn't all that interested in them either. At sixteen, you're still half a child. I only went as a favor to my cousin because I liked him so much.

In the fascist era, people listened to foreign radio stations—Paris and London and Moscow—as much as they could with their little radio sets, to hear how people abroad saw the situation in Germany. When you experience something yourself, it is different from how foreign countries see it. And what did they know about the situation? So part of the discussions that took place dealt with these radio broadcasts. They also had the broader overview, while we only had a small one from Dresden or from our suburb. That was indeed very interesting back then. Anyway, not long after this they only met once in a while.

So did nothing happen to your cousin for the rest of the time until 1945?

That was very strange, I have to say. At first he was unemployed. Then he got a job again as a lathe operator and worked in a factory in Dresden where my father had also worked. That was at a company called Maschinenfabrik Grossman. At one time that had been a general engineering works, but three years or so after the Nazis came to power, they were put to work making preparations for war. I think they did something with torpedoes. Anyway, while my cousin was working there already in 1941, they brought in some Russian girls as workers. They brought in those foreign workers everywhere, and this particular group of them was placed under the supervision of my cousin. He was a very good skilled worker and knew how to get along well with people. So I assume that they trusted him not to do any political work with them.

Did they put pressure on you in school to join the League of German Girls [BDM]?

We were constantly getting enlistment orders in school [for the BDM]. You were supposed to report and join up. But my mother always said, "You'll be sorry if you go." And since in Übiger we had a lot of workers, left-wing oriented workers, there were many students in my class who said that they preferred sports and that they would never join up. In the end, almost half the class refused to join. So, my class succeeded in this. But that hardly was possible for the classes after us, as they were put under a lot of pressure to join. Still, my sister also did not join the BDM even though she was three years younger than me.

And then, after 1936, I was an apprentice and I only went to school twice a week. [The rest of the time] I was working in a small factory. The boss, who had previously been a manual worker, and was in the SA and always came to work in a uniform, continuously asked me why I wasn't in the BDM. My answer always was that it didn't interest me because I was an enthusiastic athlete and I practiced every day. And, in fact, this was true.

In the department where I worked later on, my boss was a former SPD man and another man working there was a former communist and had been in Hohenstein concentration camp. So there was no profascist atmosphere there and that suited me fine. Still there was one guy, the air raid warden, who was said to have denounced a lot of former workers holding leftist opinions. He was a very nasty individual.

[Where I worked,] one could easily notice from conversations that the people I was working with were not very pro-Nazi, especially because of the war. At first, the war had progressed positively and you could see immediately who was a fascist. They had maps and stuck little flags in them when the Wehrmacht moved forward. So one knew who was a pro-Nazi and with whom one could or could not speak and make critical comments.

Did you have any fears about being turned in?

No. Well, God, one was cautious nonetheless. One knew that every now and then somebody was picked up. One heard that every now and then, and one never really knew what became of it. For example, I was always telling my mother, "Mother, be quiet. You are always talking. Your talking will cost you life and limb." She was always cursing about every possible kind of situation and about what she had heard. She didn't mince words. So I was always saying to her, "You know that a couple of Nazis are also living in our building and they might report you, so calm down a bit." I was afraid for my mother. But she would say, "No, they should just as well hear everything. The way they act is scandalous." That's simply the way she was.

In Dresden, I was in a group of performing athletes. They called themselves the District Show Group of Saxony. We were selected for this because we were good athletes. Almost all of the athletes in my group were women from the former workers athletic associations because we had trained more intensively than those from the middle-class athletic associations. Whereas we had been more involved in competitive athletics, for them athletics were more of a leisure activity.

We were invited to all kinds of Nazi events as a show group and we were always forced to listen to speeches. We would stand there, and sometimes we would make ourselves rather unpopular, because we would be giggling when they were making some of those dumb speeches. We were just young girls at the time, and we could be rather silly. I can remember one time when [*Reichssportführer* Hans von] Tschammer gave a speech at a large athletic event. It was so bombastic that we almost laughed ourselves to death. We were constantly giggling and we didn't know why were giggling. But we couldn't restrain ourselves because it was all so idiotic.

Did you ever hear of a person being denounced by someone you knew but wouldn't expect this of?

No. The [only] person I knew who had denounced somebody was a colleague where I worked. I knew that. He even bragged about it. Our factory had two vacation rooms in Radewalde in [what is called] Saxon Switzerland. They were on a farm and it was inexpensive for us to go there on vacation. We young people went there almost every weekend and we did a lot of hiking. We had good relations with the people there and the farmer's wife was always saying to us, "Be careful, your air raid shelter warden was just here again, and he told me that so-and-so had said something against Hitler, and that he was going to send him to where he belongs."

She was always saying to us, "Be careful. Don't talk freely. He works in your department. Don't say anything when he is around." So we knew [that he was dangerous]. Two or three [colleagues] had disappeared from our factory, apparently because of denunciations by this man. So he is the only one I knew about absolutely. But there was also that guy who had caused that house search at my cousin's place. I also knew who he was. But, otherwise, you usually did not find out [who had denounced whom].

What did you experience of the persecution of the Jews?

Just across from us there was a small fabric store that had a Jewish owner. You knew that because of his name. I was still an apprentice at the time of the *Kristallnacht*, when the Nazis, especially the SA, went around the city destroying all the shops. And those of us in our office were in the immediate vicinity when we watched them smashing up that shop over there across from us. The owner, who was a small, elderly man, and his wife were intimidated and just stood by and wept.

One of my colleagues and I then said to our boss, who was a Nazi, "Well, Herr Klose, do you think this is right? We think it's outrageous." We basically put him under a bit of pressure. And then he said, "I can't approve of that either." Even he thought that things had gone too far.

After this the shop was closed. They had stolen everything and cleared it out, and then the two Jews were picked up and they disappeared and never showed up again. I didn't know them personally. I only knew them by sight.

When did you first hear about the mass murder of the Jews?

At home, at my parents' place, we had some acquaintances. The husband had been locked up because he was a communist. His wife was a friend of my mother. While he was behind bars, my mother supported her because she wasn't doing very well. When he was released again, he was called up to work in a factory where they were producing those "miracle rockets." This was located in a mine tunnel somewhere, and they had brought in all kinds of Russian prisoners of war, Jews, and concentration camp inmates and forced them to work there under completely miserable conditions and produce these weapons. And he was put to work there. He was some kind of specialist, a construction worker.

I don't know where it was. It must have been somewhere in the middle of Germany. I heard about this from my mother, who had heard about it from her friend—they were actually not supposed to talk about it, as it was all strictly confidential. Just before the end of the war, he was given leave and he came to visit us and he said, "Listen, I have to tell you this. I can hardly stand it any longer. It is impossible how those people are being abused there. They have driven them down into those tunnels and forced them to work under SS supervision, and one after another of them is dropping dead because they simply don't get enough to eat."

And then he also went on to tell us about how they had been in camps, and about how they were so decimated that there were ever fewer and fewer of them. Only the strongest were sent to work; the others were annihilated. That was something he knew about already, and that was how I heard about it.

Did you also believe it at that time?

Actually, I didn't believe it 100 percent. I thought it couldn't be true, that nobody could be that brutal. I didn't completely believe it at first. It was unimaginable for me. But since the same thing came from other sources and also from foreign radio stations as well—sometimes we listened to Radio Moscow and Radio London, who always made those German broadcasts, above all London—and since they had also confirmed it, and with rather exact information, we then said, "That has to be true." We had always doubted it a bit and said that nobody can really be that cruel. But since we knew how cruelly they had treated my cousin, we then said, "Then it must really be true."

WINFRIED SCHILLER

Auschwitz was not so very far away from us.

Born in 1928, Winfried Schiller was raised in the city of Beuten in Upper Silesia. His father, a doctor at a home for the handicapped, told his children about the murder of the Jews in the fall of 1944 after he was arrested and released.

We first came to Cologne in 1945. [Before that we lived] in Beuten in Upper Silesia. With 130,000 inhabitants, it was thought to be a big city at the time. I was born there.

Did you know who the [Nazi Party] block leader was? Were you afraid of him?

Yes, we knew who he was. It was known basically everywhere that so-and-so was the block leader. We weren't directly afraid of the block leader. But one was certainly aware not to say things that could get you into trouble. So you avoided saying anything against the party or anything like that. My father was a strict Catholic and that is the way we were brought up. That's why we were aware that the regime was not very pleasant. They [the Nazis] were opposed to the [Catholic] religion. You were raised by your parents to be careful and not to make any comments about the party or any of those people, including the block leader.

[Our block leader] was a normal human being. He naturally toed the party line, but he was not unpleasant. He didn't put pressure on people, at least not to my knowledge. I don't believe that the man who was the block leader in our neighborhood denounced very many people. He didn't do that, not to my knowledge. This man was otherwise rather reasonable; not all of the party's supporters were manipulative. But the local *Ortsgruppenleiter* [the block leader's superior] would denounce people, and he was therefore much more dangerous.

My father was always under some kind of surveillance anyway, because as a Center Party representative before 1933 he had opposed the National Socialists. Back then, he had been a municipal representative in the Center Party, the Catholic party. So, he was suspect to the Nazis anyway.

After the attempt on Hitler's life, my father was arrested. That was traced back to the *Ortsgruppenleiter*, because he had certainly known that my father was in the Center Party. So he was arrested. They kept him in jail for two days. But, through the intervention of others, my father was set free again.

Who arrested your father?

The Gestapo came with two men and then they arrested him. They barged into the house, showed their identification, and asked, "Where is your desk and your office?" One stood in the door and the other did the searching. But my mother said that she would only take them to the room they were looking for if the one who was carrying out the search did not plant evidence against him. They did that, you know. So he searched the place very superficially and then said to my father, "We have to arrest you." We didn't know at first what the reason was. That came out only later.

That all took place after the assassination attempt of July 20, 1944. In the days that followed, there was a lot of commotion. So that must have happened at the end of July.

How did the Gestapo men act?

Correctly, but very firmly—the way it was with the police and so on. They didn't go around shouting and yelling; rather, they acted correctly. Nevertheless, my father was very agitated. All of us were. We knew about the assassination attempt and that it had failed. Everyone, of course, had known that. But why they arrested my father and what was now in store for the family, we didn't know at first. They arrested him without giving any reason for it.

Did your father tell you about his interrogation?

He wasn't interrogated at all. They just put him in jail, and his belt, suspenders, tie, and so on were all taken away from him. All of his pockets were emptied, and then he was in jail, in a regular city jail. And then two days later, he came back out.

We had a distant cousin who was a bearer of the Order of Blood, which means that he was one of the first party members. They had that golden party badge. The first fifty or one hundred members got that golden party badge. Anyway, he lived in Munich and my mother got him going for us. He probably was the one who somehow gave the direction to have my father released. That must have been how it happened.

So did your father go back to work?

Yes. My father was the head doctor at a large home for the handicapped. He was an orthopedist and worked with the disabled, especially handicapped children, and the Nazis did not especially like this either. So, there were difficulties.

[But] he hadn't personally been hampered because of this. He had some acquaintances and colleagues, in particular Jewish colleagues, who had even received the Iron Cross during World War I, who were then arrested. But that had all taken place during the Jewish pogroms. They were good friends of my father, who, to his great sorrow, were arrested. He was powerless; he couldn't do anything about it.

Did you talk about this in the family?

Yes. When my father had talked about this, he told us to, "Keep your mouth shut! None of this is to get around."

Then, as children, we inevitably had to join the Hitler Youth. You couldn't avoid it. I then managed to do the following: Since we were very musical at home, we joined the local Hitler Youth orchestra. And that was also considered service, but not service to Hitler; rather, we played music. And that's where I was. Naturally the orchestra had to play on official occasions, but music was our way out.

You said that you often heard conversations about political issues at home. Back then, could you talk about political topics with others?

Yes, my father had done that. When people came over to visit us, they were close acquaintances and friends, and they indeed did discuss politics. They talked about the regime and all matter of things. My father did not fear being denounced. He was of the opinion that these were good friends. They didn't toe the Nazi line.

Were there people in your neighborhood who were somehow not to be trusted?

I experienced this in school. There were teachers in the secondary school whom one had to be careful around. They kept their ears open to hear whether anything was going on. But otherwise, in the immediate neighborhood, not really.

Did these teachers ask the pupils what their parents were doing? Whether they, for example, listened to foreign radio broadcasts?

We weren't asked about this directly. It may have happened that there were trick questions as to whether anybody listened to foreign radio broadcasts. I can't remember that we were pushed or somehow forced to say something about our parents. But, in the Hitler Youth, it could happen that the leaders would ask such questions. They did that, but it wasn't done in school. Still, I'm not aware of any kids from my area or my school who tattled on their parents.

How was it with foreign radio broadcasts? Was it especially dangerous to tune in to them?

We listened to them occasionally. We listened to the BBC German-language broadcasts. We had a huge Blaupunkt radio. This was no "people's radio." They couldn't receive the broadcasts [in my area]. It was a huge Blaupunkt, with shortwave and so on. Father sometimes listened to the foreign news broadcasts in the evening, late in the evening.

We didn't tune in for the music broadcasts, we had those ourselves. Besides my father had a large record collection, so he listened to music on his own. Thus, when we tuned in, it was for the news. This was not the biased news that the Nazis spread. Rather we tuned in to the BBC to hear what was accurate and important. But we didn't do this very often. Father didn't listen to the foreign news broadcasts often. Not regularly.

I also listened sometimes in the later years because my father discussed these matters with us. And, as a doctor, he already had some connections with the concentration camp at Auschwitz, which was not so very far away from us.

How far away was Auschwitz?

Oh, I don't know exactly. I could be wrong, but about forty, fifty, or sixty kilometers. In any event, Auschwitz was less than one hundred kilometers from us. Every now and then, one thing or another got through to us about how the Nazis had numerous people in the camp. But, about the actual gassing or the elimination of the Jews, that was not known right up until the last days of the war. But that the Nazis interned people there, that the camp was full of people, that was definitely known.

Did you hear rumors about the persecution of the Jews or their destruction?

Actually, very little at first. Only in the last years of the war was when the rumors got through about things like the concentration camp inmates being tortured and that they were dying so wretchedly. About the actual consistent gassing, we did not know. Then, when the Russian invasion came and the German army had to retreat, the concentration camp was evacuated. Then there came a great flood of concentration camp inmates in their striped clothes. It ran through Beuten toward Silesia. It was only then that the extent really became known.

Did your father hear anything about it? Perhaps in his capacity as a doctor?

We didn't hear about it, not us children. But my father heard about it, and then he told us about it as well.

What did he tell you?

About the destruction, that the Jews . . . That every enemy who does not somehow support the Nazi regime can end up in the concentration camp and that he will be killed there. That's what he told us. That must have been in autumn of '44. This was after his arrest. His deep religious sensibilities caused him a lot of trouble. He spoke with us about these issues on occasion in order to show us how important it is to have a strong faith and good religious sensibilities—that things like this were the work of Satan and so on. He talked about these matters with us in order to educate us.

[But] he always told us again and again, "Don't talk to others about this." And, we didn't, either. No. Father just said, "If this becomes known, then we could meet the same fate. So, keep your mouth shut!"

How did your father find out about these things?

I suspect that the news came to him from his patients. My father had a lot of patients from eastern Upper Silesia, from former Poland, the part that Adolf had later made the [General-] Government. So he had treated many Poles and their families and had also lent them his support. I suspect that it was those patients who came from over there—there was no longer any border—who told him about this.

Did he only talk about Auschwitz? Or did he perhaps talk about other concentration camps and other "actions" against the Jews?

As a child, I experienced the pogrom and the persecution of the Jews and the burning of the synagogues and so on. That the synagogues stood [in flames], that the Jews had to wear their stars, that the shops were broken into—we experienced all of that. And it was also known that there were other concentration camps. The names Dachau and Buchenwald were known subliminally. In particular, Auschwitz, because that's where people were killed. That was known.

And did your father speak with you about this only once or several times?

Oh, he had certainly talked about it several times. It came up quite often, especially when he somehow received news from his patients. So the topic came up again and again. Father was heavily preoccupied by it.

Did you personally hear other rumors about the annihilation of the Jews?

I don't believe there were many people who knew about it. But there were certainly rumors. There were certainly rumors. But I can no longer determine to what extent they were true or not. I don't know. I don't know. But, by that time in the autumn of '44, it was no longer a rumor. It was knowledge. To my father that was knowledge. And yes, he told it to us quite clearly.

Could you talk a bit more about your family's political views?

At first, my parents weren't against the Nazis. They were neutral or took a wait-and-see position. I remember that whenever Adolf gave a speech on the radio, and he spoke about Providence—he spoke about that often—then my parents would say, "You see, he isn't at all as religious as one thinks he is." Anyway, this neutrality faded between 1934 and 1938, and my parents' internal opposition grew. My father never encouraged us to join the Hitler Youth or the [Nazi] Young People. Father never pushed us or said, "You have to join." He always remained neutral. But his neutrality grew to aversion and rejection in 1938, when the synagogues were burned and the shops were smashed. As Jews were being consistently sent off and annihilated, this became opposition for my parents and then for us as well.

Did you notice opposition to Hitler from other people as well? Did you see, for example, anti-Nazi graffiti or fliers?

No. There was no underground movement.... That is to say, in my hometown, in the area where we lived, there was no resistance. It wasn't there.

In general, what was your life like in the Third Reich?
Was it bad, was it good?

In principle, our life was not really so bad, at least until we entered the final years of the war. Sure, there were food ration cards. Of course there were the food rations and so on. But, because my father was also paid in kind, we were never in need. Whether we needed butter or a goose or meat, we weren't in need. As a large family, we always got preference on the special vacation trains and we could ride on these from Silesia to the Baltic Sea and have a vacation. We children actually have no bad memories about this time until around 1943 to 1944. We had a wonderful and good life, except some of those discussions when our father pointed out to us that some things were not in order politically. But, for us personally, school went well, we had our lessons, and the teachers— okay, they were drafted. We didn't have any problems in Upper Silesia with bombings such as Cologne had. Not at all. We were the so-called Reich air raid shelter. There were no bombs. We simply didn't experience the terror from the skies. To that extent, we had a really peaceful youth. For us it was a normal life. That is to say, we children did not suffer any dire distress.

WITNESSING AND PARTICIPATING IN MASS MURDER

ADAM GROLSCH

In two days, 25,000 men, women, and children.

Born in 1920 and raised in a Catholic family in Krefeld, Adam Grolsch became a radio operator in the German army on the Russian front. In his interview he describes in detail how he personally observed the mass murder of thousands of Jews in Pinsk in October 1942 and heard about the gassing of Jews from the BBC while he was on the Russian front.

I didn't listen to the BBC before the war. But later, during the war, I listened to it very often. While I was a soldier in Russia, I worked as a radio operator, and then we listened all the time to the BBC in the evening. Otherwise, prior to this when I was in Germany before the war, I am not aware that many people listened to the BBC.

You in fact listened to the BBC in Russia as a soldier?

Yes.

Did you have to do that as part of your duties?

No. Some people had to do that as part of their duties, but that was something we were allowed to do. We would sit there at night by the radio and we'd always listen to the BBC or also to some other [stations], but I don't remember their names.

Why did you listen to the BBC?

Because I was already very skeptical back then as to whether the Wehrmacht reports were correct. Again and again we noticed from what we heard from the other side that all of that could not have been correct, so we then often listened to the BBC. But, in so doing, we also noticed that the BBC also exaggerated sometimes.

And then there was another variant of the BBC, the name escapes me at the moment, which was this famous soldiers station. Anyway, we called it the soldiers station. They were always telling dirty jokes, so that the soldiers would stay tuned in. Thus they didn't only broadcast the news; they always mixed in some of the dirtiest jokes you could ever imagine.

The broadcasts came from England. The [announcers] were Germans who were working in England. Probably they were German Jews. We would always be alerted by the BBC's call sign, those four tones: pom, pom, pom, pom. Then we'd always tune in to the BBC.

There were two or three of these soldiers stations. I believe one of them was called the Soldiers Station West [Soldatensender West], and there was one for Russia. Anyway, all of them were introduced by those tones. We listened mostly because of the news, but also because of the absolutely wonderful jokes that they told, which were sometimes political. But they were always rather mild. After we had heard them, we would then go right away and recite them to others.

Did you explain to those others that you had heard the jokes from the BBC?

For heaven's sake, no! It depended on whom you were talking to. If you knew they were people you could trust, then we told them. But not, for heaven's sake, to others, as that was not allowed and you could get the death penalty.

What kind of radio set did you need to receive these broadcasts?

You could practically get them with every type of normal radio set. We had all kinds. But the regular soldier didn't have any set whatsoever. Where was he supposed to get one?

The radio set was equipped for radio telephone. The programs were intentionally aimed at the frequencies we listened to, so that means that they also popped up on the frequencies that were reserved for official use. They would just pop up and say, "Hello, Lindley Fraser is back again. Today, I have just slipped in next to you in this sector, and I hope you can understand me well." And then he'd start in. He was actually one of the moderate ones; indeed he was somewhat moderate.

Did you have to try intentionally to receive the BBC, or did you just get it anyway?

I'd switch around here and there. It wasn't all that simple. We had to search the waves anyway. That was what the radio operator did anyway. As a radio operator, you always had to switch around back and forth through certain wave frequencies to see whether there were any emergency notices.

So, was it possible to get the BBC with a common *Volksempfänger* [people's radio set]?

You could, but I heard about others who had been arrested by the Gestapo for that, people who listened to London with a *Volksempfänger*. There was this friend of some of my fellow soldiers in Leimke, back in Germany. They told us when they came back from Germany that he had been arrested for doing that.

Did you also get to go on furlough during the war?

Absolutely not, not one single time. But I was given leave once to get married. At the time, I was a new recruit. I was drafted for the Russian campaign right after I finished my studies. I was never in France; I was always only in Russia. I was among the first ones to go over the Russian border, which was the Lithuanian border at the time. I was there from day one. And I was outside of Moscow in the winter campaign. I took part in the retreat from Moscow, and then, because I was no longer fit for combat, I was suddenly assigned to be a communications engineer. I received a special rank and was attached to the high command of the Wehrmacht as a specialist for radio equipment. I then went through Russia to the Ukraine, and there I had to oversee all of the radio posts [in my sector].

So I was in Russia from 1941 until 1945. After being forced to retreat in the Ukraine, we were disbanded and became regular soldiers once again and were sent up to the front. There I was a radio operator for an artillery battery. This was a post that was directly next to the artillery, a forward position, that passed on orders to shoot and so on. It wasn't at all pleasant.

May I pose another question regarding the BBC? Did many soldiers in Russia listen to the BBC?

There were only a few who listened to it as radio operators, as I did. I was then a special officer, an engineer. This meant that nobody could give me an order except the specialists from the high command of the army. We were deployed as engineers. We were to look after the technical posts and could listen to everything we wanted. That's how it worked.

Did you hear reports about Stalingrad and the like?

Yes. I took them quite seriously at the time; they appeared to be quite credible.

Did you believe the BBC reporting more than the German?

No, I can't say that. Well, the German reporting was very clever. But, if you could read between the lines, you could sometimes recognize the truth as well. For example, the expression "German retreat" was a contradiction in terms. One could see what was happening. However, I must say again, that when I wasn't working as an engineer, I had to work the radios and I would also receive the official news from the higher authorities to those below them, and the truth was there about what was happening. Thus sometimes what came on the radio was the truth about how these or those guys were surrounded, had no more weapons, and so on. Of course, one heard that.

The BBC must have built up an absolutely amazing information network. Above all, names were named in full. We were always thinking, "How did they find out that kind of information?" They reported information from occupied Russia, and I could reassess it, since I was in a position to do so behind the front.

I had permission to travel all over the place. But how could those guys know that in this place in Russia that this and that man, and this and that woman had done this and that? That's never been cleared up for me.

Perhaps you could tell us a bit about your childhood? You were born in 1920, right?

I was thirteen when Hitler came to power, and I have to say that as a thirteen-year-old, I knew little about politics. My father died in 1933. He was unemployed at the time and was actually for Hitler. That's nothing new to you, though. Everybody will confirm it for you. Hitler had gotten the unemployed off the streets. He understood that first and foremost. My father didn't get to experience this. But that is what his expectation was. "None of the others is doing anything. Hitler will take care of it. He will give the unemployed something to do." Today I understand this, but I didn't understand it back then as a thirteen-year-old, that this was only possible to do by creating jobs that could eventually only exist by going to war.

My mother was a woman for whom Hitler was a god. For her, Hitler was the Lord God. Everything he said was right. The führer could do everything. And she wasn't alone. Everybody else in the neighborhood, especially many, many women [agreed with her]. What the führer said was both just and the real truth and it had to be that way. I lived at the time in a suburb of Krefeld, in Borkum, but I heard basically the same things from many of the people I knew. So when you hear as you often do today how they had all been against him, that is absolutely not true. I can't at all remember that the masses were against Hitler. But I come from a home and a neighborhood where we were all mostly for Hitler, especially because of the jobs he created, the autobahns that were built. That is all nothing new is it, that the masses were in fact for him?

But what I did not like personally was that the free youth movement, which I had joined when I was still a youth, was banned. I had been a member of the Kittelbach Pirates and then after that the Nerother and the Path Finders. After 1933, everything was banned little by little, but that's another story. But, back then, I still went on a lot of trips with these youth groups that were strictly forbidden. But then, at the same time, I also had to join the Hitler Youth.

I think I was first in the Young People, then in the Hitler Youth. You automatically became a member. At school those who were not in it were looked at funny. More than anybody, the teachers immediately did an about-face [and embraced Nazism]. It is rather amazing from today's point of view that Hitler was so strongly supported by the teachers and the German middle class. This was not the case, however, when he was still struggling, not before '33. They were all against him then. But after '33, [they discovered that] he was actually just what the country needed.

What was the political climate like back then? Did you live in a lot of fear?

If you weren't trying to make waves, like in politics or something like that, you didn't feel threatened. To the contrary, I have to say. What I often heard was, "Finally, you can go out once again in the evening on the Gladbacher Strasse." Previously that had been the red section of town. At one time, there had been five or six sections of Krefeld where no upstanding citizen, above all no woman, would have dared to go in the evening. [That was because of] the criminals and also because of the way it was in general in these places. You'd be abused there. And everything was red there, blazing red. Red, of course, means the German Communist Party. And if anyone they recognized as a noncommunist went through there, he would be beaten up. It was that bad in those days. But when Hitler came to power, it suddenly got quiet. As we now know, of course, he did this by sending them all off to concentration camps. But, at that time, people thought, "*Mensch*, you can finally go out here again."

But what about the Gestapo; didn't you know about them?

I only found out about them once I was with the troops. But before this, one did know about the SS. That is to say, the SS was involved with the Jews. But there were rumors that they [the Gestapo] were up to something, that they hauled people off to cellars.

I would have never joined the Nazi Party, but not because I was a hero. I didn't want to join the party, because they had outlawed the literature I loved and they had made it illegal to travel abroad and the like. That's why I was privately against the party back then. But my mom thought that the [Nazis] were super, that everything they did was wonderful and fantastic and she couldn't understand it when I was sometimes critical of them.

Nevertheless, I went on trips with some remaining members of the free youth movement to places like Oberwesel on the Rhine, and we ended up getting into fights with the Hitler Youth leaders. We beat the daylights out of them, and, if we had been caught, it would have been the end for us. To that extent, we knew that the Gestapo existed. Back then, one had to restrain oneself and not make too many negative remarks. To that extent, I certainly knew that it was dangerous. But, strangely enough, I had little fear, I would have to say.

What did you know about the mass murder of the Jews?

That affected me enormously. It was in fact a key lifetime experience. After I had taken part in the winter campaign against Moscow and was no longer fully fit to fight at the front, I was then frequently deployed as an engineer and had my base in Pinsk, which is today in Belarus. And then one morning, after I hadn't been there for more than five or six days, there was a huge racket going on outside and I said to myself, "Man, what's going on here?" Otherwise it had been very quiet there where I had been living in the town in an old church where we had our quarters. And Pinsk had a ghetto, a Jewish ghetto with around 25,000 inhabitants.

Back then, the Ukrainians and the White Russians didn't like the Jews either. They hounded them and hated them just as much as the Nazis did, just not in this way. In short, I then set out with a friend, and with my own eyes saw how the people there were slaughtered; in two days, 25,000 men, women, and children, and in the most beastly way. I saw how they had to undress in front of the tank traps and many other things. And the absolute worst thing I saw was how this man took a screaming baby and beat it headfirst against a wall until it was dead.

Of course, the Germans were the ones who ordered this, but the ones who carried out the orders were mostly Russians: Cossacks and Lithuanians and Latvians. The auxiliary troops provided the force, but that doesn't relieve the Germans of responsibility. One called them *Hilfswillige* [voluntary helpers], or *Hiwis* for short. They were mostly Lithuanians, Latvians, and Estonians, and they carried out the worst jobs for us, the dirty work. They did everything they were ordered to do. And that was something I experienced.

And then while I was standing at the edge of the pit, suddenly they saw me, just as it is shown in the film *Holocaust.* That was no exaggeration, as it had been just like that. And then they saw me standing there with another [guy who was with me]—both of us were wearing uniforms—and then a number of them suddenly came up and grabbed us and took us under arrest. And then standing just near to us was the local commandant, who was an officer and the local commandant for the city of Pinsk. He suddenly saw us there as well, and, in short, if he hadn't been there, we also would have ended up in the pit because that was all top secret. Nobody was supposed to know what was being done there.

They had dug it all out and there were all of these corpses. Then they [the Jews] had to undress. Mothers were still carrying their children, usually in one arm. And then they would have to go up there, and they shot them. I saw everything, everything.

Afterward I went into the buildings [where the Jews had been kept], and it was horrifying. There were still people who were standing down there in the toilets, in the sewer trenches where the feces were. They were hiding, and they had only stuck out their heads and peered out and they thought they had gotten away. But then the Poles came along and stole everything they could. This was not like the Germans would do. And then they said, "There's another one in there. There's another one down there." And then they shot them all. It was horrifying. What an experience that was! I just thought to myself, "something like this just can't happen."

That was in 1942, in October 1942. I can only say that after this experience I sat down and wrote a letter to my wife. That is to say that after I had seen all of that, I then wrote, "If there is any God at all, then Germany should never be allowed to win this war."

Weren't you afraid to write such a letter?

Oh, yes, but I was so shocked. I'm telling you this because that was such a [terrible] experience for me. "Something like this just can't happen," I thought. "How can one do something like that?" This undressing, this standing there stark naked, and those ditches, and then when you saw those guys, who were mostly Cossacks, standing there behind them and shooting them all down with their submachine guns! And then they would hand back their submachine guns and get new ones fully loaded. I have always said that if there were ten or fifteen guys standing up there, let us say twenty, then each one must have shot more than a thousand people in this short period. It was utter insanity!

Afterward we got to know them back at the radio post. They were always drunk. There was no other way to do it. They were running around drunk all of the time, those guys. And their boss was an officer from Düsseldorf. Unfortunately, I have forgotten his name.

Their boss who had organized all of this, was he in the Wehrmacht or the SS?

He was in the Wehrmacht. Wait a moment, no, stop, that was the SD. That was new for me at the time. Yes, they had done that. This man from Düsseldorf belonged to the SD. But among those people who did all that, this Holocaust there, only the bosses were Germans. The others were Hiwis. They did the dirty work. But they did this gladly, apparently. I am not certain about this exactly. But that was a real experience.

How did you manage to see all of that?

There was a loud noise. I was living right next door to the ghetto. I'd been there for six days and I remained there after that. That was my base of operations, where I was living and where I continued to live for quite a while after that. And then one morning there was a loud noise, and I thought to myself, "What is going on here?"

So you heard this loud noise and the submachine guns?

No, not just yet actually. Well, yes, there was also some shooting, but mostly a lot of noise. You suddenly heard this horrible racket and screaming and crying. When I think about it, it's horrible.

And now it is just coming back to me that there was already snow on the ground, a light powdering of snow. And then there was an endlessly long and wide procession of people and there were guards escorting them with carbine rifles and submachine guns. Oh, man! Let's say there were five hundred people on the road. They were sent out in batches, not all at once. There were perhaps ten guards for these five hundred people. We said to ourselves, "Good heavens! If they had all run at once, those ten men would have been able to shoot only fifty or sixty at best. The others would have made it into the forest. It wasn't that far away. They would have been in the woods. And the Germans wouldn't go into the woods. That's where the partisans were. They didn't go there. It was too dangerous for them."

But the people went submissively to their fate and trotted along, and they knew exactly what lay before them.

How far outside of town were the ditches?

They were about two or three kilometers away. Later, when it was all over, we went there once again. We often had to drive out there because there were disruptions, problems with the lines. They had already fixed everything up; it had all been neatly graded. One couldn't see anything anymore. Everything was flat, done with extra care so that you wouldn't notice.

Were the Jews dressed when they were marched to the ditches?

They were still dressed, but people were constantly walking past them, looking to see whether they still had a watch on, or were wearing jewelry or something else, things that were always being snatched. But they were dressed when they arrived at the ditches.

It was always a long line, but they came up in batches. I estimate that there could have been a thousand in each batch. I don't know anymore. But I have never understood why, as there were also men along with them, that not a single one of them had the mettle to run away.

So, [going back to the beginning of all of this,] you heard a racket outside and then you went into the ghetto?

Yes, and then we saw what was going on there and how another group of people was being assembled. It was all cordoned off, but we got in despite that. We showed our IDs, our special IDs, [and then we said,] "We have to enter. We have to check something." In fact we were lying. And then they said to us, "Good, okay." So we had then made our way in and then we saw that this procession of people was heading out and we became curious: "What is going on here? What are they doing with them?" So we then followed along after them, right along with one of these batches of people. And the Ukrainians and the Russians, the guards, didn't do anything. They had simply thought, "Well, okay, let them follow along with them." When we arrived, we saw the huge ditches. They must have been made in advance. There couldn't have been any other way.

When the shooting started, could you hear it all?

You could even see it, see it and hear it. We were standing right below the ditches. They were [mounded up] somewhat higher. They [the Jews] were led up to this mound of dirt, and there were those guys standing there with the submachine guns at the top. And then they were shot down and they simply fell right in.

What did the remaining people do?

Absolutely nothing. One row of them were crying, especially the children being held in their arms. The little children being held in their arms, they were crying. And then something happened. One of those guys went over to them and snatched a child from [its mother's] arms and threw it against a wall. Such [awful] things were happening there that one should simply not be allowed to think about them anymore. There were some who were crying, perhaps a hundred, but not very loudly. They were simply resigned to their fate, especially since they had been forced to go up there stark naked and they knew that now it was the end.

Mensch, but if a hundred of them had somehow attacked, even though there were those guys with the submachine guns, they could somehow have gotten away. But I don't know if I would have had the courage to do this in such a case. I just don't know.

What did the soldiers think about this? Did you discuss this with your friends?

They simply didn't believe it. That was a so-called top secret that nobody was supposed to know about. And then the local commander—who was a Wehrmacht officer responsible for the entire Wehrmacht post in the area, but who didn't have anything to do with combat troops as that was, of course, a rear area and there weren't any combat troops there—was there, by coincidence, and he noticed us there as well and didn't think that this was such a bad thing presumably. I can't really say. Anyway, he then came between us [and those guys who were holding us] and said, "Halt! You are not supposed to be here. These people are under my command and so on." He saved our lives. Later, he had us report to him and he ordered us to remain absolutely silent about this. For, if we talked about it, he couldn't do anything more for us.

So you didn't really pass on what you had experienced to the other soldiers?

Not a lot, I believe. But I don't know anymore. Yes, here and there, sure, if I knew that it was someone I could trust. The others who had been present there had all been aware of this as well, every soldier who was there in Pinsk, and that was more than a few. Still, they hadn't quite seen it like the both of us. [But] they all were aware of it. It was something that everyone would notice. But hold on a second. They had worked that all out very cleverly. Now it is coming back to me. Yes, everyone saw that the entire Jewish ghetto was empty after a few days. Suddenly the barriers were gone and it was open. And then all of those Poles were constantly running around and searching and searching to see whether they could find anything they could use. The ghetto was empty. And then there was this official communication that they [the Jews] had all been sent back to work in Germany and all over the place. And we, for heaven's sake were not allowed to speak with anyone about what had really taken place.

It was just like that in other places as well. That didn't only happen in Pinsk. [For example,] I was with the armored spearhead that went over the

Memel River at 4:00 A.M. [on June 22, 1941]. And when we entered that first Lithuanian town—I've forgotten the name, but it's directly behind the border—I thought to myself, "What the heck is going on here?" This was because when we looked around we saw bodies all over the place hanging from the trees, people who had been hanged. And then one guy came up to us who spoke good German and said, "We've already taken care of things here. All of the Jews from this town have already been strung up." Before the Germans got there, the Lithuanians had already strung up all of the Jews.

Of course, we found out later that they had done this in order to get hold of their things. They had robbed them all. They had exploited the situation: "Hitler is against the Jews anyway. We'll kill them and then we'll take all of their stuff."

We had crossed the border early in the morning and entered that town around noon. There were perhaps twenty [dead Jews]. It was a small town. However, I have since heard that it was like that everywhere. And the Lithuanians, Estonians, and Latvians—those who were the ones who had later been mostly involved in all of the shooting of the Jews—had done that with great enthusiasm.

Finally, one last question about the BBC. When you were on the front, did you hear BBC reports about mass murder and gassing?

Yes, I heard that as well. I can still remember this because I later saw those [gas] vans. But I heard about it too. I had by chance seen those vans. They were parked in Rowno [Rivne] and nobody knew what they were. They were those large and long mobile trailers attached to trucks. That is to say, they were mobile gas chambers for smaller operations. My attention was drawn to it by the BBC.

Where I saw it was in Rowno. Rowno was in the middle of the Ukraine. But previously we had heard about such things from the BBC, like about mass shootings of Russians. That was what I knew about the best. They had also explained how they had also done that with small groups [of people] and with such vehicles as well. That was such a thing to hear that you wanted to see for yourself if that was really the case. And then I ended up seeing two or three of those things in Rowno, parked near the harbor. I often had to go to Rowno to get replacement parts for the radio post. That could have been in 1943.

HANS RUPRECHT

We have to carry out some "cleansing measures" here.

*Born in 1915 and raised in an upper-middle-class family in Cologne,
Hans Ruprecht was a Wehrmacht officer during the war in the Crimea.
In 1942 he had to organize a squad of troops to cordon off the local popu-
lation from a mass shooting of Jews.*

My father was a self-employed entrepreneur and stemmed from the so-called
middle class. I was born in Wuppertal, and we moved to Cologne in 1918.

We thought that Hitler was an outsider. For those of us in middle-class
society, he wasn't a German. He was an Austrian. How could an Austrian in
Germany pull off such a development? That remains incomprehensible for me
to this today.

Hindenburg said, "What does that corporal want?" But Hindenburg was too
old. He was as old as I am today, and he couldn't control the situation any
longer. Furthermore, the population in Germany at this time was basically
impoverished. The unemployment was alarming. For us, as self-employed entre-
preneurs, the situation was also very difficult. But, when you promise someone that
he will get economic growth, a reduction in unemployment, and things like that,
he is easily inclined to give in to these temptations. That there would be such grave
political and military consequences, and that the National Socialists would strive
to dominate Europe after they had achieved dominance in Germany, were dangers
that the people did not recognize at the time because they couldn't assess them.

Hitler was a masterful politician and diplomat. What he achieved is what
is so fascinating about this man, things that nobody in Europe had been able
to achieve at the time. He battled against unemployment. He strengthened
German unity. He brought the Germans to a certain level of dominance.

I left home at eighteen in 1933–1934 and completed my education. Then I
worked at an engineering works, and at a paper factory, and so on. So I didn't
know much about what was going on back at home.

**You were a Wehrmacht officer during the war and had a special
experience in the Crimea. Could you elaborate on that a bit?**

Yes, but that was a coincidence. At the time, I was deployed in the Crimea, at
the harbor of Yevpatoria. And then a number of individuals and small groups of
older men, who were evidently Jews, kept coming to us and they would try to
feed themselves by trying to gather up the table scraps and other leftovers from

our mess hall. [I didn't know] where these people came from, whether they were Tartars, or if they were people from the bottom levels of society, or if they were people who were uprooted by the war for whatever reason, who had more or less come to this area by chance.

In any case, I became acquainted with a group of perhaps forty to sixty of them, although I didn't know any of them personally. I only saw these people coming and going, over and over again, and I thought to myself that they were just poor devils going from place to place in order to survive and that we could offer them what we had left over.

I belonged to a unit that was not so tightly organized as those larger units. It was composed of three [artillery] batteries spread out along the coast by Yevpatoria, which was actually a medium-size vacation town with an industrial zone. Because of the physical distances involved, we could not always get together [very often]. The highest-ranking officer there was a captain or a major, who commanded or led or administered or in any event supervised these three batteries. We concentrated primarily on the Russians' night attacks, and thus we often had to sleep during the day.

Anyway, these people really stuck out as a group of poor, badly nourished people, and they were always talking in a language that I couldn't understand. They could neither speak English, nor any other Western, civilized language, but we understood enough to know that they were being forcefully persecuted.

One day a call came in from an SS officer. I don't know what his rank was. In any event, he said, "We have to carry out some 'cleansing measures' here. You will not be affected by this as we can carry them out ourselves in a remote area to the north of the city. However, we do need to isolate the population from these measures." And then I said, "What is this all about?" To which he replied, "You must know, of course, that we are eliminating 'inferior creatures,' and also people who don't fit within our framework."

So that was my experience. Nevertheless, I said, "I can't force anyone from my unit to take part in this." "Ah, go ahead and ask them," he said. "There will certainly be some people who will be willing to do this on a voluntary basis." I then thought this over and proposed it to my commander.

They had already dug out the pits or had them dug out by these people in the meantime. I heard about this again and again from people who understood something of the babble of languages and they had heard about it from those who had been forced to do the digging. So it had already become clear to me what was going on with this whole affair. But I had also spoken about it with my commander.

The preparations dragged out over several days, and eventually these people began to suspect that they were going to be shot. How they reacted to this surprised me, however, inasmuch as these people were rather resigned to their fate, or should I say, indifferent. They were so bad off anyway. Mostly these were older people, in a state of health that they were not fresh and flexible and mobile or ready to run away. Rather they simply gave up and waited for what was going to happen. Still, I cannot really judge to what extent that was comprehensible and understandable for them.

Anyway, I asked around among those in my battery and noted the people who would be willing to take part in such a cordoning commando and they were then posted in such a way that they wouldn't actually have to be directly next to the unpleasant business. The SS men did that themselves. Instead, the streets that led to the residential area of the city center and the industrial district were cordoned off. That's where they were posted by the SS men.

And then one day, the shooting commenced. The incident lasted about half an hour or an hour until it was over. With that, the whole thing was over and done with. There were no written records or written instructions or regulations or anything that had to be followed. It was completely carried out without any written [orders].

How did you get your instructions for this?

They simply just called me or my commander.

Were you called or your commander?

He was called.

And then he informed you that you had to do this, correct?

Yes, and I had to do it too. I had to [have] these men [get ready] at a specified time. They then were picked up with motor vehicles and taken to where they were to be dropped off. They then had to stay there until a detachment came to pick them up.

But your cordoning commando had been voluntary, correct?

It was voluntary, yes. But the men who went to do the cordoning basically knew what it was all about. As a consequence, they were well informed about those kinds of situations that became taboo here for a long time after the war, and that people didn't want to admit having been witness to. They didn't divulge it either. Basically, they had taken part in this because of the monotony one experienced there. In the place where we were, sometimes nothing would happen for weeks. And, of course, that was an event in which they said, "Oh well, before you die of boredom here, why don't you go? Maybe you'll experience something or other." You know, at all executions, of royal families or whatever, it has always been the [ordinary] people who are the big onlookers and they often applauded what took place. You see it at traffic accidents as well. If there's a traffic accident, then there are people there who you just can't believe have the time to spend there. They only do this because of their curiosity or the thrill of participating, seeing, or comprehending something unusual.

Were there men who refused to go?

Yes. A whole bunch refused, but I think about twenty people from my unit went.

How many refused? Can you give an estimate?

There were about sixty men [in our unit]. So perhaps a third took part.

How was it for the forty people who didn't take part? Was it a problem for them? Were they considered cowardly by the others?

Those were people who were convinced that an injustice was taking place. There were also those who didn't need this thrill of knowing more than was absolutely necessary about a thing such as this. That was too much for them.

Can you explain further how it happened?

We always had an assembly in the morning, a kind of gathering. Then it was announced that a cordoning detachment had been requested by the SS, but they would not have to be involved directly in the affair. They would simply take up a position so as to isolate the whole thing from the public. Many immediately said, "No, that's not for me." It was said from the start as well that all of this was voluntary. Some people expressed curiosity. Some were bored and said, "Oh, well, maybe you can see something." Normally you couldn't leave your garrison.

On the day this happened, had you heard about anything like this before?

No, it was new for me too. This was the first direct, unmistakable experience [I had] with something like this. We already had suspicions, but we basically never had any details. Yes, we had already suspected [something like this]. But that was the only time I was personally involved in this way.

Were there any Gestapo men or anyone who said, "You must not talk about this?" Or did you simply know that yourself? How was that?

There was no Gestapo with us. Nevertheless, the whole matter only came up once. The request came from the SS, and they made it very clear that we couldn't dodge this request. It wasn't my decision either, rather that of my commanding officer. He then spoke to us officers and said, "We don't have any other choice. I've also contacted the superior commands. As the Wehrmacht, we have to accept that we will have to provide a cordon for this project and find sufficient volunteers who are prepared to make this possible."

Many of those [who took part] didn't see anything at all. They did indeed hear shooting, and possibly also screams or something. But, you know, at a distance of five hundred meters, even a scream dissolves and becomes imperceptible. The shooting wasn't supposed to be heard, right! But if someone wanted to find out where the shooting was coming from and went in that direction, he would be prevented from getting there by this cordon. And they also brought those people who were going to be the last ones to be shot and had them throw dirt on top of those who had already been shot before in the end they were shot themselves. Then the last commando came, and that was all filled in by a motor vehicle.

Does this mean that you saw all of this only from a distance of five hundred meters?

Not even that close, much farther away. The city lay flat on the coast, and beyond the city began an elevation of mountainous terrain. It was in this area that the shooting took place, and I only know of one shooting.

You can describe all that happened very well. Was this operation discussed afterward among the troops?

No. Well, you know, I was the only officer in this group of seventy. I also had my own room. I lived in my own room. As an officer, you have to keep a certain distance from the troops. Consequently I didn't participate in the conversations with the troops and also not with those who took part in it. So I didn't take part in what might have been said between those who had gone there and those who had not gone there.

But then how do you know that they threw dirt on top of the victims and later drove over the pit with a bulldozer?

You know, that was in 1942, and now it's 1994. What I want to say is that this incident touched me very deeply. But it was basically clear to me that with the power the Nazi regime had over everything, only the combat soldiers of the Wehrmacht could stay free of this.

Can you estimate how many of the men who knew something about this incident had the possibility of taking leave during the war and going home for a while?

Yes, they all had the possibility.

And could you provide an estimate of how many talked about it with their wives, children, relatives, cousins, and friends?

I can't estimate that.

What was said about such events in general?

I have to say something here. When you get into such a situation and cannot get out of it, a process of suppression sets in. And you shut it out [of your mind]. But you can never forget it. Even if you didn't experience the event as such, you could make a picture of it for yourself about what had taken place from the illustrated photographs of shootings you would see in the newspapers after the war. Therefore, one has to assume from the start that this incident was comparable to the other incidents that were published later. And that is why those people who had even volunteered [to take part in such events] have possibly said, "I don't know anything at all," in order to provide a protective covering for themselves.

Were you afraid to talk about it when you went home on leave?

No. When I was on leave, I never talked about it.

ALBERT EMMERICH

There are three hundred Jews lying in each grave.

Born in 1907 in Wolgast, Albert Emmerich grew up in Stettin (today, Szczecin, Poland) and became a typesetter. He was a policeman in Nazi Germany in the small city of Eberswalde, and also, for a while, a concentration camp guard at Dachau. In 1943, he was sent to the Ukraine, where he observed many atrocities carried out against both Jews and the local Ukrainian population.

I was not drafted into the military. Right after the war started, I was drafted into the police as an auxiliary policeman, and I experienced all kinds of things. I was drafted like a soldier, but into the police instead of the military. As an auxiliary policeman, I had to carry out police duties, patrol the streets, and make sure that the blackout was observed during air raid warnings.

I was born in 1907 and was a typesetter by trade. In 1939, I was thirty-two years old. In 1939—it must have been in the autumn—I was transferred to Hohenstadt in the Sudetenland, where a police regiment was being set up. That was Police Regiment 1. [The men] were all young people, between eighteen and twenty-six, who had volunteered for the police—or was that a bit later? I don't know anymore. In any event, the regiment went to the front, and I was able to go back home.

I was in Eberswalde near Berlin, where I was employed in a printing house. We had a [police] instructor there, who said to me, "Man, you could go on active duty." I responded, "Stop it! Active? With your low wages and with my wages? Your salary? No, I'm not going to do that." But he kept pestering me. Then he said, "Listen, you don't really believe that you will stay here forever? You'll also end up on the front. Your wife will continue to receive your salary, and you'll get your soldier's pay as well." So, in 1941, I went on active duty with the police, took the training course at the police school in Berlin-Schöneberg for three months, and left with a promotion.

Then I went to the Ukraine. I won't forget the place. It was called Liuboml'. It was close to Kovel'. An active-duty comrade, an older fellow, had been there, and they shot him. It was partisan territory, a wooded area, and they shot him. And now I was to go to Liuboml' as his replacement. That must have been in 1943. The older comrades who had been there from the start familiarized me with the work. They were from Silesia.

Then one day, a younger fellow, around twenty-six to twenty-seven, said to me, "Come here, I want to show you something." It was a gravel pit. He took me there. Gravel pits always sit deep in the ground. Then he said, "Look at that. There are three mass graves. Those are Jews. There are three hundred Jews lying in each grave." "I was there as well," he said. "We had to shoot the people. They were forced to undress, no matter whether they were old or young, or whether they were babies or women with babies in their arms. They all got a shot in the back of the neck. None of us received a submachine gun. They got a shot at the nape of the neck with simple revolvers and were forced to undress beforehand. Then the next three hundred were ready. They had to dig their own mass grave again and then their turn came later. A few days later, they had to stand on the edge of their grave, and then they were shot. It was awful." Well, I thought, "Those Nazi bastards!"

They [the policemen] were supervised [during the shooting] by the Gestapo. Those were the SS men from the Secret State Police. They assigned them the task. Then I arrived. . . . The Gestapo had ordered the police to shoot those people. And anybody who didn't do so could be shot himself.

How did it happen that the man from Silesia told you this?

We were in our lodgings and we were drunk. In the morning when we got up, we immediately received schnapps. So we were all drunk.

I also recall another incident, when I was still in Hohenstadt in the Sudetenland, when I got sick. The doctor of our unit was a dentist and he didn't know what to do with me. So he sent me to Munich, to Dachau, to a police hospital. And that was also where the concentration camp at Dachau was. I was there for four weeks for observation and treatment and I didn't have anything to do all day. And then they said to me, "Since you don't have anything to do, you can reenforce the guards." The concentration camp inmates [I watched] were in a camp where there was also an agricultural enterprise and they had to do gardening.

Once an inmate came along who was about to drop dead—he was weaving and couldn't walk right—and I said to the one SS man who was there, "What's wrong with that guy?" "Oh," he said, "During the lunch break, we simply strung him up by the legs for two hours." [The reason for this was that] in the mornings the prisoners had to sing while standing in place and this guy hadn't sung. You can imagine what was up with him.

And then there was also something else [that I remember]. It was on a really hot day and the sun was burning down. The prisoners were forced to stand for hours with their faces looking at a wall that was three and a half meters high, whitewashed, and about seven to eight meters wide. They were all dressed in dark clothes, really dark, either dark blue or black and they fell over like flies in the heat. Then they got a bucket of water over the head and a kick in the backside and were forced to stand up again. Such were the methods the SS used. . . .

And then came the war, and I was, as I said, in Liuboml'. And then I was deployed to the front in the spring of 1944. We had to carry out an attack on a village in the Ukraine, and that's where I was wounded. I was shot in the arm and the lung. I went first to a military hospital in Warsaw and then to a military hospital in Silesia. After I was there for three months, I was sent to a hospital back home in Eberswalde, where I also spent another three months. When I was released from the hospital, I had to return to the police and report to Captain Ehmke. By this time I knew what was up in Russia and the Ukraine. The Russians were coming closer and closer.

I need to mention here that I did not belong to the Nazi Party and that this captain had faith in me. One day he closed the door and said to me, "You were just in Russia. What is really going on there?" Then I said to him, "If the Russians keep coming closer, then I can only advise you to get out of here and go as far west as you can with your family, because what the Nazis have done there will have bitter consequences." And he did just that.

Sometime after that I was transferred to Potsdam as a military instructor, and I received a group of recruits. The Russians kept coming closer and closer. And then I told my family that they had to head to the west. We couldn't get a peaceful night's sleep anymore. It was always alarm, alarm! And then, when we got over to the west, along the Elbe, I told them, "Listen, I'm now going over to the Yanks. I'm not going to do this any more. I can't sleep any more." And then we were taken into captivity in an American prison camp in Ludwigslust.

[After the war,] in June 1946, I began serving in the police again. First I was a traffic cop and then I went to Schleswig-Holstein to head up a village police post. In March 1949, I began working as typesetter again. On July 1, 1954, I came here to Cologne, where I became a department head, a chief typesetter. That's where I was until 1972, up until my sixty-fifth year, when I retired.

Let us return to the Nazi period. You said that what the Nazis did in the Ukraine and Russia would have bitter consequences. What did you experience there yourself?

In effect, nothing. In effect, little.

But then how did you come to this conclusion that what the Nazis did there would have bitter consequences?

With the shooting of the Jews, and then in Dachau and how they treated the people there. As a result of that, we said, "this is going to have bitter consequences." After Hitler occupied the Sudetenland and Austria, he then started the war in 1939 and it lasted until 1945. And what they did during that time in the occupied territories, for example, in the Ukraine! Hitler had promised the Ukrainians a free state, and the Ukrainians were happy. They invited us to breakfast as police officials. But then something else came along and he didn't do what he had said. Then the battle with the partisans started and the Germans were forced to shoot them.

One thing that I recall was a real partisan-controlled village. When the Germans drove through it in small trucks, the partisans shot at them and only a few of them managed to return back on foot to Liuboml'. So what were the consequences? Well, the German artillery was called up. The village lay in a valley. The Germans went in first and took all of the animals, everything, cows and sheep and pigs. They brought out everything. Then they shelled the village. Nobody came out of there alive, [including] the women and children. There weren't any young men there. They were with the partisans. There were only old people, women, and children, shot to pieces. And because of things like that I said, "Man, that's going to have consequences."

Did you actually see the shelling of that village?

I was there when it happened.

Did you have a function?

Me? No, no. I was just a policeman doing patrol duty. There was a curfew, and we went to the village at night to patrol it. Otherwise, we didn't do anything.

Referring to your description of the shooting of the Jews at the gravel pit, was the Wehrmacht also involved there?

Oh, no. Those were policemen, they were all just policemen. And the Gestapo, as I already said, had ordered them [to carry out the shooting]. Of course, not every shot was lethal. And then the man explained [to me] that "they were all lying there in blood and we had to go down there and wade in the blood up to our ankles and give them the mercy shots."

What was your work routine in Liuboml'?

It would begin at 8:00 A.M. in the morning after we were woken up at 7:00 A.M. Then we would go out on patrol and so on. We would drive through the surrounding villages, usually with four men, in an all-terrain vehicle. There was one guy there who wasn't a 100 percent Nazi, but a 300 percent Nazi. And there were certain areas where you weren't supposed to go. But one time we drove through one of those areas anyway and a young man in his early twenties was running, and the [300 percent Nazi] yelled out at him, "Stand still! Stand still!" But he didn't stand still and he kept on running. Then the [300 percent Nazi] raised his rifle and shot him. He let go a volley and just blew him away. And we were not allowed to say anything about what had happened.

Why couldn't you say anything about it?

Because then it would have been our turn. You weren't allowed to say anything.

Would it have been tolerated, if you had shot as well?

Yes, of course. And then I remember how [the locals] were forced to collect livestock and potatoes for the soldiers, for the Wehrmacht. At the time we were accompanying them and had to ride along as protection. When they arrived in this one village, there was an old man sitting on a bench in front of a house. The Gestapo noted exactly who had delivered potatoes and grain and so on and who hadn't. There were these three men from the Gestapo with us, and they went up to [the old man] and spoke to him. What was said, I don't know. In any event, they spoke to him, and he shook his head, and then one turned his gun around and struck him dead with the butt. It was because of those kind of things that I said, "That's going to have bitter consequences."

Were you ever forced to do such things yourself?

No. Never. Thank God, no. But I would have had to do it, if they had ordered me to.

Why do you think that man from Silesia showed you those gravel pits and told you about them?

I don't know. In any event, he said, "Come along. I'm going to show you something." "Okay, fine," [I said]. Then he went with me to the gravel pits. They were fifty meters long. In every one of them lay three hundred Jews.

Was he an officer?

No, he was a normal policeman, just like us. He had been there since 1941, but we didn't get get there until 1943.

Was your friend from Silesia allowed to talk about it? Wasn't it supposed to be kept secret?

The way it happened was that we were taking a walk and then he said, "I'm going to show you something." Nobody there, none of the comrades, knew anything about it. There were about fifteen or twenty of us there.

Did you ever swap stories about such experiences with your colleagues?

No, no. You know, one guy didn't trust the other. It was a complete rarity for him to show me that place near Liuboml', those mass graves. The Jews had to undress before they had to stand on the edge of the pits and they had to leave all of their things behind. After the shooting was over, the Ukrainians who had been standing up above on the side of the pits came down and took their things. It was no love affair between the Jews and the Ukrainians. Most of the Jews had capital, money, and the Ukrainians were poor devils.

WALTER SANDERS

I not only told my parents about that, I also told others when I was on leave.

Born in 1920 and raised as the son of a civil servant in Krefeld-Ürdingen, Walter Sanders was a communications officer on the Russian front during the war and unexpectedly had a conversation with Hitler. He describes the horrors and atrocities he witnessed and shared with family and friends when he was on leave during the war.

When I started at the *Gymnasium* in 1930, I became a member of Neudeutschland, a Catholic youth group for *Gymnasium* students, but it was dissolved in 1933. Then I joined the Hitler Youth in 1934–1935. I had to do this; it was obligatory. When I was eighteen, I joined the NSKK (the National Socialist Motor Vehicle Corps). That was a fantastic association inasmuch as it had little to do with National Socialism. We met twice a month in a bar and had something to drink. I didn't even have a uniform.

I wasn't in the party, although, as a civil servant candidate, I was supposed to be. I asked them if they could wait until I completed my military service and they accepted that. Then the war came, and I was able to get around joining the party. This was almost impossible for me as a civil servant, but I was able to do it. Through my parents, I had a different view of things politically, certainly not a National Socialist one.

In 1939, I was drafted. After the Polish campaign, I was stationed with the occupational forces. Then, in 1941, it heated up again and I was in Russia from the first day of the invasion. . . .

[After a time,] the Russians broke through our division, and in a few days it didn't exist anymore. Those of us who survived were put on a train to eastern Prussia for re-outfitting. I got enormously lucky when I landed in a communications regiment. That meant a farewell to combat. I went back to Russia, but to an army command group that was far away from the war, about five hundred kilometers from the front. That was the highest [field] command, directly under the high command of the Wehrmacht. The army group had around a million and a half soldiers.

I held a special position there. There were around ten work places next to each other where all the staff officers were connected. The field marshal was there, the head of the General Staff, and all of those guys with those red pants, the General Staff officers. I had those as well. I had been administered a special oath and had to listen in on the conversations that were held.

At the time we were stationed in the Caucasus, and the Sixth Army [in Stalingrad] also belonged to us. From the Caucasus to Berlin or to eastern Prussia where Hitler sat, amplifiers were built into the communications network everywhere. Otherwise, it all wouldn't have worked. But if one broke down, the entire line would go down. When there was a conversation with the führer, when Hitler called the field marshal, I had two lines. I can still remember that the code name for that was Anna. We were called Fortuna, and Office Anna was the führer headquarters in Rastenburg. And Office Zeppelin was Berlin, the Wehrmacht command.

When Hitler would call us, I would be on the line and I would first hear from a first lieutenant who was my counterpart where Hitler sat. Immediately everything else on the line would then be interrupted, I would call for the marshal, and then he would have everybody who had those red pants on gather around me.

I'd like to tell you something about Hitler. That guy was unbelievable. You have to imagine it: The army group covered an enormous expanse of territory, a front sector of at least five hundred kilometers. You just can't imagine the way in which he would juggle with those divisions and those regiments. Our own field marshal couldn't keep up with him. He needed four men to do this. Hitler had the maps in his head. It was amazing. It was amazing, I tell you. I don't like the guy, but what's true must remain true.

[And then one day] the line went down, and suddenly I had Hitler on the telephone. He was still trying to get through and yelling, "Hello! Hello!" "Please excuse me, my führer, the lines went down," [I answered]. "That can happen, my comrade," he said. He had such a deep voice. And then this happened again three or four more times during our conversation. "We're slowly getting to know each other already," he said.

Just between us, the communications officer was standing just behind me and he was almost wetting his pants. "Calm down," I said. "He's not all that angry. He could have reacted very differently."

Hitler understood that I couldn't do anything about this, and that nobody else could. This happened to me a couple of times. Those were my conversations with the führer. I think he showed more humor with the lower ranks than with the high-ranking officers. He had a different attitude toward them. I don't know this, but I assume it was the case.

One thing that I have never understood is how such people, who had to have been high-ranking officers in World War I, could have behaved like such school children vis-à-vis Hitler. You can't imagine such obedience. Except for Field Marshal List, who once contradicted him [in my presence]. But that was the first and only exception I experienced. Guderian is supposed to have done so as well. I read all the books about it later. You can't imagine this slavish obedience, the fear they had of him.

Could you now tell us about your experiences back at home before the war?

My best friend here in Ürdingen was a Jew. [His family] had a horse dealership right behind our house on the Luisenstrasse. We were at his place one evening in 1934 and the next morning they said that his father had hanged himself in a stall. Prior to this he had told my father, "It's over for us Jews. There's no point anymore." Then he went and hanged himself.

In 1938, after my friend received his diploma from the Moltke *Gymnasium*, he fled to France and then England. Today he is a citizen of France. His sister went to England and their brother went to Belgium. But he was caught and killed during the occupation of Belgium.

Their mother was a really fine woman. She had a brother in Elberfeld who had lost both eyes in World War I. For this he received the wounded medal in gold, which was a very high decoration. He had a cigarette shop, but the Nazis left him in peace and he was able to go on running his shop. Their mother would go there and take care of him. They even received ration coupons just like—I now have to utter that word—Aryans. So I thought they would make it. But, at the end of 1944, the brother died, and, the day after the funeral, they nabbed the woman and sent her to Theresienstadt. We never heard from her again. It's tragic.

There were a lot of Jews in Ürdingen, but they were all working in the trades. One case involved some friends of my parents. The husband was a plumber and he had a small shop here on the Niederstrasse. During the *Kristallnacht*, they smashed in his windows. So what did he do? He put on his black suit and his World War I medal and swept the broken glass away from the street. And then his neighbors came and helped him while some SA men who were there made an about-face. Apparently they were ashamed. That was the feeling he had, he told me afterward. But that didn't help him any in the long run. . . ."

What happened on the thirtieth of January 1933, I can still remember perfectly. My parents had been at the movies. They went to the cinema at 8:00 P.M. and came back at 10:00, and I said to them, "Hitler has just become the Reich Chancellor. It was just on the radio." "For heaven's sake," was their first reaction. My father had to howl with the wolves. He was a civil servant. He was an inspector, later a senior inspector. Whether he wanted to or not, he had to. He had fought in Africa, was in the Herero uprising in Southwest Africa in 1902–1904. He was a kind of "protected species" during the Nazi period. He came to an accommodation [with the new order]. What was there left for him to do? It may sound strange today, but what was he supposed to do then?

We were a mixed family. My mother was Catholic, my father was Protestant, and I was Catholic. I was an altar boy, and my father made sure that I got to church on time. And heaven help me if I wasn't there. Then there was hell to pay. He went to his Protestant church, and my mother went with me to the Catholic church at 10:00 A.M. This never gave us any difficulties whatsoever.

I don't believe [that my father stood behind the new political order]. Not my father, and certainly not my mother. My mother was always skeptical. I don't want to say that she loved the Weimar Republic. She didn't. Those were insane times, four or five governments per year. It was madness. And how those communists, or red front warriors, or whatever they were called, carried on here blowing their little trombones (*Schalmeien*)! And then there was the SA—they were also here before 1933—and both sides would beat each other up. Those were the circumstances, and they were dreadful. I'm convinced that a whole bunch of normal, well-behaved citizens put a cross [next to the Nazis in the Reichstag election] and said, "Thank God order will finally prevail." That's the way it was at the beginning. And, above all else, one can hardly imagine how, presto, Hitler got rid of the unemployment of 7 million people in just a few years.

When I consider the time between 1933 and 1939 before I had to leave, one could live pretty well here in Ürdingen. There had not been many infringements, save for the situation with the Jews. I had some colleagues, whom I worked with later at the city treasury, who were Center Party people and they were not harassed. When I was in the Hitler Youth, they didn't have to ask us for a long time whether we wanted to join the SA, SS, NSKK, and so on. We could choose whether we wanted to or not. So I chose the NSKK because you are in good hands with your drinking buddies. I knew them all; one of them was a doctor. So what we then had was a kind of small motorcycle club and we were allowed to travel around, and that was something.

But weren't people in Ürdingen afraid of the Gestapo, the police, or the Nazis?

Not that I knew. Now things like that were not broadcast widely, except for when they applied to Jews. That's a chapter in itself. Even though it was done on the quiet, when the Gestapo came in the night and took the Jews away, one would know about this on the next day: "My God, they picked up the poor devils after all." But people were rather cautious in discussing such matters. Nevertheless, among the people I knew, there were not only people who supported this, there were also people who were against it. But, nevertheless, I didn't know of a single case in which one had people taken away by the Gestapo. Things must have been worse in Krefeld; it was larger. But here, things like that would have gotten around in Ürdingen. They did indeed grab a few communists though. They were sent to concentration camps, but they eventually came back. After about a half a year or so, they would come back, chastened.

What did people think happened to the Jews who were taken away?

The worst. You can't imagine what the agitation against the Jews was like. There was a newspaper called *Der Stürmer*. It was something you just can't imagine, and it was spewed out week after week. And then there were the [anti-Semitic] films, such as *Jud Süss*, which I saw myself. We had to go to see it because of school. We had to go there as a group. That was indeed a kind of agitation. So when the Jews were deported, we knew that something was going to happen to them.

How was it at your *Gymnasium?* Were racial theory and anti-Semitism actually taught there?

The *Gymnasium* principal had a party badge, but he was anything but a party comrade. There wasn't a single Nazi teacher at our school [with the exception of a teacher who came there later]. Of course, they had to teach what was prescribed and racial theory was also taught, but in a subdued manner, not à la *Der Stürmer* or the like. They had to do this, but they did this in a really subdued way. As teachers, they had to be in the party. But there was not one of them about whom I could say, "That was a Nazi." There were people from every level of society here in Ürdingen, and the teachers knew exactly where one came from and what one's father said and so on. But not a word was said about any of that in class. To that extent, my school years at the Ürdingen *Gymnasium* were not overshadowed by National Socialism.

What was it like with the Jewish shops while you were in Ürdingen?

All their shops were still open, but there would be a sign out front, "Don't buy from Jews." But we did so anyway. Nobody went broke—until they were closed later. They went on selling their goods. We had a horse butcher, a large department store, a garden shop. There were all kinds of things here. There were a lot of Jews who had something here. They went on selling until '38. Only then did it happen.

Wasn't anybody afraid of the SA? In Cologne, they took pictures of people shopping at Jewish stores.

They did that sometimes, but it was known when they would be there. Then nobody would shop at Jewish stores. I tell you, it was liberal here. It could even happen that an SA man would call and say, "Don't let yourself get caught there tomorrow." Not all of those who were involved in the party were enthusiastic Nazis. The shops were open, but of course business got much worse. That's clear. A large part of the population wouldn't go there anymore out of fear, but the [Nazis] couldn't watch the stores from morning to evening. You noticed that there were ever fewer Jewish shops as the Jews still had the opportunity to leave the country. And there were many who did this, above all the younger ones. Eventually they were all gone. The older ones stayed, and the younger ones left, so that in '38, not so many of them were rounded up. The bulk of them had left already. Many of them were well off, and they had relatives everywhere. The Jahn family had relatives in Belgium, England, and France. It wasn't any problem for them to get out. And, at the beginning, the [Nazis] would let them go, and often they could get out of Germany. To the contrary, that was even encouraged.

Were people sad that the Jewish community was getting smaller?

There were some scoundrels among them, just like among us Christians. There were some I couldn't stand, but there were those among us as well. There were the same kind of louts among them as among us. But, for the most part, it was very much regretted. Most of Ürdingen's Jews were middle-class people and businessmen. They were in the veterans association and what all. The people in Ürdingen and the Jews would all say *Du* to one another. We didn't even know that a Jew was something different from us. [When a Jew was picked up by the Nazis, it was said,] "My God, he was picked up. He's gone. He didn't do anything." Or, "She was such a good woman." And then it all would be talked about. The Nazis did all that very secretly and silently and nobody had seen them doing it. Usually they came for the Jews in the night or during the early morning hours.

How do you know that? Did people observe this from their windows?

People living in the same building had noticed this happening. Not only Jews but also Christians, of course, were living in the apartment buildings. Those who took the Jews away were not people from Ürdingen. The Gestapo was in Krefeld, and they always came in civilian clothes, not in SS uniform. They did this very clandestinely. And then, when this would take place during the day, it would be thought they were just being summoned for questioning. That's what we kept hearing. There were no public beatings [of Jews] that took place here. But I can only report on what happened before the beginning of 1938. I don't know what took place after this, as I was no longer here.

But I did experience the pogroms in Russia. They were something horrible. I said there and then to myself, "If there is a God, then this is going to come back to haunt us." For example, when we were advancing into Russia, we passed by an abandoned mine and there were SS men walking along next to the Jews and throwing them into the shaft while they were still alive.

Were they then killed immediately?

I assume. By SS men, but not by [SS men who were] Germans. The Poles, by the way, were beating them themselves. The Jews must have been greatly hated and also in Latvia and Estonia. The Waffen-SS had recruited them there and they were the worst. And I often saw those columns of Jews. [But there was also some opposition to this.] One time I was in a small town and the Jews, one thousand of them or something like that, were being marched on foot to some camp and were being guarded by the SS. And whoever was not able to go on any longer was beaten to death and there were corpses lying all over the place. But then the [Wehrmacht] colonel [who was in charge] went over and said, "If you show up here again, then we are going to shoot you." After that, the SS men made a detour around the town. There were German officers who couldn't abide this. But what could they do against it?

I then said to my comrades, "If there is a Lord God, may he have mercy on us." Those were human beings. And my comrades agreed with me. I wouldn't know of any of my comrades who would have said, "Serves them right." But what are you to do?

The way the eastern Jews were treated was the worst, much worse than here, which was exemplary in comparison. There were huge numbers, millions, of Jews over there. They were basically still the real Jews running around with those caftans and their little locks of hair. It was not a pleasant sight; let us say, it was a sight that was foreign to us. We had never seen Jews like this. We hadn't known Jews like that. We didn't have that kind running around here. I don't know of a single Jew who ran around like that in Krefeld. And those Jews over there were driven like livestock, and whoever was unable to go on was beaten with truncheons and was shot. Later, a couple of wagons would come by and pick them up and take them away. It was terrible. That was in the second half of '41. After that I was with the army group and there was nothing like that there.

What was the relationship like between the SS and Wehrmacht?

That was no friendship. During one terrible winter I was transferred to the SS Division Das Reich. They were almost surrounded, but we had to go there. I was with them for two months. When we arrived, we were greeted by an SS captain, and then he said to us that the only good Russian is a dead Russian. He only spoke of Jews as vermin. So we then knew what was up. I was happy to get back out of that heap of shit, to use proper German. There wasn't any friendship between us and the SS. They were a kind of people unto themselves. They were brutal. I don't know about any atrocities committed by members of the Wehrmacht against the civilian population. I never experienced that, neither in Poland, nor in Russia. Perhaps that happened somewhere, but not on a large scale, I would say.

But in the SS, later the SS Police Division, [it was different]. They were deployed behind the front. They only carried out manhunts. They were only there to catch the Jews. That was beyond our comprehension. How often did we say to ourselves that they [the Jews] were in better hands here at the front than they would be if they were back there? There was a sense of injustice among us, but you had to be very careful [with what you said]. You didn't know what your buddy was thinking. There was one guy with me who had been in the civilian SS and later joined our unit. He always acted as if [he belonged], but we never trusted him. He was just a few years older than me. He would boast that he had been a concentration camp guard sometime after 1933 or 1937 or something like that. And he told us all kinds of things about the Jews and the communists.

What did he tell you exactly?

How things had gone there and how they had beaten up the inmates and so on. He would brag about it. But they wouldn't beat them to death, and, after a certain time, they would get out, except for a few. Most of them were communists as the Jews were not there yet. It was mainly communists that they had there. They [the Jews] were [still] there in Poland.

Have you ever heard of the Warsaw Ghetto? That was a city that was as large as Krefeld. I went through there when I went to Warsaw. The Polish campaign was in '39. I had still been in Schwerin at the time, and then I went to Poland in early '40 to the Warsaw garrison barracks. During the time I was in Poland [from around March or April] 1940, the ghetto wasn't closed. It was still in the beginning phases. What it was like later, I don't know. When I went into town, we drove through this ghetto. It took perhaps twenty minutes to drive through. What you saw there was enough. The streetcar windows were open, so you could see outside. I don't know what it was like later on, but what one saw back then was bad enough. You saw these ragged, emaciated figures, just skin and bones wasting away. It was clear that they hardly had water to wash their beards with and so on.

The worst thing for us was to see the children, such tiny children, such poor little creatures, and how they would sit there holding out those tin cans. Their heads consisted only of eyes. But what eyes and what tiny faces. That was what was most distressing. You could have cried when you saw those children. It was dreadful. But what could you do? Because of this, you could have doubts about religion. How can a God allow something like that? But that wouldn't have done anything for them.

Did you ever see any possibility back then to do something against it all?

No. Then you would have been sent away yourself. Nothing, nothing. We already had enough difficulties in Russia. How often had we given those Russians [who were living in such pitiful conditions] some of our bread? Although that was strictly forbidden, the head of our company looked the other way and didn't say anything. And we also had given some chocolate to the children. That was also strictly forbidden. That was fraternization. But we did it anyway.

But you couldn't get close to the Jews. The streetcar didn't stop and you couldn't get off it. It rushed through. And you couldn't throw anything out from the windows. They were closed. You couldn't help them there. If you had been hiding something to throw out to them, it would have been your turn next. This was because the SS who were guarding them were swarming around everywhere. And there was also an SS guard on the tram to make sure that nobody jumped on or off the tram or whatever. There was nothing you could do. You saw only misery. More than anything, I remember those children. Those big eyes looked at you and you didn't understand the world any longer. Poor little creatures of three, four, or five years of age. Those children were the most appalling thing I saw.

Did you ever write to your parents or tell them about what you experienced?

You were not allowed to write. Tell them? I not only told my parents about that, I also told others when I was on leave—like good friends and relatives here. But you didn't come home all that often. I was here three times on leave. Of course I talked about it. But I knew with whom I was talking.

And what kind of reaction did they have?

For the sake of those who say today that they didn't know anything about it—a large part of the population did know about it. Perhaps [they didn't know] that it was quite as brutal as it was in reality. But they knew that there were concentration camps. They knew that Jews were kept there. And later, word got around that they were gassed. It wasn't for nothing that it was said in those years, "Take care, otherwise you'll go up the chimney." That was a familiar figure of speech. It circulated everywhere in Germany. [An expression like] "otherwise, you'll go through the chimney" doesn't come about by chance.

Part THREE

JEWISH SURVIVORS' SURVEY EVIDENCE

+8+

EVERYDAY LIFE AND ANTI-SEMITISM

In the final words of his interview, William Benson, who left his home in Leipzig in 1937 and fought during the last years of the war with the partisans in Italy, states, "They should make a big park out of all of Germany, a beautiful park—the location is perfect—and use all the Germans as fertilizer. That is what I felt and what I still feel." In a similar vein, Ruth Mendel, who was raised in Frankfurt and survived Auschwitz concentration camp, laments near the end of her interview, "There were two Germanys, and too bad there weren't a hundred of them, broken up into little pieces." Such sentiments, though not held by all Holocaust survivors, reflect what many survivors continue to feel today about the Germany that uprooted their lives, murdered their families and friends, and left them with tortured memories that have lasted a lifetime.[1] These expressions of anger and bitterness not only arise from experiences of hardship and loss but also stem from a deep sense of betrayal by a country and a people most German Jews once proudly claimed as their own.

Time and again in interviews we conducted, German Jewish Holocaust survivors told us about how very German and deeply integrated into German society they and their families had once felt and how difficult it had been to come to terms with becoming outcasts in the new German society after Hitler's takeover in January 1933. Although they were not asked explicitly about this, about one-third of the survivors described the pride their fathers and uncles took in having been decorated or wounded frontline soldiers in World War I.

Henry Singer, formerly of Berlin, explains that many Jews "were fanatical patriots for Germany . . . so patriotic they would give their life for Germany." Another third of the interviewees volunteered that they had blond hair and blue eyes or "didn't look Jewish." Some even referred to themselves as "very Aryan looking" (as did Ernst Levin, who was raised in Breslau) or "looking like any other Aryan" (as did Thomas Green from Mannheim). Werner Holz, who was brought up in Krefeld, took it a step further and criticized Hitler and many other top Nazis for themselves not measuring up to the Nazi racial stereotype, whereas he himself "was blond" and "had more of a German face than they did."

Near the beginning of his interview, William Benson explains, "Some of those German Jews were more German than Jews. They had medals and were really gung-ho—real, real Germans, especially the rich ones—because Hitler was against communism." Later in his interview, he recalls his confusion when youths from Leipzig first called him a Jewish pig: "I was only a kid. I didn't know what I was, Jew or not Jew. . . . We were very integrated. Especially in the business where my father was, they were always very integrated. My father had German friends and they even came to our house—businesspeople, customers. My father always entertained. And that is why my father perished—because he believed in his Germans. . . . Even in 1942, when he gave himself up, he still believed in them."

Perhaps Thomas Green summarizes best the views of the majority of the survivor population about the situation they faced and the shock and bewilderment they felt when Nazism took over the German nation they loved so much: "The German Jews before 1933 were totally assimilated. There were instances of anti-Semitism even under the kaiser. But, in general, it was a blooming time for German Jewry. The assimilation went so far as to present a danger of Jews disappearing eventually as a religion. It took Hitler to awaken the German Jews to the fact that they are really Jewish. . . . It came to us German Jews as a tremendous shock that this anti-Semitic policy was introduced. It took us such a long time to grasp this new direction. It was unthinkable. Because we were so utterly German—more German than some of the Germans themselves—we couldn't understand that there should be a difference among people because of religion or race. . . . There is no Jewish race. You were a German citizen of Jewish belief. It took us by surprise. And because of that so many people perished."[2]

Whereas Green expressed views that represent the majority of survivors we interviewed for this book, others were far less positive in their assessment of the historical situation of German Jewry prior to the Nazi takeover. For example, Josef Stone, the son of a Jewish salesman from Frankfurt, asserts, "A Jew was always a Jew in Germany." And Hermann Gottfried, whose father was a professor of law in Berlin, reckons, "Ninety-nine percent of Germans either were anti-Jewish or were *Mitläufer* [fellow travelers] and continued going along with it." Henry Singer, whose father was a master tailor in Berlin, tempered his remarks by saying, "They were not all bad. The majority, yes, but you cannot condemn all of them because the majority was bad." Yet he concludes, "The anti-Semitism in Germany was there before Hitler came to power. He just openly sanctioned it, and he also asked to kill."

These examples show that while all Jewish survivors of Nazi Germany were plagued with the same anti-Semitic governmental policies, their assessments of the plight of German Jews in the Third Reich vary widely. This divergence of opinion is due in part to the markedly different personal experiences individual Jews had in contending with official anti-Semitic policy, and to the different treatment they received from their German neighbors. While some Jews experienced relatively little anti-Semitic bigotry before or after Hitler and even received considerable help and support from their fellow German townspeople at crucial moments,[3] others encountered constant persecution from German neighbors, classmates, teachers, and work colleagues throughout and sometimes before the Third Reich.

This division of experience and opinion reflects a raging debate among Holocaust scholars over the prevalence and virulence of popular anti-Semitism in Nazi Germany.[4] Whereas some scholars insist that German society and nearly all Germans had long been imbued with a pathological hatred of Jews that Hitler did not create but only unleashed, others maintain that the history of popular anti-Semitism in Germany was similar to that of other European countries. Even under Nazism, they argue, Germans were divided in their attitudes toward Jews, giving the Jewish population "mixed signals" that complicated the painful decisions on which their survival often depended.[5]

Although there is no evidence that resolves this debate conclusively, the data presented in this chapter sheds considerable light on the questions that lie at the heart of this debate: How much and what specific forms of popular anti-Semitic discrimination and persecution did Jews experience in the Third Reich? Did the size and nature of the communities in which they lived account for any significant differences in the popular anti-Semitism they encountered? How can Jews' relations with their German fellow citizens before 1933 best be characterized, and how did these relations change over the years of the Third Reich? And, finally, how much sympathy, help, and support did Jews receive from the non-Jewish population, and who were those who offered such sympathy, help, and support?

The Survey and Oral History Data

Before attempting to answer these questions, we need to examine the evidence we will be using, for it is unusual and in some ways unique. Most studies dealing with the persecution of the Jews in Nazi Germany have relied primarily on either archival documents originally generated by the perpetrators (e.g., police and judicial investigations and case files, court records, newspaper accounts, mood and morale reports compiled by the Gestapo and SD, Hitler's and other Nazis' speeches and pronouncements, etc.)⁶ or biographical accounts from the victims in the form of memoirs, diaries, and sometimes oral history interviews.⁷ In contrast to these efforts, our study is based exclusively on an unprecedented and systematic social-scientific survey that we administered to a large number of Jews who lived in the Third Reich and on in-depth interviews that we conducted with a large and representative sample of the survey participants. A brief discussion of the design and administration of our study and of the backgrounds of the people who participated in it follows.

We began our study in the fall of 1994 by constructing a written twelve-page questionnaire with fifty-four separate questions pertaining to survivors' demographic and socioeconomic backgrounds and their experiences with and knowledge of anti-Semitism, terror, and mass murder in Nazi Germany. Since most survivors do not live in Germany and most understand English, the questionnaire was written in the English language.

We sent the questionnaire to two separate groups of survivors in 1995 and 1996. Aiding us in the administration of the larger survey was the United States Holocaust Memorial Museum, which, in the early months of 1995, endorsed our study in a cover letter and mailed our written questionnaires to a thousand German Jewish survivors whose names, addresses, and identities the museum held in confidence.⁸ Whereas the survivors in this larger group lived in cities and towns spread across Nazi Germany, the survivors in the smaller survey conducted a year later lived in Krefeld, a modest-size community on the Rhine River not far from the Dutch border. The names and addresses of these people were provided by a Krefeld survivor and they included all ninety-four Krefeld Jews who were presumed to be alive when we mailed out the questionnaires in the early winter of 1996.

A total of 507 survivors filled out and returned the questionnaires, 463 from the larger group and 44 from the smaller one. Although the nearly identical response rate we received—slightly over 46 percent—for both surveys compares favorably with the response rates of other types of surveys, it would be even higher had we not sent the questionnaires to an unknown number of people who were either deceased or too infirm to respond. Nevertheless, we were pleased with the response and thankful that roughly 81 percent of those who responded indicated willingness to talk with us personally and provided contact information. Eventually we conducted lengthy interviews with fifty survivors and selected twenty for publication. Finally, we were pleased to receive such a favorable response from both groups of survivors since it would be useful to compare the two groups.⁹

Broadly speaking, the survivors who took part in the survey are representative of the Jewish population in the Third Reich except that, by necessity, they are somewhat younger than most Jews were at the time and a slightly higher percentage of them had emigrated to other countries before World War II. Otherwise, in terms of gender, socioeconomic and political backgrounds, experiences with discrimination and terror, and places of origin, they mirror the Jewish population living in Germany during the Nazi period.

Like most Jews living in the Third Reich, most of the participants in our survey were relatively well educated, came from middle- to upper-middle-class business and professional families that typically supported liberal political parties in the Weimar Republic, and lived in either Berlin, where over one-quarter of them resided, or in another large city like Frankfurt, Cologne, Hamburg, Munich, Dresden, or Düsseldorf. Fewer than 10 percent lived in small towns.[10] In terms of their gender and age, 56 percent are male, 44 percent female, and their median year of birth is 1922.

Similar to most Jews in Nazi Germany, approximately two-thirds of the survivors we surveyed left Germany before World War II began in September 1939.[11] Emigration, however, did not necessarily guarantee the Jews' security. Although nearly half of the survivors who left before the war made emigration difficult managed to make their way to safe havens like Great Britain (26 percent), the United States (17 percent), or Palestine (4 percent), one-third initially went to neighboring countries on the Continent, for example, the Netherlands (11 percent), Belgium (9 percent), France (7 percent), and Poland (6 percent). Many were swept up later in the Holocaust. Of those who emigrated before the war to France, Holland, Belgium, or Poland, 29 percent were deported during the Holocaust and 40 percent became concentration camp inmates in places like Auschwitz, Dachau, Buchenwald, Sachsenhausen, Westerbork, and Gurs. Nevertheless, the situation was considerably worse for those who remained in Germany. Over two-thirds were eventually deported to ghettos or concentration camps; of those who had not left before September 1941 when emigration became impossible, only one-quarter were not deported and many only managed to survive by going into hiding (see, for example, the interviews of Rosa Hirsch, Ilse Landau, and Lore Schwartz).

Although the economic boycotts, Nuremberg Laws, and other discriminatory measures caused many Jews to flee the country in the first several years of Hitler's rule, most held on to hopes that the situation would improve and chose to remain in Germany. But this changed dramatically during the *Kristallnacht* pogrom of November 9–10, 1938, when across the country Jewish synagogues were set ablaze, Jewish homes and businesses were vandalized, and between 20,000 and 30,000 Jewish men were rounded up and carted off to concentration camps where they were informed that their release depended on leaving the country with their families forthwith.[12] Whereas Jewish emigration before November 1938 had been a relatively small but steady stream, after *Kristallnacht* it became a tidal wave. In 1939 alone, 154 of the survivors in our study left Germany, representing nearly half of all survivors who left the country in the 1930s and nearly one-third of the entire survivor population.

Several of the survivor interviews in this book demonstrate in graphic detail how the anti-Jewish pogrom was perhaps the defining moment when German Jews finally realized that any hopes they entertained about Germany returning to its senses were illusory. Of the twenty survivor interviews we decided to publish, five involve Jews who left the country within a year after November 1938, but nearly all survivors who were still in Germany at the time remember the "night of broken glass" with intense pain, bitterness, and sorrow.

Popular Anti-Semitism and Anti-Jewish Discrimination

Certainly *Kristallnacht* served as a wake-up call for the Jews of Germany. Many ordinary Germans either participated in it or accepted it. Some added insult to injury by scoffing and jeering at the bewildered Jews, like Josef Stone in Frankfurt, as they were rounded up and marched through the streets on the following morning. Nevertheless, questions remain about the broad popularity of the pogrom and about the extent of popular anti-Semitism that infected the German population.

When, in 1988, Ian Kershaw published a well-received study of German popular opinion in Bavaria, he pointed out that reactions to the *Kristallnacht* pogrom were mixed, but he stressed evidence indicating that a great number of Germans disapproved of it: "A broad swell of disapproval, unmistakable despite the intimidation, found muted expression in the comments of reporters. Most people were too afraid to speak openly, but muttered invectives and words of disgust at the barbarity of the action and shame and horror at what had taken place could be observed in Munich as in other German cities. . . . Goebbels's claim that the pogrom had been the 'spontaneous answer' of the German people to the murder of vom Rath was universally recognized as ludicrous."[13] Twelve years later, however, when he published the second volume of his acclaimed Hitler biography *Hitler 1936–1945: Nemesis*, his assessment of the popular German reaction to *Kristallnacht* had become more negative in tone. Although he continued to argue that the pogrom was "organized and carried out by the Party" and that "many ordinary people were appalled" by it, he now placed greater stress on popular approval: "Ordinary citizens, affected by the climate of hatred and propaganda appealing to base instincts, motivated too by sheer material envy and greed, nevertheless followed the Party's lead in many places and joined in the destruction and looting of Jewish property. Sometimes individuals regarded as the pillars of their communities were involved. . . . Schoolchildren and adolescents were frequently ready next day to add their taunts, jibes, and insults to Jews being rounded up by the police, who were often subjected to baying, howling mobs hurling stones at them as they were taken into custody."[14]

If Kershaw's assessment of *Kristallnacht* changed modestly in tone and emphasis between 1988 and 2000, it probably stems from his conscientious weighing of the mountain of new scholarship and historical evidence on the Third Reich and the Holocaust that appeared in the interim.[15] Still, despite all that has been learned over the years, many questions remain that a systematic survey of the experiences and opinions of the people who lived through the Nazi period can help clarify.

How then, on balance, did the Jewish survivors we surveyed assess their relations with and treatment by the German population? What do they tell us about how virulent, widespread, and popular anti-Semitism really was among the German population? We might begin with an analysis of the survivors' appraisal of the pre–1933 situation.

As explained at the beginning of this chapter, most of the people we interviewed stated that they and their families had felt well accepted and integrated in German society. Only a few believed that anti-Semitism was especially prevalent in Germany before the Nazi takeover in January 1933. This, if confirmed by the more systematic survey data, would help explain why so many Jews decided to remain in the country for so many years in hopes that normalcy and decency would return. It would also indicate that a "unique eliminationist antisemitism" did not prevail among the German populace and German society prior to 1933, as Daniel Jonah Goldhagen boldly insists.[16]

Whereas most of the questions in the survey deal with survivors' experiences during the Nazi period, two questions relate to the pre–1933 situation—one involving relations with their non-Jewish school classmates and the other with their families' treatment by non-Jews in their communities; the answers to these questions do not point toward a German society full of anti-Semitic prejudice before Hitler came to power. First we asked the following question: "During your school years in Germany, how would you describe the manner in which you were treated by non-Jewish pupils in your class?" A list of possible responses was provided ranging from "mostly friendly" to "mostly unfriendly." Of those who finished their schooling before 1933, one can conclude that most Jews appear to have gotten along well with their non-Jewish classmates before Hitler came to power. Thus, of the sixty-seven survivors born before 1916 and who had therefore completed their primary and secondary schooling before the Nazi period began, 55 percent characterized the treatment they received from their non-Jewish fellow pupils as being either "friendly" or "mostly friendly," and only 16 percent rated the treatment they received as being either "unfriendly" or "mostly unfriendly." The rest of the survivors in this age cohort had either no relations with non-Jewish pupils or described their relations with them as a "mixture of friendly and unfriendly." The situation worsened considerably for those who went to school during the Nazi period itself. For example, only 32 percent of those born between 1920 and 1924 rated their relations with non-Jewish pupils as either friendly or mostly friendly, and this declined to 17

Table 8.1   Family's Treatment by Non-Jews Before and After 1933
(By Type of Community)

	All of Germany %	Berlin %	Medium-Size Cities %	Small Towns %	Catholic Cities %
Before 1933					
Friendly or mostly friendly	69	59	71	68	76
Mixture of friendly and unfriendly	14	22	16	5	14
Unfriendly or mostly unfriendly	3	3	2	10	3
Other (too young, etc.)	14	16	11	17	8
After 1933					
Friendly/ no change	10	9	8	8	14
Mixture of friendly and unfriendly	11	14	7	14	10
Worse/ hostile	58	52	61	70	55
Other (too young, etc.)	21	24	24	8	22
N of cases	**471**	**122**	**99**	**40**	**78**

NOTE: Medium-size cities include 33 cities with populations of between 50,000 and 200,000 inhabitants; small towns include 39 small towns with circa 10,000 or fewer inhabitants; Catholic cities include Aachen, Bonn, Cologne, Düsseldorf, Krefeld, Mainz, Munich, and Würzburg.

Table 8.2   Family's Treatment by Non-Jews Before and After 1933
(By Gender, Year of Birth, Year of Leaving Germany)

| | Gender | | Year of Birth | | | Year of Leaving Germany | | |
	Male %	Female %	1895–1919 %	1920–1925 %	1926–1932 %	Before 1938 %	1938–1939 %	After 1939 %
Before 1933								
Friendly/ mostly friendly	68	71	74	71	63	71	71	66
Mixture of friendly and unfriendly	16	12	16	16	10	15	15	11
Unfriendly/ mostly unfriendly	3	3	6	2	3	4	1	5
Other	13	14	4	11	24	10	13	18
After 1933								
Friendly/ no change	10	10	15	10	5	14	9	6
Mixture of friendly and unfriendly	9	13	8	11	12	8	7	23
Worse/ hostile	61	53	59	61	49	48	67	39
Other	20	24	17	18	35	29	18	32
N of cases	**262**	**194**	**95**	**251**	**112**	**96**	**227**	**86**

percent among those born after 1924. The picture these figures paint of a mostly positive relationship between Jews and non-Jews that only soured after Hitler came to power is confirmed by answers to questions about how the survivors' families were treated by non-Jewish citizens in their communities both before and after 1933.

The two tables (shown on pp. 270 and 271) provide strong evidence that it was not only Jewish schoolchildren who experienced positive relations with non-Jews in the pre-Hitler years. These tables summarize the responses that different types of survivors gave to questions we asked about their families' treatment by non-Jews. As the figures at the top of the first table indicate, more than two-thirds of all survivors say that their families had either friendly or mostly friendly relations with their non-Jewish fellow citizens before 1933; only 3 percent had unfriendly or mostly unfriendly relations. Moreover, as the evidence in the two tables shows, this overwhelmingly positive assessment was shared by Jews who lived in communities of different sizes and religious backgrounds, by both male and female Jews, by younger and older Jews, by Jews who left Germany in the 1930s, and by Jews who lived in Germany throughout the entire Nazi period. Although some might think that these Jews were viewing their families' past lives in Weimar Germany through rose-colored lenses, the consistency of this pattern of responses among different subgroups of the survey population is striking.

The only significant percentage (10 percent) of survivors to say that their families were treated in an unfriendly or mostly unfriendly manner by non-Jews before 1933 had lived in small German towns, but survivors from small towns represent only a small minority of the survivors in general. Even though this percentage is higher than it is for Jews who lived in other types of communities, the percentage of small-town Jews who rate their families' treatment as primarily positive is somewhat higher than it is for Jews who lived in Berlin, and about equal to that of Jews in general before 1933.

If, as the data show, most Jews cherish positive memories about their relations with Germans before Hitler assumed power, few hold romantic thoughts about what they experienced in Germany between 1933 and 1945. Although many Jews received help and support at critical moments from German friends and acquaintances during the Nazi years (as will be discussed more fully later in this chapter), it did not prevent the lives of all Jews in Germany from becoming more and more of a nightmare as time went on. But was this nightmare primarily brought on by the ever intensifying anti-Semitic policies of the National Socialist government and inflicted on the Jews mostly by the Gestapo, police, and other Nazi officials? Or were German civilians crucial agents in adding to the misery of their Jewish neighbors, classmates, and colleagues? In the opinion of the Jews who lived in Germany during the Nazi years, how popular and widespread was anti-Semitism among the German population, what forms did it take, and how quickly did it take hold?

The short answer to these questions is that in the experience of most Jews, popular anti-Semitism in Nazi Germany was powerful and strengthened with continuing Nazi anti-Jewish policy and legislation. But this general sentiment was not shared by all Jews, and some had far better experiences than others with the non-Jewish population. Even Jews from the same city often had quite different views and experiences. Thus, while Helmut Grunewald of Cologne says that, with the exception of his own personal friends, "otherwise, anti-Semitism was everywhere," Karl Meyer states that "in Cologne, they never had this anti-Semitism." Part of the difference between their viewpoints probably stems from the fact that Meyer managed to emigrate to safety in Shanghai in early November 1938 and was spared the tragic experiences of *Kristallnacht* and the Holocaust, while Grunewald remained in Germany until early 1943, when he was deported to Auschwitz concentration camp.

The length of time Jews remained in Germany is, however, not the only determinant of the severity of the anti-Semitism they experienced. Indeed, some Jews who left Germany in the 1930s view the popular anti-Semitism they encountered as more intense than Jews who remained in Germany during the war years. Recall the views of Hermann Gottfried, who left Berlin for Great Britain in April 1939 on a children's transport, and compare them with those of Ilse Landau, who originally came from the small city of Düren outside of Cologne and remained in Germany during the war and went into hiding with her husband in Berlin in January 1943. While Gottfried bitterly remarked in his interview that "99 percent of the German population were either anti-Jewish or were *Mitläufer*," Landau began her interview by saying, "We were very much loved. We didn't have any enemies in Düren at all." She later followed this up with similarly positive comments about her experiences with Germans during the war years. About her time working as a forced laborer at Siemens in Berlin, for example, she said, "The foremen and foreladies were German people. They were marvelous to me."

The varied opinions of the four people above reflect the broad spread of opinion among survivors in general. But the fact that Grunewald and Gottfried better represent the majority opinion than Meyer and Landau is made clear in the figures presented in the bottom half of Tables 8.1 and 8.2. After we asked the survivors how their families were treated by non-Jewish citizens before 1933, we then asked them the following question: "After the Nazis came to power in 1933, was there a change in the treatment your family received by most non-Jewish citizens in your town? How would you describe this change?" Table 8.1 provides figures for how survivors from different types of German communities answered this question, and Table 8.2 does this for survivors of different individual backgrounds.

The figures show that after Hitler took power in 1933, the once positive relations between Jews and non-Jews deteriorated. Whereas over two-thirds of the survivors' families before 1933 had friendly relations with non-Jews in their communities, after 1933 nearly two-thirds had relations that the survivors described as clearly worse or even hostile; only about one in ten of the survivors' families continued to experience good relations with non-Jews in their communities. Not only did relations between Jews and non-Jews become worse in general after 1933, they declined dramatically in all types of communities. Although the decline was somewhat more precipitous in small towns and medium-size cities than in large, Catholic-dominated cities, very few Jewish families in any German communities after 1933 maintained friendly associations with non-Jews.

Jews from all types of communities say that their families' relations with non-Jews deteriorated after 1933, and this was also true of Jews of all types of individual backgrounds, with a few modest exceptions. Thus, as the figures in Table 8.2 show, Jewish men and Jewish women held similar views on this issue, as did Jews of different ages. Still, it is not easy to explain why the youngest survivors were the least likely to say that their families continued to enjoy positive relations with non-Jews after 1933. Perhaps they had not lived in Germany long enough to develop the kind of lasting friendships that many older survivors had with non-Jews before Hitler came to power. But this is only conjecture. However, it makes intuitive sense that the assessment of survivors who left Germany in the first years of the Third Reich was somewhat more positive than among those who left later or did not leave the country at all. It also strongly suggests that the relations between Jews and non-Jews not only became worse almost immediately after 1933, but they continued to worsen over time. The fact that only 6 percent of the survivors who remained in Germany after 1939 continued to be treated in a friendly manner by non-Jews in their communities after 1933 clearly points to a sour relationship that developed over the years between Jews and their non-Jewish neighbors and former friends and colleagues in the Third Reich.

Although the large majority of survivors say the treatment they and their families received from non-Jews became ever worse after 1933, this does not necessarily imply that they believed all Germans around them were ardent Nazi supporters. In fact, in a subsequent question in which we asked the survivors to rate how their German neighbors "were disposed toward National Socialism after 1933," only one-third answered that "most were for it," and roughly another one-third described the support for National Socialism among their neighbors as "mixed."

But, if most survivors did not think their German neighbors were particularly attracted to National Socialism, they also did not think that many of them opposed Nazism either. As Table 8.3 shows, only 3 percent of the survivors say that most of their German neighbors were against National Socialism, and survivors from different types of communities and different types of personal backgrounds were again largely unified in this viewpoint.

Table 8.3   Disposition of Non-Jewish Neighbors Toward National Socialism
(By Type of Community)

	All of Germany %	Berlin %	Medium-Sized Cities %	Small Towns %	Catholic Cities %
Most for	33	37	30	33	29
Some for, some against	35	31	36	53	37
Most against	3	4	2	0	4
Don't know	29	29	32	14	30
N of cases	**471**	**122**	**96**	**38**	**99**

(By Gender, Year of Leaving Germany)

	Gender		**Year of Birth**			**Year of Leaving Germany**		
	Male %	Female %	1895–1919 %	1920–1925 %	1926–1932 %	Before 1938 %	1938–1939 %	After 1939 %
Most for	39	26	32	34	34	29	32	39
Some for, some against	34	36	33	40	22	23	37	42
Most against	3	3	5	3	2	7	2	3
Don't know	24	35	30	23	42	42	29	17
N of cases	**240**	**178**	**87**	**230**	**103**	**84**	**211**	**78**

There is, however, one significant caveat in regard to how the survivors assess the extent of National Socialist support among their German neighbors, and this points once again toward the conclusion that Jews believe that anti-Semitism became increasingly popular and widespread among the German population over time. Survivors who had lived longer in Nazi Germany were considerably more likely to view National Socialism as having gained a large degree of support among their German neighbors than survivors who had only experienced a few years of Nazi rule; in fact, among survivors who were still in the country after 1939, over 80 percent believe that their German neighbors were either fully in support of the Nazi movement (39 percent) or at least mixed in their support (42 percent), and this compares with a total of only 52 percent among those who left the country before 1938. Thus, since anti-Semitism was a major component of the Nazi movement, and since the longer Jews lived in Germany the more Nazi support they detected among their German neighbors, the conclusion follows that most Jews who were there to witness and experience it believe that anti-Semitism became ever more palatable and popular among their German neighbors over the years.

The evidence pointing toward a rapid deterioration in Jews' relations with non-Jews and toward a growing support for the National Socialist movement among the Jews' German neighbors provides largely subjective indications of growing anti-Semitic popular sentiment in the Third Reich. To provide more objective information about the explicit types of anti-Semitism that Jews suffered and to help assess the involvement of the German civilian population in anti-Semitic behavior, we posed the following question near the middle of the questionnaire: "What kind of harassment or discrimination did you personally experience during the Third Reich?" We then provided a list of twelve types of anti-Semitic discrimination and harassment and asked the survivors to indicate which they had personally experienced. Among these were several that applied to the German civilian population (verbal taunts and threats; physical beatings; spying by neighbors, coworkers, and fellow pupils; home vandalized; and family's business vandalized) and several others that applied to Nazi officials (verbal taunts and threats, physical beatings, spying by the police, being sent to jail, being sent to a concentration camp). Tables 8.4 and 8.5 summarize the responses.

Even though the specific types of discrimination and harassment on our list constitute only some of the myriad types of persecution Jews experienced in Nazi Germany, it was the unusual Jew who did not suffer any persecution. Only 11 percent of the survivors experienced "none of the above," but more than half experienced three or more types of persecution. More often than not these involved discriminatory acts committed by German civilians. Nazi leaders and officials may have set the Third Reich's campaign against the Jews in motion,

Table 8.4 Types of Persecution Experienced (By Type of Community)

	All of Germany %	Berlin %	Medium-Size Cities %	Small Towns %	Catholic Citites %
From civilians					
Verbal taunts or threats	63	63	65	70	44
Physical beatings	22	22	24	22	18
Spied on by neighbors	19	20	26	22	16
Spied on by coworkers	5	3	5	3	7
Spied on by fellow pupils	15	10	18	22	10
Home vandalized	25	15	41	46	34
Family's business vandalized	24	26	36	30	23
From Nazi officials					
Verbal taunts or threats	27	19	24	43	23
Physical beatings	10	8	11	8	16
Spied upon by police	8	6	13	8	10
Put in jail	11	10	15	11	15
Put in concentration camp	27	26	33	35	23
None of the above	11	15	8	0	18
N of cases	**406**	**106**	**85**	**37**	**61**

Table 8.5   Types of Persecution Experienced (By Gender, Year of Birth, Year of Leaving Germany)

	Gender		Year of Birth			Year of Leaving Germany		
	Male %	Female %	1895–1919 %	1920–1925 %	1926–1932 %	Before 1938 %	1938–1939 %	After 1939 %
From civilians								
Verbal taunts or threats	68	56	43	67	69	49	67	69
Physical beatings	30	11	21	19	27	20	21	19
Spied on by neighbors	18	21	8	21	23	7	19	31
Spied on by coworkers	4	5	11	5	1	0	4	11
Spied on by fellow pupils	17	12	13	17	14	11	15	16
Home vandalized	24	26	24	25	25	14	25	30
Family's business vandalized	26	23	19	30	17	14	25	30
From Nazi officials								
Verbal taunts or threats	30	22	25	28	25	16	27	40
Physical beatings	13	6	17	8	11	11	4	19
Spied on by police	8	9	6	7	13	4	5	21
Put in jail	12	9	17	12	5	10	7	19
Put in concentration camp	27	28	29	25	31	19	12	66
None of the above	10	12	17	9	11	22	12	1
N of cases	**236**	**169**	**72**	**223**	**111**	**74**	**203**	**83**

but for many Jews the faces of persecution they most commonly saw were not those of people dressed in Nazi uniforms. They were those of their neighbors, classmates, teachers, coworkers, and townspeople wearing civilian clothing. The interviews provide numerous examples of this, Jews being isolated by their teachers in the front or back rows of classrooms, being called names like "dirty Jew" and "Jewish pig" by neighboring children and adults, being jeered by crowds of onlookers as they were marched or carted off to deportation trains, having their homes and shops destroyed by greedy civilians as well as Nazi storm troopers during the *Kristallnacht* pogrom, and being accosted and beaten up in the streets by the local population.

Table 8.4 shows that nearly two-thirds of survivors endured "verbal taunts or threats from German civilians" during the Nazi years, which was more than twice as common as "verbal taunts and threats from Nazi officials." While verbal abuse might be a relatively mild form of anti-Semitic behavior in comparison with other forms of anti-Semitic persecution, the ratio of civilian to official acts of persecution was more or less the same for more severe forms of discrimination like spying and physical beatings. The issue of spying will be discussed in more detail in the next chapter on state-sponsored terror and mass murder, but for present purposes it is significant to observe that more than twice as many survivors believe they were spied on by civilian neighbors (19 percent) than by Nazi police authorities (8 percent), and neighbors were only some of the civilians who spied on them. Even more disturbing, 22 percent of the survivors (30 percent of males and 11 percent of females) suffered physical beatings from German civilians, and this was nearly three times the percentage of those who suffered beatings from Nazi policemen or other officials (8 percent of the total, 13 percent of males, 6 percent of females) even though 11 percent of the survivors spent periods of time in Nazi jails and 27 percent in concentration camps.

Approximately one-quarter of the survivors' homes and businesses were vandalized in anti-Semitic acts that German civilians commonly participated in, suggesting that official Nazi anti-Semitic policies found a strong popular base among the German citizenry. Although anti-Semitism was unquestionably widespread, it was more prevalent in some kinds of communities than others and Jews of some backgrounds fared somewhat better than Jews of other backgrounds. As the figures in Table 8.4 show, Jews who lived in communities with a majority Catholic population reported lower percentages of several types of civilian-based discrimination (in particular verbal taunts and threats) than Jews who lived elsewhere. Also Jews who lived in large cities received better treatment in several ways than Jews who lived in small communities, and this is probably one of the main reasons why many Jews moved from small cities and towns to larger cities like Berlin during the Third Reich. Small-town Jews, as the evidence shows, were more often verbally insulted or threatened by both German civilians and Nazi officials, more of their homes were vandalized, and they appear to have been spied on more often by their neighbors and schoolmates than Jews in big cities like Berlin, or in Germany in general. Perhaps the most important indicator that small-town Jews received worse treatment than Jews in larger communities is that every single survivor from a small German town experienced at least one type of discrimination and harassment listed in Tables 8.4 and 8.5. But many survivors from larger communities answered that they had not experienced any of the types of persecution listed (15 percent of survivors from Berlin, 8 percent from medium-size cities, and 11 percent from all types of communities).

Several of the survivor interviews provide additional evidence that small towns were especially inhospitable for Jews. For example, Rebecca Weisner of Berlin describes being sent in 1938 at the age of twelve to stay with her aunt in Stralsund, a small city on the Baltic Sea, where, she says, about twenty Jewish families lived. When she got off the train, she says, "All [the Jews] were beaten up. They were already beaten up on the streets by the Germans. I don't know how they knew they were Jewish, but being that it wasn't such a big place, maybe they knew that. They didn't arrest them, but they were beaten up. This happened in every small town in Germany."

If the size and religious makeup of German communities were significant factors in determining the relative prevalence of anti-Semitic activity, what can be said about the gender and age backgrounds of the Jews, and to what extent did popular anti-Semitism gain intensity over time? The evidence provided in Table 8.5 helps answer these questions.

As the percentages reported in the first five columns of the table show, the gender and age backgrounds of the Jewish survivors accounted for modest differences among them in the relative amount of anti-Semitism they experienced, but Jews from both genders and all age-groups suffered heavily from anti-Semitic activity perpetrated against them by both German civilians and Nazi officials. For example, even though more Jewish men than Jewish women suffered verbal and physical abuse from both German civilians and Nazi authorities, a strong majority of both Jewish men and women suffered verbal abuse of some kind and a considerable minority of both Jewish men and women endured physical beatings. Although younger Jews were more likely to experience civilian taunts and threats and physical beatings, they were less likely to be beaten by police authorities, spied on by coworkers, or put in jail. Finally, whether they were male or female or older or younger Jews, there was essentially no difference among them in their likelihood of having their homes or family businesses vandalized or being sent to concentration camps.

Far more significant than considerations of gender and age in determining the amount of anti-Semitism that Jewish survivors experienced, however, was the length of time that the survivors remained in Germany. The evidence presented in the last three columns of Table 8.5 provides yet another indication that popular anti-Semitism grew more intense and virulent over the years of Nazi Germany. By almost every measure of discrimination and harassment listed on the table, the longer Jews remained in the country, the more overt anti-Semitic persecution they experienced. Although fewer than half of the survivors who left Germany before 1938 endured verbal taunts or threats from German civilians, over two-thirds of those who left after this time experienced such abuse; while only 7 percent of those who left the country in the early years of National Socialism believe they were spied on by their German neighbors, 4 percent by the police, and none by coworkers, these percentages rise to 31 percent, 21 percent, and 11 percent respectively among those who remained in Germany after 1939. Similar to these figures are the increased percentages of those who suffered verbal abuse from police authorities among those who left the country after 1939, and the increased percentages of those whose families' homes and businesses were vandalized. A kind of bottom line is provided in the final cell of the last row of the table, which shows that nearly every Jew who remained in Germany after 1939 suffered at least one kind of anti-Semitic persecution listed on the table.

The only survivor who was in Germany after 1939 who experienced none of the forms of persecution listed was a man born in Breslau in 1912. With only an elementary school education, he rose to become a midlevel manager by the early 1930s. During the Nazi years he married and moved to Berlin, where he remained until early 1945, when he was deported to Theresienstadt. Although some might consider Theresienstadt a kind of concentration camp, he apparently did not. Hence he probably answered "none of the above" because he believed that none of the forms of persecution applied to him. From his answers to other questions on the survey, we find he believed that most of his neighbors were against National Socialism and that he enjoyed friendly relations with them both before and after 1933, relations that he described as "friendly support." Moreover, during the Third Reich he went into hiding in Berlin and received help and support from several people, most importantly from a forty-year-old policeman whom he considered a "friend."

Help and Support from German Civilians

This man may have been unusual; nevertheless he was only one of many survivors who received help and support from German civilians during the Third Reich. Indeed, if many German civilians participated in anti-Semitic acts that worsened the plight of the Jews, a considerable minority of other German civilians did what they could to help Jews endure the hardships they faced. In the interviews we conducted, we encountered several examples of this. Some German civilians supported Jews in minor ways, such as an older Quaker man who showed his sympathy for the Jews' plight by putting a yellow handkerchief in his coat pocket and attending Jewish services on Friday evenings in Nuremberg during the middle of the war years. As Herbert Klein explains at the end of his interview, "This was somebody who helped. He didn't help you by trying to hide you or something like that. He just wanted to show his cooperation, his sympathy." Others helped Jews in major ways, sometimes involving huge personal risks, by tipping them off about impending police raids or providing them with food, shelter, and money, or helping them hide and avoid being sent to a concentration camp. Whatever kind of help or support was offered, it was greatly appreciated. Often it made the difference between survival and death.

Sandwiched between questions on the survey dealing with how their German neighbors had been disposed toward National Socialism and what types of discrimination the survivors personally experienced, we asked the following question: "Did you ever receive significant help or support from non-Jewish Germans in your town or city during the Third Reich?" If the answer was yes, the survivors were asked to indicate the year and month this occurred, the nature of the help or support they received, the gender, age, and occupation of the helper, and the type of relationship they had with the helper.

Most survivors answered these questions (432 out of 507). Of those who answered, 166, or 38 percent, answered in the affirmative that they had received significant help or support from non-Jewish Germans. Typically the help or support had not come during the earlier years of the Third Reich, as fewer than one-third of those who had received it indicated that it took place before November 1938. Thus most of the "significant help or support" that the respondents received came in the later years of Nazi Germany, when, arguably, Jews needed it most to survive. In fact, nearly two-thirds (61 percent) of the survivors who were still in Germany after 1941 answered that they received significant help or support from German civilians.

Typically the help or support the survivors received was truly meaningful: 41 percent of the instances of help or support involved helping them to escape or go into hiding, 29 percent involved providing them with food, and 10 percent involved warnings about roundups, deportations, or other police actions. The remaining instances were more minor in nature, but they were nonetheless significant gestures, for example, safeguarding the survivors' possessions, providing them with financial support, helping them find work, vouching for them during police and Gestapo investigations, and sometimes merely displaying friendship or compassion toward them.

Just as help came in many forms, so too did the helpers themselves. When the answers the survivors gave concerning the helpers' gender, age, and occupation are tabulated, no clear prototype emerges. Nevertheless, most helpers appear to have acted alone (73 percent of the cases of help or support involved either an individual man or woman). Individual male helpers outnumbered individual female helpers, by a modest margin. Most helpers were middle-aged and few were very young or very old (only 10 percent were below thirty, 7 percent above fifty-five; the median age was forty). And, finally, the helpers came from all types of occupational backgrounds. Over sixty different occupations were listed for the 146 helpers whom the respondents identified with a specific occupation. Like the Jews they helped, few helpers (26, or 18 percent) came from the ranks of the working classes, whether skilled or unskilled, and only three were farmers. Most held either middle- or upper-middle-class managerial or professional positions, and many were in government service. While eleven were teachers or professors, only two were clergymen (one a Catholic priest and the other a Catholic monk). Perhaps the biggest surprise is that the most frequently named profession of all was policeman, of which there were sixteen.

Helpers, therefore, typically came from the same kinds of social and economic backgrounds as the Jews they helped. This is probably to be expected, since meaningful contacts and bonds are more likely to develop among individuals from similar backgrounds. Furthermore, most of these contacts seem to have been of long duration. When asked about their relationship to their helpers, the most frequent answer given was friend (35 percent), and the next most frequent answers were neighbor (24 percent) and coworker or colleague (10 percent). Like the helpers who were friends, neighbors, coworkers, or colleagues, many of the rest were people the survivors knew well, such as relatives (3 percent), teachers (3 percent), and former fellow soldiers (1 percent). Only 20 percent of the helpers were described as strangers or acquaintances, or others with whom the survivors had an "indirect relationship."

Conclusion

That a large percentage of Jewish survivors received significant help and support from non-Jewish German civilians during the Third Reich cannot compensate for the fact that a greater percentage of Jews received none. If roughly one-third of the survivors were helped by Germans, about two-thirds could not find a single German willing to help them, and one can only wonder about the Jews who did not survive. The help and support that many Jews received cannot obscure the fact that most Jews suffered systematic and pervasive anti-Semitic treatment from both the German government and its officials and from great numbers of German civilians. It grew worse over time, and most Jews were forced to leave Germany before the Holocaust or perished in it. Nevertheless, the help and support that many German civilians provided should not be overlooked. Had it not been offered, even more Jews would have died in the Holocaust. Sadly, however, many Jews, with fond memories of their once positive relationships with their non-Jewish neighbors and with a strong identification with the German nation and its history and culture, probably perceived a mixed message about what their fate would be if they remained in Germany, and thus the help and support they received sometimes served, if unintentionally, to make this mixed message more perilous.

The evidence, then, points to a mixed conclusion about the extent and degree of popular anti-Semitism in Nazi Germany. Certainly it does appear to have been widespread and also to have gained acceptance and support over time. While some Catholic communities may have fostered it less and some small towns and cities may have fostered it more, all German communities provided ever more fertile soil for anti-Semitic behavior as the years progressed. In all German communities, the relations between Jews and non-Jews deteriorated rapidly after Hitler came to power and grew ever worse in the Nazi years. In all German communities Jews became ever more vulnerable targets of popular persecution and discrimination. By the war years, there was nary a Jew living in Germany who had not suffered at least one form of discriminatory treatment perpetrated by German civilians, ranging from verbal and physical abuse to spying and the destruction of their property. But even if only the rare Jew did not experience anti-Semitic treatment from German civilians, this does not mean that all Germans had become raving anti-Semites. Since the Jewish population never constituted more than a tiny fraction of the German population, only a minority of Germans probably took a direct part in overt anti-Semitic activity. Furthermore, even if most survivors say that their once cordial relations with their German neighbors turned sour over time, most do not believe this was because their German neighbors had all become ardent Nazi supporters.

Despite some bright spots, the picture of popular anti-Semitism in Nazi Germany painted by the survivor evidence is an unattractive one. Even if some Germans continued to remain friendly toward Jews, and even if some Germans offered them aid and assistance, and even if Germans were mixed in their support for National Socialism, nearly all Germans went along—many actively, most at least passively—with the anti-Semitic policies and measures fostered by their government and offered no meaningful protest against them. As Ian Kershaw once explained, "The road to Auschwitz was built by hate, but paved with indifference."[17]

+9+

TERROR

Nazi crimes against humanity ultimately claimed the lives of millions of people from many national, social, ethnic, and religious backgrounds all across Europe, but the Jews were the foremost targets. From the beginning of the Third Reich in January 1933 to its end in May 1945, Hitler and his Nazi regime plied a policy of terror and discrimination that led to the economic and social death of German Jewry in the peacetime years of the 1930s and then culminated in the attempt to annihilate the entire Jewish population of Nazi-controlled Europe during World War II. This chapter examines the experiences German Jews had with the Nazi terror apparatus, and the following chapter details what they knew and experienced during the Holocaust.

In the questionnaires and face-to-face interviews we conducted with both Jews and non-Jews who lived in Germany during the Nazi years, our questions concentrated on three major areas: everyday life under National Socialism, the nature and application of terror at the local level, and the extent of knowledge that people had about the mass murder of the Jewish population while it was taking place. With non-Jews, the first set of questions we asked about everyday life focused on whether they supported Hitler and National Socialism and why. With Jews, on the other hand, it would have made no sense to ask such questions, since Hitler and National Socialism were obviously abhorrent to them. Therefore, the questions we asked of Jews about their everyday lives in Nazi Germany concentrated more on how they got along with and were treated by the non-Jewish population in their communities and on their loss of identity as former patriotic Germans in a society that no longer considered them worthy of citizenship and eventually of life itself.

If the questions we asked of Jews and non-Jews were different in regard to their everyday lives under National Socialism, this was not true of the other two major areas of interest in our surveys and interviews: terror and mass murder. Thus the questions we asked of Jews and non-Jews about their experiences with and understanding of the Nazi program of terror and mass murder were largely identical, which permits an important comparison of the answers these two groups gave that will be found in the conclusion of this book.

Among the most significant types of questions we asked about terror and mass murder are the following: How widespread was the climate of fear in Nazi Germany? Were there great numbers of spies and civilian denouncers providing the Gestapo and other Nazi authorities with damning information about the activities of the citizenry? How often did common citizens break the Nazi laws? How often did these illegal activities rise to the level of true resistance activity? What ultimately happened to the people who had cases started against them? Were the Nazis successful in keeping their program of mass murder a secret from the Jewish and non-Jewish populations? How much information did the civilian population have about the Nazi mass murder policies, and how and when did they get this information?

Fear of Arrest and Involvement in Illegal Activities

Although recent research has shown that the Gestapo and other official organs of terror in Nazi Germany had more limited manpower and resources than once believed, the Nazi terror apparatus certainly had the means to inspire fear and dread in the hearts and minds of Jews and other selected targets.[1] Considering the fact that Jews in Nazi Germany were plagued by an ever growing number of laws, ordinances, and decrees that proscribed their activities more than any other group in the German population, it is remarkable that the fear of arrest alone did not eventually overwhelm nearly all Jews to the point that they could no longer function as human beings.[2] By the middle of the war years, the fear of the Gestapo "had become a general Jewish psychosis," according to Victor Klemperer's diary entry for August 29, 1942. Klemperer was a Jewish professor of romance languages from Dresden.[3] Nevertheless, as Marion Kaplan elegantly shows in a recent book and as the interview narratives in this book attest to, most Jews continued to carry out their lives throughout the Nazi period with dignity and often with courage as well.[4]

Despite the decorous manner in which most German Jews conducted themselves, fear was an ever present feature of life for them in the Third Reich. Over time the amount of fear that most Jews perceived grew in a nearly linear fashion. Clear evidence of this is presented in the table on page 288, which summarizes the answers we received to the following question we asked in the Jewish Holocaust survivor questionnaire: "In the period before you had to leave Germany, or in the city in which you lived in Germany, did you personally have fear of being arrested by the Gestapo, or did you have no fear of this happening to you?"

The percentages found in the table relate to a number of separate analyses we made to determine the level of fear of arrest that different types of survivors had during the Third Reich. Thus, although a strong majority of all survivors had a great deal of fear, some survivors experienced the fear of arrest more powerfully and more constantly than others, and there were even some survivors who said that they did not personally fear arrest at all. Among the total survivor population who took the survey, over three quarters indicated that they had feared arrest, and usually the fear that they had held was a constant fear (47 percent) as opposed to an occasional fear (30 percent). The percentages for both male and female survivors are strikingly similar to these figures. Although Jewish women might have been expected to have a lower fear of arrest than Jewish men because in most societies of the past and the present women have far lower arrest rates than men, this did not turn out to be the case; 76 percent of the women and 77 percent of the men reported fearing arrest by the Gestapo, and, once again, the fear that plagued their lives was something they typically experienced more on a constant than on an occasional basis.

While gender made essentially no difference in survivors' level of fear, factors such as the age the survivors reached while they were still living in Germany, the size and predominant religious background of the communities in which they lived, and especially their length of residence in Nazi Germany did account for some significant differences among them. Since the median birth year of the survivors was 1922 and over three-quarters of them had emigrated before the outbreak of World War II (typically in either 1938 or 1939, when over 50 percent left the country), this means that the majority of the survivors were in their early to middle teenage years when they lived in the Third Reich. But, even among these relatively young people, the fear of being arrested by the Gestapo was something that most felt, though somewhat less constantly than survivors who were eighteen or older and thus bore full criminal liability.

Most survivors in both groups not only feared their own arrest but also experienced a great deal of fear that members of their immediate family would be arrested even if they were not. Thus in addition to the question we asked the survivors about their own level of fear, we also asked them to indicate if they feared that someone in their family would be arrested. When these percentages were tabulated, the results for the two groups were almost identical. Among the survivors who were under eighteen when they lived in Germany, 88 percent feared that the Gestapo would take members of their family under arrest, and 91 percent of those in the eighteen and older group of survivors feared it.

Table 9.1   Fear of Arrest among Jewish Survivors (By Gender, Age of Leaving Germany, Religion and Size of Community, and Year of Leaving Germany)

	Constant Fear (%)	Occasional Fear (%)	No Fear (%)	N of cases
All survivors	47	30	23	**461**
Men	44	33	23	**229**
Women	45	31	24	**167**
Eighteen or older when left Germany	53	31	16	**161**
Seventeen or younger when left Germany	40	33	28	**243**
Catholic cities	34	42	24	**71**
Large cities	44	33	23	**178**
Medium-size cities	43	30	27	**86**
Small towns	52	35	13	**31**
Left Germany before 1939	33	35	32	**175**
Left Germany between 1939 and 1941	51	32	17	**180**
Still in Germany after 1941	71	18	11	**55**

Note: Large cities include Berlin, Cologne, Dresden, Düsseldorf, Frankfurt, Hamburg, Leipzig, and Munich; medium-size cities include 33 cities with populations of between circa 50,000 and 200,000 inhabitants; small towns include 39 small towns with 10,000 or fewer inhabitants; Catholic cities include Aachen, Bonn, Cologne, Düsseldorf, Krefeld, Mainz, Munich, and Würzburg.

Fear of arrest was a regular feature of Jews' lives, whether they lived in communities inhabited by majority Catholic or Protestant populations and whether they lived in large cities with hundreds of thousands of inhabitants or in cities and towns with smaller populations. Still, the religious makeup and size of the communities in which the survivors lived did account for some modest differences in how much and how frequently they feared arrest. While there was very little difference in the overall level of fear between survivors from predominantly Catholic communities in Germany and survivors generally (76 percent versus 77 percent), survivors from Catholic communities appear to have feared arrest less constantly than was typical of the overall survivor population (34 percent versus 47 percent). This may be attributable in part to the somewhat more positive climate of relationships between Jews and Gentiles in Catholic communities that was noted in the previous chapter. But it also stems from the very high percentage of former Krefeld residents among the survivors from Catholic communities.[5] If the Krefeld survivors are taken out of the mix, the overall level of fear among those from Catholic communities becomes slightly higher than that of the general survivor population (80 percent versus 77 percent).

The size of the communities in which the survivors lived in Nazi Germany accounted for a more significant difference in their fears. Most survivors lived in relatively large urban areas, and the level of fear among those who lived in either large or medium-size cities was almost identical to that of the entire survivor population. But survivors who had resided in small towns indicated on the survey that they had experienced considerably higher levels of fear. The percentage of survivors who feared arrest on a constant basis was nearly 20 percent higher among those from small towns than those from larger communities; in addition, the percentage of survivors from small towns who feared arrest not at all was only about half that of survivors from medium-size and large cities.

Why did Jews from smaller towns have higher levels of fear? One reason may be the heightened level of popular anti-Semitism there, as mentioned in the previous chapter. Perhaps Jews from small villages and towns worried that they stuck out more than Jews from more anonymous urban settings did. Since their comings and goings and their habits and opinions were more noticeable to their predominantly non-Jewish neighbors and other townsfolk, they may have been easier targets for civilian denunciations that could get them in trouble with the Nazi authorities. But, it should also be mentioned, there was not a greater police presence in their communities. Previous research has demonstrated that most small towns in Germany had no Gestapo officers present and consequently the political police work in these communities had to be performed by modestly staffed regular police forces.[6] Thus the greater fear of arrest that small-town Jews experienced must have resulted more from their heightened fear of being reported to the authorities by their anti-Semitic neighbors, classmates, and work colleagues than from their fear of being persecuted by the interventionist efforts of the Nazi police.

Whatever differences among the survivors are attributable to their ages and communities, they pale in comparison with the most significant determinant of the survivors' level of fear—the length of time they lived in Nazi Germany. In the peacetime years of Hitler's reign in the 1930s, the survivors' fear of arrest was more typically intermittent than constant. But after the *Kristallnacht* pogrom in November 1938, when thousands of Jewish men in communities across Germany were carted off to concentration camps for the first time, the fear of arrest among Jews grew dramatically. As the figures in the table demonstrate, only one-third of the survivors who left Germany before 1939 felt constant fear of arrest before leaving the country, while the other two-thirds were divided almost equally between those who had occasional fear and those who had no fear. But after the war broke out, the survivors' fear of arrest escalated rapidly. Nearly three-quarters of the survivors who were still in Germany in 1941 when the doors to emigration slammed shut and the Holocaust began in earnest say they lived in constant fear of arrest.

It is nevertheless astonishing that 29 percent of the survivors residing in Germany at the beginning of 1942 maintain that they did not fear arrest at all or did not fear it on a constant basis. Perhaps some of these people interpreted the question too literally. Whereas they might have feared being arrested by some Nazi policing body, they might not have feared being arrested directly by the Gestapo. Still, most of these people were eventually deported and sent to concentration camps, and thus it is hard to fathom how any Jew would not have lived in constant fear of arrest.

Nevertheless, several interviewees said they felt no fear of arrest even though family members had been arrested, sent to concentration camps, and put to death. One such person is Margarete Leib. In the spring of 1933, shortly after Hitler came to power, Margarete Leib was a university student in Berlin in her early twenties who had returned to her parental home in Karlsruhe after hearing that her father, an attorney and former SPD Reichstag deputy, had been arrested and placed in investigative detention. In the weeks that followed, she and her mother were allowed to visit her father daily and bring him food while he was in a local jail. But then on May 16, she personally observed how he and six other SPD politicians were forced into an open truck and paraded through the streets of Karlsruhe past screaming crowds of onlookers en route to a small concentration camp in the surrounding countryside. He was murdered ten months later, hanged with packaging cord attached to a window frame. While this experience might have made her deeply fearful for her own life, she says that she was not afraid. Rather, she went back to Berlin, joined an underground resistance group, and helped produce and distribute anti-Nazi literature before emigrating to France in 1936 and later to the United States in 1941.

Lore Schwartz provides an even more extreme example. Raised the daughter of a shoe store owner in Gera, she was only seventeen when her father died on December 7, 1938, five days after returning from Buchenwald concentration camp. During the war she made her way to Berlin and found work at the Jewish Hospital. Although this temporarily spared her from the deportations, in early 1943 she too was about to be deported when she chose to go underground. At about the same time, both her mother and her fiancé were deported to concentration camps in Poland. After learning that her fiancé had been taken to Auschwitz, she actually went there herself and for two days tried to get the guards to allow her to visit him under the pretext that she had promised to help a lady in Berlin locate her son. After this highly unusual visit to Auschwitz, she returned to Berlin, where she worked in a massage parlor and was hidden by a woman whose husband was both a pimp and a member of the SS. In June 1944 the Nazis finally arrested her and sent her first to Theresienstadt and later to a number of other concentration camps before she was liberated from Bergen-Belsen on April 15, 1945. Obviously, given the harrowing saga she related in her interview, she had great reason to live in constant fear of arrest. Near the end of her interview, however, when she was asked if she had lived in fear all the time, she responded, "No, not at all. Nothing would have happened really, except that they sent you away. I knew that I couldn't live through the war through what I did. I had the feeling . . . I had nothing to lose but myself. I was all alone. My mother was away; my father was dead; my brother was in England. What else could have happened?"

If these two women's narratives provide extreme examples of fearlessness, several other interviewees also said they had not been afraid even though they too had strong objective reasons to fear arrest. Karl Meyer, for example, who was born in 1915 and raised in Cologne, was also a member of a resistance organization. But he also said that he had no fear of arrest, at least until he was arrested in August 1938 by the Cologne Gestapo on suspicion of high treason. Even though he had worked for a few years for the Rote Hilfe resistance organization, which provided aid to German socialists and communists in exile, he says that he ended up being "lucky." He was let out of jail and allowed to emigrate to Shanghai on November 6, 1938, just three days before *Kristallnacht*. Had he not left at this opportune moment, a Jewish man with his background would probably not have survived. But at that time "nobody knew about the impending doom," he said.

Several other Jews we interviewed also said they did not fear arrest, even though some of them knew about the impending doom. Helmut Grunewald of Cologne, for example, intrepidly played illegal jazz in bars in Cologne and Mönchengladbach before he was arrested in December 1942 and sent to Auschwitz. But most of the interviewees, just like most survivors in the larger survey population, had indeed spent much of their time in Nazi Germany living

Table 9.2 Involvement in Illegal Activities among Jewish Survivors (By Age, Gender, and Year of Leaving Germany)

| | Left Germany between 1933 and 1939 | | | | | | Still in Germany After 1939 | | | | | |
| | All Ages | | | Over Seventeen When Left | | | All Ages | | | Over Seventeen When Left | | |
	Men	Women	All	Men	Women	All	Men	Women	All	Men	Women	All
Member of illegal youth group	19%	14%	17%	29%	21%	26%	18%	16%	17%	27%	21%	24%
Listened to illegal radio broadcasts	31	19	26	46	30	39	37	40	38	46	61	52
Told anti-Nazi jokes	15	11	13	19	13	17	27	13	20	30	21	26
Criticized Hitler	16	20	18	23	25	25	27	22	24	30	29	29
Criticized Nazis	21	21	21	35	30	33	35	22	28	42	29	36
Spread anti-Nazi flyers	2	1	1	6	2	5	4	2	3	6	4	5
Helped people threatened by Nazis	5	6	5	14	8	10	18	13	16	21	18	19
Active Resistance Activity	3	1	2	4	2	3	2	2	2	3	4	3
None of the above	34	43	37	21	28	26	39	31	35	24	21	24
N of cases	201	141	351	52	53	106	49	45	96	33	28	62

Note: The N of cases listed under the "all" category is generally higher than the total of men and women because a few people did not list their gender status on the questionnaire.

in fear of arrest. And, for almost all of the interviewees who were still in Germany after 1941, the fear was constant.

More typical of the Jewish survivors in regard to the fear they felt were people like Ilse Landau and Rosa Hirsch of Berlin. Even though Ilse Landau actually jumped off the train deporting her to Auschwitz, she says that she "always, always, had fear. There was never a moment when we saw that we were secure, never." And even though Rosa Hirsch also displayed great courage while going into hiding during the Holocaust, she states in her interview, "You always were afraid. You didn't talk to other people. Even among yourselves, you only whispered because they say walls have ears."

As a final example, Ruth Mendel was barely a teenager when she was deported to Auschwitz from her home in Frankfurt in April 1943. Expressing the numbing fear that most Jewish youth must have felt when they realized their parents could no longer protect them, she explains, "I always had this feeling that my father would be able to protect me, protect us. When you're a child, you feel your parents are almighty. But I realized then that your parents cannot. . . . Of course we were afraid. We always wanted to be inconspicuous. We didn't want to awaken anything or anyone."

If most Jews, for good reason, did indeed fear being arrested, this obviously did not stop great numbers of them from taking considerable risks. Most did not jump from a deportation train like Ilse Landau, voluntarily take a trip to Auschwitz to try to get information about a loved one like Lore Schwartz, or play illegal jazz in bars during the war years like Helmut Grunewald; most probably preferred to remain as inconspicuous as possible, as did Ruth Mendel and her family. Still, as our evidence will demonstrate, most Jews who lived in Nazi Germany found it impossible not to break one or another of the multitude of Nazi laws that enmeshed them. Some even broke the law on a daily basis. Evidence for this is found in Table 9.2 about the survivors' involvement in illegal activities during the Third Reich.

In one question we asked in our survey, we provided a list of activities that were illegal in Nazi Germany and asked the survivors to indicate which of those activities applied to them. Although the list contains a variety of forbidden activities ranging from listening to foreign radio broadcasts and telling anti-Nazi jokes to taking an active role in resistance activity, it does not attempt to cover all possible outlawed behavior. In particular, it does not contain offenses that applied only to Jews and not to non-Jews, for we eventually wanted to compare the amount of involvement in illegal activities of these two different groups. Thus, for example, it does not include offenses that large numbers of Jews committed such as refusing to wear the Jewish star when they went out in public after September 19, 1941.[7]

Clearly most Jews did not simply buckle under to Nazi authority, and many displayed considerable courage and took direct action against their oppressors.

In fact, the table demonstrates that a clear majority of Jews of various backgrounds took part in forbidden activities during the Third Reich. Usually their transgressions were relatively minor. Only relatively small numbers, as the table shows, disseminated anti-Nazi literature or actively worked against the Nazi regime in other ways as members of underground resistance organizations. Still, given the risks involved, the number of survivors who did take part in such extremely dangerous activity is noteworthy and there are at least four examples of survivors who were involved in underground resistance among the interview narratives featured in this book.[8] Furthermore, female survivors were equally as likely to take part in resistance efforts as male survivors, and the percentage of both female and male survivors who were involved in these activities rose among those who were still in Germany during the war years, when they could expect to be put to death if caught.

Jews commonly took part in other types of illegal behavior such as belonging to illegal youth groups, listening to forbidden foreign radio broadcasts, telling anti-Nazi jokes, providing aid and support to Nazi victims, and criticizing Hitler and the Nazis in discussions with acquaintances. Even before the war, offenses such as these could lead to lengthy confinement in jails and prisons for non-Jews as well as Jews. But being arrested for such offenses during the war years was, especially for Jews, often tantamount to a death sentence, as the Nazis considered such behavior injurious to the success of the German war effort and punished it severely. Nonetheless, roughly two-thirds of the male and female survivors took part in one or more of the types of illegal activities enumerated on the table; this was equally true among those who remained in Germany during the war years and those who left the country sometime during the 1930s.

Listening to forbidden foreign-radio broadcasts was the most common offense committed by the survivors. During the war years, this most often involved tuning in to the German-language broadcasts of the BBC, which previous research has demonstrated could be received all across Germany and even in places as far away as Pinsk on the eastern front.[9] Although the Nazis threatened all German citizens with the death penalty for this behavior, and even though it was especially difficult for Jews to gain access to the BBC broadcasts as their radio sets were taken away from them during the war, more than half of the survivors (52 percent) who were over seventeen years old and still living in Nazi Germany during the war years say that they tuned in to these broadcasts. This, as it turns out, was almost the same percentage as that of the non-Jewish German population that listened to the BBC during the war, as demonstrated by our survey evidence relating to the German populations from the cities of Cologne, Krefeld, Berlin, and Dresden.

The number of survivors who took part in the other types of illegal behavior listed on the table was also quite large. For instance, among those who were over seventeen and still living in Germany during the war years, about one-quarter joined illegal youth groups, over one-third criticized Nazis in discussions with acquaintances, and more than one-quarter criticized Hitler and had related anti-Nazi jokes to others. These figures are similar to and sometimes higher than the percentages of the regular German population from the cities we surveyed who took part in such activities. Finally, considering that the percentage of survivors who had involved themselves in the most serious illegal activity listed on the table—taking part in active resistance and belonging to an illegal organization—was also somewhat higher than that of the non-Jewish population from the cities of Cologne, Krefeld, Dresden, and Berlin, the conclusion follows that Jews were every bit (and often more) likely to stand up against the Nazi regime than were others among the German population.[10]

Spying, Denunciation, and Police Persecution

As prime targets for discrimination and persecution, Jews had special motivation to oppose as well as to fear Nazi authority. That many Jews courageously took grave risks in opposing Nazi authority does not mean, however, as anti-Semitic Nazi propaganda alleged, that they were in the habit of acting illegally or that they simply threw all caution to the wind. Not only were Jews one of the most traditionally law-abiding groups in the German population, with historical crime rates that were well below most other groups of German citizens, they were especially cautious with whom they spoke.[11] As several of the interviewees related to us, "We kept to ourselves."

The caution Jews usually exercised in speaking with others is also borne out in the survey. When we asked the survivors to compare how openly they believed they could discuss political topics with Jewish and non-Jewish friends and neighbors, upwards of two-thirds answered that they had felt it was advisable not to speak about political topics even with Jewish friends and neighbors they knew well. This applied equally to survivors who had left Germany in the 1930s and to survivors who had remained in Germany during the war years. With non-Jews, even those considered friends, the survivors displayed great caution. Only 7 percent of those who remained in Germany during the war indicated that they felt they could speak openly with non-Jewish friends, and only 1 percent felt that they could do this with non-Jewish neighbors.

Cautious as most Jews were, the Nazi authorities waged a campaign of terror and persecution against them that had no comparison with that carried out against any other group in the German population except perhaps the communists. But, whereas the pressure against the communists subsided and many former communists were supposedly "healed" and reintegrated into German society after the mid 1930s, when the communist threat had been eliminated, it only increased over time against the Jews, reaching a crescendo after the war broke out when the Nazis tried their utmost to eliminate the entire Jewish population. Well before the war started, however, Jews were commonly spied on, arrested, charged with offenses real and imaginary, and punished with a severity that few "ordinary Germans" ever experienced.

One of the issues touched on briefly in the previous chapter is spying. As we saw earlier, a relatively large percentage of the survivors indicated that they were spied on by neighbors (19 percent), fellow pupils (15 percent), coworkers (5 percent), or police (8 percent). Furthermore, the percentage of survivors who were spied on increased in a linear fashion with the passage of time. For example, only 7 percent of the survivors who left Germany before 1938 believe that they were spied on by their neighbors, but the percentage rises to 19 among those who left the country between 1938 and 1939, and to 31 among those who were still in Germany after the war began. Similarly, the percentage of survivors who say they were spied on by the police rises from 4 percent among those who left in the earliest period to 21 percent among those who were still in Germany after 1939.

The finding that Jews were regularly spied on in Nazi Germany would surprise few people. Still it runs counter to a popular current in recent scholarship which maintains that spying in Nazi Germany was far less common than has commonly been assumed. The Canadian historian Robert Gellately, for example, who made a detailed study of Gestapo case files in Würzburg dealing with the issue of race defilement and friendship displayed toward Jews in an influential book on the Gestapo he published in 1990, reports that he found only one case that began with a report of a Gestapo spy and concludes that "paid informants or agents are conspicuous by their absence."[12] Although other recent work on Gestapo case files in other cities uncovers a greater incidence of spying when other kinds of cases are considered, the dispute over the prevalence of spying warrants more detailed consideration.[13]

In the survey questionnaire, therefore, we not only asked people to indicate if they believed that they had been spied on, we also posed several other questions that aimed to uncover how much depth of knowledge they had about Gestapo spies. Therefore, in addition to asking them to cross off if they had been spied on from a list of possible experiences with discrimination, we also asked them directly in a separate question if they had either known or assumed that people in their neighborhoods or places of work had been involved in spying. And, if they had, we asked them to provide specific information about the backgrounds of the spies they knew the most about.

The answers the survivors provided strengthen the conclusion that spying was often employed against Jews in the Third Reich; moreover, it became more prevalent over time. Among the survivors who left Germany in the 1930s, even though many of them were young at the time, 13 percent say that they had direct knowledge of Gestapo spies in their neighborhoods and workplaces; an additional 28 percent relate that they had reason to assume that there were spies working for the Gestapo in these places. These figures rise to 20 percent and 32 percent, respectively, among those who were still in the country after 1939. As one would expect, though, younger survivors had less knowledge about spies than older survivors. Among survivors who were younger than twenty when they left the country, only 12 percent knew of spies in their neighborhoods or workplaces and an additional 27 percent assumed that people were spying on them.

Further evidence that the survivors' knowledge of Gestapo spies is based on more than conjecture is that most can provide a number of details about the backgrounds of the people they either knew or assumed to be involved in spying. Broadly speaking, the typical profile of a person survivors identified as a Gestapo spy is a middle-class, adult male between the ages of twenty and fifty who was directly affiliated with the Nazi movement either as a party member or as a member of the SA or SS and who was also either a neighbor or a work colleague of the survivors. Thus among those whom survivors identified as known Gestapo spies, 85 percent were male and 15 percent were female. Only 10 percent were younger than twenty years of age and only 6 percent were older than fifty. The youngest person identified as a spy was thirteen and the oldest was seventy-five. The median age of spies was just over thirty, but there was an almost equal distribution among spies between the ages of twenty and fifty. Although the spies came from a wide range of occupational backgrounds, relatively few were common workers (only about one-third); most held middle-class positions in business, government, or the professions. Only 16 percent of the spies were thought to have no affiliation with the Nazi movement; slightly more than one-third were identified as regular Nazi Party members (34 percent); another slightly more than one-third were thought to be members of either the SA or SS (38 percent); 6 percent were members of either the Hitler Youth or the League of German Girls; and another 6 percent were identified simply as Gestapo. Finally, only 7 percent of spies were people who had no relationship with the survivors. Nearly 50 percent were neighbors and 25 percent were work colleagues. Ten percent were either domestic servants or employees, and the remaining few were either teachers or building superintendents (*Hausmeister*). Only one spy was identified as a friend, and one was said to be of Jewish background.

Even if many of the survivors believe that they were spied on and can furnish a number of details about the people they believe acted as Gestapo spies, this does not necessarily prove that the individuals they identify were in fact spies. But even if the survey evidence in itself cannot prove definitively that spying against Jews was indeed a common practice in Nazi Germany, one cannot challenge the firmness of the survivors' convictions. Thus, in the in-depth interviews we conducted with the survivors, we heard time and again how they had to be especially cautious during the years they lived in the Third Reich because they knew at the time that they were being spied on. The phrase "all the walls had ears" became a common refrain in these interviews. One example of this comes from a Jewish woman born in Hamburg in 1914, who relates the following about the Jewish men she knew who returned from concentration camps after being rounded up during the *Kristallnacht* pogrom: "They were not allowed to speak about what they went through. They had to sign a paper when they were released from the camps—either Buchenwald or Sachsenhausen or Dachau—that they were not allowed to speak about it. But some of them did. They couldn't speak loudly [though], because all the walls had ears. If they still had maids, they all had ears. They were paid by the party to talk about what was happening in these families."[14]

However much spying was conducted against the Jewish population, there can be no disputing the fact that the Nazi police authorities were far more likely to start cases against them for alleged criminal activity than they were to start cases against most other people in the German population. This has been established elsewhere by detailed investigations of Gestapo case files, and it is supported further by the survey and interview evidence in this study. Whereas, for example, only 2 percent (30 out of 1,342) of the respondents in the surveys we conducted of the ordinary German population of Cologne and Krefeld indicate that they had been interrogated either by the Gestapo or another policing body during the years of Nazi Germany on the charge that they had committed an illegal act, this happened to more than 13 percent of the people who took part in the Jewish survivor survey. Although this suggests that Jews were more than six times more likely to have cases started against them than non-Jews, it considerably underestimates the real difference between Jews and the rest of the German population in this regard. To begin with, while nearly all of the people who participated in the Cologne and Krefeld surveys had lived in Nazi Germany for its duration, most of those who were involved in the survivor survey had only lived in the country for a few years before emigrating abroad. Thus, if one considers only those survivors who were still in Germany after the war began, the percentage of Jews who had been interrogated by the Gestapo on the charge that they had committed an illegal offense rises to 19 percent. This would mean that Jews were nearly ten times more likely than non-Jews to have cases started against them. But even this figure underestimates the true difference between Jews and non-Jews. Many of the survivors who remained in Germany after 1940 were either too young to have criminal charges brought against them or had been deported to concentration camps before the end of the Third Reich. Had they remained in Germany throughout the war or had they been older when they were deported, their chances of having a criminal case brought against them would have been considerably greater. If we, therefore, only consider those survivors residing in Germany after the war broke out and reaching the age of seventeen before they left the country, the percentage of survivors who had cases started against them rises to 27 percent (24 percent for male survivors and 30 percent for female survivors). In sum, this means that our survey data indicate that Jews may have been at least thirteen times more likely than non-Jews to have cases started against them for alleged illegal activity.

Beyond demonstrating that Jews were frequently spied on and charged with illegal activity in Nazi Germany, what else does the survey evidence tell us about the Jews' brush with the Nazi legal authorities? What kinds of offenses, for example, were Jews charged with committing? What sources of information, in addition to spying, did the Gestapo and the police use to start cases against the Jews? And what was the final result of the cases brought against the Jews?

The survey evidence shows that most criminal cases initiated against Jews involved relatively minor infractions. This, however, was more typical in the prewar period than in the war years. In the 1930s, only one-third of the cases started against the survivors involved offenses that the Nazis considered especially serious, most commonly including race defilement (*Rassenschande*), spreading anti-Nazi propaganda, and illegal attempts to flee or hide from the authorities. The remaining two-thirds of the cases against survivors at this time constituted a hodgepodge of illegal behaviors that were severely punished only on occasion, such as minor violations of the pervasive legislation discriminating against Jewish business and economic practices, and of the laws and decrees that limited Jews' contact with non-Jews or restricted their freedom to travel or their rights to speak their mind about Nazi policies and leaders.

During the war years, however, the cases initiated against the survivors typically involved far more serious allegations and cases involving minor infractions slowed to a trickle. Seemingly by this time survivors had learned to do their utmost to avoid being implicated in any kind of unlawful activity. But this was not always possible. Thus the cases started against them often involved attempts to flee the country or go underground, illegal relations with non-Jews, illegal resistance activity, libel or slander of Nazi authorities, and failure to wear the Jewish star (which became mandatory for German Jews in the fall of 1941).

Given that Nazi policy toward the Jews escalated from destroying their livelihoods to destroying their lives and that the crimes the Jews were accused of in the war years were more serious than in the 1930s, it comes as no surprise that the punishments handed out to alleged Jewish offenders followed the same trajectory. Nevertheless, some people would not expect to learn that the Nazis did not always throw the book at Jews who were accused of violating the law. In the 1930s, in fact, nearly two-thirds of the Jews in our survey (64 percent) who had cases started against them soon had the charges dropped. They were let go immediately after being interrogated by the Gestapo or other police authorities, with no further action taken against them. This probably suggests that the evidence against them was weak. But it also implies that the Nazis were not at that time keenly interested in punishing the Jews with utmost severity. Further evidence of this is that an additional 8 percent of the Jewish survivors in our survey who had cases started against them in the 1930s were tried and subsequently acquitted by Nazi judges. Only 16 percent were sent to a concentration camp or placed in so-called protective custody.

This comparatively lenient treatment contrasts sharply, however, with the treatment they received in the war years. After the war broke out, the Gestapo usually acted as the final arbiter and judge in cases involving Jews and the result was often life-threatening for the accused. Among the survivors who had cases that took place in the 1940s, none were passed on from the Gestapo or the police to the courts and the percentage of cases in which charges were dropped against them fell by nearly half to just over one-third (36 percent). What most typically transpired, therefore, was that the Gestapo simply bypassed the court authorities in cases involving Jews during the war years and placed the Jews directly in protective custody and sent them on to concentration camps. Clear evidence of this is that at least one-half of the wartime cases involving survivors who took part in our survey ended in this fashion.

While the severity of the punishment alleged Jewish lawbreakers received depended largely on the time period when the cases took place, the manner in which the cases started against them also played a role in determining their fate. In the questionnaire, survivors who indicated that they had been interrogated by either the Gestapo or the police on the charge that they had committed an illegal act during the Third Reich were subsequently asked to specify how the cases had originated against them. Next to this question, we provided a list with eight possible answers they could chose from. Three of the possible answers involved what might be construed as denunciations from civilians ("accusation/report from a neighbor, coworker, or relative"); three other possible answers involved information coming from official sources ("accusation/report from a Gestapo spy, a member or official of the Nazi Party, or a police roundup"); and the remaining two possible answers were "other" or "I don't know." Table 9.3 summarizes the answers the survivors gave.

Although the information provided in the table about the sources of information used to initiate criminal investigations is based on the experiences of only 86 Jewish survivors who themselves were interrogated by the Gestapo or the police on the charge that they had acted unlawfully during the Third Reich, it permits a number of key observations about the manner in which the Nazi terror apparatus operated. Furthermore, this information corresponds closely with a detailed study of the archival records of all existing Gestapo case files involving Jews in a typical German city (Krefeld) that one of the authors of this study conducted in the course of his research on his recent book, *Nazi Terror: The Gestapo, Jews, and Ordinary Germans.*[15]

The Gestapo had many different sources of information at its disposal for starting cases against Jews, and no single source of information predominated over the entire period of the Third Reich. Among the most significant sources were accusations stemming from German civilians, which in contemporary research on the Third Reich are commonly referred to as "denunciations."

Table 9.3   Origin of Gestapo and Police Cases Involving Jewish Survivors

	All Cases (%)	Cases in 1930's (%)	Cases in Wartime (%)
Civilian Denunciations			
Accusation/report from neighbor	9	17	–
Accusation/report from co-worker	12	21	23
Accusation/report from family member or relative	–	–	–
Official Sources			
Accusation/report from Gestapo spy	12	8	15
Accusation/report from Nazi Party	6	–	8
Gestapo/police roundup	17	21	39
Other	11	13	15
Don't Know	33	21	–
N of cases	**86**	**34**	**13**

They often stemmed from such base motives as a desire to gain the favor of party officials or petty personal quarrels between neighbors and coworkers. But, as the table shows, they seldom arose from family disputes. These denunciations helped the Gestapo and the police begin over 20 percent of the eighty-six cases against the survivors in our survey. That such denunciations were numerous is attested to by several of our interviewees. Herbert Klein of Nuremberg, for example, relates a story in his interview about his sister's elderly mother-in-law, who was denounced during the war by a neighbor for not observing the blackout restrictions after she had unintentionally turned on the lights in her apartment one evening. "It was always like that," Klein insists. "These Germans could not wait to get a feather in their cap."

Common and deplorable as denunciations were in Nazi Germany, their importance should not be overestimated. Their prevalence does not prove, for instance, as several scholars have recently maintained, that the Gestapo was primarily a reactive organ with such limited resources and manpower that it merely sat back and relied almost exclusively on the civilian population for its information.[16] Not only does our questionnaire evidence show that the Gestapo utilized many other sources of information to begin its cases throughout the

Third Reich, it shows that civilian denunciations were most plentiful during the prewar years, when most cases against Jews did not lead to draconian punishments. They were considerably less common during the war and the Holocaust, when any criminal case initiated against a Jew might result in death.

The evidence in the table, therefore, points to a terror apparatus that combined both reactive and proactive strategies in maintaining law and order and combating the targeted enemies of the National Socialist regime. During the 1930s, when Nazi policy called for putting pressure on Jews to force them to leave the country, the Gestapo may have been content to act mainly in a reactive fashion. Evidence for this is that a higher percentage of the cases started against the survivors in the 1930s began with accusations made by the civilian population (38 percent) than by information the police authorities received from official sources (29 percent). This overlaps neatly with the study mentioned above of Gestapo case files involving Jews in the city of Krefeld, where 41 percent of the Krefeld Gestapo's cases began with civilian denunciations in the 1930s. But during the war, when Nazi policy toward the Jews turned to mass murder as a "final solution to the Jewish problem," the Gestapo actively set in motion its own limited but still considerable resources to help decimate Germany's remaining Jewish population. Correspondingly, the table shows that civilian denunciations became far less important sources of information in starting Jewish cases, as most of the information the Gestapo and the police used to initiate cases against Jews during the war came from spies, Nazi Party members and institutions, and, above all, from Gestapo and police roundups. Taken together, these official sources of information made up 62 percent of the wartime cases in the survivor survey, and this does not exhaust the Gestapo's official sources of information. Many cases against Jews also began with information the Gestapo gained from forced confessions they beat out of people under interrogation, house searches, or other Nazi control organs that are only partially subsumed under the "other" category in the table.

Spying, denunciations, and Nazi police repression contributed heavily to the persecution and ultimate destruction of Germany's Jewish population, but it was not necessary for Jews in Nazi Germany to be spied on, denounced, or accused of wrongdoing by the Gestapo or the police to meet a dire fate once the Holocaust began. We now turn to perhaps the most sensitive part of our entire study—the carrying out and supposed secrecy surrounding the so-called Final Solution.

✛10✛

MASS MURDER

Since the war and the Nazi regime came to an end in 1945, it has been an article of faith among the German population that very few people in Germany knew about the Holocaust as it was happening. Holding to this belief offered many benefits to the citizenry of postwar Germany. It helped many avoid being prosecuted for crimes against humanity. It helped many others deal with their children's questions about what they had done in the war. It probably helped still others justify their own past lives to themselves. It arguably helped Germany and Germans regain acceptance into the family of nations and mankind.

Holding to the belief that few had known about the Holocaust as it was happening also may have offered some advantages to Jews, especially German Jews. Some may have felt better about the country they had been raised in and the people they had known as neighbors, colleagues, classmates, and sometimes friends. Others may have found it easier to deal with the nagging question of why so few Jews openly revolted against Nazi authority.

Indeed, when we began our efforts to survey both Germans and Jews, we were not certain that it was possible or even a good idea to ask people questions about what they knew and experienced during the Holocaust, and this was true for both non-Jews and Jews. But, at the possible risk of having fewer people answer our surveys or agree to be interviewed by us, we decided that we had to push ahead and ask a battery of questions to both groups about their knowledge of and experiences with the Holocaust, since this might be one of the last chances available to gain such information from firsthand witnesses about this darkest period in modern history. Although we are sorry that our questions brought back painful memories, we are heartened by the fact that so many German Jews and non-Jews agreed nonetheless to take part in our surveys and interviews and answered our questions with candor and openness. Although there are many caveats to be noted, what they in essence told us is that the Nazis' "terrible secret," as the eminent historian Walter Laqueur has called it, was not especially well kept.[1]

The Deportations

To demonstrate that large numbers of both Jews and non-Jews eventually became quite well informed about the Holocaust as it was happening, we might begin with a consideration of how the deportations to the ghettos and concentration camps were carried out. Everyone in Germany knew well that the Jewish population was in decline during the war years, just as it had been before the war began. It was obvious for all to see. Ever fewer Jews were on the streets or in the stores and one could read in the daily newspapers about apartments and homes vacated by the Jews and about the auctioning off of their property. But how much was known about the deportations that were carting the Jews away by the trainload? Did they depart from shadowy locations in the darkness of night so as to be kept secret from the public? Or were they organized and carried out in a more transparent manner? If people did find out about the deportations somehow, where did they think the Jews were going and what did they think would happen to them when they reached their final destination?

Our surveys and interviews help answer these questions. Among the 507 Jews who responded to our survey, 118 indicated that they had been deported at some time during the Third Reich. From a follow-up question we asked about the exact dates of deportation, we know that at least eighty-one of these people were deported after September 1939; most of the others were deported either in the fall of 1938 or in early 1939 in the deportation of stateless Jews to Poland or in the wake of the *Kristallnacht* pogrom. Not all of the eighty-one survivors who had been deported during the war years, however, were deported from Germany itself. Many had already left the country during the 1930s and were subsequently deported from one or another European country. Thus, if we only consider the survivors who were deported during the war years and from Germany itself, we are left with a total of fifty-four people, many of whom we interviewed in depth and several of whose interview narratives are included in the pages of this book.

Even though the fifty-four survivors who were deported from German communities to the ghettos and concentration camps make for a relatively small
sample, it forms a large enough group of people to reveal much about how the
deportations were carried out in Germany and what was known about them.
Among the people in this group are an almost equal number of males and
females. They range in age from adults in their thirties to young children, with
a median age of about twenty at deportation; most were old enough to be aware
of what was taking place. They were deported from Berlin, Frankfurt,
Hamburg, Leipzig, Breslau, Mannheim, and other cities all across the map of
Germany. They include people who were deported in each of the war years,
with over half of the deportations taking place before the fall of 1942 and most
of the rest in late 1942 or sometime in 1943. The places to which they were
deported were many and varied. Fourteen were sent off on transports to
Auschwitz, twelve to Theresienstadt, nine to Riga, eight to Gurs, and the rest
to other ghettos and concentration camps across Europe.

Although these people vary in age and gender and were deported from many
different localities and at different times to many different ghettos and concentration camps, one thing that nearly all of them have in common is that the
deportation was carried out in the open. We know this because we asked them
explicitly in the questionnaire if they had been deported "in the open," and, of
the forty-nine who answered the question, 92 percent answered in the affirmative. Only four people answered that their deportation had not been carried
out in the open.

But what exactly does "in the open" mean in this context? We intended it to
mean, of course, that their deportations had been carried out in such a way that
others could have witnessed them and that knowledge about them could have
been spread by word of mouth around the country. That this is what the
respondents also understood by the phrase "in the open" was made clear when
we conducted our in-depth interviews. In a number of these, the survivors
provide detailed information about their own deportation. They reveal that
from the first deportations to the last, there was very little secrecy surrounding
this crucial aspect of the Holocaust. Far from being shrouded in secrecy, the
deportations commonly took place in the full light of day and in full view of
considerable numbers of civilian onlookers as Jews were carted off on open
trucks or marched through main city streets to public train stations, where they
were herded and sent off to their final destinations.

Max Liffmann, for example, was deported from his home in Mannheim in
the fall of 1940 in the first wave of the large-scale deportations of the war.
Unlike most of the larger deportations that departed for eastern ghettos and
concentration camps, however, his deportation train took him and thousands of
other Jews from Baden to the concentration camp erected at Gurs in the

French Pyrenees. Nineteen years old at the time, he was working as a secretary for the Reich Association of German Jews when, on the afternoon of October 20, 1940, his boss informed him that he and his mother were to be deported on the next day (his father had already left the country in 1938) and sent him home to pack. When the next day came, he and his mother closed up their apartment, the police took the key and put a seal on the door, and two Gestapo officers in civilian clothes escorted them to the main train station in Mannheim. Hauling "whatever we could carry" of their belongings on their way, he explains, "Many people saw us when we walked through the street." At the train station they then waited for two or three hours: "Eventually there were three and a half thousand people at the train station. Among them were children and old people—my wife's grandmother was ninety-two years old. They were all so stunned. Nobody knew what was coming next. But I said to whomever I saw that to my knowledge we were to go to France. That was a positive, yes, but we didn't know what was going to happen tomorrow."

This was certainly true of the earliest deportations, but over time more and more became known about them, especially because they continued to be organized "in the open." By January 21, 1942, when a transport of Jews from Leipzig departed for the Riga ghetto, Herta Rosenthal, who was on it with her parents, had already "heard about deportations from other cities." So too, presumably, had many non-Jews from Leipzig by this time, but that did not necessarily engender compassion for the fate of the Jews. Taken in the morning hours by truck from a former school building, where they had been assembled, to Leipzig's Bayrischer train station, the sixteen-year-old Herta Rosenthal and her fellow Jews were jeered by a swarm of onlookers as they passed by. In her words, "Everybody saw it, and they were screaming bloody murder. All the Jews were leaving Leipzig, and they [the Germans] were happy, a lot of them. They were standing there laughing. . . . They brought us during the day, not at night. There were both SA and ordinary citizens there."

Slightly over a year later when teenage Ruth Mendel was deported from her home city of Frankfurt to Auschwitz, most of the main deportations of German Jews had already gone and she and her family had heard a lot about them. "That was pretty late. Because by [the end of] 1942, most of the Jews had been taken away and they were not in Frankfurt anymore. So then they started picking on the ones that were left and they found us—we were thirty-seven in a crowd that were sent to Auschwitz . . . we were aware. Every few days, my friends were taken away. What they told us was resettlement. My parents must have known [what this meant], but they didn't tell me. . . . We were children; we didn't know what resettlement meant. At first, the very first people were taken to Lodz. Once in a while from the ghetto somebody did get a postcard back, but very few, and then you didn't hear from them anymore."

In describing her own deportation, she relates that she and her family had to leave their apartment and were housed in ghetto-like conditions with other remaining Jews in Frankfurt at the former Jewish orphanage. Just before they left their apartment, as she explains, "different Nazis came to buy my parents' furniture for three marks or whatever—a sensible bargain. It was really disgusting. They fingered everything and they were so anxious and so eager to get anything. Their eyes would open up. They wanted this and they wanted that and they were grabbing everything."

Her deportation to Auschwitz followed several months later. Like the other deportations mentioned above, it took place in broad daylight: "One morning we were marched to the train station. It was for Hitler's birthday on April 20. . . . He had already suffered a defeat in Stalingrad and also in El Alamein, and I think he was in a bad mood. To make him feel better for his birthday— that's probably what we were told later on—they tried to give him a birthday present and make Germany *judenrein* [Jew-free]. . . . When we left the orphanage, we had to walk through the streets to the train station, one of the commercial stations. It was early in the morning. If people were watching, I didn't notice. When we got to the station, it was a beautiful, bright day."

Hannelore Mahler was a young mother of mixed parentage who was deported from Krefeld via Berlin to Theresienstadt in September 1944. Like so many other deportations that had left German cities over the previous four years, Hannelore Mahler's deportation was carried out in broad daylight and witnessed by many of her townspeople. In her case, it was especially difficult for the citizens of this predominantly Catholic Rhineland city not to bear witness. In what must have been a forlorn scene, she and the last remaining Jews of Krefeld were marched through the streets, carrying their belongings, to a large building in the center of the city lying about seventy-five yards away from the central train station. From there they were put on an open truck and taken to a train station in the nearby city of Düsseldorf to be deported to the east. Along the way, they were led past Krefeld's main Catholic church, just as the main Sunday mass was getting out in the late morning. In her words: "After the war, they all said, 'We didn't know about it.' [But in September 1944,] when we were arrested, we were marched past the main church, the Dionysiuskirche, with our Jewish stars and backpacks, and I was pushing the baby carriage with my little son in it. And, exactly then, the mass let out, and, yes, they all saw [us]! We had been assembled at the police station on the Hubertusstrasse in a former school. And then, on Sunday morning, the twenty to twenty-five of us were led on foot through the middle of the street to the courtyard of the Hansa-Haus, and there I met my mother. We had walked through the city along the Westwall [boulevard] and crossed the Dionysiusstrasse just as the people got out of mass and were leaving the church. Indeed, they had to have seen us."

These examples from Mannheim, Leipzig, Frankfurt, and Krefeld clearly indicate that from the earliest ones leaving in the fall of 1940 to the last ones leaving in the final year of the war the deportations were very often carried out "in the open." Jews and non-Jews alike could not have failed to be aware of them. An awareness of the deportations, however, does not necessarily equate with an awareness that the result of the deportations would be mass murder. We now need to ask what did the Jews themselves believe was to be their intended fate and, more broadly, how widespread was the Jews' knowledge about the mass murder that was taking place and exactly when and how did that knowledge become widespread?

Knowledge about Mass Murder

Our survey and interview evidence sheds considerable light on these questions. Summarizing this briefly, it shows that most Jews, both in Germany and in other countries, did become aware that the mass murder of the Jews was being carried out well before the end of the war and that the information about the Holocaust came to them from many and varied sources. Furthermore it shows that Jews not only learned about the mass murder when they physically became swept up in it, but that considerable numbers of the deported Jews knew, even before they were deported, that the Nazis were systematically murdering the Jews of Europe. Finally, it shows that while many Jews at the time of their deportation did not want to believe they were under a death sentence, many Jews fully expected that they themselves would soon be killed.

In the questionnaire, the survivors were asked a number of questions about what they knew about the mass murder of the Jews, and when and how they came to know it. They were also asked a number of other relevant questions about their knowledge of and experiences during the Holocaust, such as if they had ever been deported and when their deportations had occurred and where they were taken. The answers they gave to these questions were then systematically analyzed and cross-tabulated with other pertinent background information that they had also provided in the questionnaire.

The first question we asked the survivors regarding what they had known about the Holocaust is the following: "Before the end of the war, did you suspect, hear about, know about, or not know about the mass murder of the Jews?" We asked the question in this form because we hoped that the answers we received would indicate the depth of the survivor's knowledge. Thus we assumed that people who answered that they had only "suspected" it would have been people who had only heard rumors about the mass murder or had only surmised that the mass murder was taking place, but did not have concrete

Table 10.1   Level of Knowledge of the Mass Murder of Jews (Prior to the End of the War) among Jewish Survivors

	Suspected (%)	Heard About (%)	Knew About (%)	Didn't Know About (%)	N of Cases
All survivors	12	26	43	20	**460**
Survivors who left Germany before June 1941 and were never deported (by first country of exile)					
USA	14	24	31	31	**49**
Great Britain	19	23	33	25	**73**
Palastine	10	10	20	60	**10**
Poland	–	–	100	–	**2**
The Netherlands	12	24	40	24	**25**
Belgium	14	29	38	19	**21**
France	18	41	35	6	**17**
Other Countries	11	34	26	30	**47**
Total for all survivors exiled in the countries listed above	15	27	32	26	**246**
All survivors still living in Germany after June 1941	11	18	64	7	**55**
Survivors still living in Germany after June 1941 but never deported or put into concentration camps	20	50	20	10	**10**

information to confirm their suspicions. Those who answered that they had "heard" about it or "knew" about it, on the other hand, were assumed to have received relatively believable information about the mass murder or even to have observed it taking place themselves. Finally, given these three choices for answering the question in the affirmative, those who answered that they "didn't know" about it could be assumed to be people who really had not even received any information about the mass murder before the war ended and had not even suspected that it was taking place before they learned the truth about it sometime after the end of the war.

The information in Table 10.1 shows that it was the unusual German Jew who lived through these years without finding out about the mass murder before it ended. Of the 507 survivors who took part in the survey, 460 answered the question, and only 20 percent of these people answered that they had not known about it, while 80 percent answered that they had suspected it, heard about it, or known about it. Moreover, most of the survivors obtained relatively believable information about the mass murder as it was taking place, since only 12 percent answered that they had only suspected it; 26 percent answered that they had heard about it and 43 percent had known about it.

Most of these people, however, were not living in Germany itself when the mass murder was taking place, having emigrated to another country sometime before the German invasion of the Soviet Union in June 1941, when the large-scale murders of Jews commenced. Still, as the table shows, there were only limited differences between those who had left the country and were living abroad during the Holocaust and those who remained in Germany while it was going on. Among the 246 survivors who answered the question and had emigrated before June 1941 and had also never been deported during the Holocaust, only 26 percent answered that they had not known about the mass murder and only an additional 15 percent answered that they had only suspected it at the time. This leaves a clear majority of 59 percent who either heard about it or knew about it. These percentages compare with 7 percent of the fifty-five survivors who remained in Germany after June 1941 and answered in the questionnaire that they had not known about it and 11 percent who had only suspected it. But, independent of whether the survivors remained in Germany during the Holocaust years or emigrated earlier, the large majority of the Jewish survivors in both groups answered that they had either heard or known about it before the end of the war (82 percent among those who had remained in Germany; 59 percent among those who were living abroad).

From these figures, one can conclude that believable information about the mass murder of the Jews became widespread before the end of the war, and that those who had any interest in finding out the truth about what was happening could usually have done so without great difficulty. Other scholars have argued

Table 10.2   Year (Prior to the End of the War) that Survivors First Heard or Came to Know Something about the Mass Murder of Jews

	All survivors (%)	Survivors who left Germany before June 1941 and were never deported (%)	All survivors still living in Germany after June 1941 (%)	Survivors still living in Germany after June 1941 but never deported or put into concentration camps (%)
Before 1940	13	13	12	–
1940	7	7	12	33
1941	16	13	10	–
1942	26	26	21	17
1943	17	17	26	33
1944	18	21	12	17
January–April 1945	3	2	7	–
N of cases	**260**	**126**	**42**	**6**

these points on the basis of various types of evidence, but never before has this kind of direct testimony been employed as proof.[2] Thus, as the table shows, news about the mass murder of the Jews was received during the war by Jews who had emigrated to almost every corner of the world. Among former German Jews residing in the United States, only 31 percent did not know before the war's end; among those residing in Britain, the percentage of those who did not know was 25 percent; and among those in the Netherlands, Belgium, and France, the percentages of those who did not know were even smaller. Even survivors who had emigrated to countries in Africa, South America, and Asia received the tragic news as well (see the percentages under the "other countries" category).

As Table 10.2 demonstrates, the news about the mass murder of the Jews took time to leak out around the world, but by 1942 or 1943 most German Jews and former German Jews had received the information. The figures in this table relate to the second question we asked the survivors about the mass murder: "At what time before the end of the war did you first hear something about or come to know something about the mass murder of the Jews?" After we asked this question, we then asked the survivors to specify the year, and, if possible, month, when they obtained their information.

From the answers the survivors provided, it appears that the information about the mass murder may have come slightly later on average to Jews who were still in Germany after June 1941 than to Jews who had emigrated to other countries. Presumably this was because Jews in Germany had more limited access to needed channels of information than Jews outside the country had and because the Nazi leadership tried to keep the Holocaust a secret from both the German Jews and the German public generally, while foreign countries had greater motivation to expose the truth about the mass murder that was taking place.[3] Thus, although information about the mass murder started to reach many Jews in Germany in 1941 and 1942, it was not until 1943 that most German Jews became fully aware that mass murder was taking place. Of course, by this time, most of the Jews who remained in Germany after the Soviet invasion could not have avoided becoming aware of the tragic events, since most of them were now caught up in the Holocaust, having already been deported to the ghettos and concentration camps where the murders were being committed. But, even for the small numbers of survivors who remained in Germany and were never deported during the war years, 1943 was also the year when the greatest number of them appear to have gained their awareness of the mass murder.

What were the most important sources of information that Jews in Germany and Jews living in other countries received about the Holocaust? To determine this we next provided the survivors with a list of possible sources of information about the mass murder and asked them to cross off from the list as many of the sources that they had personally received. This information is presented in Table 10.3 below. Furthermore, as a kind of truth test, we also listed as possible answers to our question about their sources of information, "I don't know anymore" and "I first heard something or knew something after the war was over." Compelling evidence that the survivors were consistent in answering about their knowledge of mass murder before the end of the war is found in the very low percentages of those who answered that they didn't know anymore where they had received their information or that they had first heard something after the end of the war. Among the great majority who heard or knew about the mass murder as it was going on, most gained their information from media reports, family members, or Jewish friends and acquaintances, although some found out about it in a variety of other ways. Since the percentages total up to more than 100 percent, clearly many had multiple sources of information. This was true of Jews who lived outside of Germany and Jews who remained in Germany. Among those who stayed in Germany during the Holocaust, however, their own personal observations were the single greatest source of information; 52 percent answered that they "saw it happen," and another 41 percent learned about it from people who were in con-

Table 10.3   Source of Knowledge (Prior to the End of the War) among Jewish Survivors About the Mass Murder of Jews

	All survivors (%)	Survivors who left Germany before June 1941 and were never deported (%)	All survivors still living in Germany after June 1941 (%)	Survivors still living in Germany after June 1941 but never deported or put into concentration camp (%)
Radio broadcast	29	35	13	40
Family member	26	31	13	20
Jewish friend, coworker, or neighbor	17	18	18	30
Non-Jewish friend, coworker, or neighbor	6	5	14	50
Saw it happen to myself	18	6	52	–
Others in a concentration camp	18	8	41	–
Other	7	9	2	–
Don't know anymore	7	11	–	–
First heard or knew something after the war was over	12	15	7	10
N of cases	**507**	**277**	**56**	**10**

Note: The percentages exceed 100 because multiple listings were possible.

centration camps. Nevertheless, even among Jews trapped in Germany, radio broadcasts (usually from the BBC), as well as information received from family, friends, and acquaintances were all important sources of information; four out of the ten German Jews who remained in Germany but were never deported, for example, had heard radio broadcasts informing them about the mass murder, and five had received information from non-Jewish friends.

The conclusion to be derived from the evidence presented above—that most survivors eventually became informed about the mass murder while it was still taking place and that they obtained this information from multiple possible sources—does not, however, indicate that Jews who were swept away in the deportation waves knew about the Holocaust before they were sent off to the places where the murders were being committed. Neither does it indicate that they believed they themselves and those sent off with them were destined to become victims of the mass murder. To determine what the deported Jews knew at the time of deportation, one needs to compare the exact dates they provided for their deportation with the exact dates they gave for when they first heard about the mass murder. If the date they gave for when they had first heard about the mass murder fell prior to the date they gave for when they were deported, this would indicate that they had known some things about the mass murder before they were deported, but it does not prove that they had also believed the information they had received. To ascertain what they had actually believed at the time, we need to refer to the specific testimonies the survivors gave in their in-depth interviews.

Nearly one-quarter of the survivors in our survey were deported during the years of the Third Reich. Of the 118 who had been deported, 101 provided a specific year and usually month when their deportation had occurred. But only slightly more than half of the survivors (54 of 101) who had been deported and provided their deportation date had been deported after the Soviet invasion commenced in June 1941. Of those deported earlier than June 1941, most had been deported either as stateless Jews to Poland in the fall of 1938 or from Baden to Gurs concentration camp in France in the fall of 1940. Of the fifty-four survivors deported after June 1941, most who had been sent off between the second half of 1941 and the first months of 1942 went originally to ghettos established in Lodz, Minsk, and Riga, and most of the rest who had been deported later originally went to either Auschwitz or Theresienstadt.

Since large-scale mass murder did not begin until after the invasion of the Soviet Union, Jews who were deported before June 1941 could not have heard about what truly constituted mass murder at the time of their original deportation. But those deported after this date could indeed have received word about it already, and, as time passed, ever greater numbers had in fact heard about it before their own deportation. Thus, if we consider only those survivors who were deported after June 1941 and gave a specific date of both their deportation and when they first learned that mass murder was taking place, a total of forty-three survivors remains in our sample.

When we compare the dates these forty-three survivors gave for their deportation and when they came to know about mass murder, it turns out that 31 percent of those who were deported from Germany itself and 27 percent of those who were deported from other countries had known about the mass murder before they were deported. Although several others in both groups indicated in their survey responses that they had become informed about the mass murder in the same month and year that their deportation took place, this cannot be assumed to mean that they gained this information prior to the time when their transports left for the east.

Having demonstrated, nonetheless, that many of the survivors who were deported after June 1941 had received information about the mass murder before they were deported, we now want to pinpoint when they had first received this information. To do this, we might first attempt to determine what the survivors deported in a given year had known about the mass murder before they were deported. When we do this, we find that none of the survivors deported in 1941, either from Germany or elsewhere, appears to have known about the mass murder and that the majority of the survivors who were deported in 1942 still did not know (of the seven survivors deported in 1942 from Germany who provided specific dates for both their deportation and for when they had come to know about mass murder, only two had already known at the time of deportation; and only one of the two survivors deported from outside of Germany who provided both dates had known). Thus it was not until 1943 that a significant number of the survivors in our sample knew about the mass murder before deportation and not before 1944 that a clear majority who were deported in that year knew in advance about what was transpiring.

While the information above demonstrates that most of the survivors deported before 1943 did not know about the mass murder in advance of deportation, it also shows that some of them who were deported in 1942 had already known about it. Further evidence that prior word about the mass murder of the Jews had reached at least some of the survivors deported in 1942 or even before that time can be provided when we examine the specific dates the survivors gave for when they had first heard about the mass murder. Of the ten survivors deported from Germany who knew about the mass murder before deportation, eight indicated that they had come to know about it before 1943: three in 1942, one in 1941, two in 1940, and two before 1940. Whereas one might hold doubts that someone could have known about the Holocaust before the middle of 1941, the fact that several survivors who had not yet been deported say that they had known about the mass murder in either 1941 or 1942 cannot be disregarded. Confirmation that many Jews did indeed know about the mass murder at such an early date was provided to us in several of our face-to-face interviews. In addition to this, the wartime diary of Victor Klemperer also demonstrates that considerable information about the Holocaust had already reached many German Jews in these early years.[4]

Bear in mind, however, that the Jews we are focusing on here survived the Holocaust while most Jews in Nazi-occupied Europe did not. Often they survived because they were deported at a later date and thus had to endure a relatively shorter period in the concentration camps. Typically they were Jews living in special circumstances; either they were born into mixed marriages between Jews and Gentiles or they worked in crucial war-related industries that offered them some protection for a while. When all of this is taken into consideration, it leads to the conclusion that even though many and possibly the majority of Jews who were deported in or after 1943 knew about the mass murder before their own deportation, most Jews who were deported prior to this time did not know about their intended fate before they were carted away. And, since most German Jews were deported before 1943, this means that most who were deported during the Holocaust probably were not aware that they were to be killed, even if they had held grave suspicions about what was in store for them.

On balance, therefore, our survey evidence indicates that the news about the mass murder became relatively widespread among the Jews still living in Germany between the latter months of 1942 and the early months of 1943. For additional support for this conclusion, we now turn to the interview narratives of the Jewish survivors. Several were either deported after the Soviet invasion had commenced or somehow survived the war and the Holocaust without ever being deported, usually because they had gone into hiding. What did these people know and what did they believe?

In nearly every interview with survivors who were still living in Germany after the Holocaust had begun, we asked when they had first learned that mass murder was taking place, whether they had believed the information, and, if they had been deported, what they had expected was going to happen to them at that time. About one-third of the people who were deported appear not to have heard about the mass murder before deportation. Most of the rest had heard, often quite a lot. Still, among those who received information about the mass murder prior to deportation, there remains a noticeable division between those who believed it and those who did not.

Herta Rosenthal and Herbert Klein are probably typical of many German Jews who were deported in 1942 and 1943. Although both heard rumors that gave them reason to fear the worst, neither really knew about the mass murder before deportation. As already noted, Herta Rosenthal was a sixteen-year-old teenager when her transport left her home city of Leipzig and took her and her parents to Riga. After she described the sordid scene in which many onlookers screamed and laughed as the Leipzig Jews were being deported, we asked her where she had thought she was going to be taken and what she had expected was going to happen to her. Her response indicates that she knew very little at the time: "My father said that if they send us to Poland, we're lost. We didn't know what was going on. We didn't know about Auschwitz. We knew about Buchenwald, Sachsenhausen, but the other we didn't know. We thought of Poland, because you heard from people who were deported in 1938 and came back that there was a big problem with the food and the cold. So I didn't know anything. I was so numb. Then they said that we're going east and my father said they're going to send us to Russia. Then we were on the train and we went to Königsberg. In Königsberg we stopped. But they didn't send us to Russia."

Since the recently established concentration camp at Auschwitz did not receive its first transport of Jews until late March 1942, and the first gassing of Jewish deportees did not take place there until early May 1942, the Rubinsteins could hardly have known "about Auschwitz" prior to their deportation in January 1942.[5] By the time Herbert Klein and his family were deported a year and a half later in June 1943, one might expect Jews like the Kleins to have known much more about the Holocaust. Nevertheless, Herbert Klein says that he and his family did not know about the mass murder at the time of their deportation, even though his father, as the head of the Jewish community in Nuremberg, was in a position to know more than most Jews. Perhaps his father knew more than he let on to his family and wanted to shield them from fears about what they might be facing. Perhaps he believed that it was pointless to worry them because he expected that their deportation to the so-called paradise ghetto at Theresienstadt would protect them from the worst. Whatever the case may have been, Herbert Klein was apparently not much better informed than the Rosenthals when he and his family left together with what he called "the last ones" to leave Nuremberg. As he explains, "We knew that in concentration camps like Dachau people got killed. My father sometimes had to open caskets and identify people with shot wounds [that indicated] if they had been shot from close distance. I mean, one knew that. And one knew about all kinds of accusations and things like that. But nobody knew that [the Jews were being systematically murdered]."

Although Herbert Klein possessed relatively limited knowledge about the Holocaust (and this may have been typical of many other Jews at the time), Helmut Grunewald and Ilse Landau, also typical of many Jews who were deported around the time Herbert Klein was deported, were much better informed. Not only had they already heard about the mass murder before they were shipped off, they believed what they heard.

Like Herbert Klein, both Helmut Grunewald and Ilse Landau had special circumstances that explain why they had not been deported earlier. Grunewald was the child of a mixed marriage between a Jewish father and a Catholic mother; Landau held an important job at the Jewish hospital in Berlin. Prior to March 1943, when he was deported from his home city of Cologne to Auschwitz, Helmut Grunewald had been in a Cologne jail for several months. Although his father ended up not being deported with him, he too had been arrested by the Gestapo along with his son in December 1942. Soon after their arrest, they were interrogated by the Cologne Gestapo; at one point his father blurted out, "I don't know why you want to interrogate me. I know that I'll be sent to Auschwitz and be gassed anyway." When we asked Grunewald how his father could have known this, he explained that his father had a large number of contacts in Jewish and non-Jewish circles (his own father-in-law was a Cologne policeman), and that by December 1942, when he and his father had been arrested, both Jews and non-Jews had already become aware of Auschwitz and the gassing and mass murder that was taking place in Poland. As he put it, "That people were being murdered in Auschwitz and in Poland in general was evident anyway. And it was also already known that Auschwitz was very clearly an extermination camp." Since we wanted to be sure that it was not only his father who had known this, however, we asked him repeatedly about his own level of knowledge. Each time he unhesitatingly answered, "Yes, I also knew it. One already knew about that. Something like that gets around quickly. It gets around very quickly. . . . In Jewish circles, one already knew about the Polish Jews. [And] we believed it. We knew that it was true." As proof, he referred us to a standing exhibition at the National Socialist Documentation Center in Cologne, which includes a postcard he wrote at the time of his deportation and handed to a stranger to put in the mail: "I am now being sent to Auschwitz. I don't believe that we will ever see each other again." Finally, when we asked him to confirm to us yet again that on the deportation train he fully expected to die when he reached Auschwitz, he stated firmly, "Yes, of course. Everybody thought that."

Ilse Landau had that same expectation when she was on the train to Auschwitz at around the same time. And, as noted previously, she decided to take her chances with the cold and the elements and intrepidly jumped off the train en route. Nevertheless, to be certain that she expected to be murdered if she remained on her deportation train and did not jump off, we asked her about this directly. Her reply was convincing: "Yes. They all would be gassed."

To conclude our discussion about what Jews knew and believed at deportation, we can refer to our interviews with Ernst Levin and Hannelore Mahler. Their sentiments may be the most characteristic of German Jews deported in the last years of the war. By the time of deportation, both had heard many things about the mass murders. Nevertheless, both told us that they had tried to deny to themselves what they had many reasons to believe was true. They held to the hope that the news was too unbelievable to be true and simply refused to believe it.

Before he was deported to Auschwitz in January 1943 "on the last transport from Breslau when the city decided to become Jew free," Ernst Levin had been working in a war-related industry. He had already heard many things about the mass murder of the Jews. He knew, for instance, that many deportations had already left for the east and he heard "frightening" things about "what was going on with the Polish Jews." More specifically, he heard about transports to Treblinka and Auschwitz. This information came from a variety of believable sources, including secondhand accounts provided by Jews and non-Jews. "Word filtered out," he said, from German troops returning from Poland. He also heard things from a non-Jewish woman at work whose Jewish husband had already been killed. Beyond this, he also had firsthand information. About a month before his transport was assembled, he had received a startling letter that somehow got through to him from a close friend who had been recently deported to Treblinka telling him that "here is a camp where the people are being treated with chemicals."

Despite all of the information he received, he says that he and many other Jews could not bring themselves to believe it. In his words: "Word was filtering out. It was filtering out that transports were leaving for the east from the ghettos. It was known at that time that these transports went directly to Auschwitz. Terrible, terrible! But people really did not want to talk about it. When the German Jews learned about it, they really refused to believe a lot of it. The German Jews themselves would say, 'This is atrocity propaganda. That can't be so. After all, it's the twentieth century and we're German.'. . . They didn't believe it primarily because they did not want to believe it. Who can blame them?"

Hannelore Mahler also did not want to believe what she knew must have been the truth. When she was rounded up in September 1944 with the last of Krefeld's remaining Jews and transported to Theresienstadt, she already knew what to expect, but she steadfastly held on to the hope that it was not true. Several times in her interview, she repeated that she and other German Jews had been aware that the end was probably coming for them but had not wanted to believe it or talk about it, even though they sometimes did. In her final words to us, she poignantly put the situation in relief: "Since we ourselves could have been the next ones, or were—we were practically on the list to be mowed down—we did not want to believe it, because we could have been next. . . .Everyone knew it. Everyone thought that it was so. But we did not want to talk about it, because you could be there yourself. When one suspects that those, who had been arrested and taken away and had never been heard from again, had not been sent to a sanatorium, you can almost compare that with someone who is about to be tested for cancer. One just doesn't talk about it, even though everyone knows that it is so."

Conclusion

Whether or not they wanted to talk about it and whether or not they found it hard to believe, the tragic news about the mass murder of European Jewry had spread far and wide among the Jewish population both inside and outside of Germany by the last years of the war. As Helmut Grunewald explains in his interview, information of this nature "gets around quickly." Spread inside Germany by word of mouth along the "Jewish grapevine," it came from many credible sources, including, but not limited to, German soldiers on leave from the front who sometimes spoke with loose lips about what they had witnessed, German citizens who remained in contact with their Jewish friends, BBC German-language radio broadcasts that could be received throughout Germany, and even from the letters of eyewitnesses that somehow managed to get through. Jews who were taken away in the earlier deportations from Germany or from elsewhere in Nazi-occupied Europe usually could not have had more than suspicions about their fate. But those who were on later transports or those few who were never deported had often been quite well informed about the reality of the mass murder before they were physically exposed to it. As our survey and interview evidence shows, nearly all of these Jews knew about earlier deportations from their own and often from other communities, especially since so many of the transports departed in broad daylight, not under cover of night and fog. Many also eventually received word about the mass shootings of Polish and Eastern European Jews, and probably most had become aware of the mass murder that was taking place in the concentration and death camps.[6] In the later months of 1942 and the early months of 1943, many Jews who were still living in Germany could even identify by name and location some of the most notorious death camps like Auschwitz and Treblinka, where they knew that Jews were being gassed.

Knowing about the Holocaust, or even experiencing it firsthand, was only part of what Jews in Nazi Germany came to know and experience. Subjected to terror and persecution like no other group, they lost their families, friends, occupations, identities, money, and freedom. But this did not happen overnight. Gradually at first, the faces of most of their German countrymen turned from friendship to indifference to outright anti-Semitic hostility. Although some Germans continued to display friendship and compassion toward Jews (more than a third of the survivors in our study say that they received significant help or support from their German countrymen during the Third Reich), they were in the minority; there were many times fewer Jews than non-Jews in Germany and nearly two-thirds of the survivors received no help whatsoever. Still, the mixture of support, indifference, and hostility the Jews experienced made it difficult for many of them to believe that their worst fears would come to pass.

Many of the survivors who took part in our study say that they were among the "lucky ones." They say this even though over one in ten of the survivors had criminal cases started against them by the Nazi police, nearly one in four endured deportations, more than one in four suffered in concentration camps, over nine in ten lost most of their property, and almost all lost loved ones—and this is not to mention the physical beatings, spying, and other indignities that had plagued their daily life in Nazi Germany. In view of the horror, trauma, and loss they experienced, one can understand why not all survivors chose to tell their children "to forgive, but to never forget" and, like William Benson, prefer to tell them instead: "You never forgive, you never forget."

Part FOUR

✢ ✢ ✢

"ORDINARY GERMANS'" SURVEY EVIDENCE

+11+

Everyday Life and Support for National Socialism

Adolf Hitler and the Nazi Party rose to power with remarkable speed and in the face of powerful leftist opposition. In the space of only four years, between May 1928 and July 1932, the Nazi vote in national Reichstag elections grew from a mere 2.6 percent to 37.4 percent and finally surpassed the Social Democratic Party, which had previously been the strongest party in Germany.[1]

Although another Reichstag election half a year later brought a minor drop in the voting totals, the Nazi Party had nonetheless become so important politically that, on January 30, 1933, Adolf Hitler was named chancellor of a coalition government and this soon led to the end of the Weimar Republic. In the last Reichstag election of the Weimar Republic that took place five weeks later in early March 1933, the Nazi vote reached 43.9 percent. This was, however, only a partially free election and must be seen as a special case: Communists, who were accused of having set fire to the Reichstag building shortly before the election, were de facto banned from voting and their party's functionaries were incarcerated; other political parties were also greatly hindered.

With the March 1933 election, the Nazi Party received nearly half of the votes cast but the share of the vote received by parties that opposed the Nazis still remained high. The Communist Party (KPD) garnered 12.3 percent of the votes, the SPD 18.3 percent, and the Catholic Center Party 11.2 percent. Taken together, all of the parties that could not be assigned to the national-conservative camp and opposed the Nazis polled almost as many votes as the Nazis. And, if the number of eligible voters are considered instead of only those who voted, the potential for opposition was even greater. In short, the Nazis still faced considerable potential opposition.

In the years that followed these elections, to what extent did the Nazi regime succeed in making itself truly popular among the German population? Did it win over supporters from the other parties and opposition groups, either completely or partially? Or did it rely primarily on force and terror to maintain its hold over German society because its support remained limited to a minority of Germans?

Such questions have long attracted interest and attention from historians and the general public, but the possibilities for answering them in the past were circumscribed. Survey research as we know it today that would allow a more precise picture did not exist in the Third Reich. Although American social scientists carried out some surveys during the war and shortly afterward among prisoners and civilians (e.g., psychological warfare research and U.S. strategic bombing surveys), they were too limited in thematic scope and time perspective to allow a broader picture. Nonetheless, they do provide some important basic findings (discussed later).[2]

Historians have not made use of these survey data. Whether this was because they did not know about the material or because they did not feel competent to use it is unknown. To measure public opinion in the Third Reich, they have instead leaned on traditional sources of historical inquiry such as diaries and autobiographical memoirs as well as secret reports of public opinion produced by the Security Service of the SS (SD) and other offices of the Nazi state and, to a lesser extent, on the mood and morale reports of the SPD in exile.[3]

These are indeed important sources of information, but their significance is limited by their failure to provide any quantitative statements about German popular opinion in general and about subgroups of the population in particular. A further shortcoming is that they rely on remarks made by citizens in public or in the vicinity of an informant. Naturally, these sources cannot provide a precise picture of private opinion, since the expression of opinion was often hampered by fear of punishment. In a society where divergent political opinion is under threat of repression, a broader consensus than that which really existed might easily be perceived.

Another reason for the difficulty in assessing public opinion in Nazi Germany is that very few historians and social scientists after the war questioned retrospectively those who had lived through the Nazi era. Only journalists, writers, and documentary filmmakers usually conducted such interviews, which historians often viewed skeptically. The systematic questioning of contemporaries—in the form of oral histories—did not begin to find its way into historical research on the Nazi era until the late 1970s and 1980s.[4]

As much as this development was to be welcomed in principle, the actual practice—when applied to the general population—was not without problems. Mostly the empirical basis was limited to a small pool of respondents, often arbitrarily chosen. The approach that had proven so successful in social science research—involving questionnaires and large representative samples—was neither applied nor taken into consideration. We think this was mostly because historians were largely unfamiliar with the tools of survey research, including the selection of samples and the conduct of quantitative analysis.

In the Federal Republic of Germany, the impulse for retrospective research into the Nazi era by means of empirical surveys based on a large pool of respondents came from nonacademic, commercial, public opinion research institutes that sometimes acted on their own, but more often were initiated and financed by the media and other organizations. The first inquiry to assess former Nazi support, involving only a few questions, was made by West Germany's Institut für Demoskopie Allensbach (Allensbach Institute for Public Opinion Research) in a small study of around one hundred respondents in 1947. This was followed in 1949 in the context of a study of popular anti-Semitism that employed a broader sample and range of topics.[5]

Given the dependence of nonacademic, commercial survey research on public debate and finance, a long time passed before retrospective questions about National Socialism's acceptance were posed to a large part of the West German population. This first occurred in 1985 at the fortieth anniversary of Germany's surrender in World War II, when Germans were debating whether the end of the war signified a defeat or a liberation for the German population. The survey, carried out by the Allensbach Institute, relied on face-to-face interviews and involved 715 people born in or before 1930.[6]

To measure the extent of National Socialism's acceptance, the survey used several questions, each tapping different dimensions of identification with the Nazi regime. For our survey, we have adopted these questions in slightly modified form. This gives us the advantage of being able to place our own findings, ascertained at the municipal level, in a comparative national context. Our study, however, encompasses more topics than the Allensbach and other surveys. It poses several series of questions about various important issues in the Nazi era that researchers have not yet addressed in representative surveys. From this point of view, therefore, our study makes up for what was missed in the past. Our study also distinguishes itself by being the largest: more than three thousand Germans, born in 1928 and earlier, responded to our survey questionnaires, which had been sent out to a random sample of the population, with up to three reminders.

We administered our main surveys by mail for methodological reasons. More than other types of survey research, mail surveys provide respondents with a feeling of anonymity and encourage them to be more open to sensitive questions. Also, in mail surveys, respondents have more time to recall the past and this improves their ability to remember. In addition to this, the response rates in mail surveys are at least as good as in face-to-face or telephone surveys if they are carried out properly. In fact our surveys received response rates of between 45 and 50 percent, which are generally considered very admirable in survey research dealing with older populations in large cities. Thus, in conformity with professional standards in survey research but in contrast to the usual practice employed in much oral history research, we chose our samples so that they would be truly representative of the German population. Still we also utilized the best techniques of oral history research in our study as we also carried out in-depth, face-to-face interviews with a sizable number of the respondents to the written surveys, chosen in part randomly and in part because they represented people from especially interesting and important sub-groups of the original survey population.

As discussed in the introduction to this book, our study is based primarily on four large and individual surveys that we carried out with representative samples of the people living in four German cities: Cologne, Krefeld, Dresden, and Berlin. The choice of cities was determined by several criteria: political significance, prevailing confessional makeup, and the availability of other studies for comparison. Berlin was the center of power in the Third Reich. It was the capital where the ministries were located, and it was the city with the largest number of Jewish inhabitants. Dresden is an eastern German city in the state of Saxony, once the stronghold of social democrats and communists. While most people in Dresden and Berlin were Protestants, the majority of the people in the Rhineland cities of Cologne and Krefeld were Catholics.

In the Allensbach Institute study, as well as our own, people who were young in the 1930s and early 1940s were naturally overrepresented in comparison with the Third Reich's population. The majority of older people from that era have since died. This might at first be seen as a problem for making inferences about the past. We can, however, compensate for this age bias and control for it by breaking down our respondents into different age-groups whenever it seems appropriate. Thus, those born between 1923 and 1928 make up the youngest age-group in our survey. By the war's end, they were between sixteen and twenty-three. The oldest age-group is made up of people born in 1910 or earlier. They were twenty-two or older at the beginning of the Third Reich in January 1933 and thirty-four or older at the end of the Third Reich in May 1945.

Partial Dissent and Extensive Consent

To measure popular support for the Nazis, we used the following three questions adapted from the Allensbach Institute survey: (1) "Was there a time in your life when you believed in National Socialism, or did you never believe in National Socialism? (2) Was there a time in your life when you admired Hitler, or did you never admire him? (3) Many failed to see everything that happened under Hitler in the Third Reich. Many did not know about it. When you now think back on the views and ideals in those days, what applies to you? Respondents were then given several possible answers that they could choose, ranging from support to rejection and including variations of indifference and ambivalence.

The three questions are intended to gauge Nazi sympathies. They offer a generalized orientation without implying an acceptance of all of the features of National Socialism. Furthermore, respondents who said they had believed in National Socialism didn't necessarily have to embrace anti-Semitism—just as those who rejected National Socialism didn't have to be free of anti-Semitism. Similarly, the statement that one supported National Socialism did not inevitably mean active, continuous participation in National Socialist organizations and activities. A person's support may have applied only partially and may have been expressed more in words than in deeds. Importantly, identification with Nazi ideals and support for National Socialism must not have lasted to the end of the Third Reich. As we know from the literature—as well as from our own data—many initially enthusiastic Nazi supporters became disillusioned and some even became active opponents of the regime or did things that helped help Jews escape death during the Holocaust.[7]

From other sources, based on SD reports and other kinds of data, we know that several people became increasingly disillusioned in the long run, and that the greatest drop in popularity occurred in 1943, when the German army in the east was defeated at Stalingrad. At the end of the war probably a majority of people who had once supported National Socialism had less sympathy for it than previously.[8]

We will first address the responses to the three questions posed in the nationwide survey carried out by the Allensbach Institute in 1985. Listed in Table 11.1, they show that a rather high degree of sympathy for National Socialism eventually prevailed among the German population and that this sympathy exceeded the Nazi Party's share of the vote in the last Weimar elections.[9] Around 59 percent of those surveyed admitted that they had once believed in National Socialism, 51 percent said they had supported National Socialism's ideals, and 41 percent indicated that they had admired Hitler.

Table 11.1   Attitudes Toward National Socialism

A. Believed in National Socialism

	National Allensbach Survey (1985) (%)	Cologne Survey (1994) (%)	Krefeld Survey (1994) (%)	Dresden Survey (1995) (%)	Berlin Survey (1999) (%)
Yes	59	45	54	58	54
No	32	49	42	37	43
Neutral*	9	6	5	5	3
N of cases	710	828	349	620	803

*Don't remember or other.

B. Admired Hitler

	National Allensbach Survey (%)	Cologne Survey (%)	Krefeld Survey (%)	Dresden Survey (%)	Berlin Survey (%)
Yes	41	33	38	43	32
No	34	65	59	54	66
Neutral*	24	2	3	3	2
N of cases	705	801	351	576	819

*Don't know, other, difficult to say.

C. Shared Nazi Ideals

	National Allensbach Survey (%)	Cologne Survey (%)	Krefeld Survey (%)	Dresden Survey (%)	Berlin Survey (%)
Yes	51	36	43	66	65
No	22	55	47	28	32
Neutral*	27	9	9	5	3
N of cases	715	634	265	587	804

*Don't know, too young, difficult to say, or other.

Table 11.2   Sympathy for National Socialism (Percentage)

	Total	Weighted Total*	
Positive	30	18	
Mostly Positive	26	31	NOTE: The scale is based on a combination of the three indicators as listed in table 11.1.
Ambivalent, neutral	11	9	
Mostly negative	16	18	
Negative	16	25	
	100	100	
N of cases	(715)		

*Weighted for the demographics of 1938.

The responses to the three questions regarding sympathy and support for National Socialism are, as to be expected, not independent of one another. Those who answered yes to one question were more likely to answer yes to the others as well. But not everybody who judged the regime positively or negatively answered all of the questions identically. Some may have admired Hitler for his foreign policy successes in the early period of the regime while rejecting National Socialism in general. And others may have approved of the basic ideas of National Socialism—for example, the idea of the "national community" (*Volksgemeinschaft*)—without accepting all National Socialist ideas.

In order to create an overall measure for National Socialist support, it makes sense to combine the three indicators in the form of an index or scale that differentiates the responses according to the degree of support. In creating the scale given below, we labeled respondents as "positive" in their attitude toward the Nazi regime when they answered all of the three questions affirmatively, and we labeled people as "negative" when they answered all three questions negatively. Those who answered two of the three questions positively or negatively, we labeled as "mostly positive" and "mostly negative" respectively. For example, when somebody answered negatively once but otherwise answered positively, he or she was then ranked as "mostly positive." This also applied to those who expressed themselves positively only once but otherwise neutrally ("I don't know"; "undecided").

As can be seen in Table 11.2, only a portion of the respondents answered all three questions either positively or negatively. Mixed attitudes prevailed. In this respect our findings are not unique, for modern societies usually number only a few people who are true "ideologues" with fully crystallized attitudes; most people have mixed attitudes and beliefs. Politics for most people is distant from their everyday lives. They give little attention to it and they don't care about being politically well informed.[10] In the 1930s and 1940s, given the lower level of education in the population compared with today, this tendency may have been even greater.

In the nationwide Allensbach Institute survey, 30 percent answered all three questions positively and another 26 percent were "mostly positive" in their answers. In contrast to this, 16 percent were uniformly negative in their responses and 16 percent "mostly negative." The remaining 11 percent of those surveyed were classified as ambivalent or neutral. Either they could not remember what their views had been, were undecided, or gave no answer. Strictly seen, the percentage of ambivalent people is underestimated by our procedure because a number of them—who showed a neutral, indifferent, or ambivalent attitude but answered at least one question positively (or one question negatively)—were placed in the category with a mostly positive (or mostly negative) attitude vis-à-vis National Socialism.[11]

The correct percentage of respondents who can be considered to have supported the Nazi regime depends on the criteria chosen. If one goes by the percentage of those who consistently judged the Nazi era positive or mostly positive, then the share of former Nazi supporters in the Allensbach survey would be 56 percent of the respondents. But if one included those who judged the Nazi era partially positively, ambivalently, or were undecided (i.e., those who did not give a decisively negative answer), the figure rises to 84 percent. This means that a majority of respondents, if sometimes only partially or temporarily, saw some positive sides to National Socialism. Even most of those who never accepted the Nazi regime outright appear to have found at least some positive aspects to it.

As already mentioned, the survey relied to a large extent on people who were relatively young at the end of the war, and younger people, as will be demonstrated, were disproportionately receptive to National Socialism. To determine what beliefs the German population held during the years of National Socialism, our national sample has to be made to resemble the age distribution that existed in Germany during the Third Reich. We have attempted to do this by estimating the pattern of answers on the basis of Germany's demographic structure in the late 1930s.[12] The result is remarkably stable, even if the percentages vary slightly. The fact remains that a majority of Germans identified with the Nazi regime at least temporarily.

What characterized the national-level data generated by the Allensbach survey was also replicated in the main by our larger and more recent four-city survey. Thus, as can be seen in Table 11.1, where the results of our four-city survey are reported next to those of the Allensbach survey, there was overall a high degree of support for National Socialism in general and similar nuances as far as various degrees of support are concerned. At the same time, the populations of the four cities did not all support National Socialism to the same

Table 11.3 Sympathy for National Socialism by City and Residence Before 1945 (Percentage Positive and Mostly Positive)

	Cologne	Krefeld	Dresden	Berlin
Respondents total	36(865)	45(372)	55(653)	52(853)
Lived there before 1945	31(407)	39(146)	55(399)	48(554)
Moved there after 1945	39(458)	49(226)	54(254)	58(299)

NOTE: This table lists the proportion of respondents expressing a positive or mostly positive attitude toward National Socialism. Those who are negative or ambivalent make up the rest of it. The number of respondents, which form the basis of evaluation, is listed in brackets. Same questions, as in Table 11.2, used for the construction of the scale.

degree. The strongest support for National Socialism was found among those surveyed in Dresden and Berlin, where the percentages of the people who answered that they had "believed in National Socialism," "admired Hitler," and "shared Nazi ideals" were at about the same level as or sometimes even higher than in the nationwide Allensbach survey. Among the people we surveyed in Krefeld, and especially in Cologne, however, we found a relatively lower level of support for National Socialism than in either Dresden or Berlin, but the level of support was still considerable. These local variations became even more pronounced, as can be seen in the Table 11.3, when the respective respondents were restricted to those who had lived in these places during the Nazi era itself.[13]

It is worth noting that more or less the same variations that we observe in our data in the level of support for National Socialism among the people in these four cities also existed in late Weimar elections. Thus the Nazi's share of the vote in the early 1930s was lowest in Cologne and Krefeld and highest in Dresden. This means that the milieus that originally favored the rise of the Nazis remained the same milieus where the Nazis eventually received the most support during the Third Reich itself.

The Social Bases of Support for National Socialism

Which people were most supportive of National Socialism? What kind of social profile did they have? Past attempts to answer these questions often involved more conjecture than solid facts. Data based on election statistics and data on the social characteristics of voting districts in the early 1930s as well as data on the social profile of Nazi members have provided important—yet somewhat limited—information about the beginnings of the Third Reich, but little about its later years. For later periods, basic impressions based on nonquantifiable reports by the secret state police or other organizations have been used in the scholarly literature.

Our survey data allow a much more precise and quantitative picture. As can be seen in Table 11.4, the level of sympathy that the respondents had was highly correlated with their gender, age, and religious background, and somewhat less with their educational background. Whereas male, Protestant, and younger respondents were mostly in sympathy with National Socialism, female, Catholic, and older respondents were considerably less likely to have been pronounced supporters of National Socialism. Thus, as the table shows, between 48 percent and 68 percent of the male respondents in the four cities we surveyed provided answers demonstrating that they were mainly in sympathy with National Socialism, while for female respondents the percentages ran in a range between a low of 28 percent in Cologne and a high of 47 percent in Dresden. Similar variations were found when we considered the age and religious backgrounds of the respondents. Whereas in all of the cities except Cologne and Krefeld, an absolute majority of the youngest age cohort surveyed (i.e., those born between 1923 and 1928) report that they had mostly supported National Socialism, among the older cohorts of respondents only about a third or fewer answered that they had been mostly in sympathy with the Nazis. And, finally, whereas a majority of Protestant respondents in all of the cities except Cologne had once given their support to National Socialism, the range of Nazi supporters among Catholics varied between a low of 31 percent in Cologne and a high of 45 percent in Dresden.

Whatever the reasons were for women in our survey to have been less supportive of National Socialism than men, the fact remains that our findings are different from what many authors once argued in the past. Among others, Wilhelm Reich, in his 1933 book *The Mass Psychology of Fascism*, as well as the sociologist Theodor Geiger, took the position that the rise of the Nazi Party relied primarily on female voters. Later authors, based on visual impressions of mass meetings and rallies, also argued that women were more enthusiastic for National Socialism than men. That such assumptions were wrong could be seen already in the Weimar election statistics, which show that women were in no way more inclined to vote for the Nazi Party than men. Our data underscore this further and show clearly that the Nazis never succeeded in winning over a majority of German women, even if it cannot be said most were against them either.

In regard to the varying support that the Nazis received from different age-groups among the German population, various factors were at work. Probably most important was the Nazi Party's recruitment of youth in the period before Hitler came to power. The party understood itself as a party of youth, and many of its functionaries were in fact younger than those in other parties. Against this

Table 11.4   Sympathy for National Socialism by Social Characteristics and City
(Percentage Positive and Mainly Positive

	Cologne	Krefeld	Dresden	Berlin
Sex				
Male	48(333)	57(152)	68(246)	60(479)
Female	28(531)	37(223)	47(397)	42(360)
Year of birth				
Until 1910	23(102)	35(37)	42(82)	17(47)
1911–16	21(161)	35(63)	39(118)	35(91)
1917–22	37(237)	48(133)	56(176)	47(258)
1923–28	45(361)	50(141)	65(262)	62(440)
Education				
Low	33(499)	44(220)	48(355)	52(447)
Medium	34(177)	42(65)	58(173)	52(197)
High	47(111)	50(46)	80(29)	49(90)
University	40(194)	51(89)	71(83)	51(120)
Religion				
Catholic	31(526)	35(225)	45(60)	43(89)
Protestant	44(269)	61(124)	58(518)	54(630)

Basis: Scale as Table 11.2

Education: Low=Volksschule; Medium=Realschule; High=Gymnasium backdrop, the Nazis projected a youthful image and appealed to youthful rebel-liousness. Second, the strong support given to the Nazis by the younger people in our survey also probably reflects the Nazis' strong efforts to mold the new generation for the benefit of the regime after its seizure of power, through direct and indirect influence, such as through schools and the Hitler Youth (which was compulsory for youth after 1936). Finally, receptiveness to Nazi ideology was also facilitated by an openness to new things found among young people in general. Young people are characteristically less committed to previous conditioning than older people; they can be more easily molded. They make up, in the words of the sociologist Karl Mannheim, society's "mutation potential."[14]

Before the Nazis seized power, Catholics were strongly inclined to vote for their own Catholic party, the Catholic Center Party. Membership in the Nazi Party was even forbidden by the Church for some time. Under these conditions Catholics might be expected to keep a certain distance from the new regime, even when their party ceased to exist. Furthermore, the regime intervened in what was traditionally considered church matters, such as the existence of parochial schools, crucifixes in classrooms, and Catholic youth groups. The Church criticized this publicly and to its members. On the other hand, some Catholic clergymen praised the new regime for its opposition to communism. In 1933 the Vatican and Hitler agreed on a concordat, giving many Catholics the feeling that the new regime might not be so bad. Whatever the pro and cons, in the end, as our data show, the reserve among Catholics persisted during the Third Reich.

With regard to schooling, there was a modest tendency among the better educated to be more in support of National Socialism than the more poorly educated. This tendency was not very strong in Cologne, Krefeld, and Berlin, but it was more pronounced in Dresden. Why education had a greater effect in Dresden than among those surveyed in the other cities is unclear. Possibly leftist—especially Marxist parties—were so strong in the area around Dresden in the Weimar Republic that the middle and upper classes felt endangered and perceived the Nazis as a desirable alternative to socialism and communism.[15]

A further reason for the observed relationship in Dresden might be that National Socialism spread most successfully in populations where the bour-geoisie as a local elite also succumbed to it. That better-educated people were no more immune to National Socialism than the less educated calls into question the widely held belief that tolerance and enlightenment are more likely to be found among people who have a higher education. It is the content of socialization that counts, not the degree of sophistication.

In this context, it is particularly important that National Socialism, with its racist ideology, picked up on a widely held line of biological thought that draped itself in modern scientific findings. In the early twentieth century, principles of genetics and heredity came to enjoy widespread popularity and merged in turn with crude variations of social Darwinism. Aggressive expressions such as "struggle for existence" and "survival of the fittest" corresponded with this thinking, which was also applied to reshaping society.[16]

Reasons for the Nazi Regime's Popularity

What was the popularity of National Socialism based on? Taking the statements made in the oral history interviews we conducted as a measure, Hitler's personality without a doubt played a significant role. This concurs with the views of other authors who credit Hitler's charisma and speak of a Hitler myth that existed among the German populace.[17] Starting early on, the Nazi Party contributed to the myth making by intensively promoting a cult of personality centered on Hitler. The introduction of the Hitler greeting—"Heil Hitler!"—belonged to this cult as well as the oath of allegiance taken by the party membership and later by the civil service and the army. The renaming of streets and squares for Hitler shortly after the seizure of power also belonged to the cult of personality around Hitler, as did the national celebration of his birthday.

Whether the Hitler myth really won over the support of the German population, however, is not entirely certain. In the Allensbach Institute survey and in our own surveys we discovered that the percentage of respondents who answered that they had once believed in National Socialism generally was often considerably higher than the percentage of respondents who answered that they had "admired" Hitler (see Table 11.1). A possible reason for this might be that Hitler had become such a vilified figure in the postwar world that few people would admit having admired him but found it more acceptable to admit once believing in part of the Nazi program. Another reason could be that some Nazi ideals had a stronger appeal than Hitler himself had. Whatever the case, Nazi propaganda certainly portrayed Hitler as someone with both human and superhuman characteristics. As we found when we conducted our face-to-face interviews with the survey respondents, many Germans once credited Hitler for several positive accomplishments and often acquit him for having been responsible for what they construe as negative aspects of National Socialism. Some examples follow:

> For us, Hitler was a really special personality. We somehow felt protected by him. I have to say, we gladly followed his orders. What he organized back then was all right to us. As a man—dictator is wrong—he was a leader one had to respect, because he had brought us so much good.[18]

The führer was the highest idol of the entire party, the youth party, and all of its organizations. He was an idol that was emulated and served. And everything that a young man wanted to do at the time had to be done for him.[19]

The führer was [in the eyes of the population] always a good man. If something bad happened, it was always said: "If the führer knew about it, something like that wouldn't happen."[20]

People's fascination with Hitler also became clear in our respondents' reports about his radio addresses in the 1930s, for which people often had to gather at work and elsewhere):

On important occasions, the führer spoke [and this was broadcast on radio]. The streets were empty then. Everybody hung on the first radios that were available. People met in groups because not everybody had one then: "You can listen at my place. The führer is speaking from then until then."[21]

Hitler's charisma, beyond the propaganda, is also visible in reports about his public appearances where some of the respondents were present. Fanaticism among the population was often quite pronounced.

Hitler was supposed to come in '36, when the Rhine bridge was dedicated. We stood on Friedrichsplatz in Krefeld. It was completely full of people. They were all for [National Socialism]. They were all for it. And I didn't hear anybody who was against it back then. They were all for it. And we were also for it.[22]

The enthusiasm that Hitler provoked in many people also becomes clear in the reports of those who came into his immediate vicinity. One respondent was standing outside the Reich chancellery when Hitler appeared. Even though a political event was being celebrated—the avoidance of war in 1938 through the Munich Agreement—the masses' choice of words, "dear Führer," shows the intensity of the emotional bonding with Hitler:

I was standing beneath the balcony of the Reich chancellery in Berlin when he returned from Munich and where he had managed to avoid a war for the Sudetenland. He was received triumphantly. . . . . Hundreds of thousands of people stood on the streets and cheered the führer who had saved the peace. . . . We were standing under the balcony and calling out all those phrases, "Dear Führer, be so kind, come to the window!"[23]

Another respondent from Dresden once had to provide an honor guard with other members of the Hitler Youth to welcome Hitler. "Because I was blond," he reported, "[Hitler] stroked my head. And I was proud. I was proud."[24]

Another one of those surveyed saw Hitler drive by in a motorcade and described having a "sublime" feeling come over her. And one woman, who saw Hitler up close, was impressed by his "beautiful blue eyes." Even during the interview, she fell into rapture:

> One time I did see Hitler very close up. My daughter was still very small. She was born in 1937, so it must have been in 1938 or it could have been in 1939. Anyway, the war hadn't started yet. [Foreign Minister Joachim von] Ribbentrop lived here in Dahlem and he had a large house and it was his birthday. I think it was April 30. I was taking a walk with my daughter and kept hearing "Heil! Heil!" And I thought, "Huh?" As I drew nearer, I saw a couple of people standing in front of a driveway and I said, "What's going on here?" "The führer is in there," [was their answer]. I got curious and remained standing there for a while, and then I saw him driving out in an open car. He had beautiful blue eyes, like Enzian (a flower), and he was suntanned.[25]

Another female respondent described the kind of deep impression that Hitler left even on those who opposed National Socialism and how much his eyes impressed people. She relates how her mother—who was opposed to the regime—ended up in the presence of Hitler, and how, contrary to her own convictions and in the heat of the moment, she became a part of the applauding crowd even though she was simultaneously seized by dark foreboding. She too was impressed by Hitler's eyes—so kind and patriarchal in appearance, that one might call him "father."

> We lived on Potsdamer Platz, and my brother wanted to see the linden . . . the trees that had been transplanted roots and all. That was interesting [to him]. So my brother and my mother walked up to the commuter rail station Unter den Linden. [The street] was full of people there. Then my mother saw that we could get through [by walking] between the cars. Then something happened: Suddenly she was standing in front of Adolf's car. [All at once, she started feeling strangely.] She had a kind of handbag and put it away and raised her hand. It was the only time [she ever raised her hand in the Hitler greeting]. He then nodded to her and waved. But the SS was suddenly there and surrounded her. They pushed her on. She later said, "That man is extremely dangerous. He has eyes that you can say father to. But what's behind the eyes . . . "[26]

If some made Hitler's magnetic personal appeal responsible for National Socialism's popularity, others in our interviews mentioned specific measures and events that they saw as the regime's positive achievements. Not infrequently, however, they also credited Hitler for these accomplishments. Going by the results of our interviews and our questionnaires, the reduction of the mass unemployment dominated as the Nazis' most important achievement:

Then Adolf came to power with his new idea. For most that was indeed better. People who hadn't had a job for years had a job. And then the people were all for the system. When someone helps you get out of an emergency situation and into a better life, then you're going to give them your support. Do you think people would then say, "This is all such nonsense. I'm against that." No. That doesn't happen. How things were done later on is something else.[27]

I didn't find it at all horrible [when Hitler came to power]. That was a time of great unemployment. My father wasn't unemployed, but I had understood that many people were unemployed, and that the unemployed suddenly had work. . . . What I knew from my parent's stories, I always understood as something positive.[28]

Today, young people say, "Were you stupid? How could you listen to all that?" But it was different then. . . . You have to go back to this time: the bitter poverty, stew once a week, and everything else that was happening. . . . You can't imagine that today. It wasn't like today. If I were to hear [Hitler's speeches] today, I would say the man was crazy. He wasn't. Not for the people back then. It was the zeitgeist.[29]

In our survey, we not only asked people if they had believed in National Socialism, shared its ideals, and admired Hitler, we also asked them to specify which features and accomplishments (if any) of National Socialism they had found to be particularly positive. As possible answers, we provided them with a list of eight features and accomplishments of National Socialism and asked them to choose the three that were most important to them. Their responses are displayed in Table 11.5.

In the table one notes that the respondents considered the reduction of unemployment the Nazis' most positive accomplishment. Even among people who say they opposed the regime, there was a majority who crossed this off on the survey. After the seizure of power, Hitler in fact significantly reduced mass unemployment in a short period of time. In late 1932 and early 1933, unemployment had reached its highest level in Germany. Roughly one year later, the figure had been cut in half, and by 1936, a shortage of workers, especially skilled workers, was beginning to make itself felt. By 1938, there was no longer any unemployment worth mentioning.[30]

Another feature of National Socialism that a great number of respondents rated positively was the construction of the autobahn highways. With this large project, the Nazis realized something that Weimar government officials had discussed but had not yet begun. The large number of people who were involved in the construction of the autobahns (in 1936 around 125,000 people) and obtained their first job under the new regime contributed significantly to Hitler's reputation as the leader who overcame unemployment.

Table 11.5 What People Like Best About National Socialism by City (Multiple Response as Percentage)

	Cologne	*Krefeld*	*Dresden*	*Berlin*
Fight against unemployment	62	63	69	65
Less crime	57	59	42	56
Construction of highways (Autobahn)	40	43	58	47
Support of families	36	40	34	29
Community feeling	26	27	21	27
Idealism	15	14	10	11
Overcoming of powerlessness	12	15	13	15
Jews less powerful	4	5	2	*
Other	4	3	4	4
Nothing	20	21	13	16

*Not supplied as category in questionnaire

Until 1933 there was the period of unemployment. And then Adolf basically got the unemployed off the streets with the measures he took, like building the autobahn. The people were content. They had a job, but what they did, well, that's another question.[31]

At first, it was said [Hitler] will bring us work. We thought, "If he does that, that'll be super." But the construction of the autobahn [was also something positive for us]. . . "The construction of the autobahn will give all kinds of people something to do." But you didn't know why [Hitler] was building autobahns. He already had an eye on the war. We didn't think about that.[32]

Partly in the context of fighting poverty, partly in the context of family policy, 29 to 40 percent of respondents named support of families with lots of children as an important achievement of National Socialism. "He helped poor families with lots of children. Families with lots of children got preferential coupons for foodstuffs, for clothing. They could buy them for less," said one of those surveyed.[33] And another reported, "We had five children in our family. Those with lots of children were promoted, as was done back then. I can still remember it exactly. For five children, we had three beds, so to speak. Two children slept in one bed. Then we got the money or a check to buy beds."[34]

For many Germans, the reduction of unemployment, the construction of the autobahns, and social policy measures merged to form a picture of something being done for the little guy. Against this backdrop, Hitler's government became a benefactor for the population's welfare in many people's minds. This was a crucial factor in the establishment of the Nazi regime's legitimacy, since economic performance counts heavily in the development of a political system's legitimacy, regardless of whether it is a dictatorship or a democracy.

Thus, just as the economic upswing in West Germany in the postwar era legitimized the new political system—and favored the establishment of a democratic order—the reduction of unemployment and the economic upswing in the 1930s promoted the legitimacy of the Nazi regime.[35] This development was probably accelerated in part by the population's low level of identification with the Weimar Republic and the social and political crises that accompanied the German experiment with democracy between 1918 and 1933.

Another one of the regime's important achievements for many of the respondents was the reduction of criminality. One might expect their views in this regard to have been shaped by their present-day conditions and by the disproportionate fear of crime generally found among older people. But present-day worries about criminality do not solely explain why so many respondents endorsed the statement about crime. The fact that acts of violence and street battles between different political groups, which had been a nearly constant feature of the Weimar Republic, suddenly stopped with the establishment of the Nazi regime also contributed to this verdict. For many Germans, street fighting for political reasons and criminality had merged because they often had not felt safe on the streets where they lived during the Weimar years.

We lived near Sproedentalplatz, where the Krefeld fair is held. That's where political marches were always being held by all kinds of parties. They would then march past our place as well. There was a lot of turmoil on the streets. There was a sigh of relief when things settled down [in 1933]. Conditions were better. Order ruled the streets. Women were also able to go through town without anything happening like [it would] today.[36]

In comparison with the factors named above, relatively few of the respondents found any of the other features of National Socialism on the list nearly as positive. Thus they assigned relatively little prominence to foreign policy triumphs ("Germany became strong and powerful once again"), "the strengthening of idealism among the people," "the strengthening of a sense of community," or to the Nazi's anti-Semitic policies ("The Jews were no longer so powerful"). This is not to say that these things were always fully unattractive to most people—but in the context of the other features they could choose from the list we provided, they were accorded a more subordinate position by most people and thus were not considered one of the three most attractive features of National Socialism.

Some of the events that might have impressed many German people and led to Nazi success in late Weimar elections may have faded in the minds of our respondents, such as the consequences of the Versailles Treaty and the war reparations after World War I. Nevertheless, many of the people we interviewed mentioned such things. Some recalled the occupation of the Ruhr region by foreign troops in retaliation for unpaid war reparations, and the subsequent humiliations they experienced. Others—especially in the Rhineland—remembered the German reoccupation of the Rhineland, which in the wake of World War I had been declared a demilitarized zone, a situation annulled by the arrival of German troops in March 1936. Indeed many Germans were proud that Germany had once again become an autonomous state under Hitler. In light of this, even many critics of the regime were unable to conceal their respect.

We were at work. . . . All of a sudden in the afternoon, [the news] reached us: German troops have entered Cologne. Well that's just great. Thank God! . . . We are something again. . . . There was nothing left of the Versailles Treaty for us to fulfill. Now we have our own troops here.[37]

Older people—those I associated with—were never enthusiastic [about Hitler]. They said, "That won't turn out well." On the other hand, [positive things] were said. Hitler left the League of Nations. Then came the universal draft and the occupation of the Rhineland. . . . Then we said, "That's the right thing to do. Here in Germany, in our country, we can do what we think is correct." And those payments that we had to pay England and France, those reparations from World War I, the Germans were forced to pay them. People said, "It's right to fight them."[38]

Whatever relative ranking the respondents may have ascribed to the various features of National Socialism that were included on our list of possible answers to the question we asked them, it is particularly striking that so very few people answered that they found the regime's anti-Semitic policies especially to their liking. As displayed in Table 11.5, that "Jews were no longer so powerful" was the response that was crossed off the least frequently on our list. Although a few people we interviewed mentioned anti-Semitism as something they and other Germans had once found attractive about National Socialism, they were rare exceptions. We doubt that Nazi anti-Semitic policy was really as uninspiring to the German population as our evidence seems to indicate. Probably our surveys and interviews with non-Jews uncovered so little evidence of overt anti-Semitic feeling because few people would ever want to admit that they once supported policies that eventually led to the mass murder of millions of Jews. Hence, in this But even more important in this context might have been that respondents had to choose their most important reasons and in relation to them anti-Semitism did not figure so prominently even though it may still have been prevalent.

Most importantly, about the answers the respondents from Cologne, Krefeld, Dresden, and Berlin gave to our question about the features of National Socialism that they found to be "positive," is that only a fifth or fewer of the respondents in each of the cities answered that they found "nothing" at all positive about National Socialism. This would indicate that something like 80 percent of all Germans admit that they had been at least attracted to some aspects of the Nazi program, a figure that jibes rather squarely with that percentage of Germans we reported earlier in this chapter who had answered in the 1985 nationwide Allensbach Institute survey that they had at least been partially attracted to Nazism.

Conclusion

Based on nationwide survey data and our multicity study, we have shown that National Socialism did indeed gain widespread popularity during the Third Reich. However, as has been shown as well, the popularity was not universal and for many Germans was only partial. Only a minority of Germans, it appears, fully believed in National Socialism, admired Hitler, and were strongly committed to most Nazi ideals, though most Germans certainly found at least some things that were to their liking about National Socialism and very few were truly against it.

In this respect our findings resemble the findings that were carefully collected by the American Psychological Warfare division during the war and the Strategic Bombing Survey Division after the war—in selected areas and cities and with somewhat more limited questions. Here too those fully committed to the Nazi ideal—called "black" in these studies—were a minority, as were the "whites." The majority fell into the group of the "gray"—somewhere in-between "black" and "white."[39]

Of course many former Nazis at the war's end or right after it, disillusioned by what had happened in the meantime, gave up many of their Nazi beliefs. But data from earlier periods, as far back as 1943, collected among prisoners of war showed the same pattern of a broad—but partial—endorsement of the Nazi system. Hard-core Nazis constituted a minority among them as well. The majority had mixed feelings with strong tendencies in favor of National Socialism.

What the strategic bombing survey also showed was the fact that the Catholic Rhineland—where two of the cities we studied are situated (Cologne and Krefeld)—were the areas where resistance to Nazism was highest. In other areas of Germany, especially in the north, the Nazis seem to have enjoyed far greater popularity. This can also be seen when the Allensbach survey, which we made use of initially, was broken down by region.[40]

The fact that people were often—despite criticisms of the Nazi period—attached to at least some aspects of National Socialism is also documented in surveys that were carried out right after the end of the war. When asked in October 1948 if there were some things they especially disliked about National Socialism, 78 percent answered yes. But, at the same time, 57 percent also agreed that "National Socialism was a good idea that was poorly implemented." But when asked whether there was something they disliked, 99 percent said yes. Given their mixture of attitudes, it is no wonder that this positive attitude toward the idea of National Socialism lasted for many years. Only in the course of the 1950s and 1960s did the share of positive answers gradually decline due to the inevitable generational shift that was taking place. The generations that expe-rienced the Third Reich and could see something good in National Socialism were successively replaced in number by the postwar generations. The Nazi gen-eration has slowly died off over time and is now almost completely gone.[41]

Our evidence, though somewhat more limited in our non-Jewish surveys than in our Jewish surveys, questions if the appeal of National Socialism was primarily due to its anti-Semitism. The reduction of unemployment and crime and the spread of social welfare support appear in our surveys to be especially important in accounting for the Nazis' popularity. This is also in accord with reports compiled by the Nazi agencies and the Social Democratic Party in exile.[42] The influence of economic factors especially has also been shown to help account for the Nazi Party's ups and downs in Weimar elections. In addition to this, others have shown that the original growth in Nazi Party membership was closely linked to the prevailing economic conditions at both the national and the regional levels.[43]

✛12✛

TERROR

The early phase of the Third Reich was a precarious one for the Nazi regime. Although the Nazis had received the highest percentage of votes in the last Reichstag elections, the other parties still posed a potential threat to the new regime. However, in the wake of the Reichstag fire, within one month after Hitler's coming to power, the Nazis took drastic steps toward eliminating all political opposition. The first wave of arrests began immediately after the fire and was directed primarily against members and functionaries of the Communist Party who were accused of setting the fire.

For these arrests, the SA rapidly opened concentration camps all over Germany—in schools, hotels, and even youth hostels. Among those held in concentration camps were groups such as the communists—which had regularly engaged in street fights with the Nazis, often with considerable casualties. But some who had opposed the Nazis less violently, such as social democrats and unionists, were also arrested. The Jews were not specifically targeted at this point. If some Jews were arrested, it was usually due to their political convictions.

In general, the early concentration camps existed only a short time; nonetheless, several thousand people fell victim to all kinds of violence as the Nazis consolidated power in 1933. Around 100,000 people were arrested and temporarily jailed.[1] Even when these initial detainees were released—some after a long term of imprisonment—their freedoms were still constricted, and they remained under surveillance.

346

One of our respondents from Dresden, whose relatives, both male and female, had been members of the Communist Party, reported that his father was taken to the concentration camp in Hohenstein near Dresden in 1933: "It was around five or six months. Then he came back. . . . Once a week he had to get in touch with the mayor [to show] that he hadn't left [Dresden] and was always there. He had to report to the mayor's office because a police station was there."[2]

The attack on members of other parties, however, did not eliminate all opposition. After the Communist and Socialist Parties were banned, many of their members decided to work undercover against the regime. While these groups were loosely connected, they were nevertheless centrally operated to a considerable extent (the communists from Moscow and the exiled Social Democratic Party from Prague).

Our findings from Cologne and Krefeld show the extent to which political activities were carried out, especially in a communist setting. In the Krefeld and Cologne surveys we asked respondents to specify their parents' political orientation. Of respondents who identified their parents as "communist," nearly half (46 percent) said they knew people personally who had actively opposed the regime. Among those who identified their parents as "social democrats," this figure was still 25 percent. In the remaining categories—including the Catholic Center Party—these figures were lower; less than one-sixth (approximately 16 percent) of these respondents personally knew people who actively opposed the Nazi government.

Of course only a fraction of the original members of the outlawed political parties took the dangerous route of underground opposition. Many withdrew from political life because they saw no possibility of mounting a successful opposition to the Nazi regime, since the leaders of their organizations were arrested or went into exile. Many refrained from opposition because they did not want to endanger themselves and their families—or because they found ways to benefit to some extent from the new regime. And this regime was well suited for such "defectors." From the very beginning, the Nazi regime's strategy was to exert terror on those it considered to be a threat while at the same time trying to win over those it did not consider true opponents.

Harassment by the new regime was not limited to former functionaries and members of the banned political parties and unions. Even those who made snide remarks about the state and its representatives risked arrest and punishment. The *Heimtückegesetz* (law against political libel and slander) of 1934 greatly curtailed freedom of speech and made the prosecution of such criticisms of the Nazi regime and its leaders possible. As a rule, these new types of offenses were not punished severely, but sometimes they were, and they were plentiful in the early Nazi years. In 1937 alone, 17,200 cases were initiated.[3]

Despite this relatively large figure, our survey evidence shows that most Germans had little contact with either the newly established Gestapo or the other organs of Nazi terror. In one of the most important questions dealing with the issue of terror in our survey, we asked the respondents to tell us if they themselves had ever been arrested or interrogated by either the Gestapo or the police during the years of the Third Reich and if they personally knew other non-Jewish people who had been either arrested or interrogated in the course of a criminal investigation. We then provided them with a list of different types of people (including relatives, friends and acquaintances, work colleagues, neighbors, and others) and asked them to indicate which if any of these types of people they had known personally had cases started against them. Those who neither had a criminal case started against them nor knew anyone personally who had been arrested or at least interrogated were asked to indicate this as well. The responses we received to this question are displayed in Table 12.1.

The evidence provided in the table shows that only 47 of the 2,601 people who answered this question in the four cities we surveyed were ever arrested or interrogated by either the Gestapo or the regular police during all the years of the Third Reich. This means that an average of less than 2 percent of the non-Jewish people in these cities—even though many of them hailed from former left-wing backgrounds and most (as will be shown below) had broken the laws of the Third Reich in the course of their daily lives—were ever accused of wrongdoing in Nazi Germany, much less punished for such activity. Only in Cologne, where sympathy for the Nazi movement was lowest among the four cities, was the percentage of respondents involved in criminal cases higher than 1 percent. Older respondents had somewhat higher rates, yet a systematic relationship with age did not exist. The basic results remain the same.

If this evidence calls into question the long-held notion that terror was ubiquitous in Nazi Germany, the evidence in the table showing that most survey respondents did not personally know anyone who had ever been accused of committing an illegal act calls it further into question. Only in Dresden, which lies in Saxony, where communist and socialist activity was perhaps more pronounced than in many other regions of Germany, did more than 30 percent of the respondents answer that they knew somebody personally who had been arrested or interrogated.[4] Thus, in the other three cities, over 70 percent of the respondents knew nobody at all who came afoul of the Gestapo or the police.

Still, it was not unusual for people to know someone who had been arrested or interrogated, and in most instances the people they knew had acted individually as opposed to in a group. In the few cases that involved groups, typically they were associated with former political parties, especially the social democrats and the communists. Among the more typical cases involving individuals who acted alone, the people who were referred to were equally divided

Table 12.1   People Known Personally by Respondents Who Were Either Arrested or Interrogated for Illegal Activity

	Cologne (%)	Krefeld (%)	Dresden (%)	Berlin (%)
I myself	3	1	1	1
Family members	10	9	9	8
Friends, acquaintances	13	13	11	11
Work colleagues	3	1	4	2
Neighbors	8	6	9	*
Other people	6	9	7	5
Nobody	70	74	69	76
N of cases	**767**	**340**	**631**	**857**

*Not asked in the Berlin survey

among the respondents' relatives, friends, acquaintances, and neighbors in each of the four cities.

In a follow-up question, we asked respondents to specify the reasons for the cases that had been started against them or others they had known, and these reasons varied widely. When an arrest involved membership in one of the former political parties, it was more often the Communist than the Socialist Party. Members of the Center Party were seldom mentioned—even in the Catholic Rhineland. However, church activity was often mentioned as the reason for Gestapo involvement, although it was never as decisive a factor as the underground political opposition of groups such as the communists or socialists. Among the other cases, many involved illegal statements of opinion against Hitler and the Nazi regime, and many involved doubts about Germany's ultimate victory in the war. Political activities deemed by the regime to be especially dangerous—such as high treason, sabotage, or active resistance—made up only a minority of the cases.

Among respondents who had been arrested or interrogated by the Gestapo or the police, a broad spectrum of activities were the causes for suspicion—from maintaining contact with forbidden youth organizations to direct or indirect participation in active political resistance. Some of the respondents were also interrogated because their fathers had engaged in political activities against the Nazis and they were suspected of knowing about or being involved in those activities as well.

From another follow-up question, we learned that the arrests or interrogations that the respondents recalled were spread out over the years of the Third Reich. The first large wave came in 1933, the year that the Nazis came to power, when they carried out mass arrests in an attempt to crush existing political parties and organizations. There was a reduction in the number of arrests and interrogations that the respondents mentioned in following years, but their number began to climb again in the second half of the 1930s. The highest number of arrests and interrogations the respondents mentioned was reached during the war years between 1942 and 1944, and these numbers correspond to the numbers of internments in concentration camps.[5]

After we asked the respondents to tell us why and when they or others they knew had been arrested, we then asked them to specify how these cases had been initiated and we provided a list of possible answers to choose from, including various types of civilian denunciations as well as police raids, Gestapo spies, and reports from the Nazi Party. Thus, when the respondents were asked how the Gestapo or the police had found out about the alleged illegal activity, around 40 percent in Cologne and Krefeld identified informants in their immediate surroundings—primarily neighbors—followed by colleagues and finally by relatives and family members as the cause. Another 25 percent of respondents mentioned Gestapo spies, 11 percent police raids, and 11 percent notifications from the Nazi Party. These figures are similar to those given by the respondents in Dresden (we did not ask this question in the Berlin survey). This evidence, which shows that voluntary reports from fellow citizens often provided the Nazi policing authorities with the information they used to begin criminal cases against alleged wrongdoers, jibes with evidence found in earlier studies based on Gestapo and Nazi criminal court records.[6]

Although some scholars have argued that these civilian denunciations reflect the high degree of consensus that existed within the Nazi regime, more importantly they underscore the difficulties the Gestapo had in gaining direct access to people's private lives as well as the Gestapo's general lack of interest in pursuing such access. The Gestapo knew that most cases begun by civilian denunciations involved only trivial offenses and generally it did not want to waste its own limited resources on policing such minor matters.[7]

Based on the evidence provided by the survey respondents, the number of people who had cases started against them through information provided by Gestapo spies was notably high. But the extent to which these putative spies were in fact spies remains unclear, for many people may have assumed they were being spied on by Gestapo agents and surrogates when in fact the information that was used to initiate cases against them came from civilian denunciations or party officials. In fact, the Gestapo had a limited number of spies, and they usually concentrated on organized political groups and targeted enemies like Jews. We suspect that in many cases the real informer remained unknown to the respondent, so that he or she could only imagine that information from a spy triggered the arrest.

Above all, spies were named as the source of the Gestapo and police information in cases involving unlawful activity associated with church matters. In many cases, the alleged spies may have been Gestapo officers who attended church services dressed in civilian clothing and took notes on the sermon. In small communities, where everyone knew everyone else, the village policeman occasionally fulfilled this function:

> The village policeman. He stood in the back of the church and listened. We were already wondering why the man was standing there. He wanted to hear what the pastor said. He wasn't there to worship. He only went to listen in. But our pastor was a very intelligent man, and he already knew you shouldn't say too much.[8]

Aside from cases involving the church, spies mostly were mentioned in cases directed against the members of former political parties. This is not surprising. These organizations were suspect to the Nazis from the start, and people who had been active in them were also suspect.

What did the respondents believe happened to the people they knew who had cases started against them by the Gestapo or the police? Not all respondents knew the final outcome. Perhaps some of them only recalled the most spectacular cases, especially those involving severe punishment. Nonetheless, the respondents' subjective perceptions of what happened in the cases they were aware of are at least as important as the objective situation.

From the answers they gave to a question we asked about what happened to the people they had known who had cases started against them by the Gestapo or the police, the respondents said that 36 percent of the people mentioned in the Cologne and Krefeld surveys were soon released after their initial arrest or interrogation. While this was what the respondents believed to have been the most frequent outcome in these cases, the rest of the cases often resulted in more dire outcomes for the accused persons. Thus, according to the respondents, 10 percent of the cases resulted in the accused persons being sent to jail or prison, 21 percent in their being placed in "protective custody" or sent to a concentration camp, and 4 percent in their being executed. The remaining respondents mentioned other outcomes, such as a combination of various measures, sometimes even including court acquittals followed by confinement in a concentration camp.[9]

In Dresden, the number of those who were released without being sentenced or sent to a concentration camp was similar, around 31 percent. The percentage of people in Dresden who were placed in protective custody or were sent to a concentration camp, on the other hand, was 37 percent and thus somewhat higher than among respondents from the Rhineland. The share of those executed in Dresden was around 7 percent. The reason for stronger repressive action presumably lies in the fact that the leftist political opposition was more strongly organized in Dresden, and therefore subjected to more persecution.

Some of the released prisoners who were mentioned by the respondents were people whose offenses could not be proven or whose complicity in delinquent acts was doubted by the Gestapo. In many cases, this was because accusations were based on suspicions and false assumptions and often malicious intent by the accusers. The Gestapo was well aware of this problem. Although denunciations against political dissidents were welcomed, false accusations meant extra work and detracted from other activities. Having limited personnel, the Gestapo sought to discourage false accusations.

According to the respondents, the Gestapo occasionally took the popularity of the person in question into consideration. Possibly the Gestapo feared that measures taken against a popular individual could result in public unrest and could potentially threaten the legitimacy of the political system. Thus, for example, one of the Cologne survey respondents reported that a popular priest who was critical of the Nazis was repeatedly arrested and repeatedly released.

The gravity of the offense was also decisive. While the Gestapo often treated less serious offenses with leniency, especially in cases involving what it considered to be thoughtless outbursts of opinion made by otherwise loyal citizens, it would proceed ruthlessly in punishing those it considered truly dangerous. Thus, for example, when priests or clergymen were too outspoken in their opposition to the Nazi regime and openly condemned measures taken against Jews or against the Church—as was the case of Minister Lichtenberg in Berlin—their popularity made little difference.[10]

During the Third Reich, the politically controlled press strove to make the Gestapo appear legitimate and all powerful at the same time. The media portrayed an institution that dealt harshly but fairly with criminals, traitors, and agitators, and this helped deter the regime's enemies while silencing the rest of the population. Regardless of the press image, many people considered the Gestapo brutal and violent. Ample evidence for this is found in our survey data. When we posed a question in our Cologne and Krefeld surveys about popular awareness of Gestapo torture practices during interrogations, 28 percent of respondents answered that they had been aware of it, and another 14 percent answered that they had suspected it. Thus the proportion of those who associated the Gestapo with violence and torture amounted to 42 percent.

People who came in direct contact with the Gestapo were the most likely to have heard about the use of torture. Only a small fraction of respondents were subject to violence themselves, but others who had been interrogated by the Gestapo or had visited imprisoned friends and relatives found out about these torture practices secondhand. Thus, according to our survey, the percentage of respondents with knowledge of torture rises with the number of people they knew personally who had come into conflict with the Gestapo.

In addition to this, the existence of concentration camps on German territory was no secret. Mention of concentration camps often appeared in newspapers, especially in the early years of the Third Reich.[11] Naturally, this was done in a way that sought to legitimize the new regime. Hence concentration camps were presented as correctional facilities, where criminals, "work-shy" individuals, and political opponents were given their hard but just punishment; finally they would learn to do real work. The camps were portrayed in the popular media as model rehabilitation facilities.

Many people therefore had a false impression of what was happening in the concentration camps. The fact that not only political enemies but also "work-shy" persons and criminals were among the concentration camp detainees—and even made up the majority for some time in the 1930s—no doubt led some to equate work camps (which also existed) with concentration camps.[12] Thus several respondents did not perceive the concentration camps to be necessarily condemnable. "Detainees were brought there, but that was entirely natural," one interviewee stated. Another interviewee explained that the people in the camps simply "were criminals or something."[13] One interviewee added, "One assumed that they were guilty of theft, robbery, or murder, or something."[14]

Large numbers of people who were incarcerated in the 1930s were eventually released. In the summer of 1933, more than 26,000 people were being held in large and small concentration camps and prison-like facilities. These were mostly political opponents. Two years later, in the summer of 1935, fewer than 4,000 inmates were still locked up in the camps, which shows the extent to which the Nazis had established themselves and no longer feared organized resistance.[15] In the following years, the figures started to go up again, and the number of those affected finally reached—over the entire period of the Third Reich—a considerable size. Although great numbers of people who were sent to concentration camps were either Jews or specifically targeted enemies like communist and socialist opponents of the regime, more than half a million Germans, according to one estimate, spent time in a concentration camp between 1933 and 1945.[16]

Released inmates were told not to disclose any information about what took place in the concentration camps. They had to pledge in writing not to report anything about what they had seen and experienced. Otherwise, they faced severe penalties, including being sent back to concentration camp. Some inmates, though, did not bear external marks of the pain they had suffered, and what they related about their experiences in the camp was rather reserved:

> The father-in-law of my oldest sister, he came into a concentration camp in '36 because of communist activities. He had handed out fliers. Then they interned him. They talked of work camps for reeducation. He came back out after two years, that's when they released him. Then he worked in the moor. He never said anything about torture. My father asked, "How was the food there?" "Good," he said, "normal. We had to work there, all day. 'Work sets you free!' was written up there." And when he was released, he said nothing more [about his experiences in the concentration camps].[17]

Those who bore marks of violence when they left the concentration camps warned those who saw them not to say anything to others, lest it cause problems for released inmates. "We knew that there were concentration camps," reported one of the Berlin respondents. "One day, they came and picked up our employee. He came back without fingernails or toenails. We were strictly forbidden to say a word about it."[18]

Fear as an Instrument of Control

In light of the large number of individuals arrested by the Gestapo and temporarily detained in concentration camps and the cruelty of the Gestapo's conduct—especially where the extortion of confessions was concerned—many authors have assumed that the fear of falling into the hands of the Gestapo constantly plagued everyone in the Third Reich and concluded that fear and terror were the decisive factors in shaping the German population's everyday behavior.[19]

Our survey evidence, however, does not support this assumption and conclusion. When we asked the people in our survey if they had lived in fear of being arrested by the Gestapo during the Third Reich, only a minority of the respondents responded affirmatively. As shown in Table 12.2, the percentage of respondents in each of the four cities we surveyed who said that they had "always" feared being arrested by the Gestapo was remarkably consistent and varied from a low of 3 percent in Berlin to a high of 7 percent in Krefeld. In addition to this, the percentage of people who said that they had "occasionally" been afraid of being arrested was also consistently low among the four cities, ranging from 13 percent in Berlin to 20 percent in Dresden. This strongly suggests, of course, that the majority of German citizens did not fear arrest. In

Table 12.2   Fear of Arrest by Gestapo

	Own Fear of Arrest				Fear of a Family Member's Arrest			
	Cologne (%)	Krefeld (%)	Dresden (%)	Berlin (%)	Cologne (%)	Krefeld (%)	Dresden (%)	Berlin (%)
Constant	5	7	5	3	9	9	9	7
Occasional	19	17	20	13	29	26	22	22
None	77	76	76	83	62	65	69	71
N of cases	**851**	**372**	**613**	**812**	**839**	**366**	**604**	**805**

fact, between 76 and 83 percent of the survey respondents in the four cities answered explicitly that they never feared being arrested by the Gestapo for any reason.

After we posed the question about the respondents' own personal fear of arrest, we then asked them if they had feared the arrest of a family member. As Table 12.2 demonstrates, the answers we received demonstrate that not only did most Germans not fear arrest for themselves, most did not fear that members of their families might be arrested either. Between 62 percent and 71 percent of the respondents in the four cities reported that they had never feared that anyone in their own family circle (*Familienkreis*) would ever be arrested.

Not only do our data indicate a consistent lack of fear among people who lived in different German communities, we also found that respondents of different gender, age, educational, and religious backgrounds all reported consistently that they had not feared Gestapo arrest. Minor caveats here are that Catholic respondents in each of the four cities feared arrest somewhat more than Protestant respondents, and female and older respondents tended to have slightly more fear than male and younger respondents in the majority of the cities. The respondents' educational level made no consistent difference whatsoever in the level of fear.

Because our evidence shows that only a small fraction of the respondents were ever arrested or even interrogated by the Gestapo or the police during the years of the Third Reich and that a majority did not even know anyone personally to whom this happened, it does not seem at all surprising that people who answered in our surveys that they had been in sympathy with the Nazi regime answered negatively to the question we asked about fear of arrest. But it is somewhat surprising that a majority of those who say that they had opposed the regime would also say that they had not feared being arrested by the Gestapo. While the level of fear among those who had opposed the regime was slightly higher than among those who had supported it, the difference between

Table 12.3   Occasional or Constant Fear of Arrest (By Gender, Year of Birth, Education, and Religion)

	Cologne (%)	Krefeld (%)	Dresden (%)	Berlin (%)
Gender				
Male	22	17	24	16
Female	24	27	24	18
Year of Birth				
Before 1911	32	28	22	26
1911–1916	22	33	31	23
1917–1922	23	24	26	17
1923–1928	22	18	21	14
Education				
Low	26	24	26	18
Medium	17	24	24	14
High	18	23	23	12
University	28	26	17	19
Religion				
Catholic	26	29	27	22
Protestant	18	15	22	15

these two groups was rather modest. In Cologne, 90 percent of the respondents who were pronounced supporters of the Nazi system claimed not to have feared arrest; among those classified as consistent opponents, the proportion was lower, but it still only amounted to 60 percent.

It is possible that some respondents were deceiving themselves concerning their feelings, turning their earlier experiences into positive ones in the process of looking back and overestimating the "normality" of their everyday lives back then, while underestimating their level of fear. Indeed, not everybody who once violated the law and feared punishment will remember the particular situation and the feelings it produced. But those who were repeatedly exposed to such a situation will be more likely to remember the fear associated with such moments. From this perspective, generally dominant experiences should be reflected in our respondents' answers.

Table 12.4 Involvement in Illegal Activities Among German Respondents by City

	Cologne (%)	Krefeld (%)	Dresden (%)	Berlin (%)
Member of illegal youth group	6	7	2	4
Listened to illegal radio broad-casts	46	47	40	49
Told anti-Nazi jokes	33	35	24	32
Criticized Hitler	15	15	14	11
Criticized Nazis	21	21	17	16
Spread anti-Nazi fliers	3	3	2	2
Helped people threatened by Nazis	12	14	11	11
Active resistance activity	1	1	1	1
Other	1	1	2	4
None of the above	37	36	43	43
N	**842**	**367**	**615**	**904**

Why was fear of the Gestapo so uncommon among the German population? The most important reason is probably because the majority of citizens supported the regime or at least conformed to the system. When they violated Nazi laws, they did so in a manner that guaranteed the most secrecy and the least risk. Realizing the specific risks involved, they developed coping mechanisms that usually enabled them to avoid punishment. The assumption therefore is that conforming behavior and selective risk and information management does much to account for the lack of fear that respondents remembered.

Concerning conformity, two lines of empirical evidence are of interest. First, many respondents, when asked whether or not they had feared being arrested by the Gestapo, answered "no", since they had done nothing wrong. Second, behavior that was most likely to be met with heavy sanctions and actually was associated with fear was too infrequent among them to raise the overall level of fear among the population.[20] In other words, most people did not behave in ways that they believed would put themselves in real danger.

This does not mean, however, that most Germans refrained completely from activities that were considered illegal in the Third Reich, because in fact a majority of the respondents told us that they had indeed been involved in at least some kind of illegal activity during the Nazi period. People understood the difference between the forms of illegal activity that would place them in true danger of being punished and those that would not. Therefore, when we asked people about forms of illegal behavior that they had been involved in and provided them with a list of possible answers ranging from trivial offenses like offering criticisms of the regime or its leaders in the course of conversations with friends and acquaintances to real acts of political disobedience like belonging to an underground resistance group, we learned that only a tiny percentage of the respondents had ever actively resisted the regime even though most people, as shown in Table 12.4 (57 percent in Dresden and Berlin; 63 percent in Cologne; and 64 percent in Krefeld), had broken Nazi laws in one way or another.

Thus, whereas only 1–3 percent of the respondents in the four cities had ever taken part in serious acts of political opposition such as distributing illegal fliers and leaflets or joining an anti-Nazi resistance organization, much higher percentages of people had committed minor infractions such as participating in illegal youth organizations (2–6 percent), retelling anti-Nazi jokes (24–35 percent), criticizing Hitler (11–15 percent) and other Nazi leaders and policies (16–21 percent), or offering help to people who were threatened by the Nazis (11–14 percent). Far and away the most common form of illegal activity that German citizens involved themselves in, however, was listening to illegal foreign radio stations. Nearly half of all the respondents in the four cities surveyed reported that they had done this at least on occasion even though this was strictly forbidden during the war years and could result in stiff punishment, including death.

One reason why so many people broke this law without any great fear of arrest was that they only listened sporadically. Those who listened to foreign radio stations did not necessarily start doing so the moment the Nazis came to power, or when the BBC began its German-language programming. And those who listened did not necessarily do so on a daily basis. In our Berlin survey, for instance, only 14 percent of those surveyed said that they had listened regularly to foreign broadcasts. A larger percentage, 36 percent, said they had listened only occasionally.[21]

A much more important reason, however, why listening to foreign radio broadcasts did not appear to arouse much fear lies in the individual's sense of control. As opposed to being involved in direct resistance activity, which might easily be found out, radio listening was easier to keep secret and less likely to come to the attention of the authorities. The risk of detection could be minimized by turning down the volume, putting a pillow on the speaker, or huddling under a blanket while listening. As one not atypical Berliner told us, "Later, during the war, we put a pillow over the radio set and listened to the BBC. We did that in secret. There were Nazis living above us and below us. We couldn't let them find out about this. We just had to listen closely and we always hoped that this would soon be over."[22]

Hence the danger of detection was quite low so long as one listened secretly and did not tell anybody about it. In a number of cases, however, people did talk with others about what they had heard. What they divulged and to whom depended on the level of trust they felt. In this way they acted as they generally did in their everyday interactions with both ordinary citizens and Nazi Party officials, such as the ubiquitous Nazi Party block leader, who typically supervised forty to sixty households in their residential areas.[23] Thus most of our respondents believed that they had to be careful in how they acted and what they said in front of certain people within their intimate social circle as well as with people generally.

The respondents' level of openness vis-à-vis another person varied according to their prior knowledge or assessment of that person. If they knew that someone was a Nazi sympathizer, they refrained from making statements on certain subjects and behaved "diplomatically," as one respondent called it. They emphasized their similarities and suppressed differences. With strangers, however, things became more complicated and they would usually display considerable caution. People under these circumstances had to infer loyalty toward the system from appearances and behavior. For example, they would notice if the person in question had said "Heil Hitler" on entering a store or had made critical remarks about the regime.

The caution that most people displayed toward others with whom they spoke is reflected in the statements of one of our interviewees from former East Berlin who compared his experiences in the communist period with those in the Nazi era: "In the course of time, all people became cautious. They simply didn't speak with people anymore. It was similar to when one knew that someone belonged to the Stasi here [the former German Democratic Republic]. Then people were careful too. We all knew each other from work, so you knew that certain individuals [had contacts with the Stasi], same as with the Nazis."[24]

So what is the conclusion? In contrast to what has often been portrayed in the literature, the Gestapo was not an institution that governed the thinking and daily behavior of most citizens. Most Germans did not live under constant fear of being picked up, interrogated, beaten, or sent to a concentration camp by the Gestapo. As is evident in many of the interviews we conducted (see, for example, our interview with Hubert Lutz from Cologne), many people instead experienced a kind of "normality" in their daily lives in the Third Reich, albeit a normality that depended on their acceptance of the Nazi regime and their keeping their heads down and not acting conspicuously. From this perspective, most Germans did not live in fear. But they knew well that rash, politically unacceptable remarks and corresponding behavior could lead to serious punishment and possibly endanger their lives. Many people, therefore, retreated into their own private sphere and often turned a deaf ear to political issues. Unlike Jews, anti-Nazi activists, and other targeted enemies, however, they had the option of retreating in this way.

+13+

MASS MURDER

From Social Exclusion to Deportation

Although Jews did not predominate among those arrested, beaten, or sent to concentration camps in the beginning years of the new regime, their humiliation and exclusion from German society began almost immediately and worsened as time wore on. Not all of the measures the Nazi state took against the Jews were immediately visible to the entire German population, but many of them were carried out in full view of the public and showed clearly the kind of status the Jewish population was going to have during the Third Reich. Furthermore, the propaganda found in the daily newspapers and public speeches by Nazi politicians made it unmistakably clear that the Jews were to be regarded as Germany's true enemies.

Anti-Jewish measures that were widely visible to the public began with a one-day boycott of Jewish-owned stores on April 1, 1933, continued throughout the 1930s, especially with the passing of the Nuremberg Laws, and culminated in the "night of broken glass" (*Kristallnacht*) in November 1938. That nationwide pogrom marked a turning point in Jewish persecution as Jewish shops, facilities, and people were for the first time, aside from the boycotts, the targets of widespread, barbaric violence.

Although *Kristallnacht* was a one-time event, it marked an important threshold, and the pace of anti-Semitic measures accelerated. While regulations restricting Jews' freedom and increasing their social isolation proceeded apace in the following years, perhaps the most important measure to exclude the Jews from German social life came in September 1941. From that time onward, Jews aged six and older had to wear a yellow Star of David placed visibly on the outside of their clothing whenever they went out in public. Those who failed to comply were punished.

Already in the 1930s, non-Jewish Germans were discouraged from associating with Jews and could be punished if they did.[1] Now they could even be sent to a concentration camp, and the penalties for not complying became stiffer. Although these measures increased the social isolation of the Jewish population, many Germans continued their contacts with Jewish friends and colleagues.[2] With the introduction of the "Jewish star," many people were astonished to see how many Jews were still living in Germany. "This quarter— Lindenstrasse–Richard Wagner St.–Engelbert St.," said one Cologne respondent, "was a purely Jewish quarter. The poor devils had to wear the Star of David. One saw for the first time how many there were, [people] whom I as a child would have never seen."[3] Another, who lived in Berlin at the time, said, "When the Jews were forced to wear the yellow star, only then did it occur to us at all how many there were."[4]

The reactions of the German population to the introduction of the Jewish star were varied. Many Germans, as documented in our interviews as well as numerous memoirs written by Jews, were ashamed of the measure and displayed solidarity and empathy with the Jews. The diary of the Dresden professor Victor Klemperer, for example, includes detailed descriptions of how some people he hadn't known previously turned to him offering words of consolation and how others offered their seats in streetcars to him. His experience was far from uncommon, since many Jews who lived in Berlin and elsewhere at the time made similar reports.[5]

Other Germans, however, were less willing to associate with Jews. For example, one of the Krefeld interviewees who said that he had seen people wearing the Jewish star on several occasions explained, "I didn't know them. We knew they were Jews. However, we weren't allowed to speak to them. We weren't allowed to have any ties to them."[6] But if many Germans showed restraint and avoided contact with the star-wearing Jews, they did not always do this because they were anti-Semites. Indeed, in the interviews we conducted, negative reactions to the introduction of the Jewish star were common.[7]

What we heard in these interviews corresponds closely with contemporary reports by foreign newspaper correspondents, autobiographies, and other sources compiled by David Bankier in his book *The Germans and the Final Solution*.[8] They also correspond with the findings of a representative survey of the German population conducted in 1949 by the Allensbach Institute in which the respondents were asked whether they had seen the Jewish star and how they had responded to the requirement to wear it. In a subsequent, in-depth analysis that we conducted of the original Allensbach data, we found that older people disapproved of the star much more than younger people, and that Catholics and women were more opposed to the measure than Protestants and men, as were people from urban than rural areas and midsize towns.[9] It also made a difference if the respondents had previously maintained friendly contacts with Jews. In general, therefore, the pattern we found in this regard closely resembles that of Nazi supporters described in Chapter 11. Those who were least supportive of National Socialism were least positively disposed to the introduction of the Jewish star.

The extent to which non-Jewish Germans sustained their initial disapproval of the star, however, is uncertain. In his diary, for example, Klemperer noted that the initial acts of solidarity with Jews over this measure dwindled as indifference for the measure grew and occasionally included hatred toward Jews, especially on the part of children and young people.[10] Remarks made in our interviews suggest that at least some of those who were at first bothered by this measure ultimately came to terms with the situation in the long run. "For a couple of days, one swallowed hard," as a respondent put it, and then one accepted it. After all, "there wasn't any changing it."[11]

The introduction of the Jewish star was the prelude to the deportation and murder of Germany's Jews. A month after it was introduced, Jewish emigration was prohibited and the deportations to the east began. If the introduction of the star made clear to Germans how many Jews were still in the Reich, this labeling also helped make Germans aware of their disappearance. The stars became "thinner and thinner," said one respondent, meaning that fewer and fewer Jews appeared in the streets. Another stressed the sudden appearance and then disappearance of the stars in the cityscape: "When the Jews at some point in the war were forced to wear their Stars of David, one noticed how many Jews were in Germany and how much [they] . . . were restricted in their way of life, and then how they grew fewer in number."[12]

When the deportations to the east began in October 1941, Jews were usually informed of the date of their transports in advance, by either the local Jewish community or the Gestapo. Sometimes even the transport destinations were announced. In November 1941, for example, Cologne Jews selected for deportation were handed a leaflet by the local Jewish community leadership telling them that another transport was to leave on December 8 heading for Minsk. They were also told how to prepare for their "journey," and what they could bring with them. As part of the deception, people who were elderly, single, and infirm were directed to report to the welfare department of the Jewish community so that they could be placed in a home for the elderly.[13]

In the early deportations, similar information was also provided in other cities. Thus, given the circumstances, it is no wonder that Jews as well as non-Jews who learned about these deportations did not necessarily perceive them to be transports leading to death. The conditions under which Jews headed for the trains, therefore, appeared rather peaceful at first.[14] Those selected for deportation usually walked or took streetcars to the collecting points or the train stations where the transports to the east originated. Sometimes they did so without police or Gestapo escort. Once they had arrived at the train station, they sometimes boarded normal passenger cars. Other times they were loaded onto freight or cattle cars. For smaller transports that left Berlin for the Theresienstadt ghetto, railway cars were attached to normal trains bound for Prague.[15]

The situation changed, however, once Jews gained awareness of the true intent of the transports. Soon the Gestapo started showing up unannounced at people's homes and forcing them to the deportation trains. In Berlin, the city with the largest Jewish population, forcible deportations were the rule from October 1942 onward.[16] Occasionally this led to spectacular scenes with streets being cordoned off, houses combed by the Gestapo, SS, and regular police, and large numbers of Jews being rounded up, loaded onto trucks, and taken to the collection points.

The reactions among our interviewees who witnessed the deportations were mixed. Those who witnessed the early deportations often had been told in advance about them by the deportees or had seen people wearing Jewish stars heading for the collection points. One Krefeld interviewee, for example, realized one morning on the way to work that a group of women and children, all marked by the Jewish star and carrying baggage, was heading to the train station.[17] Others, like an interviewee from Berlin, saw Jews who were guarded by people in uniform "being taken out of buildings" and then being "loaded on a truck, and driven off."[18]

A native of Cologne who reported something similar had only vague ideas at the time of what was happening to Jews:

> A big bus drove up. It was right in the inner city, on the Ring [road]. The [Jews] came out with bag and baggage, with suitcases, and other belongings and [got] in the bus. I didn't hear them scream or cry. Their faces were sad . . . I just looked and was very astonished. I was somehow depressed. The entire building was emptied. I believe that the SA or something like that was standing there. Then they were driven off, driven away. And we didn't even know where they were going. We thought to a [concentration] camp.[19]

In other cases, the use of force was highly visible, especially when entire streets were blocked and searched. A Berlin respondent, Ruth Hildebrand, whose interview is also in this book, reports:

I also saw the Jews being picked up. Nobody was allowed to go out into the streets as they were all cordoned off from one corner to the next, and there were trucks waiting there [to take the Jews away]. Nobody dared to say anything. We were all standing out on the balcony; that is, all of us women, since our men were not there.[20]

In every city, the starting point on the road to death was the train station. Whenever it was possible, officials tried to shield the transports from public view by organizing them in the early morning hours or later in the evening, when fewer people were in the streets. But at train stations with large numbers of people coming and going, both in the morning as well as in the evening, it often was impossible to keep them hidden from the public. As a result, many people witnessed what took place. But they did not necessarily know at the time that the transports were to lead to the imminent annihilation of the Jews. To some, they appeared almost "normal." As one person reported, for example, Jews were still carrying suitcases and backpacks:

I experienced that once here at the train station in Krefeld, in '42, in the autumn. It was a coincidence. There was a train [full of] Jews. It was outside the main hall, somewhat in front of the train station. I saw it at a distance of twenty to thirty meters, but one couldn't go over there. The area was cordoned off. I thought to myself, "Aha, they are being forced to leave."[21]

The events did not strike this interviewee as especially dire: "They had baggage, backpacks, and so on. . . [There was] no screaming, nothing. [It was] as if they had to take a trip. But one did have the impression that they had to go." But, for another Krefeld interviewee, the situation appeared far more ominous, especially since the baggage that Jews were carrying was left behind:

My mother saw them transported from the freight station. The baggage that individuals were allowed to carry was loaded separately in a freight car. When the train pulled out, the freight car stayed there. It didn't go with them. [My mother] was shocked. It was awful. If the baggage stayed there, one could imagine [that something bad was going to happen to them]. . . . Whether they would come back or be murdered, one didn't know at the time.[22]

Fleeing Underground and Finding Help

As the deportations continued, suspicions about the fate of the deported Jews mounted. Since few people heard anything from them after they had been taken away and ever more information about the murder of Jews in the east filtered back into Germany, more and more Jews began evading the transports and fled underground. Although Jews went underground throughout Germany, the greatest number of Jews who went "illegal" was in Berlin, where it is estimated that five thousand Jews lived in hiding during the war. Most of them went underground at the time of the "factory action" in early 1943, when all Jews remaining in Germany and working in industry were to be arrested in one sweep. Some four thousand of the eleven thousand potential victims in Berlin managed to elude the sweep.[23] Although it had been prepared in great secrecy, information about it leaked out, and many Jews went underground after being warned by people working in offices involved in the action or by being otherwise informed. Others fled once they noticed the operation unfolding.

Until recently, there was little systematic research about the experiences of the Jews who fled into hiding or the help they received in the process, which was often crucial for their survival.[24] For example, the Jews who went into hiding needed to find accommodations. And, because they always had to worry about being discovered, they often had to move repeatedly from one hideout to another. Also they had to find food, and, at a time when foodstuffs were rationed, this was only possible with ration cards. Thus Jews who had gone underground often had to rely on non-Jews who would offer them their own precious cards or would purchase foodstuffs on their behalf.

One of the people whose interview we have included in this volume, Stefan Reuter, met a Jewish woman who later became his wife after she went underground in February 1942. She had done this after receiving a message from the police ordering her to appear with her suitcase at a certain police station at a given time. Like Reuter, she was a communist and was involved in political activities against the regime. Most, but not all, of the help she received over the ensuing three years of the war, which enabled her to survive, came from communists. Yet one of the persons who put her up for a while turned out to be an opera singer who was also a member of the Nazi Party.

The number of assistants who were needed to enable a Jew to survive underground is hard to say. Some sources suggest a rather high figure. Some Jews who survived in hiding have spoken of between fifteen and twenty helpers, but that is not necessarily the upper limit. Herbert A. Strauss, later the founder of Berlin's Center for Research into Anti-Semitism, once tried to put together a detailed list of all the people, Jewish and non-Jewish, who helped him survive in hiding. For a period of seven months, he came up with over fifty people. For all of Germany, some estimates put the number of helpers in the tens of thousands.[25]

The circle of helpers usually overlapped, as a number of small groups of people would time and again provide shelter for Jews in hiding. Communists, who could rely on their connections from their earlier political work, and people from church communities usually occupied key positions in the networks supporting

Jews. Hence, in light of the overlapping circles of helpers, it is almost impossible to estimate the number of helpers based on the number of surviving Jews.

Nevertheless, we know from our Berlin survey that many Germans helped Jews try to escape the Holocaust, for 15 percent of the survey respondents from that city told us that they had met people, either during or after the war, who helped Jews in hiding during the war years. Although most Jews who went underground did not survive in the end, many did. In Berlin alone, about fourteen hundred of the estimated five thousand Jews who went underground were still alive when the war ended. For the entire Reich, an estimated ten to fifteen thousand Jews went underground, of whom between three and five thousand survived.[26]

Most Jews who did not emigrate but continued to live in Germany during the war years, however, did not go into hiding and did not survive. Those who did survive often had the support of non-Jewish helpers among the German population who showed compassion for the Jews, often at considerable personal risk. As mentioned in Chapter 8, over 60 percent of the Jews we surveyed who remained in Germany during the war years and survived the Holocaust had received what they construed to be significant help and support from the non-Jewish population.

The Spread of Information About the Holocaust

From the surveys we conducted, we know that a large number of people in Germany came to know about Nazi crimes against humanity such as the Gestapo's use of torture during interrogations and the killing of handicapped and mentally ill persons in the Nazi euthanasia program.[27] But how many Germans came to know about the most egregious Nazi crime of all, the murder of the European Jews?

Since the murder of the physically disabled and mentally ill took place on German soil, it was more likely that news of the killing would spread among the German public. But this cannot be said about the murder of Jews. The conditions surrounding this crime were different. Most significantly, the murder of Jews took place in occupied territory in the east, where the spread of information could be better controlled. Those first affected by this campaign of mass murder were Polish and Russian Jews. In time, Jews from other occupied countries—Belgium, France, Serbia, Hungary, and so on—were also sent to their death in occupied Poland.

Jews were massacred as early as 1939, both during and after the invasion of Poland. Yet the mass murder operations at this point in the war were not fully systematic. The systematic destruction started in 1941 with the German invasion of the Soviet Union. As the German troops moved eastward, they were followed by four *Einsatzgruppen*—special task forces made up of personnel from the Gestapo, SD, Waffen-SS, and the Order Police—who carried out mass shootings of eastern European Jews. Within months after the launching of the Russian campaign, German Jews were drawn into the process of destruction as well. The first transport of Jews from the Reich to the east took place in October 1941. At almost the same time, daily transports of up to a thousand people began heading to the Litzmannstadt ghetto (Lodz). A second wave of deportations to Riga, Kovno, and Minsk followed a bit later. Starting in mid-July 1942, transports of German Jews to Auschwitz got under way.

In the early phase of the murder of the Jews, when the *Einsatzgruppen* were conducting mass shootings in open fields and forests, the German army sometimes assisted by setting up cordons or providing additional shooters. Under these circumstances, German soldiers, just like local Polish and Soviet citizens, often saw what happened and thus represented a potential source of information about the killing. This changed in the course of 1942, as the murder was increasingly confined to the extermination camps, where the personnel were sworn to secrecy under threat of death.

Although the questions of how many people knew about the murder of Jews and how they came to know it have often been raised, they have never been answered sufficiently. Our survey and oral history evidence offer detailed information about the answers to these questions for the first time.

In our written surveys we sought to determine not only if the German population came to know about the mass murder of Jews during the war years, but also how and when they received their information. In the face-to-face interviews we conducted with a large sample of the written survey respondents, we asked people to elaborate on the answers they had given in the written surveys. Several examples of the detailed descriptions many gave about how and when they learned of the mass murder are provided in this book, especially in Chapters 6–7.

In the first question we asked about the issue of mass murder in our mail surveys in Cologne, Krefeld, and Dresden, we asked the respondents to tell us if they had already become aware about the "mass murder of the Jews before the end of the war." Depending on the nature and believability of the information they received, the respondents would have different levels of awareness about the mass murder, and consequently we did not simply ask them if they had been "aware" of the mass murder. Rather, we asked them if they had either "suspected" that it was taking place, "heard" that it was taking place, "known" that it was taking place, or "not been aware of it" (*nichts davon mitbekommen*) at all.

In the subsequent Berlin survey, which we conducted after the Cologne, Krefeld, and Dresden surveys, we refined this question and asked it in a slightly different fashion. Here we did not ask the respondents simply if they had been aware or not about the "mass murder of the Jews"; rather, we asked them two

Table 13.1   Level of Knowledge of the Mass Murder of Jews (Prior to the End of the War) among German Respondents by City

	Cologne (%)	Krefeld (%)	Dresden (%)	Berlin (%)
Suspected	11	10	13	*
Heard or Knew About	27	27	29	28
Didn't Know About	62	63	58	72
N of cases	**802**	**362**	**602**	**923**

*Not asked in Berlin Survey.

separate questions that differentiated between their having become aware or not about two different specific types of mass murder, namely mass murder in concentration camps and mass shootings. Furthermore, in the Berlin survey we did not ask them if they had "suspected, heard, or known" about these different types of mass murder. Instead, we asked them to specify the exact year and month when they "had heard or become aware of" the mass murder or to answer that they "didn't know anymore" or that they had "first become aware after the end of the war."

Independently of how and where we asked the question about the respondents' awareness of the mass murder, however, we received answers that were remarkably consistent among the four cities. They show that information about the mass murder of Jews was indeed widespread throughout Germany. Thus, as one observes in Table 13.1, between 27 percent and 29 percent in each of the four cities had clearly received information about the mass murder before the end of the war and many others had "suspected" that it had been taking place. Stated another way, an average of about 60 percent of the respondents said that they had "not been aware" of the mass murder before the war's end.

Although these numbers can only be seen as general estimates,[28] our confidence in them is bolstered by the fact that they jibe with both a subsequent nationwide telephone survey that we conducted in 2000 and with the results of five other national surveys conducted in the past by the Allensbach Institute and other German research institutes that generally escaped scholarly notice in the past.[29] These five other surveys indicated that about one-third of the German population knew in some form or another about the mass murder.[30] As will be shown later, the somewhat lower percentages we observed in our surveys result primarily from slight differences in the composition of the age-groups that were surveyed in our own and these other surveys.

Table 13.2   Social Characteristics of German Respondents Who Knew or Heard About the Mass Murder of Jews (Prior to the End of the War) by City

	Cologne (%)	Krefeld (%)	Dresden (%)	Berlin (%)
Gender				
Male	28(312)	29(146)	34(235)	27(496)
Female	27(483)	26(213)	26(355)	30(394)
Year of birth				
1910 or earlier	43(84)	17(35)	32(69)	42(38)
1911-16	36(142)	45(53)	29(106)	26(112)
1917-22	30(222)	25(132)	31(163)	27(276)
1923-28	18(343)	25(137)	28(248)	29(473)
Education*				
Low	27(461)	24(212)	31(163)	28(485)
Medium	31(166)	34(58)	27(162)	24(206)
High	24(95)	22(45)	22(27)	30(94)
University	26(76)	34(44)	30(79)	41(121)
Religion				
Catholic	29(479)	31(217)	31(55)	31(97)
Protestant	23(247)	22(116)	27(480)	28(662)

*Low = Volksschule; Medium = Realschule; High=Gymnasium.

Note: N of cases in parentheses.

If the best estimate is that one-third of the entire population surveyed had at least heard something about the mass murder before the end of the war, what can be said about various subgroups of the survey respondents? One might expect, for example, that men found out something about the Holocaust more often than women because so many of them served in the German army or possibly because they were more interested in political matters. One might also expect older people to have been more aware than younger people, who did not yet have such extended social networks.

As can be seen in Table 13.2, men were only marginally more likely to have heard or known about the mass murder than women. However, age did account for some greater differences in most of the cities we surveyed.

Among those surveyed in Cologne, the knowledge of the mass murder of Jews more or less steadily increased according to the age of the respondent, until it reached a high of 43 percent among those born in or before 1910. In Krefeld, Dresden, and Berlin, older respondents were also usually better informed about the mass murder than younger respondents, but the relationship between the awareness of the mass murder and age was not completely linear, as it was in Cologne. Thus, in Berlin, only the oldest age-group (those born before 1910) was appreciably more aware than the younger age-groups, and the differences between the age-groups in Dresden were hardly noticeable.

Whatever accounts for these variations among the four cities—whether the different samples we used or other possible methodological reasons—it seems sensible for the purpose of further analysis to consider the four cities as a whole so as to reduce the effect of the fluctuations among the four cities we surveyed. To this end, we added up the responses from these four surveys and supplemented them with responses from a pilot study survey we had conducted in Cologne in 1993. The resulting large number of cases has the advantage of making it possible to differentiate between those born in or before 1904 and those born between 1905 and 1910.

The results provided in Table 13.3 show a marked correlation between the age of the respondents and the level of awareness they had about mass murder, with older people being more aware than younger people. Furthermore, this was true among both men and women.

Even though our results show that the differences between men and women were limited, our evidence indicates that men knew somewhat more about the mass murder of Jews than women in each of the age-groups. Since

Table 13.3 Total Percentages of German Respondents Who Knew or Heard About the Mass Murder of Jews (Prior to the End of the War)

Year of birth	Male (%)	Female (%)	Total* (%)
1904 or earlier	36(11)	27(22)	32(33)
1905–1910	39(59)	34(147)	37(206)
1911–1916	34(139)	32(278)	33(417)
1917–1922	31(350)	25(471)	28(821)
1923–1928	26(645)	25(573)	26(1218)
Total	29(1204)	27(1491)	28(2695)

* Average of the percentages for men and women
Basis: cumulated samples of the four city surveys and Cologne pilot survey.
Note: N of cases in parentheses.

considerably more women took part in our surveys than men, this means that the overall percentage of people who knew about the mass murder of Jews during the time of the Third Reich might have been higher than our initial estimates indicate. But when we controlled for possible distortions caused by the gender imbalance, this did not turn out to be the case. Thus, for the respondents as a whole, we still found that a total of 28 percent had either "known" or "heard" about the mass murder before the end of the war (see the figures in the table under the "total" column), basically the same as we found in each of the four cities we surveyed.

As mentioned above, however, earlier nationwide surveys produced a somewhat higher result. The reason for the divergence between those surveys and our surveys must lie first and foremost in the long-term aging process among the age-groups of interest to us. In the earlier surveys there would have been more people who reached their adult years before the Third Reich began than in our surveys. When we took this into account and controlled for the age factor, and when we estimated what the percentages would have been for those who were relatively older during the Third Reich than those in our sample, we found that 33 percent, or every third German, would have either "heard" or "known" something about the Holocaust before the war's end.[31] In absolute figures this means that millions of people before the end of the war either possessed concrete information about the mass murder of Jews or heard rumors about it.

Belief and Suspicion

Receiving information, however, is not the same as believing it. Although information concerning the mass murder of Jews circulated during the Third Reich, rumors about other issues in Germany's past had often turned out to be false. Frequently the Propaganda Ministry dismissed negative reporting from abroad as Allied atrocity propaganda, partly by referring to supposed or real evidence to the contrary. Consequently many people must have been suspicious about information they received concerning what was going on elsewhere. Under these circumstances, the credibility of the content and the source of the information were crucial. The less clear and more improbable the information, and the less specific and more dubious the source, the less frequently people believed the information.

In our national telephone survey, we asked about the credibility of the information that participants had received about the mass murder of Jews. Among those who said they had heard something about it, 60 percent said they had completely believed it and 8 percent said that they had believed it in part. Among the rest, 14 percent said they had not believed it at first, and 18 percent said that they had not believed it at all.[32] In the face-to-face interviews we conducted, where we also asked some of the respondents about the credibility of the information received, a majority said they had believed the reports they received about the mass murder.

The majority of our survey respondents said they first learned about the mass murder after the war ended, and their response is quite believable. There was nothing to hide from us, since our surveys were carried out anonymously and also in a way to establish trust. Furthermore, although determined opponents of the regime heard about the killing of Jews more frequently than others, a majority of the Nazis' opponents nevertheless said they had not heard anything either. Thus, among those who said they heard nothing about the murder of the Jews, there were also some people who were clearly critical of the Nazi system or had personal ties to the victims of Nazism. The idea of a systematic mass murder surpassed their imagination of what was possible in the Third Reich. As one Berlin respondent told us, many people were aware of the concentration camps in their vicinity, like Oranienburg, but were not aware that Jews were being systematically murdered.[33]

A number of the respondents who first learned about the Holocaust only after the war ended, however, suspected that it might be taking place. Nazi rhetoric had referred to the extermination and annihilation of the Jews for a long time. In the early phase of the Nazi regime, during the 1930s, people may have dismissed this as mere rhetorical flourish, and at the time systematic mass murder was not yet in the planning stage. But in the course of the 1940s, the annihilation of the Jews was mentioned more and more. Hitler's "prophecy" of January 1939—when he threatened the annihilation of the Jews in the event of a new world war—was most frequently mentioned in public starting in 1940–1941.[34]

The repeated citation of this particular speech did not necessarily mean that every German took it as a realistic threat. For many Germans, even if they had heard such speeches, the murder of the Jews was beyond their imagination. And some may have suppressed what they heard because it disturbed them. The radical nature of the language that was used in this matter was also typical in other matters, which is why the Jewish professor Victor Klemperer aptly described the Nazis' language as a language of "superlatives."[35]

But those who realized how frequently the Nazis threatened the Jews with annihilation must have suspected that this was a potentially deadly threat. In our questionnaires in Cologne, Krefeld, and Dresden, we therefore included "suspected" as a possible answer to the question about whether people had been aware of the mass murder or not. Between 10 percent and 13 percent of those surveyed said they had suspected that the mass murder of Jews was taking place. This percentage boosts the figure for those who had either suspected or clearly received information about the mass murder of Jews to over 40 percent.

Analysis of those who suspected mass murder reveals no great variations among different age-groups. The only exception is the oldest group of respondents, born in 1904 or earlier. Among these people, the percentage who had suspected mass murder was disproportionately high—21 percent, nearly twice as high as the average for all respondents. But closer examination shows that the age factor was only significant among the Cologne and Krefeld respondents.

An explanation for this could lie in the Catholic environment of Cologne and Krefeld. Many Catholics had reservations about National Socialism and may have felt that the Nazis were capable of anything, even mass murder of Jews. The bishop of Cologne, Cardinal Frings, showed the greatest courage among the Catholic hierarchy in protesting what was happening to Jews. On December 12, 1942, he issued a pastoral letter that was read widely in Catholic churches. In it, he emphasized the basic rights of men and stated that they applied also to people who were "not of our blood and do not speak our language." On August 8, 1943, he persuaded the other members of the episcopate to publish a declaration about the "ten commandments as principal rules for people to live by" (*Lebensgesetz der Völker*). This declaration asserted that all killing is bad, even if committed for the presumed public good, and specifically mentioned people of "foreign races and descent."[36]

Although vague, these statements could be seen as references to Jews. Nevertheless, they were not distinct and concrete enough to allow more than suspicion that something was happening to Jews. Perhaps more important for the development of suspicion was the Catholic Church's position vis-à-vis the Nazi euthanasia program. Catholic clergymen protested repeatedly against the euthanasia program, which might have made Catholics more receptive than Protestants to negative reports about the Nazi regime. Indeed, our survey evidence reveals that there was a remarkably strong connection between knowledge about the euthanasia program and knowledge about the mass murder of Jews. Those who said they had heard something about euthanasia were much more likely to have heard about the mass murder of Jews, and this connection was more pronounced in the Catholic cities of Cologne and Krefeld than in the Protestant city of Dresden. Those who learned about the murder of the physically disabled and the mentally ill possibly belonged to social networks where such information circulated. They were also probably more sensitive to and critical of the Nazi system and tried more frequently to get hold of information that might help undermine the Nazi regime.[37]

The Influence of Attitudes and Social Networks

Those who answered that they had found out about the mass murder of Jews were disproportionately respondents who already held strongly negative views of National Socialism. The remaining respondents with varying degrees of affinity for National Socialism differed negligibly from one another in this regard. The disproportionately high degree of knowledge about the murder of Jews among opponents of National Socialism appeared to have two main causes. First, they usually lived in social milieus that were critically predisposed to the Nazis. Second, people with negative attitudes toward National Socialism were more receptive to negative news about the regime and often searched for things that were negative about it. This is to be expected, since what is compatible with people's views and expectations is more easily incorporated into people's belief systems. This also applies to supporters of National Socialism, who were more likely to ignore or block out disturbing information about the regime.

In addition to this, our evidence shows that respondents who either resisted the regime themselves or had contact with others who resisted or had become victims of the regime typically were better informed about the mass murder than other respondents. Thus people who came from households that had once supported the Communist Party had the highest level of awareness of the mass murder in comparison with respondents who came from households with other types of political orientation. Likewise, as we found in our Berlin survey (in which we asked specific questions about this), those who came into contact with concentration camp prisoners during the war were more likely to have received information about the mass murder of Jews than those who had not; people who met people who had hidden Jews (either before or after the war) also had a disproportionately high degree of knowledge about the mass murder.

A final observation about people who gained a higher level of knowledge about the mass murder than others relates to the educational backgrounds of our survey respondents. Whereas some might expect that people who were better educated would have become better informed about the Holocaust, our evidence shows that this was not the case. In fact, as the survey evidence under the rubric "education" at the bottom of Table 13.2 indicates, there was no correlation between the survey respondents' level of education and their awareness of the mass murder of Jews. Thus people who had only a primary school education were just as likely to have found out about the mass murder as those who graduated from secondary schools or even universities. This finding indicates that information about the Holocaust spread widely among people from all socioeconomic backgrounds just as it did among people from all communities across the map of Germany. What appeared to matter most in differentiating those who came to know about the mass murder and those who did not was how an individual was politically disposed to the Nazi regime and the personal experiences one had.

Oral Accounts of Mass Murder

Both our survey and interview evidence demonstrate that people became informed about the mass murder of Jews through a wide variety of ways. Several of our interviewees, like Hans Ruprecht from Cologne, for example, provided detailed descriptions of mass shootings of Jews that they witnessed directly or indirectly. One day, while Ruprecht was deployed in the Crimea as a Wehrmacht officer, he received an order to participate in "cleansing measures." "We have to carry out some 'cleansing measures' here," he was told. "You will not be affected by this. . . . However, we do need to isolate the population from these measures."

Due to a shortage of personnel, support was needed from the regular troops. They were to cordon off the site of the killing. Soldiers in Ruprecht's unit who volunteered to take part were deployed. "And then one day, the shooting commenced. The incident lasted about half an hour or an hour until it was over. With that, the whole thing was over and done with."

Although the soldiers who had cordoned off the killing site did not necessarily witness the killing of Jews, they became aware of what was happening. As Ruprecht explained, "Many of those [who took part] didn't see anything at all. They did indeed hear shooting, and possibly also screams or something . . . but the men who went to do the cordoning basically knew what it was all about."

Another interviewee, Albert Emmerich (whose interview, like Ruprecht's, appears in Chapter 7), was stationed as a policeman in Ukraine when he found out about the mass murder of Jews. After being transferred to his region, he fell into conversation with a younger comrade who had been stationed there for some time already and wanted to show the new arrival something: "It was a gravel pit. He took me there. Gravel pits always sit deep in the ground. Then he said, 'Look at that. There are three mass graves. Those are Jews. There are three hundred Jews lying in each grave.'" Then the younger policeman described his participation in the events:

> We had to shoot the people. They were forced to undress, no matter whether they were old or young, or whether they were babies or women with babies in their arms. They all got a shot in the back of the neck. None of us received a submachine gun. They got a shot at the nape of the neck with simple revolvers and were forced to undress beforehand. Then the next three hundred were ready. They had to dig their own mass grave again and then their turn came later. A few days later, they had to stand on the edge of their grave, and then they were shot. . . . They were all lying there in blood and we had to go down there and wade in the blood up to our ankles and give them the mercy shots.

Adam Grolsch, born in 1920 and raised in Krefeld, directly witnessed a massacre in which thousands were murdered. He was stationed in Pinsk at the time as a radio operator in the Wehrmacht. One morning, he was startled by an enormous racket and wondered what was going on:

> I then set out with a friend, and with my own eyes saw how the people there had been slaughtered; in two days, 25,000 men, women, and children, and in the most beastly way. I saw how they had to undress in front of the tank traps and many other things. And the absolute worst thing I saw was how this man took a screaming baby and beat it headfirst against a wall until it was dead.

In some of the massacres, as in this one, most of the people who did the shooting came from a variety of non-German ethnic groups such as Russians, Cossacks, Lithuanians, and Latvians.[38] These were the so-called *Hilfswillige* (voluntary helpers), or Hiwis for short, who acted on orders from the Germans. Deployed at first temporarily and then as needed for all kinds of support jobs, the Hiwis became a standard institutional feature of the German occupation on the eastern front. Over time, their areas of responsibility expanded and many became formally employed in the military, police, and the SS, and many eventually became active in antipartisan activities, which very frequently, but not always, served as a cover for terror and mass killing operations.

Many of the so-called Hiwis did not have to be coerced to take part in the tasks that the Germans ordered them to perform. Their willingness to kill stemmed not just from a readiness to follow orders, but often from an existing hatred of Jews that the German occupiers exploited. The willing participation of non-German ethnic minorities in many of the pogroms and massacres of Jews gave many Germans the sense that it was not they who were responsible for the murders they witnessed, but the bloodthirsty foreigners. One of our interviewees, Walter Sanders of Krefeld, for example, described several massacres he had witnessed, including one in which foreign SS personnel were throwing Jews into an abandoned mine and another in which Jews on forced marches were being shot and beaten to death. Sanders explained that a Wehrmacht officer had made protests against these actions.

While several of the people we interviewed said they had become aware of the mass murder of Jews by directly or indirectly witnessing shooting operations and other kinds of pogroms and massacres, others had become aware of the mass murder by hearing about the killing of Jews in extermination camps. Even when the information they received about this was only vague, it was often enough to raise their suspicions. Thus, as one interviewee related,

Nobody knew in detail what had [happened] to the Jews. With the Jews, that became known to me only in the military, didn't it? There was one fellow with us who had connections to the SS. And once he said, "There are concentration camps with the Jews . . ." But he never said anything specific. He had a wonderful cigarette case. He was always saying, "This is from a Jew, from a Jew." But he never wanted to come straight out with it. He never talked about it. Later when the information about murdering Jews became known, I just remembered that.[39]

Another man found out from his uncle that "horrible things" were happening in the camps in Poland. Although he did not know the details, he could not help but suspect murder. Still, the form in which it was taking place—by starvation or some other means—remained unclear to him:

In 1944, I think, I heard about it for the first time. I was at home with my mother. Her brother, my uncle, came over. He had been drafted to watch concentration camps, in Poland somehow. He was on leave, and I was on leave. . . . They forced him to go there as a guard. And the SS, which was responsible for it, was rarely seen in the camp. The [guards] didn't go inside. He told my mother, "There are horrible things happening there." He didn't say anything to me about the terrible things. He didn't say anything about it again. He probably meant the burning . . .

What did you think? That people were being killed?

Yes.[40]

With other interviewees, additional bits of information they received over time hardened their impression that systematic murder was taking place. One woman, for example, said she had heard about the trains to Auschwitz from her husband. Soldiers had told him that they accompanied trains there and rode back afterward on empty trains. "That they were gassed, that came later. That they met their deaths there somehow, that seeped out slowly. But one didn't hear anything specific."[41]

In another case, the father of an interviewee, a policeman who accompanied trains to Poland, reported something similar:

My father. . . was brought to the police. That was around '43 or '44 or so, and he had to escort such a transport, and they had to get off the train. . . The SS then took it over. And after twelve days, the train came back empty and was then back in Germany.

So he didn't escort it to the end?

> No. . . They got off, and the SS took over and probably took the Jews to
> Auschwitz. And then he also said, "There probably isn't a single one of them still
> alive."[42]

For some time, stories also circulated about Jews being electrocuted. Since
researchers have rejected the idea that this form of killing was ever used, we
expect that gas vans were sometimes mistakenly equated with such methods.[43]
Many such vans were used until the large-scale gassing facilities were developed
at Auschwitz and other camps.

One interviewee, for example, who lived at the time near Lublin—the
administrative center of the region where the extermination camps Belzec and
Sobibor were located—told us that he had heard about the electrocution of
Jews from an aunt:

> In 1941, I went to my aunt's place, where the camp was. It came out that the
> [inmates] were killed by electrocution. . . . That was a [small] experimental
> camp. It was also guarded by the Waffen-SS. The people were then buried, but
> the current had not been effective enough. There was some life still left in them.
> There were young SS men there who couldn't take it and wouldn't join in. A lot
> of SS men ran off. Those who were captured were shot. Then a steel chimney
> was brought in, 110 meters high. And the first cremation facility was made.
> Then I was at my aunt's, and she had the window open and I said, "It smells so
> strange." . . . My aunt said, "People are being burned, Jews and Poles who were
> in prison. They are being burned, but the camp is supposed to be shut." An SS
> man who had slipped away and came through later told them about it. That's
> how I knew.[44]

Later in his interview the same man spoke specifically about events at
Auschwitz-Birkenau that he heard about through his father, who knew a Polish
inmate there by the name of Janek. Poles and Russians had been detained in
Auschwitz before it became a death camp for Jews, and there were still many
Poles there after Jews started arriving.

> They nabbed him and brought him to Birkenau. And he got out of Birkenau
> after half a year. And then he came to my father and told my father
> everything. . . . That's how we knew that Birkenau was the biggest extermi-
> nation camp.

[He] also told you about the crematoriums, everything?

Yes, everything.

Also about the gassings?

Things really got started at the end of '42. And that was what Janek could already report. Janek didn't lie to us.

You and your father, however, believed it back then as well?

My father saw what they were doing with the Jews. They loaded up the Jews near our place. In 1941, it was a hard winter. They picked up all of the Jews from our very small town. They froze to death in the railway cars.

You could see that?

My father was standing watch there. They unloaded them afterward as corpses.

For some Germans, the information they received resembled unsubstantiated rumors that they did not believe at first. But their perceptions changed once they got more concrete information. As one interviewee related, "After all, one can talk a lot." But he did finally recognize the truth when the Jewish woman who would later become his wife was selected for deportation, and he "heard in communist circles that numbers of Jews were being gassed."[45]

Others clung to the belief that the rumors did not reflect the truth until the very end. Some who heard about the extermination camps did not want to believe in systematic mass murder. One woman who lived in Stuttgart and had a Jewish mother wrote in her private memoirs about visiting a Jewish lawyer who acted as a middleman between the Jewish community and the Gestapo. She was trying to free her mother, who had recently been deported to Auschwitz. The lawyer responded bluntly, "You can file a petition, but you will not see your mother again. Auschwitz is an extermination camp." When she received notification of her mother's death a few months later—"died of sepsis and phlegm in Auschwitz"—she considered this plausible. "Later, I found out that it was just one of many death notices issued on that day. What Auschwitz meant and how our mother died is something we found out only after 1945."[46]

Other people we interviewed heard about the gassing of Jews, some in the form of rumors, others in the form of concrete information from reliable sources. Hiltrud Kühnel, for example, whose interview appears in Chapter 6, heard about this from local clergymen who spoke to her and other members of her family in their home in Frankfurt. Walter Sanders from Krefeld also mentioned that it got around that people were being gassed: "It wasn't for nothing that it was said in those years, 'Take care, otherwise you'll go up the chimney.' That was a familiar figure of speech. It circulated everywhere in Germany."

Gassing was not limited to the extermination camps. As mentioned earlier, the concentration camps were preceded by gas vans that claimed the lives of around 700,000 Jews.[47] One Berlin woman of mixed Jewish and non-Jewish background, whose mother had faced the threat of deportation, reported that in 1942–1943 rumors were spreading about the gas vans:

> Gas was already spoken about, but nobody knew exactly [how]. Then people told the Jewish people that it was said [the SS was using] trucks in which the occupants were gassed by the exhaust fumes. And that later turned out to be true.[48]

Adam Grolsch, who had witnessed the Jewish massacre in Pinsk, also witnessed two or three gas vans while he was in Rivne, Ukraine, but their function occurred to him only later: "They were parked in Rivne, and nobody knew what they were. . . . That is to say, they were mobile gas chambers for smaller operations. My attention was drawn to it by the BBC."

Finally, while some people insisted that the mass murder of Jews was something that "everyone knew about," others maintained just as insistently that hardly anyone could have known about the Holocaust during the Third Reich. Although the reality lay between these two opposing contentions, people were able to hold completely different viewpoints. This can happen because societies are not homogeneous but are made up of interlocking social networks that allow information to diffuse in some circles while not in others. Thus what might seem self-evident and be taken for granted in one social network need not be in another.[49] This must have been the case in the Third Reich, where people had to be cautious when speaking about sensitive matters because of the risk of punishment. Under such circumstances, information often remained within the inner circle of people who trusted one another.

Sources of Information: Survey Evidence

The importance of social contacts in spreading information about the Holocaust becomes all the more apparent when one considers the survey evidence. In the surveys, just as in the interviews, the most frequently named sources of information the respondents received about the mass murder of Jews came from close social contacts. The evidence for this is presented in Table 13.4.

In the written surveys, people who answered that they had found out about the mass murder were then asked to specify how they found out, and they were provided with the list of possible sources of information contained in the table. As the table shows, there were many sources, but the most important ones were people the respondents knew personally, such as family members and friends as well as neighbors, work colleagues, and fellow soldiers. Only a small minority, between 3 and 6 percent of the respondents, directly witnessed the events.[50]

Other than information received from personal contacts, the next largest source of information about the Holocaust came from foreign radio broadcasts (between 14 and 29 percent, depending on the city in question). Not surprisingly, the Dresden respondents were the least likely to hear about the mass murder from foreign radio broadcasts, probably because, as seen in Table 12.4, they were the least likely to listen to foreign radio broadcasts. What is surprising is that even more respondents, in all the cities surveyed, had not heard about the mass murder from such broadcasts, given that nearly half listened to foreign radio during the war years. What might explain this?

Certainly it is not because foreign radio stations did not broadcast reports about the Holocaust. On the contrary, foreign radio stations frequently reported on this during the the war. In fact, the British Broadcasting Service (BBC) started broadcasting news about mass shootings of Jews to the German population and in the German language as early as the fall of 1941. By the end of 1942, the BBC's German Service often broadcast lengthy, and sometimes daily, reports on the deportations and the mass murders being carried out in the concentration camps. At the same time, similar reports, which were of special interest to communists, came from Soviet radio, even though they were more difficult to receive than the BBC reports.[51]

Probably the most important reason why fewer people heard about the Holocaust from the BBC and other foreign radio stations than one might expect is that most people listened to foreign broadcasts occasionally and selectively. About half of the German population listened to foreign radio broadcasts at some point, but many only after the fall of Stalingrad. Many people were interested in hearing about the war and the German army's progress, but probably fewer people wanted to hear about the atrocities being committed against Jews. In its own research on the issue, the BBC wondered why many Germans had apparently not received information about the masacres in the east from their reporting and believed that a major reason for this was the German population's infrequent listening habits.[52]

Even if many people had heard foreign radio broadcasts about the murder of Jews, it was by no means guaranteed that the reports were trusted. As one person explained:

> We only found out about that via the BBC. And because we knew the power of propaganda, we also knew what was suspected of the BBC, that it also understood its craft

Table 13.4   Source of Knowledge Among German Respondents Who Knew or Heard About the Mass Murder of Jews (Prior to the End of the War) by City*

	Cologne (%)	Krefeld (%)	Dresden (%)	Berlin (%)
Saw it happen myself	4	5	6	3
Family member	20	20	20	26
Friend, coworker, or neighbor	24	23	23	19
In the army from fellow soldier or superior	19	24	15	17
Foreign radio broadcast	26	29	14	15
Leaflets and fliers dropped by allied planes	} 5	} 9	6	6
Other			4	2
N of cases	296	127	197	161

*Multiple responses possible

and must have made a lot of smears. One believed it only in part. There were horrible things reported there, things one could not believe, for example, the mass shootings in the Ukraine, where German soldiers were involved. When we heard that, we didn't believe it, because the Wehrmacht was always something different from the Nazis. We always believed that the Wehrmacht stood as a contrast to the Nazis.[53]

Whether one believed the reports depended not only on the credibility of the broadcaster but also on one's own experiences with the Nazi regime. The more one knew about the regime's brutality, the more one trusted the foreign reports. For example, one interviewee first found out from other Germans about the brutal conditions experienced by concentration camp prisoners in underground production facilities. Her impressions of the regime's misdeeds were then reinforced by the BBC:

Actually, I didn't believe it 100 percent. I thought that it couldn't be true, that nobody could be that brutal. I didn't completely believe it at first. It was unimaginable for me. But since the same thing came from other sources and also from foreign radio stations as well—sometimes we listened to Radio

Moscow and Radio London, who always made those German broadcasts, above all London—and since they had also confirmed it, and with rather exact information, we then said, "That has to be true." We had always doubted it a bit and said that nobody can really be that cruel. But since we knew how cruelly they had treated my cousin, we then said, "Then it must really be true."[54]

If fewer people than one might expect heard about the mass murder of Jews from foreign broadcasts, these broadcasts were, nonetheless, heard and often believed by many Germans. Beyond this, many Germans who received information about the mass murder from other people no doubt heard it from people who themselves had heard it on the radio. Indeed, other than the sources of information about the Holocaust already mentioned, all other sources were of secondary importance at best.

Flyers and leaflets dropped by Allied airplanes during the war informed only a small minority of Germans. This is no accident. Few Germans ever got hold of such fliers, since they were quickly collected by Nazi supporters and members of the Hitler Youth. In addition, the murder of Jews was never a major topic of Allied military propaganda. The Allied military command was primarily interested in projecting military superiority. Finally, when such fliers and leaflets mentioned the massacres in Poland and Russia, they usually described the victims in universal terms, without specifically naming Jews.

Hence, even though Jewish organizations had pushed early on to make the persecution and murder of the Jews a key issue, the Allied military leadership regarded it as more important to wear down the German military and undermine German morale.[55] As one person said, "They dropped fliers, but there was nothing about the poor Jews in them. There were always only matters pertaining to the war and things connected with the war. One should have said more. . . . [The Allies] probably failed here."[56]

A final issue to consider is when the German population became informed about the mass murder of Jews. Almost half of those who found out something about it did not provide a specific year and even fewer named a specific month. This is understandable, since the longer an event recedes into the past, the harder it becomes to assign a specific date to it. Furthermore, the respondents went through very turbulent times—whether on the front or at home—when it is difficult to separate events from one another and to remember exact dates.

Nevertheless, a total of 532 respondents in the four cities did provide the year in which they had first found out about the mass murder. While this was usually in the last years of the war, a considerable number of respondents had found out earlier than this: 14 percent had found out by the end of 1941, 25 percent by the end of 1942, 47 percent by the end of 1943, and 74 percent by the end of 1944.

These figures apply to all of the survey respondents, many of whom were young teenagers during the war years and were less interested in, and more often shielded from, disturbing information than the adult population. News about the mass murder of Jews came considerably earlier to those born before 1919, who were in their twenties or older when Jews were being put to death. Among the 159 respondents born before 1919 who gave a specific year when they first received information about the mass murder, 20 percent had become informed by the end of 1941, 30 percent by the end of 1942, 55 percent by the end of 1943, and 76 percent by the end of 1944.[57]

Conclusion

Although much of the persecution Jews suffered in Nazi Germany was fueled by propaganda and long-term indoctrination, the reaction of much of the German citizenry was ambivalent. Many Germans reacted negatively to the anti-Jewish propaganda and persecution. With regard to some extreme measures—such as publicly labeling Jews by forcing them to wear the Jewish star—a majority appears to have reacted negatively. Many Germans, however, were quick to accept the new situation and concerned themselves only with their own private lives and tended not to think about what was happening to the Jews. Thus it was only a very small minority—though still in the thousands—who helped Jews hide after the deportations had begun, and, even though many might have felt some pity when viewing Jews wearing the Jewish star, they preferred to keep to themselves.

Despite the regime's efforts to keep the mass murder of Jews a secret from the German population and from the outside world, news of the atrocities reached a large portion of the German public by the end of the war. A substantial minority of about one-third of the population became aware of the mass murder of Jews while it was still taking place, and most believed this information, especially because it came from persons they trusted.

What they got as information, however, was not always clear-cut enough for them to infer that systematic mass murder was taking place. Many people only got bits and pieces of information and were not aware that there was a master plan for extermination. But as much as the atrocities became a recurrent story, great numbers of Germans must have perceived a systematic pattern in it. Beyond this, their perceptions were reinforced by the frequent public utterances of Nazi leaders that the Jews were to be "annihilated" and "exterminated," even though such phraseology had an old history in Germany and had often been used when no mass murder of Jews had yet been envisioned.

It is also evident that many Germans did not want to know about what was being done to the Jews. Either it did not interest them or they wanted to suppress it from their consciousness. All too often, they were too involved in their own lives and worries, and they became blind to the sufferings of the Jews and deceived themselves about their fate.

✛ ✛ ✛ CONCLUSION

What Did They Know?

That Nazism in Germany meant mistrust, suspicion, dread, defamation, and destruction we learned from those who brought us word of it—from its victims and opponents whose world was outside the Nazi community and from journalists and intellectuals, themselves non-Nazi or anti-Nazi, whose sympathies naturally lay with the victims and opponents. There were two truths, and they were not contradictory: the truth that Nazis were happy and the truth that anti-Nazis were unhappy.

—Milton Mayer, *They Thought They Were Free* (Chicago, 1955)

"We had a wonderful and good life. . . . For us it was a normal life," concludes Winfried Schiller about his youth in the Upper Silesian city of Beuthen during the Third Reich. Another of the people we interviewed for this book, Hubert Lutz, had similar views about his upbringing in Cologne: "It was the most exciting time in our lives . . . it was a normal way of life for me." How could anyone say such things? Why was National Socialism so popular among the German people? After all, it had caused the deaths of millions and become the arch example of an evil dictatorship in modern times. Had most Germans who lived in the Third Reich somehow been filled with anti-Semitic hatred? Had

387

they been aware of the enormous crimes their country had committed while they were being committed? Didn't most Germans citizens fear that they too might ultimately fall victim to Nazi terror like their Jewish neighbors? Indeed, how might one begin to compare the experiences and perceptions of Germans and Jews who had lived in Nazi Germany?

This book tries to find answers to these questions by allowing a large and representative sample of Germans, both Jewish and non-Jewish, to speak for themselves about their everyday lives, their experiences with the Nazi terror apparatus, and their awareness of mass murder and other Nazi crimes in the Third Reich. What they reveal in the surveys and interviews in this book is not only illuminating and sobering, it challenges how the Nazi dictatorship has been commonly understood in the past. It may even help lead to a new conception of dictatorships in general. A summation of our major findings follows.

We began our surveys and interviews by asking the respondents a series of questions about their everyday lives in the Third Reich. Here we found that there was something of a Dickensian "best of times, worst of times" aspect to the Third Reich. For many non-Jews, the Weimar Republic had been the "worst of times," and the Third Reich represented much better times for them. For Jews, the situation was reversed.

Most of the non-Jewish respondents were certainly not of the opinion that the Third Reich had been imposed upon them against their will. Indeed, many shared the views of Rolf Heberer of Freithal who said that he had been "ecstatic" when Hitler came to power and that "for sixty million Germans, that was what the people really wanted." Strong evidence of this comes from our surveys, in which the majority of respondents stated that they had believed in National Socialism and shared at least some Nazi ideals. Only in the Rhineland city of Cologne, whose predominantly Catholic population had given Hitler the lowest percentage of votes among all major German cities, did the majority of respondents say that they had both not believed in National Socialism and not shared Nazi ideals. But, even among the Cologne respondents, those who had not sympathized with the Nazis only narrowly outnumbered those who had.

If the majority of the respondents had found much in National Socialism to their liking, this does not mean, however, that they endorsed everything about National Socialism. The respondents' views of Hitler himself, for example, were more often negative than positive in each of the cities surveyed. While some might be skeptical about this finding, especially since so many of the people interviewed offered glowing appraisals of Hitler's person and accomplishments, our evidence clearly shows that, in their memory of the Nazi period at least, the respondents had more reservations about the führer himself than about National Socialism in general.

Perhaps the major reason why the majority of the respondents did not answer that they had admired Hitler is because this might appear to be an endorsement of anti-Semitism. Certainly the respondents were cautious in this regard. Thus, when they were asked a question in the survey about things that they had particularly liked about National Socialism, four-fifths of the respondents answered that there had been at least some things they had liked (such as the reduction in unemployment and crime, the construction of the autobahns, and the Nazis' support of traditional family life), but almost nobody (4%) crossed off from the list of possible answers that "the Jews were no longer so powerful."

But how anti-Semitic were the Germans really? To answer this pivotal question about the Third Reich, which has been at the center of a raging debate about the very nature of National Socialism, it is best to turn to the surveys and interviews conducted with Jewish survivors. If non-Jews would have obvious reasons to be hesitant about displaying anti-Semitic sympathies, there would seem to be no reason for Jews to hold back in assessing the anti-Semitism they had experienced in Nazi Germany. After all, one does not need to conduct a survey to find that Nazi Germany represented the worst of times for these people. Still, the answers the Jewish survivors gave to the battery of questions asked of them about the anti-Semitism they experienced in their everyday lives in the Third Reich are both revealing and important.

As one can plainly see from the interviews published in this book, Jewish survivors themselves are divided over this issue. While some survivors like Karl Meyer of Cologne and Joseph Weinberg of Stuttgart say that they had not experienced much anti-Semitism from their German neighbors and townsfolk, the majority of the survivors offered harsher assessments. Nevertheless, most of the survivors also did not agree with people like the former Berliner Henry Singer, who stated that "the anti-Semitism was there before Hitler."

In our survivor survey, we first asked the respondents to rate how their families had been treated by the non-Jewish population in their communities before 1933 and how this treatment changed after Hitler came to power. The answers they gave indicate that most Jews had apparently enjoyed cordial relations with non-Jews before the Nazi years. While only 3 percent of the respondents rated their families' treatment as having been either "unfriendly or mostly unfriendly" before 1933, 69 percent rated it as having been "friendly or mostly friendly" at that time. Soon after 1933, however, the situation changed dramatically and grew ever worse over time. Thus, among Jews who were still living in Germany after the war broke out in 1939, only 6 percent answered that their family continued to have been treated in a friendly manner by the non-Jews in their communities.

Although this evidence does point toward the existence of a strong current of anti-Semitic sentiment in Nazi Germany, this does not necessarily mean that all or even most Germans were ardent anti-Semites. Somewhat indirect but still significant evidence for this comes from another question on the Jewish survey where respondents were asked to rate how their non-Jewish neighbors had been disposed toward National Socialism. Had most of the survivors answered that they believed that the majority of their German neighbors had been strong supporters of National Socialism, this would likely suggest that they had considered them to have been anti-Semitic as well. But the answers to this question were mixed. While only a tiny minority answered that most of their German neighbors had opposed National Socialism, still only about one-third reported that most of their German neighbors had clearly supported it. The majority of the survivors, therefore, either perceived a mixture of support and antipathy among their non-Jewish neighbors for National Socialism, or said that they did not know what their German neighbors' views had been.

In evaluating this evidence, one must keep in mind that most Jewish survivors in the survey had left Germany during the 1930s and had therefore only experienced the beginning years of National Socialism. Those who had remained in the country during the war years usually offered a more negative appraisal of the non-Jewish population than those who had left earlier. Not only were their subjective opinions about the prevalence of anti-Semitic sentiment among their non-Jewish neighbors and townsfolk harsher, they typically had experienced considerably more outward manifestations of anti-Semitic behavior from the non-Jewish civilian population than survivors who had emigrated. Thus, when we asked the survivors about this, we found that the longer the survivors had remained in Germany, the more likely they were to have had their homes and businesses vandalized; to have been spied upon by their German neighbors, co-workers, and fellow classmates; and to have suffered verbal taunts and threats from German civilians.

On balance, therefore, the Jewish survivor evidence points toward the conclusion that anti-Semitism before Hitler came to power had either lain dormant or had not been very widespread among the German population. After Hitler came to power, however, it became ever more virulent over time. Still, this does not mean that most Germans either harbored anti-Semitic views or acted upon them. Although our evidence shows that a large and growing number of them did treat the Jews badly, it also shows that there had been a substantial minority of Germans who had offered aid and support for their Jewish friends and neighbors. In the end, however, the majority of the German population complied with the governmental policies that made Jewish life in Germany ever more precarious and offered no protest against them.

This leads to the subject of terror which the evidence shows constantly plagued the lives of Jews but seldom those of most of the non-Jewish population in the Third Reich. Whereas the survey questions asked of the Jewish and non-Jewish populations were different in regard to their everyday lives, here they were the same, and thus they permit an illuminating comparison between the experiences of Jews and non-Jews. The most important of these were questions about the respondents' involvement in illegal activities, their fear of arrest, and their contacts with the Gestapo. The answers given by the Jewish and non-Jewish populations contrasted sharply.

Few would disagree that terror was one of the defining features of National Socialism, but the Gestapo and the other Nazi control organizations did not apply it uniformly. Rather terror was applied selectively and primarily against the Nazis' targeted enemies, above all against the Jews.

Thus, although both Jews and non-Jews often violated Nazi laws in a number of minor ways, the Nazi authorities would usually look aside in most cases involving non-Jewish offenders while proceeding ruthlessly in nearly all cases involving Jewish offenders.

Nevertheless, the survey evidence demonstrates that nonconformist activity was certainly common among both groups in the Third Reich. Nearly two-thirds of both the Jewish and non-Jewish survey respondents say that they had broken Nazi laws in one way or another. Although few respondents from either group had committed acts of out-and-out resistance such as belonging to an underground resistance organization or spreading anti-Nazi leaflets and flyers, nearly half of all respondents, both Jewish and non-Jewish, had broken the law in a variety of minor ways. Typical of these were listening to illegal foreign radio broadcasts, belonging to illegal youth groups, offering aid and support to people threatened by the Nazis, and speaking critically about Nazi leaders and policies in the company of friends and acquaintances.

Theoretically everyone who lived in Nazi Germany could have landed in deep trouble for these activities, and, given the possible risks involved, one might expect all Germans, Jewish or not, to have been fearful that they might be found out and soon have the Gestapo come knocking at their door. Jews certainly did have great fear that this might happen to them, and it often did. But non-Jews seldom had any fear of arrest whatsoever. Whereas nearly half of the entire population of Jewish survivors who took our survey said that they had lived in constant fear of arrest and nearly three-quarters of the survivors who had remained in Germany after 1941 said that they had lived in constant fear of arrest, only about 5 percent of the non-Jewish respondents said that they had feared arrest on a constant basis and upwards of three-quarters of them reported that they had absolutely no fear of arrest at all.

The strikingly different perceptions on the part of the two groups reflect a clear-headed assessment of the risks they faced. Non-Jews realized well that their non-conformity would not likely get them in trouble, and it almost never did. Although most non-Jews broke the law from time to time in one or another fashion, an average of only 1 percent of the non-Jewish respondents in the four cities surveyed had ever even been arrested or even summoned to Gestapo or police headquarters in their communities in the course of a criminal investigation against them, and most of those who had been arrested or summoned had not been punished for their wrongdoing. In addition to this, upwards of 70 percent of the non Jewish respondents did not even know anyone personally who was not Jewish who had ever been charged with having committed an unlawful act.

While only a handful of the thousands of non-Jews who took our survey had ever been sent to jail, taken into protective custody, or sent to a concentration camp even though the majority had committed illegal acts during the Third Reich, great numbers of the Jewish respondents had suffered such punishments even among those who had emigrated in the 1930s. Among Jews who had not emigrated, only a few had somehow managed to avoid incarceration. Most often these were either Jews in mixed marriages or the children of mixed marriages. A few others had gone into hiding, but the rest were all deported to concentration camps and ghettos.

The final part of this study deals with the question of what was known among the German population about the mass murder of the Jews while it was taking place during the Second World War. Beginning with what the German Jews themselves knew, the evidence shows that information about the Holocaust became very widespread among the Jewish population during the war years. This was true both of Jews who had emigrated to foreign countries before the Holocaust began and of Jews who had remained behind in Germany during the war years. The information Jews received came from many sources and usually reached them quite early on, not long after the mass murder had been set in motion. Many of the Jewish survey respondents, however, first became aware of the Holocaust when they themselves became caught up in it and had not known about it before they were deported to the concentration camps and ghettos in eastern Europe. This was especially true of those who were sent off on the earliest transports between the fall of 1941 and the summer of 1942.

Nevertheless, after these first transports had left for the east, many Jews still resided in Germany and they usually got word of the Holocaust before it was their turn to be deported. Not all of these people had wanted to know about it. Many did not want to believe what they were hearing. As Hannelore Mahler of Krefeld, who was deported on one of the last transports to leave Germany in the fall of 1944, explained, "We didn't want to believe it, because we could have been next." But news of the mass murder eventually became so widespread among Germany's Jewish population that it was almost impossible for them not to find out about it and not to believe it as well.

The survey evidence shows that by late 1942 or early 1943, most Jews who were still in Germany did become aware that mass murder was being committed. The interview evidence also supports this point. For example, consider the testimony provided by Helmut Grunewald of Cologne. Although he ended up being deported to Auschwitz in March 1943, Grunewald had first been arrested in December 1942 along with his father and taken to Cologne's Gestapo headquarters for questioning. While they were being interrogated by three Gestapo officers, Grunewald's father suddenly blurted out that he did not know why they wanted to interrogate him, because, as he exclaimed, "I know that I'll be sent to Auschwitz and be gassed anyway."

The survey and interview evidence also shows that information about the Holocaust became widespread toward the middle of the war years among the non-Jewish population in Germany. But exactly how widespread was it? On this point, the co-authors of this book have somewhat different assessments of the evidence. Karl-Heinz Reuband, a German sociologist who wrote the original draft of the chapters dealing with the German surveys conducted in Cologne, Krefeld, Dresden, and Berlin, argues that approximately one-third of the German population eventually became aware of the mass murder during the war years. Eric Johnson, an American historian who wrote the original draft of the chapters dealing with the Jewish surveys, thinks this estimate is too low.

In Johnson's view, a better estimate would be about half. He has several reasons for this. First is the age factor. Whereas Reuband bases his estimate on all of the people who responded to the survey, Johnson believes it should be based only on those respondents who had reached adulthood before the Second World War and the Holocaust began.

When people ask what the German population knew about the Holocaust, Johnson believes, they are asking about what the adult German population knew. But Reuband bases his estimate on a rather young sample of the German population—nearly two-thirds of it consisting of people who were still teenagers when the war started in the fall of 1939, and nearly one-third who had not reached adulthood when the war ended in May 1945. Since teenagers were considerably less informed about the Holocaust than the adult population was, Reuband's estimate is therefore lower than it would be had he only considered the adult population. Hence, if the estimate only included survey respondents who had reached the age of at least twenty-one when the war broke out in 1939, it would rise by several percentage points.

In Cologne and Krefeld, for example, 37 percent of respondents born in 1918 or earlier answered that they had either known or heard about the mass murder of Jews before the war was over, 13 percent had suspected it, and 50 percent say they had not received any information about it. In contrast to this, among the younger survey respondents in Cologne and Krefeld born between 1919 and 1928, only 22 percent had known or heard about the mass murder, 10 percent had suspected it, and the remaining 68 percent had not been aware of it prior to the end of the war. In the other cities surveyed, Dresden and Berlin, the older survey respondents were also considerably more aware of the mass murder at the time than the younger ones.

A second factor to consider has to do with how "awareness" of the Holocaust is defined. In our survey we did not simply ask people if they had become "aware" of the mass murder of the Jews before the end of the war. Rather, we asked them to tell us if they had "known precise details" about it (*näheren gewußt*), had "heard" about it (*gehört*), "suspected" it (*geahnt*), or not received any information about it at all (*nichts davon mitbekommen*). Reuband bases his estimate of one-third only on those who answered that they had either "known precise details" about it or had "heard" about it. Johnson believes that this excludes many people who had in fact received information about the mass murder and should be included in our final estimate.

Approximately 11 percent of the people who answered the question in the survey about their awareness of the mass murder said they had "suspected" it was taking place. Johnson argues that many of these people received the same types of information that others received who answered they had "heard" or "known" about the mass murder. Thus people who heard things from soldiers on leave from the eastern front, BBC broadcasts, or other sources could just as likely say they had "suspected," "heard," or possibly even "known" about it.

When we asked the respondents in subsequent questions about how and when they had received information about the mass murder, large numbers of those who answered that they had "suspected" it supplied the source of their information and the year in which they received it. This means they were not just surmising or assuming that the Holocaust was taking place, they had actual information to go on. Whereas it is likely that people who answered they had "suspected" it had often received less concrete information than those who answered they had "heard" or "known" about it, still they did answer that they had some awareness of it when they could have answered that they had none. Thus, in Johnson's view, the estimate of who was aware of the mass murder should include many people who answered they had "suspected" it. As already indicated, when those who say they "suspected" are added to those who say they "knew" or "heard," the percentage of people who were aware of the mass murder at some level rises to exactly 50 percent among the Cologne and Krefeld respondents born before 1919. In the other cities surveyed, the percentage was only slightly lower than this.[1]

A third factor Johnson thinks should be considered is the response rate to the survey. About half the people we mailed our survey questionnaire to did not fill it out and send it back to us. Beyond this, the specific question about awareness of mass murder was the question that the largest percentage of respondents did not answer in the entire survey. Thus, when people were asked about their age and gender, fewer than 3 percent did not provide answers to the questions. But when asked about their awareness of mass murder, over 13 percent did not answer the question. One cannot, of course, know what people who did not respond would have answered. Nevertheless, given the sensitivity of this issue, one might suspect that many of those who did not answer questions about the mass murder of Jews were people who knew things they did not want to divulge.

In Reuband's opinion, the questions that Johnson has raised concern factors that might in fact have an impact on survey results and affect the findings. However, these factors do not necessarily exert an influence and account for the described pattern.

The response rate in the German survey (between 45 and 50 percent) can be considered normal for surveys in German metropolitan cities, even if the general population rather than older age groups are taken for comparison.[2] Whether or not the topic of Nazi Germany was specifically mentioned in the cover letter to the mail respondents (heightening potential sensitivity or not) did not lower the response rate, as an experiment in our Berlin survey documented.[3] Furthermore, no tendency emerged to indicate that sensitive matters—such as having once favored National Socialism or having known about the mass murder before the end of the war—were affected by non-response. The response pattern to successive mailings that is usually taken as a yardstick for such an evaluation did not prove this.[4]

The questions on sensitive matters such as knowing about mass murder did not have atypically high rates of missing answers. Questions about the past and the dating of events generally lead to higher rates of "don't knows" than questions that refer to the present and present living conditions (everybody, for instance, knows his age). Other retrospective questions in our survey—ranging from questions on fear of the Gestapo to family influence in youth—had similar rates of non-response between 10 and 12 percent, regardless of whether the question referred to potentially sensitive political topics or not.[5]

We asked whether respondents "suspected" ("geahnt"), "heard" ("gehört") or "knew"("gewußt") about the "mass murder of the Jews." The response category "heard" and "knew" did not specify the level of information obtained, nor did we ask precise details. Some respondents chose the category "suspected" but, as further questions showed, they had apparently received some information on mass murder before the end of the war. These respondents constituted a minority, however.[6] Some misunderstanding also occurred among the group that had first appeared to be "knowledgeable" and in subsequent questions replied that they had learned about it *after* the war. The tendencies of these two groups, which go in different directions, ultimately cancelled each other out and do not alter the basic response pattern.[7]

Twenty-eight percent of our German respondents indicated that they received some information about mass murder before the end of the war. This level does not seem to have basically differed from the rate of the Jewish population living in Germany in those days *outside* concentration camps and finally being deported: Among them the rate of people who knew before deportation is about 31 percent (see p. 314).[8] To account for the fact that the respondents were relatively young in the Third Reich, which makes a difference in the overall percentage, we tried to control in our German study by grouping the data according to age and—for an overall summary—by weighting the data according to the demographics of the late 1930s.

Reuband doubts that one could extrapolate age relationships and argue that very old Germans, who are not part of our sample (because they have since died), would have had even higher rates of knowledge than our older respondents. What is more important is the extent to which different age groups are involved in social networks of news diffusion. In this respect it is of relevance that likely sources of information—German soldiers in the conquered East—were primarily in their late twenties, mostly born between 1911 and 1920.[9] This birth group is part of our sample. In accordance with the thesis of non-linear age relationships, our data, as listed in Table 13.3, in fact show that among the oldest respondents, born in 1904 and earlier, the percentage is lower than those in a somewhat younger age group.

As our extensive oral history interviews document repeatedly, when people learned about mass murder, they learned about it via a single event, such as massacres they either heard of from others or even witnessed. In Reuband's opinion, given these single instances, they did not necessarily realize (or believe) the systematic nature of the killings. Furthermore, among those who learned about the mass murder of Jews the information took time to spread. If we take those respondents as the basis of those who were able to recall a date, then by the end of 1943 (see p. 385) about half had done so. By the end of 1944, a few months before the war's end, the rate had increased to 75 percent. Applying this percentage to the estimated rate of 33 percent with some knowledge yields a percentage of 25 percent for the entire population shortly before the end of the war.

So what then is the overall rate of the German population being somewhat aware of the mass murder or at least suspicions of it *at the end* of the war? According to Reuband, we have to separate awareness from suspicion. Suspicion is not identical to information about murder; it might simply mean that people—based on Nazi rhetoric—thought it possible that such events could have occurred. In Reuband's view, the level of awareness for the whole population in Nazi Germany—with varying degrees of knowledge and clarity— was about one-third. Even if we only singled out the oldest in our sample with the highest rate, those born between 1905 and 1910—i.e., between 29 and 34 years old at the beginning of the war—the rate would be no higher than 37 percent.

In the Cologne/Krefeld and the Dresden sample, the percentage rate for "suspicion" among all the respondents ranged between 11 and 13 percent (among the oldest respondents, born 1910 and earlier, between 13 and 15 percent). Adding the percentages to the rate of respondents who heard or knew about mass murder (basis 33 percent), we get an overall percentage of 44 to 48% of people who believed or suspected that something like murder—on whatever scale and however systematic—took place.

Whatever the case, there is reason to believe that information or at least suspicion of murder of Jews, whether unsystematic or not, be it by mass shootings or otherwise, was finally quite widespread in German society. From this point of view, Reuband's estimate of awareness within the population is somewhat different from that of Johnson.

In sum, by a conservative estimate, about one-third of the German population had become relatively well informed about the mass murder of the Jews during the Second World War; by a less conservative estimate, as many as half or even more adult Germans had some level of awareness of the Holocaust. Even if some people were more fully informed than others and many had a hard time at first believing the information they received, regardless of the estimate one uses, this means that the mass murder of the European Jews was no secret to millions of German citizens while it was still being carried out. Furthermore, our evidence shows that word of the Holocaust had spread widely among people in cities and towns all across Germany and among people from all educational and socioeconomic backgrounds. Lastly, our evidence shows that the information about the extermination of the Jews reached the German population through a wide variety of sources. Many soldiers and others stationed on the eastern front had observed the actual killing of Jews firsthand and related what they had witnessed to others when they returned home on leave or vacation during the war. Many other Germans heard about it by listening to foreign radio stations like the BBC, which, by late 1942, made the mass murder of the Jews a regular feature of their German-language broadcasting. Those who heard about it from first hand sources often passed along what they heard to family members, friends, and others in private conversations.

Hence, our evidence makes a powerful case that people who kept their eyes and ears open usually had little difficulty in finding out about Nazi crimes against humanity during the Third Reich. Great numbers of both Jewish and non-Jewish Germans knew about the mass murder of the Jews, and they also knew about the killing of the mentally ill and the handicapped and Gestapo torture practices. Most people, furthermore, were aware of the serious risks involved in spreading information about such sensitive matters or getting caught undertaking other kinds of illegal activity. Although the risks were typically far greater for Jews, the majority of both Jews and non-Jews broke the law by, for example, spreading information about the Holocaust, listening to illegal radio broadcasts, criticizing Nazi leaders, offering aid and support to potential victims, and, in rare cases, involving themselves in outright resistance activity.

Most Jews lived in perpetual or nearly perpetual fear of arrest during the Third Reich. Those who survived usually did so by emigrating abroad well before the Holocaust began. Nearly all of those who remained in Germany after the war started were eventually murdered.

Most non-Jews, however, experienced a very different Third Reich. Few harbored any fear of arrest even though they too often broke the law in minor ways. Most knew instinctively that the terror apparatus was not intent on punishing them so long as they broadly accepted and went along with National Socialism, which most did. Difficult as it is to fathom, given most people's conception of dictatorship, most Germans appear to have led happy, productive, even normal lives in the Third Reich. This indicates that a dictatorship can enjoy widespread popularity among the majority even while committing unspeakable crimes against minorities and others.

✛ ✛ ✛ Notes

Introduction

1. Among the most important works on this issue are Walter Laqueur, *The Terrible Secret: An Investigation into the Suppression of Information about Hitler's "Final Solution"* (London, 1980); David Bankier, *The Germans and the Final Solution: Public Opinion Under Nazism* (London, 1992); Hans Mommsen, "Was haben die Deutschen von Völkermord an den Juden gewusst?" in Walter H. Pehle, ed., *Der Judenpogrom 1938: Von der "Reichskristallnacht" zum Völkermord* (Frankfurt am Main, 1988), 176–200; Lutz Niethammer, "Juden und Russen im Gedächtnis der Deutschen," in Walter H. Pehle, ed., *Der historische Ort des Nationalsozialismus* (Frankfurt am Main, 1990), 114–134; and Volker Ullrich, "'Wir haben nichts gewusst': Ein deutsches Trauma," *1999* 4 (1991): 11–46.

2. The scholarly literature dealing with these questions is enormous. Among the most important recent works treating these questions and the Third Reich and the Holocaust generally are Richard J. Evans, *The Coming of the Third Reich* (New York, 2004); Klaus Hildebrand, *Das Dritte Reich* (Oldenbourg, 2003); Michael Burleigh, *The Third Reich: A New History* (London, 2000); Ian Kershaw, *Hitler, 1936–1945: Nemesis* (New York, 2000); Robert Gellately, *Backing Hitler: Consent and Coercion in Nazi Germany* (Oxford, 2001); Norbert Frei, *National Socialist Rule in Germany: The Führer State, 1933–1945* (Oxford, 1993); Christopher R. Browning and Jürgen Matthäus, *The Origins of the Final Solution: The Evolution of Nazi Jewish Policy, September 1939–March 1942* (Lincoln, Neb., 2004); Omer Bartov, *Germany's War and the Holocaust: Disputed Histories* (Ithaca, N.Y., 2003); Claudia Koonz, *The Nazi Conscience* (Cambridge, Mass., 2003); Götz Aly and Susanne Heim, *Architects of Annihilation* (Princeton, 2003); David Bankier, ed., *Probing the Depths*

of German Antisemitism: German Society and the Persecution of the Jews, 1933-1941 (Oxford, 2000); Marion A. Kaplan, *Between Dignity and Despair: Jewish Life in the Third Reich* (New York, 1998); Peter Longerich, *Politik der Vernichtung: Eine Gesamtdarstellung der nationalsozialistischen Judenverfolgung* (Munich, 1998); and Saul Friedländer, *Nazi Germany and the Jews*, vol. 1, *The Years of Persecution, 1933–1939* (New York, 1997).

3. The authors are particularly grateful to the following institutions for funding the research project on which this book is based: the National Endowment for the Humanities (Collaborative Research Program), the National Science Foundation (Law and Social Sciences Program), and the Alexander von Humboldt Foundation (Transcoop Program).

4. Hannah Arendt, *The Origins of Totalitarianism* (New York, 1951); Carl J. Friedrich and Zbigniew K. Brzezinski, *Totalitarian Dictatorship and Autocracy* (Cambridge, Mass., 1956).

5. See, for example, Edward Crankshaw, *Gestapo: Instrument of Tyranny* (London, 1956); Jacques Delarue, *The Gestapo: A History of Horror*, trans. Mervyn Savill (New York, 1962); and Robert Conquest, *The Great Terror: Stalin's Purge of the Thirties* (New York, 1973).

6. See, especially, Robert Gellately, *The Gestapo and German Society: Enforcing Racial Policy, 1933–1945* (Oxford, 1990); Gellately, *Backing Hitler*; Klaus-Michael Mallmann and Gerhard Paul, "Allwissend, allmächtig, allgegenwärtig? Gestapo, Gesellschaft, und Widerstand," *Zeitschrift für Geschichtswissenschaft* 41 (1993): 984–999; Mallmann and Paul, *Herrschaft und Alltag: Eine Industrierevier im Dritten Reich* (Bonn, 1991); Eric A. Johnson, *Nazi Terror: The Gestapo, Jews, and Ordinary Germans* (New York, 1999); Gisela Diewald-Kerkmann, *Politische Denunziation im NS-Regime oder die kleine Macht der "Volksgenossen"* (Bonn, 1995); Ian Kershaw, *Popular Opinion and Political Dissent in the Third Reich: Bavaria, 1933–1945* (Oxford, 1983); and Kershaw, *The Hitler Myth: Image and Reality in the Third Reich* (Oxford, 1987).

7. Kershaw, *Hitler 1936–1945*, p. 841.

8. See, for example, the essays on social control in France, Germany, Hungary, Italy, Spain, and the Netherlands under dictatorial regimes of the twentieth century in Clive Emsley, Eric A. Johnson, and Pieter Spierenburg, eds., *Social Control in Europe, 1800–2000* (Columbus, Ohio, 2004). The authors of these essays all reject Hannah Arendt's views on totalitarianism.

9. Hubert Lutz, interview by authors, May 29, 2001, Ann Arbor, Michigan. Hubert Lutz was born in 1928 and grew up in Cologne as the son of a Nazi Party functionary.

10. For an intriguing discussion of the point about two Germanys and how most average Germans found much in Nazi Germany to their liking, see Milton Mayer, *They Thought They Were Free: The Germans, 1933–1945* (Chicago, 1955), pp. 52–53ff. Mayer was an American scholar who spent a year in Germany in the early 1950s interviewing ten common citizens in a small town about their views of the Third Reich.

11. Thomas Green, interview by authors, July 27, 1995, New York City. Thomas Green was born in 1921 and grew up in Mannheim as the son of a Jewish businessman. In October 1940 he was deported to the Gurs concentration camp in France. Although

Green's full interview, like many interviews, could not be included in the pages of this book, a transcript is available from the authors.

12. The only significant open protest against the Holocaust in Germany took place in Berlin in late February and early March 1943. See Nathan Stoltzfus, *Resistance of the Heart: Intermarriage and the Rosenstrasse Protest in Nazi Germany* (New York, 1996).

13. Much of this controversy continues to surround Daniel Jonah Goldhagen's international best-seller, *Hitler's Willing Executioners: Ordinary Germans and the Holocaust* (New York, 1996). See, for example, Norman G. Finkelstein and Ruth Bettina Birn, *A Nation on Trial: The Goldhagen Thesis and Historical Truth* (New York, 1998).

14. Gitta Sereny, *Albert Speer: His Battle with Truth* (New York, 1995). For a recent study of attempts to prosecute Nazi perpetrators in eastern and western Germany after World War II, see Annette Weinke, *Die Verfolgung von NS-Tätern im geteilten Deutschland: Vergangenheitsbewältigung 1949–1969* (Paderborn, 2002).

15. Johnson, *Nazi Terror*.

Chapter 8

1. Rosa Hirsch, for example, who survived the Holocaust by going into hiding in Berlin, relates on the last page of her interview narrative, "When the bombs were falling in Berlin, I was happy even though they could have hit me just the same as anybody else. I didn't care at that point. I rather felt, 'Let them destroy it.' If they would have wiped out all of Germany, I wouldn't have cared." Similar comments were made by survivors we spoke with whose interviews, for reasons of space, could not be included in this book. A good example is Irving Rose, whom we interviewed in New York City on July 20, 1995. Born in 1921 and raised in Dresden as the son of an owner of a chain of inexpensive department stores before emigrating to the United States in March 1938, he retains little love for the beautiful city he once called home: "Dresden was considered like the Paris of Germany and it was destroyed, part of it was destroyed. I couldn't care less. . . . As far as I am concerned, they could have destroyed the whole thing. . . . As far as I am concerned, they could have made Germany into a potato field."

2. As mentioned in the introductory chapter, Green's interview, which took place in New York on July 27, 1995, is one of many interviews we originally conducted but were not able to publish in this book because of space limitations. In his autobiographical examination of what life was like for Jews in Nazi Germany, like himself, the eminent historian Peter Gay explains that this, more or less, applied to him as well when he was a child in Berlin: "There are three ways of becoming a Jew: by birth, by conversion, by decree. Brushed by only a breath of the first, I was forcibly enlisted in the third group after January 30, 1933." Peter Gay, *My German Question: Growing Up in Nazi Berlin* (New Haven, 1998), p. 48.

3. The historian Peter Gay's family also received such help and support. As Gay writes, "My father found his closest friends in business and in sports, and his professional

associates and the soccer players and sprinters he knew and liked were nearly all gentiles. And without the help of some of them, we would probably have ended up in the gas chambers." Gay, *My German Question*, p. 49.

4. In recent years, much of this controversy has centered around Daniel Jonah Goldhagen's provocative argument that Germany was long imbued with what he calls "a unique eliminationist antisemitism." See Goldhagen, *Hitler's Willing Executioners: Ordinary Germans and the Holocaust* (New York, 1996). For prominent examples of the criticism his book has aroused, see Norman G. Finkelstein and Ruth Bettina Birn, *A Nation on Trial: The Goldhagen Thesis and Historical Truth* (New York, 1998); and the new afterword in Christopher R. Browning's acclaimed study, *Ordinary Men: Police Battalion 101 and the Final Solution in Poland* (1992; New York, 1998), pp. 191–223.

5. Peter Gay, for example, devotes an entire chapter of his book about his life as a youth in Berlin to the "mixed signals" that he and his family received. See Gay, *My German Question*, pp. 57–83. Marion Kaplan makes a similar argument about the mixed messages that many Jews in Nazi Germany received in her recent study, *Between Dignity and Despair: Jewish Life in Nazi Germany* (Oxford, 1998), pp. 4–5. As she writes, "Jews read these mixed messages with fear and hope. They thought about and prepared for emigration, all the while wishing they would not have to leave their homeland. . . . Thus, as they continued to maintain their families and communities, they clung to the mixed signals from the government as well as from non-Jewish friends and strangers—a lull in antisemitic boycotts here, a friendly greeting there. They hoped the regime would fall or its antisemitic policies would ease."

6. On documentary evidence dealing with the Holocaust in general, see, for example, Steve Hochstadt, ed., *Sources of the Holocaust* (New York, 2004).

7. Two important recent studies of Jewish persecution in the Third Reich that make excellent use of survivor memoirs and diaries are Kaplan, *Between Dignity and Despair*; and Saul Friedländer, *Nazi Germany and the Jews*, vol. 1, *The Years of Persecution, 1933–1939* (New York, 1997). Probably the most acclaimed diary of a Holocaust survivor was kept by Victor Klemperer, a professor of romance languages at the Technical University of Dresden. Originally published in German, it appeared in English translation under the title *I Will Bear Witness: A Diary of the Nazi Years, 1933–1945*, vol. 1, trans. Martin Chalmers (New York, 1998; vol. 2, 1999). For recent oral histories dealing with Holocaust survivors, see, for example, Mary J. Gallant, *Coming of Age in the Holocaust: The Last Survivors Remember* (Lanham, Md., 2002); and Joshua M. Greene and Shiva Kumar, eds., *Witness: Voices from the Holocaust* (New York, 2001).

8. The original list of these survivors was compiled by the National Registry of Jewish Holocaust Survivors.

9. Though small, the Krefeld survey is of particular importance because its results can be compared with two existing studies of the persecution of Krefeld's Jews based on Gestapo records and other archival documents. See Dieter Hangebruch, "Emigriert—Deportiert: Das Schichsal der Juden in Krefeld zwischen 1933 und 1945," *Krefelder*

Studien 2 (1980):137–412; and Eric A. Johnson, *Nazi Terror: The Gestapo, Jews, and Ordinary Germans* (New York, 2000).

10. In 1933 nearly 70 percent of Germany's Jews worked in business and commerce; over 30 percent lived in the city of Berlin alone; and 70 percent lived in cities with a population of over 100,000 inhabitants. Kaplan, *Between Dignity and Despair*, 11.

11. Of the 507 survivors, 351, or 69 percent, indicated that they had left Germany for other countries by the end of 1939. According to Wolfgang Benz's estimate, there were roughly 537,000 Jews in Germany when Hitler came to power in 1933. By the end of 1939, according to Saul Friedländer, there were only 190,000 Jews remaining in Germany. Although births and deaths are not accounted for in these figures, a rough calculation for the percentage of Jews who left the country between 1933 and 1939 would be about 65 percent. Benz, ed., *Die Juden in Deutschland, 1933–1945* (Munich, 1988), p. 733; Friedländer, *Nazi Germany and the Jews*, p. 317.

12. According to Saul Friedländer, 267 synagogues were destroyed, 7,500 businesses were vandalized, and 91 Jews were killed during the pogrom. Friedländer, *Nazi Germany and the Jews*, p. 276.

13. Ian Kershaw, *Popular Opinion and Political Dissent in the Third Reich: Bavaria, 1933–1945* (Oxford, 1983), pp. 262–263.

14. Ian Kershaw, *Hitler 1936–1945: Nemesis* (New York, 2000), p. 142.

15. In the preface to the first volume of his new multivolume history of the Third Reich, Richard J. Evans points out that between 1995 and 2000 more than 12,000 new works on the Third Reich were published, "eloquent testimony to the continuing, never-ending outpouring of publications on the subject." Evans, *The Coming of the Third Reich* (New York, 2004), p. xvi.

16. In the last chapter of his controversial book on the perpetrators of the Holocaust, Daniel Goldhagen states: "No other country's antisemitism was at once so widespread as to have been a cultural axiom, was so firmly wedded to racism, had at its foundation such a pernicious image of Jews that deemed them to be a mortal threat to the *Volk*, and was so deadly in content, producing, even in the nineteenth century, such frequent and explicit calls for the extermination of the Jews, calls which expressed the logic of the racist eliminationist antisemitism that prevailed in Germany." Goldhagen, *Hitler's Willing Executioners*, p. 419.

17. Kershaw, *Popular Opinion and Political Dissent*, p. 277.

Chapter 9

1. See, for example, Gerhard Paul and Klaus-Michael Mallmann, eds., *Die Gestapo: Mythos und Realität* (Darmstadt, 1995); Robert Gellately, *The Gestapo and German Society: Enforcing Racial Policy, 1933–1945* (Oxford, 1990); Gellately, *Backing Hitler: Consent and Coercion in Nazi Society* (Oxford, 2001); and Eric A. Johnson, *Nazi Terror: The Gestapo, Jews, and Ordinary Germans* (New York, 2000).

2. For a comparison of the persecution of Jews and other groups in Nazi Germany, see Michael Burleigh and Wolfgang Wippermann, *The Racial State: Germany, 1933–1945* (Cambridge, 1991). On Jewish persecution itself, see Saul Friedländer, *Nazi Germany and the Jews*, vol. 1, *The Years of Persecution, 1933–1939* (New York, 1997); Marion A. Kaplan, *Between Dignity and Despair: Jewish Life in Nazi Germany* (Oxford, 1998); and Raul Hilberg, *The Destruction of the European Jews* (New York, 1961).

3. Victor Klemperer, *I Will Bear Witness: A Diary of the Nazi Years 1942–1945*, trans. Martin Chalmers (New York, 1999), p. 134.

4. Kaplan, *Between Dignity and Despair*.

5. There were thirty-three survivors from Krefeld who answered the question on the survey about their personal fear of arrest, thus making up 43 percent of the seventy-six survivors in the table who came from Catholic cities. Among the survivors from Krefeld, 27 percent had feared arrest constantly, 46 percent occasionally, and 27 percent had not feared arrest at all. This may indicate that Krefeld was more hospitable toward its Jews, but that is doubtful. Survivors from Krefeld had lower levels of fear probably because nearly all of the Krefeld survivors in the survey had left Germany before the war broke out (91 percent) and all had left the country before 1942. As Table 9.1 shows, survivors who were still in Germany after the war broke out had much higher levels of fear than survivors who left the country before this time. If this important factor is controlled for, the Krefeld survivors' level of fear becomes nearly identical to that of the rest of the survivors who took the survey.

6. An example of this is the town of Bergheim. Lying about fifteen miles west of Cologne, Bergheim had a population of slightly over 18,000 inhabitants in 1939. In the town itself and in the several small villages that were attached to it, there were no Gestapo officers present. Political police work, including the control of the local Jewish population, had to be performed mostly by two regular police officers. See Johnson, *Nazi Terror*, 65–66.

7. In his interview, for example, Helmut Grunewald says that he never wore the star even though he was required to as a so-called *Geltungsjude*.

8. See the interviews of Benson, Landau, Leib, and Meyer. Although the number of both Germans and Jews who took part in underground resistance activity in the Third Reich was limited, some historians of Jewish resistance estimate that at least two thousand Jews were active in underground resistance activity at some point during the Nazi years. If the size of the Jewish population were controlled for, this would suggest that Jews were proportionately more active in underground resistance activity than non-Jews. Kaplan, *Between Dignity and Despair*, 214.

9. Ana Perez Belmonte, "'Schwarzhören' im II. Weltkrieg: Die Ahndung von 'Rundfunkverbrechen' im Sondergerichtsbezirk Essen 1933–1945" (M.A. thesis, University of Cologne, 1997). See also the interview of Adam Grolsch, who was a radio operator in the German army on the eastern front.

10. Three percent of the survivors who were over seventeen years old and still living in Germany during the war indicated on the survivor survey that they had taken part in

active resistance activity. However, fewer than 2 percent of the non-Jewish participants in the Cologne and Krefeld surveys had done the same. On Jewish resistance generally, see Arnold Paucker, *Standhalten und Widerstehen: Der Widerstand deutscher und österreichischer Juden gegen die Nationalsozialistische Diktatur* (Essen, 1995); and Konrad Kwiet and Helmut Eschwege, *Selbstbehauptung und Widerstand: Deutsche Juden im Kampf um Existenz und Menschenwürde, 1933–1945* (Hamburg, 1984).

11. On the history of Jewish crime rates in earlier periods of German history, see Ludwig Fuld, *Das jüdische Verbrecherthum: Eine Studie über den Zusammenhang zwischen Religion und Kriminalität* (Leipzig, 1885); and Rudolf Wassermann, *Beruf, Konfession, und Verbrechen* (Munich, 1907). In a more recent study of crime rates in Imperial Germany, Eric A. Johnson estimates that the Jewish murder rate in the late nineteenth and early twentieth centuries was about one-third that of Protestants and one-fifth that of Catholics. Johnson, *Urbanization and Crime: Germany, 1871–1918* (Cambridge, 1995), p. 205.

12. Gellately, *Gestapo and German Society*, p. 163.

13. See, for example, the discussion of the prevalence of spying on the Jews of Krefeld in Johnson, *Nazi Terror*, pp. 150–152, where the author finds that one-quarter of Gestapo cases started against Jews in the 1930s involved spying in one form or another and that spying against Jews became even more prevalent during the war years.

14. Anna Meier, interview by authors, July 24, 1995, New York.

15. In his analysis of the Gestapo case files for the period 1933 to 1939 involving Jews from the city of Krefeld, Johnson finds that 41 percent of the cases started with civilian denunciations and 32 percent with information coming from official sources like the Gestapo or the Nazi Party. In 27 percent of the cases it was impossible to determine what the exact source of information was that was used to start the cases. These percentages correspond closely with the percentages reported in Table 9.3 for the same period (38 percent, 29 percent, and 34 percent respectively). See Johnson, *Nazi Terror*, p. 150.

16. See, for example, Gisela Diewald-Kerkmann, *Politische Denunziation im NS-Regime oder die kleine Macht der "Volksgenossen"* (Bonn, 1995), p. 9; and Klaus-Michael Mallmann and Gerhard Paul, "Allwissend, allmächtig, allgegenwärtig? Gestapo, Gesellschaft, und Widerstand," *Zeitschrift für Zeitgeschichte* 41(1993): 992.

Chapter 10

1. Walter Laqueur, *The Terrible Secret: An Investigation into the Suppression of Information about Hitler's "Final Solution"* (London, 1980).

2. See, for example, Deborah E. Lipstadt, *Beyond Belief: The American Press and the Coming of the Holocaust, 1933–1945* (New York, 1986); Laqueur, *Terrible Secret*; David Bankier, *The Germans and the Final Solution: Public Opinion Under Nazism* (Oxford, 1992);

and Martin Gilbert, "What Was Known and When," in Yisrael Gutman and Michael Berenbaum, eds., *Anatomy of the Auschwitz Death Camp* (Bloomington, Ind., 1994), pp. 539–552.

3. Despite objections from the British government, the BBC German Service, for example, broadcast numerous news and other programs during the war providing detailed information about the mass murder of the Jews. For a discussion, see Johnson, *Nazi Terror*, pp. 441–450.

4. Even though Victor Klemperer, like other Jews, was restricted in his movement, had his radio set taken away from him, and would be in grave danger if caught discussing sensitive political events, he considered it his duty to keep a detailed record of what he knew and experienced during the Holocaust. Although his diary entries concerning the murder of the Jews became more frequent and detailed from early 1942 onward, by the fall of 1941 he had already written several times about terrible reports he was receiving from many sources about the deportations to Poland. Thus, on October 25, 1941, he writes: "Ever more shocking reports about deportations of Jews to Poland. They have to leave almost literally naked and penniless. Thousands from Berlin to Lodz. A letter from Lissy Meyerhof about it. And many stories from Kätchen Sara." And, on November 18, 1941: "The news of the Jewish deportations to Poland and Russia sound catastrophic from several sources. Letter from Lissy Meyerhof to us, from Voss in Cologne to Kätchen Sara, word-of-mouth reports. We hear quite a lot." Clearly Klemperer had heard "quite a lot" about the murder of the Jews by the end of 1941. In 1942 he heard much more. Some examples follow. On March 16, 1942, for example, he reveals for the first time that he had heard about people being killed in Auschwitz: "In the last few days I heard Auschwitz (or something like that) near Königshütte in Upper Silesia, mentioned as the most dreadful concentration camp. Work in a mine, death within a few days." And, on July 4, 1942, he writes, "The Jewish community is notified of Jewish deaths in concentration camps and in prison, the corpses and urns handed over to the Jewish cemetery. . . . In all these cases the news always spreads quickly, there are x connections between the six or seven hundred Jews still to be found here." And, for a last example among many, on August 29, 1942, he discusses how the trustee of his building had been recently taken to the Gestapo office in Dresden for being too friendly with Jews. While he was there he was told by a Gestapo officer that there were "no decent Jews" and that the "whole race was going to be exterminated." Klemperer, *I Will Bear Witness: A Diary of the Nazi Years, 1933–1941*, trans. Martin Chalmers (New York, 1998), pp. 440, 444; and Klemperer, *I Will Bear Witness*, pp. 28, 92, 134.

5. Gilbert, "What Was Known and When," p. 541.

6. Knowledge about mass murders committed in concentration camps appears to have been considerably more widespread than knowledge about mass shootings. Of the fifty-six survivors in the survey who were still in Germany after the end of 1941, only eighteen (32 percent) had heard before the end of the war about mass shootings of Jews, but forty (71 percent) had heard about mass murder in concentration camps. Among the entire survivor population participating in the survey, there was considerably more knowledge

about the mass murders committed in the concentration camps than about the mass shootings. While 325 (64 percent) of the survivors indicated that they had heard before the end of the war about mass murders in concentration camps, only 128 (25 percent) marked down that they had heard about mass shootings.

Chapter 11

1. For a thorough discussion of the rise of the Nazi Party, see Richard J. Evans, *The Coming of the Third Reich* (London, 2000); for a detailed analysis of the elections and the factors that determined the voting results, see especially Jürgen W. Falter, *Hitlers Wähler* (Munich, 1991).

2. U.S. Strategic Bombing Survey, *The Effects of Strategic Bombing on German Morale* (Washington, 1947); Helen Peak, "Observations on the Characteristics and Distribution of German Nazis," *Psychological Monographs* 6 (1945); H. L. Ansbacher, "Attitudes of German Prisoners of War: A Study of the Dynamics of National Socialist Followership," *Psychological Monographs*, 1948.

3. The SD reports have been reprinted in Heinz Boberach, ed., *Meldungen aus dem Reich: Die geheimen Lageberichte der SS, 1938–1945* (Herrsching, 1984). They are discussed in Marlis G. Steinert, *Hitlers Krieg und die Deutschen: Stimmung und Haltung der deutschen Bevölkerung im Zweiten Weltkrieg* (Düsseldorf, 1970). The reports of the SPD in exile are printed in *Deutschland: Berichte der Sozialdemokratischen Partei Deutschlands* (Salzhausen, Frankfurt/M, 1980). They are discussed in Bernd Stöver, *Volksgemeinschaft im Dritten Reich: Die Konsensbereitschaft der Deutschen aus der Sicht der sozialistischen Exilberichte* (Düsseldorf, 1993). For Bavaria, including various other reports, see Ian Kershaw, *Der Hitler Mythos: Volksmeinung und Propaganda im Dritten Reich* (Stuttgart, 1980); and Kershaw, *Popular Opinion and Political Dissent in the Third Reich: Bavaria, 1933–1945* (Oxford, 1984). For a comprehensive attempt to use the different sources and depict a total picture with regard to anti-Semitism, see David Bankier, *The German and the Final Solution: Public Opinion Under Nazism* (Oxford, 1992).

4. See, for example, the classic study by Lutz Niethammer, *Die Jahre weiß man nicht, wo man die heute hinsetzen soll: Faschismuserfahrungen im Ruhrgebiet* (Berlin, 1983). In this period several history workshops (*Geschichtswerkstätten*), often made up of laypersons, began to take an interest in oral history research, as did students in schools whose interest was promoted by various student competitions. See, for example, D. Galinski, U. Herbert, and U. Lachauer, eds., *Nazis und Nachbarn: Schüler erforschen den Alltag im Nationalsozialismus* (Hamburg, 1982). For pioneering studies on Nazi perpetrators, see Robert Jay Lifton, *The Nazi Doctors: Medical Killings and the Psychology of Genocide* (New York, 2000); Tom Segev: *Soldiers of Evil: The Commandants of the Nazi Concentration Camps* (New York, 1988).

5. See Elisabeth Noelle and Eric-Peter Neumann, *Jahrbuch der öffentlichen Meinung, 1947–1955* (Allensbach/Bodensee, 1956), pp. 127, 133. Other questions, usually limited to one or two, were asked on this period from time to time by the Allensbach Institute or other institutes.

6. For selected findings, see E. Noelle-Neumann and R. Köcher, *Die verletzte Nation: Über den Versuch der Deutschen, ihren Charakter zu ändern* (Stuttgart, 1987), pp. 390ff. The text was originally published as an article in *Die Zeit*, May 10, 1985.

7. Classic examples are the industrialist Oscar Schindler (well-known from the Spielberg movie) or Wilm Hosenfeld, a military officer (portrayed in Roman Polanski's movie *The Pianist*). On Hosenfeld, see the recently published compilations of his diaries and letters: Wilm Hosenfeld: *"Ich versuchte jeden zu retten": Das Leben eines deutschen Offiziers in Briefen und Tagebüchern* (Stuttgart, 2004).

8. In our Dresden survey we used a slightly different version of the question on support of Nazi ideals compared with surveys in the other cities. We provided an additional response category for respondents who had supported the ideals for some time but later rejected them during the Third Reich. A clear majority indicated a shift from support to rejection in this time period.

9. The data have been kindly provided to us for secondary analysis by the Allensbach Institut für Demoskopie. Thanks to its director, Elisabeth Noelle, for doing so.

10. The basic discussion on this topic is found in Philip E. Converse, "The Nature of Belief Systems in Mass Publics," in David A. Apter, ed., *Ideology and Discontent* (New York, 1964), pp. 206–261. For levels of knowledge in the population today, see M. X. Delli Carpini and S. Keeter, *What Americans Know About Politics and Why It Matters* (New Haven, 1996); W. Russel Neuman, *The Paradox of Mass Politics: Knowledge and Opinion in the American Electorate* (Cambridge, 1986).

11. It is unlikely that those who answered indecisively or could not remember were seeking refuge in neutral categories, refusing to admit their former Nazi sympathies in an interview. Further analysis showed that these people, when asked other questions about the present, were generally less interested in politics than the others were. Their behavior in answering the questions is consistent with their present attitudes toward politics and thus probably reflects their earlier orientation as well. If one assumes that those who lacked an interest in politics chose the path of least resistance and were more likely to be seen as fellow travelers than opponents, those disinterested in politics represented a latent potential for accepting the Nazi regime.

12. We did this by weighting our data according to age-groups as well as gender, under the assumption that those participating in our survey and belonging to each age-group do not fundamentally differ from members of their age-group who have already died. The estimate is inevitably tentative in that older age-groups were not available in sufficient numbers for questioning. We were therefore forced to equate those who were forty or older with the population in the preceding age-group.

13. In Cologne and Krefeld respondents who came to these cities after the war were more likely to rank among the Protestants. And because Protestants were more receptive

to National Socialism, this entailed a slight blurring of local differences on the level of all of those surveyed. In Dresden and Berlin, the effect of this influx is less pronounced because these cities were predominantly Protestant, as were those who came to those cities after the war.

14. Karl Mannheim, "Das Problem der Generationen," in Karl Mannheim, ed., *Wissensoziologie*, 2d ed. (Neuwied, 1970), pp. 509–555.

15. On the bourgeois reaction to the perceived danger, see Clemens Vollnhals, ed., *Sachsen in der NS Zeit* (Leipzig, 2000).

16. Compare Robert N. Proctor, *Racial Hygiene: Medicine Under the Nazis* (Cambridge, 1988); George L. Mosse, *Die Geschichte des Rassismus in Europa* (Frankfurt, 1990). Racist, anti-Semitic traditions—partly combined with supposed or real competition—may have made certain professions requiring higher education more receptive to National Socialism. Lawyers' and doctors' susceptibility for National Socialism, for example, may have been based on the fact that Jews were disproportionately represented in these professions.

17. Ian Kershaw, *The Hitler Myth* (Oxford, 1980); Hans-Ulrich Wehler, *Deutsche Gesellschaftsgeschichte, 1914–1949* (Munich, 2003).

18. Interview Krefeld 3280.

19. Interview Cologne 289.

20. Interview Krefeld 3369.

21. Interview Cologne 289.

22. Interview Krefeld 3131.

23. Interview Cologne 4001.

24. Interview Dresden 332.

25. Interview Berlin 672.

26. Interview Berlin 804.

27. Interview Dresden 1152.

28. Interview Krefeld 3314.

29. Interview Krefeld 3735.

30. Compare Berndt Jürgen Wendt, *Deutschland 1933–1945: Das Dritte Reich* (Hannover, 1995).

31. Interview Dresden 1152.

32. Interview Krefeld 3699.

33. Interview Dresden 469.

34. Interview Dresden 229.

35. See G. R. Boynton and Gerhard Loewenberg, "The Development of Public Support for Parliament in Germany, 1951–1959," *British Journal of Political Science*, April 1973, 169–189; Boynton and Loewenberg, "The Decay of Support for the Monarchy and the Hitler Regime in the Federal Republic of Germany," *British Journal of Political Science*, October 1974, 453–488; Kendall L. Baker, Rusell J. Dalton, and Kai Hildebrandt, *Germany Transformed* (Cambridge, 1981).

36. Interview Krefeld 3488.

37. Interview Cologne 1304.

38. Interview Krefeld 3699.

39. Ausprecher, "Attitudes of German Prisoners," pp. 12. 24; Peak, "Observations," p. 34.

40. Data here not presented can be found in Karl-Heinz Reuband, "Das NS-Regime zwischen Akzeptanz und Ablehnung: Eine retrospektive Analyse von Bevölkerungseinstellungen im Dritten Reich" (unpublished manuscript, 2004).

41. For the 1948 figures, see Noelle and Neumann, *Jahrbuch*, p. 133f. Regarding the subsequent development, see David Conradt, "Changing German Political Culture," in Gabriel Almond and Sidney Verba, eds., *The Civic Culture Revisited* (Boston, 1980), pp. 212–272; Jürgen W. Falter, Kai Arzheimer, and Harald Schoen, "Rechtsextreme Orientierungen und Wahlverhalten," in Wilfried Schubarth and Richard Stöss, eds., *Rechtsextremismus in der Bundesrepublik Deutschland: Eine Bilanz* (Opladen, 2001), pp. 220–246.

42. This is also confirmed by the postwar surveys that asked respondents to provide the most decisive factor for the popularity of National Socialism. In a nationwide survey conducted by the Allensbach Institute in June 1950, it was asked, in an open-ended question, without any possible responses provided, "What, in your opinion is the most important reason for the National Socialists coming to power in 1933?" In first place with 32 percent was the economic situation (unemployment, etc.). This was followed by 28 percent who made positive statements regarding the National Socialist program and the personage of Adolf Hitler. This includes, inter alia, his perceived determination to improve the population's situation. In third place with 23 percent was the failure of democracy in the Weimar Republic. See Noelle und Neumann, *Jahrbuch*, 134. Although the respondents were not necessarily eligible to vote in 1933, their statements at least reflect their predominant orientations.

43. On elections, see Falter, *Wähler*; on Nazi Party membership, see W. Brustein, *The Social Origins of the Nazi Party, 1925–1933* (New Haven, 1996).

Chapter 12

1. Ludwig Eiber, "Verfolgung," in Wolfgang Benz, ed., *Enzyklopädie des Nationalsozialismus*, 4th ed. (Munich, 2001), p. 285.

2. Interview Dresden 1067.

3. Bernd Dörner, *"Heimtücke": Das Gesetz als Waffe. Kontrolle, Abschreckung, und Verfolgung in Deutschland, 1933–1945* (Paderborn, 1998), p. 9.

4. For the strong leftist political base in Saxony, see Clemens Vollnhals, "Der gespaltene Freistaat: Der Aufstieg der NSDAP in Sachsen," in Clemens Vollnhals, ed., *Sachsen in der NS Zeit* (Leipzig, 2000), 9–40; and Verband der Verfolgten des Nazi-Regimes—Bund der Antifaschisten, eds., *Unsere Heimat unterm Hakenkreuz* (Pirna, 2003).

5. It is important to keep the year of a given event in perspective because we have determined that these figures are based on responses from people who for the most part became adults in the late 1930s and early 1940s and only then began to think much about their political environment. Most people who were old enough to describe the time when the Nazis came to power died long ago. But even when this fact is taken into consideration and the findings are broken up by age, a similar tendency still emerges.

6. For the case of Cologne, it can be shown that 58 percent of the cases dealt with by "special courts" *(Sondergerichte)* from 1933 to 1945 traced back to denunciations and 7 percent to anonymous accusations. The proportion attributable to the Gestapo or other National Socialist organizations amounts to 28 percent. Among Gestapo cases in Krefeld, the proportion of cases initiated by the Gestapo was higher than the proportion of denunciations in the early phase of Nazi society; from 1940 onward, however, it dropped to only half the proportion initiated by private denunciations. See Eric A. Johnson, *Nazi Terror: The Gestapo, Jews, and Ordinary Germans* (New York, 1999), p. 365.

7. Compare Karl-Heinz Reuband, "Denunziation im Dritten Reich: Die Bedeutung von Systemunterstützung und Gelegenheitsstrukturen," in I. Marszolek and O. Stieglitz, eds., *Denunziation im 20. Jahrhundert: Zwischen Komparatistik und Interdisziplinarität,* special issue of *Historical Social Research/Historische Sozialforschung* 26, no. 2–3 (2001): 219–234.

8. Interview Cologne 4002.

9. A similar pattern is found among the respondents themselves, though a somewhat lower percentage of these people appear to have been punished. Thus of the combined total of thirty respondents in the Cologne and Krefeld surveys who were either arrested or interrogated, twenty reported on what the result of their cases had been. While nine (45 percent) of these people were soon let go after their initial arrest or interrogation, one was sent to a concentration camp, two were placed in "protective custody," one was sent to jail, and the remaining seven reported other outcomes. Of course, no one completing the survey died in a concentration camp or was executed!

10. On Lichtenberg, see Ernst Klee, *"Euthanasie" im NS-Staat: Die Vernichtung lebensunwerten Lebens,* 10th ed. (Frankfurt, 2001), p. 357.

11. Compare Robert Gellately, *Backing Hitler: Consent and Coercion in Nazi Germany* (Oxford, 2001), pp. 51ff.; Sybil Milton, "Die Konzentrationslager der dreißiger Jahre im Bild der in- und ausländischen Presse," in Ulrich Herbert, Karin Orth, and C. Dieckmann, eds., *Die nationalsozialistischen Konzentrationslager* (Frankfurt/Main, 2002), 1:135–147.

12. Compare Ulrich Herbert, Karin Orth, and C. Diekmann, "Die nationalsozialistischen Konzentrationslager: Geschichte, Erinnerung, Forschung," in *Die nationalsozialistischen Konzentrationslager,* p. 26. Work camps, known as "work education camps," in which "work-shy" individuals and those who violated compulsory work programs were interned, existed in addition to concentration camps. There were more than 200 such camps with a capacity of almost 40,000 detainees. See Gabriele Lofti, *KZ der Gestapo: Arbeitserziehungslager im Dritten Reich* (Stuttgart, 2000).

13. Interview Krefeld 3488.

14. Interview Dresden 299.

15. Compare Herbert, Orth, and Diekmann, "Konzentrationslager," p. 26. On the development of the concentration camp system, see also Karin Orth, *Das System der nationalsozialistischen Konzentrationslager: Eine politische Organisationsgeschichte* (Hamburg, 1999).

16. Peter Hoffmann, *Staufenberg und der 20 Juli 1944* (Munich, 1998), p. 50.

17. Interview Krefeld 3735.

18. Interview Berlin 804.

19. For an overview of such arguments and critiques, see, for example, Gerhard Paul and Klaus-Michael Mallmann, eds., *Die Gestapo: Mythos und Realität* (Darmstadt, 1995).

20. Those who disseminated anti-Nazi fliers, helped persecuted individuals, or participated openly in resistance against National Socialism feared the Gestapo significantly more often than those who acted in conformity with the system. The highest percentage (85 percent) is found among those who had reasons for fearing the Gestapo (respondents who participated in active resistance in illegal organizations such as parties or unions).

21. Among the regular listeners, half began doing so in 1941; among the occasional listeners, two-thirds started listening to foreign broadcasting in 1941. The increasing distrust of German information sources concerning the war promoted this development. Further figures with regard to listening, based on other surveys, are found in Karl-Heinz Reuband, "Schwarzhören im Dritten Reich: Verbreitung, Erscheinungsformen, und Kommunikationsmuster beim Umgang mit verbotenen Sendern," *Archiv für Sozialgeschichte* 41 (2001): 262f. Unfortunately the results are not always differentiated according to an exact point in time. However, one finds additional evidence here that listening to foreign broadcasts began for the most part during the war.

22. Interview Berlin 715A.

23. They totaled about 2 million people and thus constituted the largest system of political control in Nazi Germany. Among their tasks was to record the political orientation of household members in their files. See Detlev Schmiechen-Ackermann, "Der Blockwart," *Vierteljahreshefte für Zeitgeschichte* 48 (2000), 575.

24. Interview Berlin 958.

Chapter 13

1. See the article reprinted in Günther B. Ginzel, ed., *"Das durfte keiner wissen!" Hilfe für Verfolgte im Rheinland von 1933 bis 1945* (Cologne, 1995), pp. 265f.

2. See Konrad Kwiet, "Nach dem Pogrom: Die Stufen der Ausgrenzung," in Wolfgang Benz, ed., *Die Juden in Deutschland, 1933–1945: Leben unter nationalsozialistischer Herrschaft* (Munich, 1993), pp. 615ff., 621; regarding the repeated reminder

to not have contact with Jews, see Karl-Heinz Reuband, "'Jud Süß' und der 'Ewige Jude' als Prototypen antisemitischer Film-Propaganda im Dritten Reich. Enstehungsbedingungen, Zuschauerstrukturen, und Wirkungspotentiale," in Michael Andel and Detlef Brandes, eds., *Propaganda, (Selbst)-Zensur, Sensation: Grenzen von Presse- und Wissenschaftsfreiheit in Deutschland und Tschechien seit 1871* (Essen, forthcoming).

3. Interview Cologne 4003.

4. Interview Berlin 958.

5. See Victor Klemperer, *I will Bear Witness*, vol. 2 (London, 1999), especially his diary entries for September 23 and 25, 1991; October 4, 1941; November 1, 8, 24, 1941; December 30, 1941; January 17, 1942; February 18, 1942. See also Inge Deutschkron, *Ich trug den gelben Stern* (Munich, 1985); David Bankier, *The Germans and the Final Solution: Public Opinion Under Nazism* (Oxford, 1992), chap. 7.

6. Interview Krefeld 3975.

7. We did not ask about this in a systematic way. Such reactions developed in the context of the interviews.

8. Bankier, *Final Solution*, chap. 7.

9. The figures are presented in Elisabeth Noelle and Erich Peter Neumann, *Jahrbuch der öffentlichen Meinung, 1947–1955* (Allensbach, 1956), p. 130. For a secondary analysis on the basis of a copy of the original data set, see Karl-Heinz Reuband, "Reaktionen der Deutschen auf die Einführung des Judensterns," unpublished ms., Düsseldorf 2004.

10. Klemperer, *Witness*, diary entry for February 18, 1942.

11. Interview Krefeld 3596.

12. Interview Cologne 958.

13. Reprinted in Ginzel, *Wissen*, pp. 285f.

14. For a fuller discussion of the deportations in Cologne, see Dieter Corbach, *Sechs Uhr ab Messe Köln-Deutz: Deportationen, 1938–1945* (Cologne, 2001); for Frankfurt, W. Wippermann, *Das Leben in Frankfurt zur NS-Zeit*, vol. 1, *Die Nationalsozialistische Judenverfolgung: Darstellung Dokumente und didaktische Hinweise* (Frankfurt, 1986); for Berlin, Beate Meyer, "Deportation," in Beate Meyer and Hermann Simon, eds., *Juden in Berlin, 1938–1945* (Berlin, 2000), pp. 171–178.

15. Wolf Gruner, *Judenverfolgung in Berlin, 1933–1945* (Berlin, 1996), p. 13.

16. Compare Kurt Schilde, *Versteckt im Tiergarten: Auf der Flucht vor den Nachbarn. Gedenkbuch für die im Bezirk in der Zeit des Nationalsozialismus Untergetauchten* (Berlin, 1995), p. 28; Hans Safrian, *Eichmann und seine Gehilfen* (Frankfurt/M, 1995).

17. Interview Krefeld 3145.

18. Interview Berlin 1008.

19. Interview Cologne 207.

20. Interview Berlin 672.

21. Interview Krefeld 3699.

22. Interview Krefeld 3238.

23. In Berlin alone there were, at the end of 1942, about two hundred firms employing more than fifteen thousand Jews. See Wolf Gruner, "Die Fabrik-Aktion und die Ereignisse in der Berliner Rosenstrasse: Fakten und Fiktionen um den 27. Februar 1943," *Jahrbuch für Antisemitismusforschung* (2002), p. 146.

24. See Eva Fogelman, *Conscience and Courage: Rescuers of Jews During the Holocaust* (New York, 1994). For Germany, see especially Beate Kosmala and Claudia Schoppmann, eds., *Überleben im Untergrund: Hilfe für Juden in Deutschland, 1941–1945* (Berlin, 2002); Wolfgang Benz, ed., *Überleben im Dritten Reich: Juden im Untergrund und ihre Helfer* (Munich, 2003).

25. For a summary by Herbert A. Strauss, *Über dem Abgrund: Eine jüdische Jugend in Deutschland, 1918–1943* (Berlin, 1999), p. 299. Konrad Kwiet, for example, estimates the number for Germany as a whole at 20,000–25,000 Germans who helped Jews hide. See Kwiet, "Rassenpolitik und Völkermord," in W. Benz, H. Graml, and H. Weiss, eds., *Enzyklopädie des Nationalsozialismus* (Munich, 2001), p. 61. With about 10,000–15,000 and the helpers who were frequently named, one would have to place the figure somewhat higher.

26. See Walter Laqueur, *Geboren in Deutschland: Der Exodus der jüdischen Jugend nach 1933* (Munich, 2000), p. 79.

27. Approximately 100,000 people were killed under the Nazi euthanasia program, a kind of precursor to the murder of the Jewish population. Of the respondents in our Cologne and Krefeld surveys, 37 percent say they either knew or heard about the killing and an additional 11 percent say that they had suspected it. In the Dresden survey, 39 percent say they knew or heard and another 11 percent suspected. We did not ask about this in the Berlin survey.

28. Thus some people who responded that they had been aware of the mass murder based their answers on less information than others. In addition to this, some people may have been confused when they gave their answers. In subsequent questions we asked about how and exactly when they had come to know about the mass murder. A few respondents said that they had first become aware after the war ended, even though they had previously answered that they became aware before the war ended.

29. In our nationwide telephone survey we asked the question as it had been asked in the surveys by the Allensbach Institute and found that 28 percent of the respondents had known something about the mass murder before the war's end. The exact question we asked in the telephone survey was: "When did you first hear something about the mass destruction of the Jews?"

30. In 1961, the Allensbach Institute conducted the first of these surveys among people age 30 and older, and 32 percent answered yes. The respective figure was 34 percent in a survey of people age 60 and older conducted by the same institute in 1988. In 1995, a survey completed by FORSA based on respondents age 64 and older came up with a figure of 35 percent, and a survey by the Forschungsgruppe Wahlen based on respondents age 65 and older came up with a figure of 32 percent. In a survey taken in 1991, the Allensbach Institute arrived at a figure of 40 percent, but this must be con-

sidered an aberration because of the sampling techniques employed. For a fuller discussion of these surveys, see Karl-Heinz Reuband, "Gerüchte und Kenntnisse vom Holocaust in der deutschen Gesellschaft vor Ende des Krieges: Eine Bestandaufnahme auf der Basis von Bevölkerungsumfragen," *Jahrbuch für Antisemitismusforschung* 9(2000): 196–233.

31. Weighing based on official statistics of the Census Bureau from 1938.

32. A further discussion is found in Karl-Heinz Reuband, "Zwischen Ignoranz, Wissen, und Nicht-Glauben-Wollen: Gerüchte über den Holocaust und ihre Diffusionsbedingungen in der Bevölkerung," in B. Kosmala and C. Schoppmann, eds., *Überleben im Untergrund: Hilfe für Juden in Deutschland, 1941–1945* (Berlin, 2002), pp. 33–62.

33. Interview Berlin 995.

34. See Reuband, "Jud Süß."

35. Victor Klemperer, *The Language of the Third Reich: LTI, Lingua Tertii Imperii: A Philologist's Notebook* (Leipzig, 1999), pp. 233, 235.

36. Wilhelm Corsten, ed., *Kölner Aktenstücke: Zur Lage der katholischen Kirche in Deutschland, 1933–1945* (Cologne, 1949), pp. 269, 303.

37. Breakdowns of the Cologne-Krefeld study by religious denomination show that there is much to say for the thesis of a pronounced sensitivity to the misdeeds of the Nazi regime among Catholics. In both Krefeld and Cologne, Catholics more frequently than Protestants said they learned something about the mass murder of Jews, regardless of whether the Catholic respondents had lived in either city before 1945.

38. Locals often outnumbered the German personnel involved in killing Jews, which in no way reduces the culpability of the Germans. See Dieter Pohl, *Holocaust: Die Ursachen—das Geschehen—die Folgen* (Freiburg, 2004), p. 133; on participation and cooperation, see also Robert Wistrich, *Hitler und der Holocaust* (Berlin, 2003), pp. 215ff.

39. Interview Cologne 696.

40. Interview Krefeld 3735.

41. Interview Berlin 672.

42. Interview Dresden 299.

43. Christopher Browning, *Die Entfesselung der "Endlösung": Nationalsozialistische Jugendpolitik, 1939–1942* (Munich, 2003), p. 595.

44. Interview Cologne 894.

45. Interview Berlin 1008.

46. Interview Berlin 772.

47. An estimated 5–6 million Jews were killed: 700,000 were killed in mobile gas vans, 1.3 million were shot, and 3 million were killed in the camps; the others died in ghettos due to starvation, illness, and other reasons. See Sybille Steinbacher, *Auschwitz* (Munich, 2004), p. 106. See also Raul Hilberg, *Die Vernichtung der europäischen Juden* (Frankfurt, 1990), p. 1298.

48. Interview Cologne 472.

49. On the construction of "reality," see Peter Berger and Thomas Luckmann, *The*

Social Construction of Reality (Garden City, N.Y., 1967). On the dissemination of information, see Everett M. Rogers, *Diffusion of Innovation* (New York, 1995). On the structure of social networks, see M. Granovetter, "The Strength of the Weak: A Network Theory Revisited," in Peter V. Marsden and Nan Lin, eds., *Social Structure and Network Analysis* (Beverly Hills, Calif., 1982), pp. 105–130.

50. In our Berlin survey, we also asked respondents if they knew anyone personally who had directly witnessed the murder of the Jews, and only 3 percent answered that they had.

51. Eric A. Johnson, *Nazi Terror: The Gestapo, Jews, and Ordinary Germans* (New York, 1999), pp. 441–450; p. 585 n. 34ff.; R. G. Reuth, *Eine Biographie* (Munich, 2000), p. 526. See also Jean Seaton, "The BBC and the Holocaust," *Journal of Communication* (1987): 53–80; and Jeremy D. Harris, "Broadcasting the Massacres," *Yad Vashem Studies* 25 (1996): 65–98.

52. BBC; Survey of the European Audiences, October 23, 1942, p. 6. National Archives, RG 208.

53. Interview Krefeld 3596.

54. Interview Dresden 1129.

55. Compare Martin F. Herz, "Psychological Lessons from Leaflet Propaganda in World War II," in Daniel Katz and Darwin Cartwright, eds., *Public Opinion and Propaganda* (New York, 1954), p. 547; Wistrich, *Hitler*, pp. 262ff. In regard to the content of the fliers, see Reuband, "Gerüchte," pp. 199ff.

56. Interview Cologne 4003.

57. Seven percent of the respondents mentioned 1939 and earlier, 10 percent mentioned 1940. Whether the respondents were thinking of mass killings in Poland or Jews killed in *Kristallnacht* or in the early concentration camps is not known. Systematic mass murder began in 1941.

Conclusion

1. Some people might consider that the best question to base our estimate on would be the question we asked about how the respondents first became aware of the mass murder of the Jews for we asked this question of all of the survey respondents in each of the four cities and because its answer requires less of a value judgment on the part of the respondents than did the question about whether they had known of, heard of, or suspected the mass murder. In the question dealing with their source of information, we gave the respondents a list of possible sources from which they might have "found out something" (*etwas erfahren*) about the mass murder before the end of the war and asked them to specify which source or sources, if any, from which they had first received information. Alternatively, had the respondents not received any information about the mass

murder of the Jews before the end of the war, they were asked to make this clear to us by crossing off the last possible answer to the question, which stated: "I only first found out something after the war" (*Habe erst noch dem Krieg etwas erfahren*). When the answers the respondents gave to this question were tabulated (and when those who said that they had first found out about the mass murder while they were prisoners of war were controlled for), it turns out that 46 percent of the survey population in the four cities born before 1919 identified at least one source of information they had received about the mass murder while the war was still going on. While this figure of 46 percent, therefore, applies to the respondents who had reached adulthood before the war began, among the entire survey population the figure was 42 percent.

2. In large cities like ours the response rate in professionally done face-to face-surveys (such as the ALLBUS) in Germany is about 45 percent.

3. We did a test with different cover letters, either stressing the study as one on old age and living conditions or on the Third Reich. An identical questionnaire, containing several questions on other topics than the Third Reich, was included in both samples.

4. We had up to three reminders in our mailings and could group the results according to time of response.

5. There is no indication that the other available nationwide surveys on that topic have a disproportionate number of missing answers; see Reuband, "Gerüchte."

6. The subsequent question on the year when they had heard confirmed this. In Cologne-Krefeld, for example, 28 percent of those with suspicions mentioned a year. Whether they thought of the year when they started their suspicions or had different interpretations remains unclear. Further questions reduced the number of knowledgeables among them even more.

7. In Cologne-Krefeld, e.g., 25 percent of those who had "heard" something wrote that they had heard about it only after the end of the war. We also constructed a consistency check variable based on four questions about knowledge and suspicion, and the overall percentage rate—measured by predominant tendencies—remained the same.

8. Even among those who were deported late—in 1944—(these are just three respondents), there are none who could clearly be seen as being informed before deportation.

9. See Christoph Rass, *"Menschenmaterial": Deutsche Soldaten an der Ostfront*, (Paderborn 2003), pp. 92, 26, 100. In his study, 11 percent were born between 1921 and 1926, 68 percent between 1911 and 1920, 19 percent between 1901 and 1910, and 2 percent before 1900.

+ + + Index

419